Building Codes

The Aesthetics of Calvinism in Early Modern Europe

Catharine Randall

PENN

University of Pennsylvania Press

Philadelphia

10 9 8 7 6 5 4 3 2 1

Published by
University of Pennsylvania Press
Philadelphia, Pennsylvania 19104-4011

Library of Congress Cataloging-in-Publication Data
Randall, Catharine, 1957–
    Building codes : the aesthetics of Calvinism in early modern
Europe / Catharine Randall.
        p.   cm. — (New cultural studies)
    Includes bibliographical references (p.   ) and index.
    ISBN 0-8122-3490-1 (alk. paper)
        1. Architecture, Renaissance—France.   2. Architecture, Modern—
17th–18th centuries—France.   3. Calvinism in architecture.   4. Calvin,
Jean, 1509–1564—Influence.   5. Architecture and state—France.
I. Title.   II. Series.
NA1045.R36   1999
724'.1'088245—dc21   99-17838
                                                                              CIP

For
Sara, best-beloved;
Andrew and Christian, sons and friends;
and my husband, Randall,
adored fellow traveler in this, the rest of life

By the grace God has given me, I laid a foundation as an expert builder, and someone else is building on it. But each one should be careful how he builds. For no one can lay any foundation other than the one already laid, which is Jesus Christ. If any man builds on this foundation using gold, silver, costly stones, wood, hay or straw, his work will be shown for what it is, because the Day will bring it to light. It will be revealed with fire, and the fire will test the qualities of each man's work . . . Do not deceive yourselves. If any one thinks he is wise by the standards of his age, he should become a "fool" so that he may become wise. For the wisdom of this world is foolishness in God's sight.

—I Corinthians 3: 10–19

Contents

Illustrations

Introduction: Calvinist Structures and the Catholic State

> Architecture is a kind of rhetoric of power.
>
> —Nietzsche

IN THE CITY of Geneva, Switzerland, stands a monument to the Reformation, an imposing tribute to Calvinist influence on the city and the epoch. However, the monolithic figures of John Calvin, John Knox, Guillaume Farel, and others push their bulk in vain against the sparse space allotted to them. Geneva has marginalized the sweep of the Reformation, backed it up against city walls, circumscribed it in a park, near university space. The Reformation now exists solely as an intellectual phenomenon from a past age. The monument's tension recalls mimetically the spatial constraint exercised by Catholics on the theological expression of sixteenth-century Protestants, as well as similar limitations placed on Calvinist artistic expression.

Many of Calvin's writings were expressly intended to reassure his followers during troubled times: *Des scandales* was conceived, at least in part, to "comfort those faithful made fearful by threats of persecution."[1] In 1548, the Augsburg Interim further imperiled the Reformed cause on the Continent, while the Huguenot diaspora from France to Geneva had already begun by 1542. It increased and nearly doubled from 1547 to 1549 due to persecutions occasioned by Henri II's accession to the throne, his creation of the Chambre ardente in 1547 (charged with incriminating those of the Reformed faith within the jurisdiction of the Parlement de Paris), the zeal of provincial parliaments to extirpate Protestantism, the censorship of books (including vernacular translations of the Bible), the surveillance of printers and booksellers, and a series of more minor irritations such as the imposition of fines, searches, and investigations. For these reasons, said Calvin, "the cause of the Gospel in France, object of [my] constant preoccupation, seem[s] ever more compromised."[2]

How did Calvinists react to threats or persecution? Did they cease their creative activity? No, they did not: Calvinist architects designed and constructed the vast majority of architectural structures built from the mid-sixteenth to early seventeenth centuries in France. While institutionally marginalized in many respects, Calvinists paradoxically populated an elite corps of artists, artisans, and architects responsible for monumentalizing Catholic demonstrations of power. So pervasive was their presence that it is difficult today to find architectural manuals penned by Catholic contemporaries or to view buildings erected by major Catholic architects. Ironically, most of the influential creators of structures—be they textual blueprints (Bernard Palissy's *Recepte véritable,* Androuet du Cerceau's collection of draftsmanly sketches and engravings of buildings, Philibert de l'Orme's *Architecture* or his *Nouvelles inventions*), actual, erected structures (by Philibert de l'Orme or Salomon de Brosse), ornamental gardens, or rusticated grottoes (Jean Bullant, Jacques Boyceau)—were either proto-Calvinists (generally termed "evangelical," for example, Philibert de l'Orme) or avowed Calvinists. Their texts and structures attest to the frustrating imperative of subordinating personal belief to public policy and financial strictures, as well as to their struggle against such constraint. In the arts of "representation," Donald Kelley instructs us, "are found the real origin and organs of social control."[3] How did these Calvinist architects "witness," display their confessional stance, within the Catholic-dominated political and religious climate?

These Calvinist creators devised strategies to subvert from within: to inscribe, via representational reconfiguration and code, their distrust of the hierarchy on the very buildings commissioned to attest to Catholic authority. Using the slim margin of artistic license available and revising from the margins, they adapted their artistic resources so as to convey a Calvinist inscription overlaying and undermining the "Catholic" monument. This ambitious, subversive, often dangerous agenda characterizes all the Calvinist creators of the period. While presenting an acceptable surface, their structures read subversively, differently than what they represent, refusing to surrender to control. "A boundary has been drawn between reading and viewing [*lisibilité* and *visibilité*], but only in order to be endlessly crisscrossed . . . in a logic of transgression."[4] If architecture comprises a structured representation of an ideology, then Calvinist architecture contradicts that, becoming a sort of anti-architecture that subverts the ideology.[5] Calvinist creators would make visible the ideology that they opposed, in order to subtly dismantle it: in their hands, its display would turn to radical criticism.

Ordinarily, "between the leader who makes displays and those who engage in them is established the difference separating a monarch from his subservient bodies. For as long as subjects admire by imitating the orders put to them in fields of ritualized life, a continuity of social distinctions can be held."[6] Calvinist creators refused to play this game; they symbolically toppled the power structure through techniques that in many respects derived from a common source: Calvin's *Institution de la religion chrestienne*. Although not customarily read as an architectural document concerned with issues of spatial assignment, the *Institution* did fill this function for Calvinist architects who demonstrated—by reference or resemblance—that they had read it, interpreted it in this way, and modeled both their theology and their structures upon it. Written from Calvin's location in self-imposed exile, dedicated to describing how the biblical blueprint for a saved world might be implemented on earth in the real space of Geneva, the *Institution* has much to say about how space is weighted, distributed, and reconfigured. Spatial vocabulary recurs incessantly in the *Institution*, as well as in numerous other of his texts. In a letter to Heinrich Bullinger dated 7 May 1549, Calvin observes, "If I were only thinking about my life and my private interests, I'd leave and go elsewhere right away. But when I think of the significance of this corner of the earth for the propagation of the kingdom of Christ, I know I am right in my concerns to protect it."[7] Calvinist architects would rehearse the spatial lexicon (boundaries, borders, overstepping, lack of space, juxtaposed structures in space, to name a few) that composes Calvin's text. His terms—"outre measure," "extravagant," "vagabondant," "hors bords"—would receive an unexpected architectural application, a hallmark of evangelical and Protestant architects: "modesty" and "simplicity" oppose "license," "caprice," "error," "useless things," and "confusion."[8] Because of the eventually more rigorous and explicit codification of Calvinism as a theological system and its actual, instead of merely virtual, institutionalization in real structures, such vocabulary of subversive structuring permeates the "second generation" of Calvinist architects, contemporaries of Théodore Beza and Calvin's *epigoni*.

Calvinist architects, particularly those of the second generation, derived justification for their covert activity from Calvin by construing his abstract, doctrinal, or ecclesiological statements in their own concrete, architectural sense, much as Calvinist epigoni found the seeds of predestination in Calvin's work and cultivated them into a full-blown doctrine.[9] From another angle, those Calvinist architects who did not clearly and openly avow their Calvinist stance (unlike du Cerceau, for example) or sympathies (de l'Orme, Bullant) could be charged, in Calvin's earlier writings, with nicodemism: a dodge employed by believers who, from fear of reprisal or to favor professional advancement, hid their beliefs under a Catholic protective cloak.[10] This group dissimulates, more than subverts. But other Calvinists are more frank about their Calvinism.

Dissimulation was not uncommon in troubled times. Mario Carpo notes that nicodemite "clandestine activity . . . was a part of the daily existence of the Reformed elites in the cities."[11] Many printers in Reformed circles, such as Jean de Tournes, disguised their beliefs and camouflaged the perspectives of sympathizers whose work they published.[12] In many cases, such figures never publicly avowed their Calvinism directly; for some, like de Tournes, who fled to Geneva in 1596, such an overt profession of faith was too risky until they sheltered within sympathetic space.

Those architects who chose to remain "underground" nevertheless built their structures on biblical foundations and laid the bases for a Calvinist statement of faith in architectural terms. One of the ways in which architects like Philibert de l'Orme crafted coded confessional manifestoes was by reinterpreting the Pauline understanding of *adiaphora*, or external, extraneous things. If true faith resides in the heart of the believer, then that which is exterior to him should not be significant. For instance, Paul allowed Timothy to be circumcised because such an external rite was unessential to faith, yet might prove persuasive in leading Jews to Christianity.[13] So outward conformity to Catholicism in order to preserve one's life or career—while anathema to Calvin—could be seen as biblically sanctioned.[14] Since the message of nicodemism actually split the apprehension of reality in two—a deeper level perceived by the elect, contrasted with the mere surface seen by the uninitiated—Serlio, Philibert, and some of the second-generation architects developed a coded, idiosyncratically symbolized language for their architectural statements.[15] One must have ears to hear, eyes to see, as the gospel says; buried beneath the surface hides the true significance, whence the importance of the Reformed attitude toward ornamentation and decoration. Calvinist architects, admirers of the biblical plain style, intentionally did not emulate it; their grotesqueries and excessive ornamentation, while culturally indebted to mannerist influences, carried a unique theological freight. Such variety and exaggeration would create disguise from abundance: an *amplificatio* of camouflage. In Serlio's case, we find, first, an explicit disavowal of ornateness; next, extremely ornamented, even bizarre, decorative schemes; finally, we realize that it means something more than surface aesthetics when an evangelical or a Protestant deliberately contravenes the biblical precepts to which he subscribes.[16]

Calvinist architecture composes what art historians refer to as a body of "peculiar problems" in late sixteenth- and early seventeenth-century art. As Calvinists, these architects and artists worked creatively with, and within, conditions of constraint curtailing their freedom of personal and religious expression—constraint which, paradoxically, constituted the very conditions from which arose a repertoire of codes and strategies circumventing constraint. First- and second-generation Calvinist architects thereby significantly contributed in surprising ways to the development of the French architectural manual, surpassing conventional expectations for the genre. Mario Carpo explicitly attributes such expansion and generic revision to the evangelical and Protestant concerns of these architects. For instance, the evangelical architect Sebastiano Serlio's "editorial project for the *Extraordinario libro* (1551) came to fruition in a very particular cultural and ideological context"[17] that determined how, and of what, Serlio wrote. "Serlio seems to privilege ambiguity, or reticence, over an outright avowal; [there are] many contradictions [in his work] . . . [as if] the author found himself surrounded by wild beasts."[18] Serlio's evangelical stance leads him to list architectural "faultes," then to propose corrections for them, thus creating a manual that is didactic both in an explicit, technical sense and in a more subtle, theological way.[19] Du Cerceau acts similarly when reworking blueprints of existing structures: he portrays them not as they are but as he wishes them to be. His revisions surpass architectural surface; they refer to a new, theologically determined value system.

While the term "Protestant aesthetics" is customarily construed as an oxymoron, this is not the case. A Protestant aesthetics of subversion, possessing its own idiom, voice, strategies, and conceptual responses to specific historical moments of oppression, existed from the mid-sixteenth through the early seventeenth centuries in France. In *The Field of Cultural Production*, Pierre Bourdieu contends that often the significance of artistic productions is misconstrued due to a failure to explore their deep, or even occulted, meanings. He says that "the work of art (like any cultural object) may disclose significations at different levels according to the deciphering

grid applied to it; the lower-level significations . . . the most superficial, remain partial and mutilated, and therefore erroneous, as long as the higher-
level significations which encompass and transfigure them are lacking."[20]
Such is certainly the case with Calvinist architectural structures. Very few
readings of them take seriously the oppositional theological stance informing their work. Until we acknowledge that foundational perspective, we
will attain no clear grasp of the intent or extent of Calvinist architectural
production. In this book I seek to remedy such an oversight and to correct
previous misinterpretations.

Chapter 1 introduces the circumstances pressuring French Protestantism, while Chapter 2 presents the city-space of Geneva as a laboratory for
Protestant solution of problems of constraint. Ideological configurations
of city-space and town planning interested Calvinist architects throughout
the sixteenth and seventeenth centuries, beginning with Serlio's designs
for private dwellings, Philibert de l'Orme's townhouses, and Henri IV's
designs for public squares. These had a profound effect on French town
planning for centuries. While in Geneva (1541–64), Calvin devised a program for the scriptural reassignment of space. Calvin's insistence on the
disjunction between heavenly and earthly realms attests to a theological
struggle to reconfigure real space so as to make metaphysical sense of
space, as well as to criticize the hostile contemporary context. Chapter 2
reads the *Institution de la religion chrestienne* spatially, establishing the paradigm imitated by many contemporary and second-generation Calvinist
architects back in France. Chapter 3 showcases the work of Bernard Palissy,
potter, ceramicist, king's architect, and contemporary of Calvin's. His *Recepte véritable* shows similarities to Calvin's *Institution* and conceptualizes a
repertoire of structuring techniques later implemented by other Calvinist
architects. Palissy's description of an edenic garden seeks to take back space
withheld by the majority culture from Calvinists, arguing that, within the
privileged space of the Calvinist text, that which cannot be realized in the
external world may yet be imagined through faith and described programmatically. Chapter 4 discusses the nature and significance of the coded
works of Philibert de l'Orme, also a contemporary of John Calvin and a
significant contributor to the development of a specifically Calvinist architectural aesthetics. Philibert devised iconographic techniques to contradict Catholic hegemony, including juxtaposition, superscription, symbolic
counter-references, and an idiosyncratic application of detail. Chapter 5
reads textually and contextually the works of several second-generation
Calvinist architects, many of them related by marriage, thus positing a veri-

table genealogy of Calvinist architecture: Jean Bullant, Salomon de Brosse, Jacques Boyceau, and Androuet du Cerceau. These second-generation Calvinist architects were forced to go underground with Calvin's agenda, since the space that Calvin appropriated and represented as Protestant Geneva did not exist in adamantly Catholic France. These architects, at times resorting to the subterfuge of nicodemism, despite Calvin's harsh assessment were Calvinist nonetheless, and their beliefs inevitably materialized on the surface of their structures—albeit often in oblique or coded ways. Their constructions, plans, gardens, and grottoes spoke an architectural language reminiscent of Philibert de l'Orme, with frequent scriptural references taking up gnomic positions on their buildings in opposition to the Catholic establishment. Their structures and their architectural manuals wielded the weapon of architecture as creative heresy: just as Serlio took on Vitruvius, daring to criticize his great predecessor,[21] so Philibert took on Vitruvius and also denounced the defective structures of Catholic architects. While Calvinist architects worked in the same artistic context as Catholics, Calvinist beliefs inflected the conventional artistic idiom of the period, generally exaggerating its tendencies. Calvinists viewed architecture as a text to be aligned with the supreme text, God's Word,[22] whose language they then applied with the goals of architectural restoration and theological redemption.

Calvinism and its offshoots articulated a persistent countercultural voice, one that catalyzed reaction to it and galvanized creative response to constraints. Absolutism maintained itself through the strategy of the imposition of visual dominance, of one sole focal point.[23] If archite(x)ture is not perfectly legible or accessible (and such is the case for specifically Calvinist architecture), then obliqueness or difficulty—manifold focal points—constitutes the germ of a Calvinist critique of Catholic absolutism. The ubiquity of early modern Calvinist architects, and the persistence of their message, mandates acknowledging them as a far more significant force in French history than that of a mere minority religious subculture. Calvinism, through its oppositional voice, in fact dialectically played a major role in the construction of an official idiom for the French absolutist nation-state.

A Context for Code

Architecture as Metaphor for Historical Situation

In an anecdote supposedly overheard by a witness to the death of Catherine de Médicis, Agrippa d'Aubigné, the Calvinist writer, emblematizes how tensions due to the political and spiritual struggles of the Wars of Religion often were expressed in architectural terms: "She turned her face toward the wall, to Marguerite, her chambermaid, whom she had allowed to retain her Protestant faith; to Marguerite who had said, *Turn your eyes to the Lord, who will lift you up*, she answered these words, *I am overwhelmed by the ruins of my house*. To understand this, you should know that prophets had predicted to her ever since her youth that she would be struck down by a ruined building, and fearing this, she always caused structures in which she lived to be shored up."[1] In his poem *Les tragiques*, d'Aubigné describes as deformed and barbarous the architectural structures commissioned by the Catholic queen. Continuing the architectural metaphor, d'Aubigné sneers at Catherine who, unwittingly, was destroying her *own* house by doing violence to that of France:

> The heretic . . . loses her judgement, unaware
> That this house is none other than the house of France,
> The house whose foundations she weakens;
>   . . . and that's also why
> She'll bring down her own work on her head . . .
> She doesn't understand, when with a thousand beams
> She bolsters her dwellings, her castles:
> Buttress or fulcrum cannot stop
> God from making of your house, your tomb.[2]

According to d'Aubigné, legend has it that Catherine was obsessively fearful that her house would fall in on her. Consequently, in every building program she required her architects to take extraordinary protective structural measures. D'Aubigné puts her on notice that "worldly architecture has nothing that is able to withstand the blows of the heavens and the great God's hand."[3] Such wording clearly exculpates Catherine's architects, nearly all Calvinists, from responsibility for any structural inadequacies in their buildings. A door opens here to the subversive structuring typical of early modern Calvinists, who are here not only exonerated but also designated as the agents of God's plan for history: retribution against Catholics.

Probably the single factor most neglected in considering sixteenth- and seventeenth-century French construction is the metaphysical perspective informing it. The confessional stance of creators inevitably inflected what they conceived the purpose of their construction to be, how they built, and how they interpreted its effect. Protestant reworkings of existing, potentially hostile political scenarios have had a vast, although hitherto little recognized, influence on the development of the Western city-state and on such issues as freedom of artistic and theological expression. Yet art historians are reluctant to take into account those theological convictions, examining only the practical and aesthetic impact of the structure rather than the spiritual imperative lying at its conception.[4] In studying sixteenth- and seventeenth-century Europe, however, political ends cannot be interrogated separately from a consideration of how religious beliefs shaped politics. In a letter to William Congreve in 1699, Joseph Addison stated that "the King has honored the Genius [of Fontainebleau] and only made so much use of Art as is necessary to Help and regulate Nature without reforming her too much."[5] It seems ironic, in reference to the style of Louis XIV, eradictor of Calvinism within France's bounds, to hear the term "reforming." Such terminology makes visible the wounds to the nation's civil unity which, unhealed, scarred the structures of its public life.[6]

A specifically Calvinist stock of subversive iconography stratified such structures, offering multiple possibilities for interpreting them, but only one correct one. In some cases, Calvinist architects insisted on a scriptural "plain style," while in others they opted for hyperbolic architectural language, deliberately adorning structures excessively to display emblems of a sin-encrusted, distorted universe. John Wyclif's 1328 translation of Genesis 19:29, "He . . . dylyueride Loth fro the subuersion of cities in whiche he had dwellid," further denigrates urban structures through mention of the "subuersion of Sodom," suggesting thereby the early development of a generalized Protestant vocabulary for states, systems, and reactions against persecution.

What terms and concerns composed this Calvinist architectural vo-

1. This many-layered substructure concealed by an ornate façade evokes Catherine de Médicis' fear of hidden structural faults in her dwellings. The ornamentation creates a surface reassurance and an impression of solidity, but actually is a form of trompe l'oeil, as the structure is assembled from a multiplicity of components and is potentially less solid from within. Philibert de l'Orme, *Architecture* (1626), 1:151. By permission of the Folger Shakespeare Library.

cabulary? What forms did it take? What were its effects? What dialogue did it engage with Scripture? Calvinist structures were in every way inextricably embedded in the context of their creation. This context was inevitably conflictual, at war with Catholic criteria for the creation of structures in an ideological way that played itself out aesthetically after arising from a theological standpoint. Thus, for instance, "building up the walls of Jerusalem," a contemporary theological reference with an aesthetic application, became an ideological code phrase for active support of the Calvinist cause.[7]

Political Constraint and Coded Circumspection

In this book I examine the period beginning with the eight Wars of Religion (the hostilities started in 1562 with the Massacre at Wassy), continuing through the time of the Catholic *Ligue* (circa 1576–89) and the promulgation of the Edict of Nantes in 1598, and ending shortly after the edict's revocation in 1685. During this period, an important contested issue was that of space. Prior to the Edict of Nantes, Calvinists had no churches of their own—and certainly none designed expressly for their services; they could only hope to appropriate a barn, such as the *grange* at Wassy, and consecrate it, or to occupy and redefine a Catholic church. The customary historical interpretation of the period of the Edict of Nantes assumes that it was a time of religious toleration,[8] despite evidence that the edict did not impose global toleration. Certain clauses restricted the practice of the *religion prétendue réformée*, the ironic term *prétendue* demonstrating that the Catholic drafters of the edict viewed the Protestant variant as *claiming* to be reformed; Catholics did not acknowledge it as such, for that would be to criticize themselves. The edict also limited Calvinist worship to only two towns per *bailliage* and to the homes of high-ranking lords. In addition, recent archival research by historians of French Calvinism documents the presence of, if not outright persecution of Calvinists during this period, at least extensive practices aimed at marginalizing them. Such im-

plicit intolerance includes being barred from public office, harassment for expressions of belief, denial of access to funds to Reformed churches, and censorship of publications. Janine Garrison maintains that Protestantism was only recognized within the kingdom by default, and that "the content of the Edict includes, in germ, many threats to the religious minority which, in any event, it explicitly set aside . . . The dubious merit of this legal text was that it recorded in black and white the antagonism of two communities, and in this way justified that hostility."[9]

Thus, while making minor concessions in order to put an end to explicit hostilities, the Edict of Nantes acted merely as a cosmetic measure or, worse, validated hostilities. By assigning only a few areas for Calvinist worship, the edict explicitly differentiated the theological schism in spatial terms, effectively establishing Calvinist ghettos. Jacques Carpentier notes that "the fact that Henri IV judged it necessary to grant to his former co-religionists the right to assemble and to retain 151 strongholds in order to permit them eventually to exercise their rights of worship shows that the Edict of Nantes is an act of political realism on the king's part and not the rendering into legal language of a true climate of toleration. The violent opposition of the law courts to the recording of the edict, the steely resistance demonstrated from a variety of Catholic quarters, attest to the same reality."[10]

Huguenots responded to such treatment by cooperating, on the surface, with Catholic expectations. However, Calvinists continued to articulate their feelings of constraint by devising coded statements. In cases concerned with the allocation of space or the construction of public structures, Calvinist architects accepted commissions from Catholic nobility, but used iconography in a subversive or ironic way to undermine—by rewriting or overwriting—the official statement of Catholic power. In this way, a state monument might seem, on cursory viewing, to confirm Catholic domination. Yet an attentive reading of the structure reveals a contradictory subtext, a sort of parasitical superscription on an ostensibly acceptable base.[11]

While hostilities alternated with periods of toleration during the early years of the Wars of Religion, "toleration" was generally short-lived, geographically limited, and elitist. Rights for Protestants often only obtained on an individual basis, generally those granted to nobility and their households. In the Edict of Amboise, in 1563, Henri de Condé, the Protestant military leader, secured his dependents' right to worship as they pleased; however, no Protestant retainer of a Catholic lord had such privilege. Protestant recusancy consequently brought reprisals: many Huguenots reverted to Catholicism out of fear or due to financial need. Protestantism was no longer a birthright: the belief system of the patriarch was not necessarily transmitted with unflagging fervency to the son.[12] Thus, those second-generation architects like Jacques Androuet du Cerceau who persisted in defining themselves as Calvinists did so in the face of criticism or reprisal, aware that their ranks were dwindling.

Catholic Reformation tactics also account for a decline in numbers. After the Council of Trent in 1563, Catholics increasingly employed seductive, sensorial iconography as well as persuasive preaching in order to counteract Protestant proselytizing. Militant, more worldly orders such as the Jesuits were created. As a result, "many Protestants feared for the future of their faith. In effect, the Catholic church in the first decades of the seventeenth century benefited from a strong revival resulting especially from reforms put in place in Catholic countries by the Council of Trent . . . The peace resulting from the Edict of Nantes allowed the clergy to begin new preaching initiatives, within the very strongholds of Calvinism."[13]

The Calvinists' awareness of losses not exclusively attributable to battlefield casualties would have two consequences. First, the polemical character of the Protestant iconographic component of the structure would increase, while a feeling of being imperiled or weakened would intensify the architect's determination to transmit the Word of God. Second, an *altered architectural vocabulary*, in which the forms of subversion were, while still pervasive, less obvious, would develop. The first few years of Henri IV's reign were far from stable, and his political temporizing and theological equivocating proved unsettling to hard-line Protestants, scriptural intransigents rather than political accommodationists. During these years, Henri IV and the duke of Sully inaugurated a massive building campaign, for which most of the structures were executed by Calvinist architects. Their structures display fascinating swerves and deviations from his programs, instead displaying their own versions or revisions.

The Calvinist sentiment of marginality was attenuated briefly from 1617 to the end of the siege of La Rochelle on 28 October 1626. During this time, some Protestant consolidation occurred, particularly along the Atlantic seaboard, due to the maritime power of the Rochelais. Protestantism began to develop several strong cities as bases. More overtly Protestant iconographic superscription of state-sponsored structures attests to greater militancy on their part. However, with the decimation of the three thousand Protestant souls in the town of Privas on 26 May 1629, the death knell for Protestantism as a real force in the kingdom sounded, and other

Protestant strongholds soon capitulated. Louis XIV suppressed all political privilege for Protestants: "They lost any hope of having any effect on the political future."[14] Now, their only outlet would be artistic; their only hope, apocalyptic. Buildings fashioned by Calvinist architects of the second generation reflect this reality.

Many instances would occur during this period of implicit and explicit persecution of Huguenots: textual and architectural documentation, as well as combinations of the two (texts that talk about how structures should be interpreted, or structures that require literary deciphering). A particularly rich textual example represents these Calvinist responses to constraint. Philippe du Plessis-Mornay, friend of Henri IV but estranged after the king converted to Catholicism in 1593, probably the most influential statesman of the Huguenot party, was to France what John Calvin was to Geneva: he penned policy, encouraged Reformed churches in France, maintained extensive correspondence with their pastors, and drafted Reformed doctrine. In response to Henri III's reliance on the Catholic *Sainte Ligue*, Mornay participated in the establishment of an oppositional body, effectively a separate Calvinist state within the Catholic realm, the *Union calviniste*.[15] Mornay paralleled the programs of Calvinist architects to erect spaces suitable for Calvinist observance, even the creation of Calvinist towns such as Henrichemont, envisioned as places set apart, where Calvinism could safely thrive.

Mornay's tract on the Eucharist asserts as an article of faith that the pope was the Antichrist, despite Henri IV's negative reaction to Mornay's stance: "The King suddenly changed markedly in his attitude toward M. du Plessis and toward Calvinism in particular, for the King took pains to persuade those near him to renounce their faith, telling them that, should they persevere, he could do nothing to advance their careers. His Majesty also took pleasure in amplifying on the obligation he felt to the pope, and the obedience he believed he owed him, denigrating all the while the Reformed church and pastors."[16] The king made these prejudicial pronouncements in 1599, a scant year after the promulgation of the Edict of Nantes. Henri IV also notified Mornay that should he publish any denigrating statements about the pope, the king would have every copy of Mornay's books burned.[17] Such strong-arm censorship attests to a policy of actively silencing Protestants.

Mornay responded by radicalizing his position, becoming a *tyrannomach*, or regicide, political pamphleteer. Unable to publish his tract *Vindiciae contra tyrannos* in France (although it eventually circulated widely there), he had it printed abroad. He also began to encrypt a significant amount of his personal correspondence in complex code, especially letters to his wife and his son, both his delegates in political and religious affairs.[18]

Mornay's letters offer a case study of the implicit and explicit constraint experienced by Huguenots during this period. Similarly, Calvinist architects would develop hermetic networks of self-protective symbols requiring a discerning readership to puzzle out their connections. Such opacity demonstrates the need for concealment on the part of the marginalized Calvinists, who would learn, of necessity, to craft the glyphs in which to convey political and theological commentary. Philippe du Plessis-Mornay's letters, begun in 1588, conclude in 1603 with the death of Madame de Mornay and in 1605 for those letters written between son and father. Of the sixty-one letters written by Mornay to his wife, twenty contain coded portions, which may be as minimal as a few lines or as extensive as half a letter. Thus, in at least one-third of the purportedly private correspondence between husband and wife, Mornay intentionally expresses himself in terms obscure to all but his intended, enlightened recipients. Letters containing the most sizable portions of code are those written immediately before, and especially during, the enforcement of the Edict of Nantes: January and April 1588, February 1589, November 1593, and February and March 1595. Therefore, Mornay's correspondence documents Calvinist concern over persecution even during a period of ostensible toleration.

Appropriately for Calvinists, "People of the Book," the code's intricacy suggests reference to a book, a text that must have been in the possession of both Mornay and his wife and, later, of their son. Was it the Bible? Was it one of Mornay's own numerous publications? The code works on a numerical system, with the occasional inclusion of a Greek or Hebrew letter, and appears consistent within each letter, although the Mornays altered the key for the code from time to time: 32, for instance, generally represents the letter *n*, while in another letter, *e* is represented both by .40. and .87. Major historical figures receive numerical ranking: the king is .1., the queen is .2., and the prince is .5. Each digit, or group of digits, is separated by a period to indicate that it should be deciphered individually before being reintegrated to construct a phrase, suggesting a complex syntax dependent on entire textual passages, a highly literary and demanding form of *bricolage*. Three-digit numerals refer to places, usually locations in which a substantial Reformed population existed or which housed a Reformed church: .264. stands for Angers, 277 for La Rochelle, and 262 for

Lyons.[19] The code thus both highlights privileged Protestant spaces and protects them, the language of the letters constituting a covert Calvinist topography.

In most cases, the coded portions serve either to give instructions to Madame de Mornay—instructions also relevant to other Huguenots—or to provide details about the movements of Huguenots within the French realm. Thus, Madame de Mornay functions as an ideal reader, an "everywoman" epitomizing a sympathetic and receptive listener to the Huguenot cause. Not surprisingly, the text often criticizes the court or contains the seeds of oppositional strategies, as in the letter of 17 February 1595, where the statement "74. 7. 17.22. 18.5. 92.4. et. 9. se reschauffent, et y en a qui les veulent persuader à .l. comme utiles à 142. 25. 50. 11" is deciphered in the manuscript as "The love affair of M. and Mme. the Count of Soissons has rekindled; some think this situation could be used in ways advantageous to the State."[20]

The body of coded text often challenges, spatially, the body of uncoded prose, creating a bizarre visual effect in which numbers proliferate and defy deciphering.[21] The code in another letter obfuscates the name of Monsieur Lomenie, who is identified, uncoded, earlier in the letter. Lomenie's encoded name protects him from recognition as the author of a statement critical of the king.

In a politically threatening climate, tactics of obfuscation or mystification offer one hiding place. Mornay's use of code contradicts the assumption that this period was unproblematic for Protestants, demonstrating, instead, the existence of considerable subversive activity on the part of Protestants, for reasons of self-protection, within France during the period of the Edict of Nantes. Mornay certainly felt uneasy enough to have recourse to code. An eyewitness records an emblematic ending to Mornay's life: on his deathbed, he uttered several indecipherable phrases, a hodgepodge of Greek, Hebrew, Latin, and French, as though recalling unconsciously the code in which he had made some of his more audacious personal and political statements.[22]

As was the case for Mornay, Calvinist architects and authors of texts concerning construction continued to create, with circumspection, and to implement a battery of strategies against constraint. Like Mornay's correspondence, their structures also contained code. This code reallocated virtual space and redetermined official monuments in a Calvinist sense, acting, as it did for Mornay, to delineate an alternative linguistic universe facilitating their outlawed confessional statement.

Alternative Architecture

The first generation of Calvinist architects, contemporaries of John Calvin, knew of his blueprint for Geneva as God's saved city and recognized the *Institution de la religion chrestienne*'s vocabulary for expressing spatial concerns. Architects such as Philibert de l'Orme and Bernard Palissy worked for Catherine de Médicis or for other Catholic patrons, and so had to contend with the interconfessional hostilities of the Wars of Religion. The cultural and religious climate during the early days of Protestantism was not, at the outset, as polarized or highly charged as it became after the Affaire des Placards; for that reason, a potential for sympathy for Protestantism existed. Theologians, authors, and architects like Guillaume Briçonnet, Lefèvre d'Etaples, Marguerite de Navarre, Clément Marot, and Sebastiano Serlio—contemporaries of Calvin, de l'Orme, and Palissy—were known as evangelicals, Catholics who wished to reform from within. Until Calvin, no alternative institutional option existed for the reforming impulse; Luther, despite his influence in France, persisted in claiming Catholic identity (although Rome declared him a heretic). Calvin, however, in establishing Geneva as an anti-Rome, provided an institutional structure in which reformist drives could situate themselves, thereby creating a specifically Protestant identity.

François Rabelais, another evangelical and a former Franciscan monk, seems to have prefigured Calvinist alternative architecture when he scripturally founded his structuring enterprise: the Abbaye de Thélème, an idealized site, only truly realizable—as is the case with the conceptions of many Calvinist architects—within the space of the text[23] (what Gérard Genette refers to as "archite(x)ture," an en-texted structure). Articulating an evangelical program, the Abbaye is very similar to the sorts of structures inhabiting Bernard Palissy's *Recepte véritable*. There are three principal areas outside the Abbaye proper: a garden, a labyrinth, and a river. An orchard, a tennis court, and an archery yard are also mapped. All these components convey a christological significance for Rabelais. The garden offers opportunity to recultivate paradise in a fallen world; pushed to its outer border, a labyrinth—a common medieval and Renaissance figure for the maze of the fallen world—connotes the confusion of man's sinful state, while a fountain recalls Christ's "living waters." Less customary are the references to the "vergier" (the orchard, site of Adam and Eve's fall) and the tennis court (Rabelais indulges in a game of protective coloration, having Frère Jean translate an enigma about Thélème as referring to a tennis match);

however, Randle Cotgrave's *Dictionarie of the French and English Tongues* provides the second meaning of *paume* as the *paulme of Christ*, while an umpire at a match is a sixteenth-century term for the Holy Spirit. The archery yard is also a reference to Christ via Pauline scripture. Rabelais makes such reference to Christian endeavor explicit: "It's nothing new that those who place their trust in evangelical belief are persecuted; but blessed is he who will not let himself be impeded [in his faith] and who will always aim straight at the target that God, through his dear son, has set for us, not allowing his carnal desires to distract or divert him." [24]

The Abbaye is in every respect an evangelical construct, structured upon a scriptural foundation. Such terms as "esleuz," "predestiné," "selon leur vouloir et franc arbitre," "non par loix," "gens libres, bien néz," "feurent reforméz par leur franc vouloir," and the biblical phraseology of such sentences as "Ainsi l'avoit estably Gargantua" [25] convey the evangelical tenor of the description of the Abbaye de Thélème. However, the Abbaye's status remains that of wish list, [26] perhaps because Rabelais does not envision a definite break with the overarching structure of the Roman church but only hopes to rectify abuses within its existing format. In its systematic structural reversal of all customary expectations governing the establishment of monastic order (it is not enclosed; only beautiful people may enter; there is no rule but nonrule: "fay ce que vouldras"), the Abbaye performs a structural correction of Catholicism, much as coded statements on Calvinist architecture criticize Catholic dominance.

One difference between the evangelical Abbaye and the Calvinist constructions that we will examine is that the Abbaye conveys an overtly critical perspective: written prior to the Affaire des Placards, it benefits from the atmosphere of humanistic tolerance emanating from the court of François I, in large part due to the influence of Marguerite de Navarre. Calvinist structures, on the other hand, use code out of necessity (rather than from a ludic impulse, as is often the case with Rabelais) and are exceptionally resistant to interpretation. Rabelais does complicate the interpretation of his Abbaye [27] by appending an *énigme en prophétie* at the end of the description. However, while appearing obscure, like code, the *énigme* is, in fact, fairly transparent: it narrates the story of the Fall of mankind, the introduction of sin into the world, the flood, Pentecost, and Christian redemption. Calvinists also employ twinned components—structure and superscription, image and commentary—to convey their perspective, but their statements are thoroughly encoded. Another similarity between Rabelais and later Calvinist architects is that they both revise architectural predecessors, appropriating what is usable and rewriting it for their purposes; Rabelais's Thélème bears similiarities in structure with Vitruvius's human microcosm as structuring model,[28] but it surpasses Vitruvius's concerns to incorporate a theological perspective.

Contemporary with evangelical re-visions of the world are other structuring enterprises by architects sympathetic to Protestantism, such as the evangelical Philibert de l'Orme. He began Chenonceau in 1515, Blois in 1515, Chambord in 1519, and Fontainebleau in 1528—all prior to the outbreak of hostilities with the Affaire des Placards in 1534, at which time liberal Reformers such as Jacques Lefèvre d'Etaples began to be edged aside by more extremist evangelicals, Lutherans, and, later, Calvinists. Anthony Blunt has noted the asymmetry of Philibert's façades at Blois and the irregular arrangement of windows and other "aberrations," attempting to account for such idiosyncrasies by observing that such "irregularity proves that although French builders had learnt the idiom of Italian decoration, they had not yet absorbed the basic principles of Renaissance architecture." Blunt here avails himself of the customary assessment of French inferiority to Italian standards to explain the oddities in Philibert's structures.[29] Yet architectural historians such as Mario Carpo, who take seriously the context (including religious aspects inflecting constructed works), have shown that asymmetry and excessive ornamentation may have ideological derivation and motivation, rather than simply showing a difference in culture or formation.

It can hardly have been the case that Philibert, with his masterful, thoroughly detailed architectural drawings and his textual display of compendious knowledge, had not adequately mastered his craft. Rather, this proto- or crypto-Calvinist architect deliberately misrepresented techniques; he implemented strategies to unsettle or deface structures in order to challenge both the view and the world-view, both the personal perspective and the metaphysics, of their viewers. And when such strange stylistic similarities exist in the oeuvres of many architects, they sketch lines of affiliation suggesting a fraternity motivated by causes surpassing the purely architectural. Thus, an architecture forming common cause with Calvinism devised a signature and camouflage techniques in response to political events such as the firm alliance of Crown with Catholicism under Henri II, an alliance that "inaugurat[ed] in arts the policy which was to be carried to its fullest development by Louis XIV."[30]

The second generation of Calvinist architects (circa 1580 to 1630) would continue the first generation's program of a subversive redetermination of structures, but would contend with somewhat different realities. In many cases, direct affiliations link this second generation with its evangelical and Calvinist sources of inspiration. For example, the architect and sculptor Jean Goujon, born in Normandy around 1510 and best known for his stunning work on the Eglise de St.-Maclou in Rouen around 1541, demonstrates in his work the influence of Sebastiano Serlio: the architectonic disposition of the arcade and base of the Fontaine des Innocents comes directly from Serlio's fourth book of designs published in 1545. Goujon's motivations for the majority of his work were not only architectural but also explicitly religious,[31] and he fled France in 1563 after his conversion to Protestantism earned him two periods of imprisonment.[32] He took refuge in Bologna, where he died five years later. Sculptor and architect for the Connétable Anne de Montmorency, he erected Louis de Brézé's tomb around 1531, constructed the rood screen of St. Germain l'Auxerrois, and worked with Lescot on the Louvre, where the "highly personalized language of his reliefs has been noted."[33] He also played a significant part in the construction and ornamentation scheme at Ecouen. Known for his deft sense of surface decoration, Goujon, like other Calvinist craftsmen, had an unnerving tendency to violate borders and limits: on some of his sculptures the upper figures break out of the field of the pediment, while the side figures extrude beyond the range of the capitals.[34]

Another convert, Ligier Richier, fled to Geneva, where he died in 1566. He emphasized decorative patterns in his work, placing a high value on detail as responsible for the coded meaning of a structure, an insistence common to other Calvinist architects, especially the influential second-generation Calvinist architect Jean Bullant. Richier's publications devote the greatest amount of space to fantastical, ornate engravings of decorative schemes, grotesques, and patterns for furniture and architectural detail.[35] He depicted skin torn like bits of parchment on the tombal figure of René de Châlons, virtually undoing the expectation of a permanent memento mori by dissolving it into remnants and shreds. While Calvinist architects shared a context with their Catholic counterparts and exhibited characteristics in common, they tended to exaggerate such traits due to their embattled Protestant perspective. Consequently, mannerism (strained, irrational, disorderly, complex, and ingenious—the anatomy of tortured thought) found its fullest expression in Protestantism.

Signature traits of Calvinist architects include multiple orders warring within the same structure, mixed forms, drastically elongated shapes, unorthodox framing, and vertical/horizontal tension. Such inherently conflictual schemas encode an ideological dissonance, a hidden agenda that calls for a response. This architecture targets a discerning elect group. Not all will hear the carefully coded message that these Calvinist architects express. As with their structures, their architectural manuals, while replete with personal anecdotes, nonetheless seem deliberately to occlude the author's point of view. Not all will be up to the task.[36] The Calvinist architect's subversive communications imitate the apparently simplistic, but in fact hermetic, biblical parable genre, for similar reasons: Jesus spoke gnomically to protect himself from persecution by the rigid, law-loving Pharisees. Yet parables do not dissimulate; their effect is subversively stronger as they speak of daily events, ordinary things and people, reworking them in a new sense utterly contradictory to the established order of things.[37] Similarly, every model that the Calvinist architect invokes, every construction he displays, is a sort of trap.[38]

Their agenda has two apparently contradictory thrusts. Protestant architects claim representationally to restore unity to the French political scene. The Calvinist architect and writer Blaise de Vigenère, for instance, states in *Images* that "just as for a poet it is not enough to know how to structure a good verse, neither for a mason is it sufficient to know how to carve just one stone: it is necessary afterwards to arrange the pieces to make a good poem or to structure the stones to make a building of which the members will correspond, and the parts duly refer to the whole, as if it were all one piece."[39] Vigenère treats structures textually, showing their description of the ideological forces that shape them, wishing for some reconciliation between the two. His comparisons between building and poem require literary deciphering.

Comparisons of structures to texts also exist in contemporary Catholic writing, but with crucial differences. Pierre de Ronsard, as an example, addresses his second book of *Odes* to Henri II, Catholic patron of several Protestant architects:

> I want to build an Ode to you,
> Structuring it in the style
> Of your renowned palaces
> Which have showy entry-ways
> And are decorated with marble
> And high gilded pillars,
> So that the facade of the work
> Will reveal, at first glance,

The entire rich building:
Thus, Prince, I want to put
On the front page of my poetry
First and foremost your virtues.[40]

The Catholic Ronsard portrays a centralized world. Unity prevails, with a consensus achieved through the use of classical orders. Everything he wants to signify is set up front, for immediate apprehension by the viewer, and his structure develops with impeccable, canonic accepted logic ("afin que"). A century later, when the style of French classicism provided the idio for the exaltation of the persona of the Sun King, the centralized aesthetics of power at Versailles worked similarly.[41] For Protestants, however, that which is displayed up front is often a ruse to lead the uninformed viewer away from the real, subjacent meaning, perceptible only to an informed reader. Causal links and narrative relationships shatter. Disharmony between word and image encourages more baroque forms rather than classical models, as is the case with Chambord, erected by a Protestant architect: "The ordering of the [pillars at Blois] remains closely linked with the structure. At Chambord, however, any unity between scaffolding and decor disappears. The decor acquires an existence unto itself . . . the crossbeams have also been recognized as devoid of any relationship to the decor."[42] Detail and ornament no longer marry with surface; instead, they disturb order, calling into question the rationale of the structure. Calvinist architectural activity is ultimately profoundly disruptive.

Another characteristic of Calvinist architects is that they often do not perceive their work to be original or creative.[43] Calvin specified that only God can create something absolutely new: "Now, creation is not in any way a transfusion, as one would draw wine from a vessel into a bottle; creation means rather to give birth to something that had never existed before."[44] Calvinists must rework preexisting structures or work from others' commands and designs. Just as they lack space for confessional expression in France, they are not free to devise their own structures.

Archite(x)tural Writing

Two Protestant authors, both using architecture as metaphor, epitomize how Calvinist architects conceived of their endeavors. Agrippa d'Aubigné in *Les tragiques* and the *Odes* (the latter written both in imitation of, and as a correction of, Ronsard's odes) enumerates Protestant criticism of Catholic structures, while Guillaume Salluste Du Bartas, in *La Sepmaine*, writes a litany of Calvinist proposals to rectify the world.

D'Aubigné berates arrogant Catholic cities:

> I have seen so many grand cities
> Whose prideful bell towers
> Pierce the sky and the heavens
> With cunning pyramids
> . . . They are proudly rich in artillery . . .

and palliates such presumption with modest Calvinist structures:

> But you, O happy city,
> Whose palace is favorable
> To much-cherished justice,
> You reign victorious:
> By you are these other cities overcome
> Who wage impudent warfare.[45]

D'Aubigné shows that structure and message should harmonize. Catholic deviance forces Protestants to work in code and to adopt distortion as a dialectical tool to correct aberrancy.

Du Bartas offers some solutions to the problem that d'Aubigné describes. His proposals are solely textual, for the real world holds no space or tolerance for the structures that he envisions.[46] Du Bartas provides the paradigm for deciphering Calvinist structures: they are written productions surpassing obvious imaged quality. On the page, the spatial distribution of Du Bartas's litanies requires the reader to visualize ways in which to fill or structure the textual spaces.[47] Content and visuals dissociate, much as schismatic detail in Calvinist architecture contradicts or redetermines surface.[48]

Recourse to strategies of coding, of writing against and around a preset text or ideology, is consistent with Calvinism's acceptance of the Bible as the unsurpassable text.[49] Any independent Protestant literary creation inevitably, and potentially blasphemously, contests with Scripture.[50] Thus, when Catholicism poses its own religious and political mandates, Protestants easily slip into the coding strategy to which they are already habituated.

Protestants may hope to insert the universe into their text, and thus reorder it, or to portray the disorder of the world in their alternative universe and thus redefine it.[51] Du Bartas resembles Calvin in the spatial deployment of his table of contents; as in Calvin's *Institution*, an architectural delineation of the subject matter builds logically, then ramifies into subdivisions and related topics.[52] Du Bartas extends the equation between text and building, playing on the disjunction between City of God and City of Man that Augustine, Calvin, and d'Aubigné recalled. Conflating terms used for texts with those used for buildings (*frontispiece* instead of *front*, *feuillet* instead of *pierre*), he states: "Some readers will stumble against the first page of this building, finding its title strange indeed . . . I refer them to the last chapter of Augustine's City of God, from which I've taken both the title, the argument and division of the book. Have no doubt that the authority of Augustine's texts acts as my safeguard . . . But, tell me, where did you learn to judge an entire palace by its frontispiece? I've not yet set in place ²/₃ of the foundations for my building. You'll only see some incomplete walls which reveal the inside of the building, and stones that wait to be aligned with the rest of the structure."[53] In this passage, Du Bartas refers to a precursor text at times, sometimes writing around that text, and acknowledges all texts' imperfection; this is a way to contradict the Catholic delusion that the world is complete and harmonious. He recalls the Calvinist motif of the *ville-refuge*, concluding that such a safe place is possible only within textual space (that of Scripture): "son texte . . . me serve de sauve-garde" [His text is to me a place of safekeeping].

Like Calvin, Du Bartas hopes to set limits (*bornes*). Overflowing its boundaries, the world's pridefulness must be curtailed and contained:

The sea . . . spills its tides over the tops of bounded mountains . . .
The power of their peaks! . . .
But see how the sea
Throws me into a thousand seas
See how its overflow makes me overflow with words![54]

The pun at the end of the above quotation demonstrates how Calvinists work creatively against and from constraint: the ocean's thrust, which Du Bartas fears, paradoxically propels him to respond with a surge of words.

Du Bartas desires to return to a primordial state of chaos, because only from that cleansing confusion will order reemerge:

This first world was a form without form,
A confused heap, a deformed mixture,
Of chasms a chasm, a poorly outlined body,
A chaos of chaos, a pile poorly gathered up.[55]

Increasingly grotesque iconography[56]—characterized by figures of over-layering, excess, marginality, and monstrosity—typifies his quest.

Exaggeration and unusual application of figures compose the architecturally revisionist Calvinist vocabulary. For instance, in the *Recepte véritable*, Palissy sculpts a series of men's bodies as supports for his grotto structures. These forms end in deformity, seeming to dissolve from a shape still imbued with proportion and sense into an amorphous mass. Such lower-body degeneration, emblem of man's fallen and sinful nature, undoes hubris. As with Serlio's evangelical architecture, Palissy's constructions provide the surface for the display of man's reprobation. "Viciousness" and "licentiousness" are multivalent terms: theologically, they evoke man's damnation; architecturally, they designate a degraded structure. In his allegories of the Good and Bad Architects, Philibert de l'Orme weds architecture to theology, indicting faulty structures as the mirror for man's crookedness and lack of alignment with God, a theater for the dramatizing of sin. Calvin, Philibert, and Palissy allude to the biblical plumb line—an architect's tool as well as a theological symbol—lamenting deviation from its standard.

Subversion is a peculiarly appropriate activity for a Calvinist architect: the earliest meaning of "subversive" is "to destroy or raze to the ground a building," according to the *Oxford English Dictionary*. The Calvinist architect erects, then symbolically topples, the edifice commissioned to glorify the Catholic patron.

2

Spatial Situations

Calvin's Prototype

> There is a correspondence of faith with the Word, from
> which faith cannot be separated or swayed . . . This
> same Word is the foundation on which faith is built and
> sustained, the foundation which, if pulled away, will im-
> mediately cause faith to tremble.
> —Calvin, *Institution de la religion chrestienne*

ARCHITECTURE RAISES the issue of space, and space would be discussed
during the sixteenth century in relation to basic theological concepts.
Catholics considered space through a "receptacle" theory: space is either
in or about something, or something is known to be in space. The Renaissance perception was relational; the Reformers subscribed to this, as well.[1]
In the relational theory, space comprises a series of interactions. This vocabulary served to break the bond between the physical and metaphysical
realms, which sought to condense the latter into the former. In the Catholic understanding of transubstantiation, for instance, the wafer was (and is)
actually and truly the body of Christ. To the Reformers, transubstantiation
was blasphemous, since the wafer was an element of the lesser, created
order.[2] To describe the relationship between the visible and the invisible
church, the Reformers forged a new language, one in which words pointed
beyond themselves to a higher reality rather than purporting to describe
immanence. Calvin wanted to move from an exclusively theological understanding of the dimensions of real space to an insistence on the interrela-
tionships between public, external, empirical space and space typified by
an inner, moral spatial dimension. Calvin's *Institution de la religion chrestienne* can be read as an innovative document concerned with ecclesiology,
theology, and the notion of space, because in it Calvin desires to locate
the visible church on earth in an approximate conjunction with that of the

perfect, invisible church. He is also concerned with the right structuring of the recessed space of the human heart.³

Calvin developed a lexicon applying biblical mandates about space to the city-space of Geneva, and to the larger scope of the church in general. His new vocabulary, along with the novel application of existing terms, enabled two generations of Calvinist architects to use his concepts in a concrete way in a vexed political and cultural situation. Calvin needed to find a space for the legitimation of the Calvinist interpretation of Scripture because he wrote from the margins. The language of the *Institution* articulates a Calvinist genealogy of architectural treatment, a Calvinist statement in architectural terms.⁴ Calvin uses para-architectural terminology to describe the relationship between dogma and ecclesiology: "it is indeed necessary that such doctrine be approved and *upheld* before the Church may be *established*, just as the *foundation must be laid* before the *building is erected*."⁵ From his doctrinal illustrations, Calvinist architects crafted tools with which they incised signature graffiti of their personal religious beliefs on public structures. Because of Calvin's theoretical texts, they were able to view space both as a bounded, empirical realm not always receptive to their real structures and as an arena of hidden, idealized possibility that they could encode with their own message.

If the Reformed grasp of space can be called relational, Calvin's is situational in a deeply dialectical sense. For him, space is always dynamic, composed of waves of tensions and dissonances rather than constituting a static container or product; it is always both itself and the shadow contradiction of itself. For Calvinism, which (in contrast with other Reformed expressions, such as the Puritans and their New World "cities on a hill") did not possess empirical space in France in which to craft a religious domain consonant with its theology, space was of necessity dialectical: it was both imperfect, even evil (Papist Rome, Catholic France), yet also potentially redeemable (otherwise, why would Calvin persist in his endeavors at reform?). In Calvin's turn toward Scripture as sole authority, he moves toward a notion of the immutability of the decree; while space is dialectical, epitomizing flawed postlapsarian humanity, the Word is enduring, unequivocal, and, as incarnation, it inhabits that same marred space. The only space for a full and perfect description of the operation and structure of salvation is, therefore, textual, the book acting as the equivalent of the invisible church.

Compelled by real circumstances of spatial limitation, Calvin presses against customary understandings of space. In Calvin's topological glossary, structures populate situational space: an inherently *architectural* project. These structures interrelate on many levels. They can be read as texts, both as texts that conform and as texts that contradict. In this way, they require an interpretive process deeper than visual. A structure has both form and content, but as Calvinist architects use the structure, it also has a third, theoretical component. This latter aspect represents the Calvinist wish list for freedom of religious expression. The theoretical aspect operates like Calvin's description of the relationship between the visible and the invisible church as a hoped-for intersection: an apocalyptic spatial overlap, one layer being real space; the other, idealized or metaphysical space. For the two layers to conjoin, it is necessary "to consider *how* and with what other *relationships* such words should be aligned."[6] For Calvin, space, syntax, and significance are superimposed on each other. Space displays the true church, its opposite, and its possible correction. Similarly, for the Calvinist architect, the theoretical dimension of a structure offers a countertext, a coded corrective to the distortions necessitated by Catholic patronage.

Calvin's understanding of space is almost a temporal construct; he does not ask *where* the true church may be found but rather *when*. For instance, he explains what happens to Christ's body at the elevation in such a way that the body is both present at the communion table and also simultaneously present in heaven, thereby safeguarding the Godhead while still making Christ's humanity available. The formulation of the *extra calvinisticum* thus provides spatial emancipation for Calvinists, because it enables something present on earth to also exist elsewhere. The *extra calvinisticum* demonstrates that something in one form can also signify, perhaps more truly, in another form. In addition, the doctrine of predestination can be considered a *spatializing* doctrine: a remnant is set aside as the "elect," while others are shifted out of the workings of salvation. Calvin says, "God has *marked out* for us two sorts of people: one from the lineage of Abraham, the other *a part separate* from that, which God *keeps* to himself like a *hidden treasure*."[7] Code works the same way. Iconography can be reconfigured so that it functions on several levels and contains multiple, even contradictory, meanings. Structures can both monumentalize a Catholic monarch and subvert their own statement by adhering to the scriptural injunction to be "in this world yet not of it." Calvinist architects would graft coded components onto structures, symbolizing the ideal, metaphysical space of protection and legitimation for Calvinists.

Calvin's treatment of space can also be discerned in his manipulation —both theoretical and actual—of the preassigned city-space of Geneva.[8]

Calvin could have razed the city and built anew. But, for Calvin, putting one space in the place of another would have been too visual and concrete a treatment of space. Instead, as with the two-layered structure of the *extra calvinisticum*, he allowed Calvinist usages and practices to redefine existing Catholic space by virtue of their presence as determinants superimposed on the city.

Calvin and Geneva: The Reformation of a City

Calvin used city-space as a laboratory. He fled Paris to the protection of Renée de Ferrare at the time of the Affaire des Placards, and was effectively in exile from Geneva at the time he composed the body of the *Institution*. This personal experience of displacement was thus an important dynamic in his textual development. The *Institution*, written in Strasbourg while Calvin was in exile, contains his theory of how Genevan city-space should be reassigned, so as to represent as closely as possible God's church on earth. Calvin's *Institution* posits the need for an intellectual structure in and through which to apprehend Scripture. The schema of the *Institution* proceeds spatially, as a sort of literary layer built upon and amplifying the original textual groundwork, Scripture, recalling thereby the raising up of a building from its foundations. In Calvin's thought, city-space contrasts with wilderness, chaos, and disorder unstructured by God's Word. Wilderness is typified by a lack of institutions, disfigured structures, and erratic movement and instability: "When the devil gains right of place, like a bad and headless horseman, he drags the church through hill and dale, makes it fall into ditches, causes it to stumble and swerve through valleys, and accustoms it to rebellion and disobedience."[9] Now stabilized in a good place, the church must make its mark on the spaces and structures around it. Calvin reconfigures city-space both as an empirical area and as an abstraction oriented toward the fulfillment of certain desiderata.

The social space inhabited by the citizenry must be aligned with textual space, both that of the Bible and that of Calvin's own writing. The introductory remarks of the *Institution* also call for order: "everything is in ruins, so that we must either absolutely despair of every human thing, or *put things back in order*"; "Although I did not regret the labor spent, I was never satisfied until the work had been *arranged in the order* now set forth."[10] For Calvin, city and church are, or should be, one and the same; he reminds his readers to "remember the captivity that they had long endured, the destruction of the city and the destruction of the temple" and uses Scripture to label space, as in his recasting of the Genevan motto: "Here is henceforth the name of the city: *God is in it*."[11] This rectified city-space then flows out to englobe the larger world. Calvin states that "the world is larger than a city. Why speak to me of the customs of the city alone? Why try to subject the right ordering of the church to a mere handful of people?"[12] Genevan city-space therefore offers a model of space shaped to a soteriologic end; indeed, Calvin's theology is inconceivable without the focal point of the city as theoretical and salvific model. Calvin's experimentations with the city-space of Geneva created a contemporary perception that Geneva was a holy city.

In theorizing Geneva, Calvin employs rhetorical spatial categories such as antithesis. He confronts Geneva in a face-off with Rome: "we put in place two Jerusalems, one opposing the other."[13] Calvin crafts a corrective diptych: by mirroring Rome's abuses, Geneva may rectify them in her own space. One "Jerusalem" exists already; it is Rome, a bastardized version of the divine city: "The Pope thereby seeks to extend his jurisdiction limitlessly, and in this he makes a gross and outrageous error . . . he tears down other churches, to build his seat on their ruins . . . Do they want to claim that the Apostolic See is in Rome? Let them show me any appearance of a true church there."[14] The other Jerusalem is in the process of being structured: it is Geneva, an existing space not yet fully detailed in accordance with the divine plan, but nonetheless the City of the Elect. Calvin designates this Jerusalem as the space within which Calvinism may thrive; it is an idealized space, toward which he projects all his aspirations for the church: "in Jerusalem . . . he has given to us a sure space . . . a space for our heritage."[15] In the Old Testament, Amos 9:1, like Calvin, envisions the reinstatement of God's Holy City in architectural terms, repairing broken walls, breaches, and fallen-down buildings: "I will raise up David's pavilion which has fallen down; I will fill in its cracks and repair its ruins . . . there is no other sign of salvation but this: . . . that David's house shall once again stand erect on its foundations."[16]

Calvin returned to Geneva from Strasbourg in September 1541. Walking the streets of Geneva, he envisioned changes in its topography to revise its earlier Catholic determination, and theorized its city-space. "To speak of Calvin is to speak of Geneva. Calvin would shape, and be shaped by, Geneva . . . To understand Calvin . . . it is necessary to come to terms with the city which occasioned and modified so much of his thought."[17] In 1537, Geneva was the largest city in a sizable region, with a population of approximately 10,300, a site crammed with preexisting structures and crowded with inhabitants. Calvin found it necessary to squeeze new buildings in, rather than finding free or neutral space for his ideal structures. Such was the case with the construction of his Academy in 1558. However, for the most part, "the architecture of Calvin's Geneva changed but little from that of the episcopal city."[18] The Upper City remained dominated by the Cathedral of St.-Pierre. Formerly, priests had clustered in the square around the cathedral, but now Reformed pastors congregated in the rue des Chanoines. Calvin spatially restructured rather than creating space, making additions that redetermined how the city-space was used and perceived rather than eliminating formerly Catholic structures. For example, he had three defensive ramparts built, the bastions of Miroud (1543), Saint-Léger (1544), and du Pin (1546), known collectively as the "Murs des Réformateurs."[19]

Calvinism superimposed itself both practically and textually on the city. He did not build a new *temple* (there was no space available) but rather redetermined the standing structure of the Catholic church by altering its interior appointments. Such a tactic is consistent with the Calvinist emphasis on interiority. Similarly, prior to the Reformation the Genevan Assembly had met in the cathedral cloister. The Reformers continued to use this structure, simply removing the wall surrounding the cathedral square (probably because such a wall designated the area as sacred space). Other alterations in the city followed the same pattern of reassigning space rather than carving out a wholly new territory. A nunnery was converted into an almshouse, and the Maison de Ville was retained as Town Hall with the simple addition of a staircase, which appears to have been a purely functional change.

The Calvinist strategy was to redetermine space by occupying it. Texts—forms of verbal inhabiting—asserted alternative significance for the area. Two registers of space are juxtaposed in Calvin's vision of Geneva. Empirical, everyday space maps a form of zoned, collective order. In addition to the space of ordinary life, the second register, formed by the ideal of conjoining secular with sacred prototype, constitutes a *theo-centric* reading of social life.[20] These two registers coexist seamlessly only within a textual universe. A conjunction beyond that of the purely textual realm would be blasphemous: "With Calvin . . . we do not find this tendency to weld the two realms together in a unity. What was 'natural,' he believed, was much too perverted by our persistent, human sinfulness ever to be trusted to lead us in its highest reaches towards the kingdom of God. Therefore Calvin simply allowed the two spheres, that of our human culture, and that of our central Christian concern, to lie side by side in their parallel coexistences, and in the tension which was bound to exist."[21]

The analogy holds for the juxtaposition of Catholicism and Calvinism, as well. These realistic compromises due to spatial constraints parallel how many Calvinists coped with curtailment of their beliefs, by finding ways to work with predefined space, to accommodate it to their needs, even though room for revision was cramped. Paradoxically, in Calvin's case spatial constraint may have facilitated the implementation of his program, because "Geneva . . . as 'political space' was unusually supervisable . . . It was possible for [Calvin] to bring his personal authority, his presence, to bear: he was always where he was most needed, for everything was within a short walk."[22] Thus, while external limitations may have affected the scope of the articulation of Calvin's blueprint for the church and for Geneva, Calvin always pushed against those boundaries, seeking to use them to his own ends. Describing his modus operandi in Geneva, he characterizes himself as one who rejects, or else reworks, constraint: "When the abomination of the papacy had been reversed in Geneva by the power of God's Word, the Council published an Edict which ordered that Geneva's religion be brought once again to the purity of the Gospel . . . Despite this, it still doesn't seem to me that a form of Church yet exists in accordance with the form our ministry would want it to take. No matter what anyone else might think, I don't believe my role to be limited so strictly that, once I've preached a sermon, my job in the city is done."[23]

Calvin reacts against strictures by developing a program to redetermine the nature of space. By calling Geneva the "City of the Refuge," he destabilizes it linguistically, intending that its city-space remain "uprooted" (déraciné, a term describing those seeking refuge), as a demonstration that the City of God can never be attained on earth. Calvin seeks always an ideal space, an elsewhere, the space of "a different country": "They want a well-founded city, of which God would be the master builder. They have all died still hoping for this, without having received the promises, but always envisioning them as from afar, and knowing and confessing that they were strangers on the earth. In this, they signified that they were searching for another country."[24] Such spatial and temporal deferral ensures that Geneva herself will not become an icon, an image to be imitated and, mistakenly, venerated.[25] A contemporary English Protestant echoed this sentiment so worrisome to Calvin: "the amount of religious knowledge is there so abundant, that one can view this city as the mirror and the model of true religion and of true piety." The Huguenot Jean Tagaut, in his poem *Protrepticon*, written as a prolegomenon to the Calvinist Jean Crespin's *Histoire des martyrs*, described Geneva as "a holy city . . . the triumphant witness . . . to evangelical truth."[26] But Calvin wants Geneva's witness, not her presence alone, to have meaning: Geneva's city-space and structures constituted a rewriting of non-Protestant space, rather than themselves absolutely incarnating God's church.

Space as Metaphor for Marginality

As "an architect of the Church,"[27] Calvin speaks a structural language. The architectural aspects of the *Institution*—"its superb organization . . . intensely systematic and organized structure"—were among the factors responsible for the text's influence.[28] In it, Calvin speaks a language that seeks to redefine space, to sculpt it as a polemical tool in reorienting theological expression.

The metaphorical network of references in the *Institution* combines literary and theological terminology. Calvin turns literary tools against Catholic usurpation of space: the See, or seat of Rome, the Pope's *siège* of authority, is debased through its literalizing as an overturned stool. In this way, Calvin subverts the figure of speech. The Calvinist plain style distills a metaphor into an ironic image, unseating the pope: "Suppose that . . . of the Popes, every seat with all four legs was overturned and toppled down."[29]

Further, the spatial terms used in the *Institution* sketch the visionary architecture of a redeemed world. Calvin insinuates his notion of redeemed space into space as currently defined and allocated. He maintains that "we are *inserted in* Christ . . . [who] has opened the kingdom of the heavens so that we may enter into it."[30] So that insertion in Christ may occur, Calvin selects scriptural passages that describe Christ spatially: "Christ is the length, height, width and depth."[31] Christ becomes the median point on an axis of which the two poles are God and the world: "we are as it were alienated from God . . . Jesus Christ is between Him and the world . . . [his role is to] lead us bit by bit to a full conjoining."[32] Christ is a vessel, a container, a storehouse, a depository, all spatial locations: "dispenser of his liberality to us . . . these gifts are committed by God in trust to him as treasure chest . . . the Spirit is distributed to each . . . according to measure."[33] The Cross demonstrates two spatial situations: the horizontal, or

Christ's humanity, and the vertical, his divinity. The intersection of these two locations makes redemption possible.

Calvin nuances this description with an analysis of the spatial situation that humanity must occupy: man must trace two movements, one vertical, the other a turning inward: "it is necessary that we *raise* our thoughts to God's promises which have been given to us, and to those *inner*, spiritual things which have been shown to us."[34] Christ's relationship to us is spatial; "he unites himself to us to retain us with him and to be mutually possessed by us."[35] "Christ by baptism makes us *participants in* his death, so that we might be *grafted onto* him."[36] Man should move toward God just as Jesus moved through terrestrial space at the Ascension: "Jesus Christ . . . moved from one place to another . . . [nonbelievers] deny this. But I ask them: How did he get up there? Wasn't he seen by eye-witnesses to be raised on high?"[37] Man stands in a spatial relationship to Christ, placed before him so that Christ may come to him, compensating through prevenient grace for man's lacks and failings.[38] Calvin develops a theory of how the distance between the two is eliminated, asserting, "it's that the Holy Spirit truly unifies things that are separated in space."[39] The link between man and God making this possible is the Holy Spirit, who acts as a channel or conduit for us.[40]

Calvin uses spatial and structuring vocabulary in many new contexts, creating new applications. His interpretation of circumcision exemplifies the spatializing action of the Word as it carves a place for the insertion of God into the believer, and, thereby, of the believer into the Lord: "Abraham . . . was the Father of the faithful circumcised . . . when the wall was broken down, as the Apostle says, to grant entry to the kingdom of Heaven to those to whom it had formerly been barred."[41] Abraham represents for Calvin the physical embodiment of a promised structuring process: God's promise establishes a holy nation, a sacred genealogy proceeding linearly through descendants: "He showed His favor *upon* him . . . His spiritual promise proceeds always as foundation and cornerstone, *linking* everything else to it . . . out of him comes the seed by which all the nations of the earth shall be blessed."[42]

Scripture, too, possesses spatial efficacy: "in reading Scripture, we find many passages that are obscure, that convince us of our ignorance. By this bridle, God restrains us and keeps us humble in order to allocate to each of us a certain measure and portion of faith."[43] Calvin exhorts believers to inhabit the space shaped by Scripture and by prayer: "It is indeed true that the Temple was in olden days dedicated by God's commandment so that prayers and sacrifices could be offered to God; but that was for the time when truth was as yet hidden under shadows; we, however, now able to see clearly, should never allow ourselves to stop short at any physical or material temple . . . we should contemplate the image of the true temple."[44]

In Calvin's description of the network of relationships between man and God and among the persons of the Trinity, spatial terms proliferate. He describes salvation as a process of *bringing together* ("colloqué en"); in his death and resurrection, Christ makes an *exchange* with us; the sacraments *send* us to the Cross; Christ does not appear to us as from afar, but rather *unites* himself with us; and Calvin exhorts the faithful to a constructive displacement: "I admonish the readers not to allow their sense to remain enclosed within narrow limits . . . but rather to try to climb as high as I can lead them."[45]

Calvin often words his concerns spatially. He asks such questions as, How am I enclosed in God? Is He in me, above me? Is the Holy Spirit in us? Around us? How is the world to be situated vis-à-vis God? What is my position, emblematic of that of all believers, in relation to, or in, the world? Calvin thereby linguistically attempts a rapprochement of two different spheres, separated in space, so that unitary space, in God, may prevail: "however if we are outside of Christ, we are separated from him . . . we should be grafted onto him . . . and don him . . . until we are made one with him."[46] Insertion is the opposite of the undesirable spiritual state of estrangement or *eslongement*: "He lives in our hearts, yet we are nevertheless so distanced from him"; "souls that are not conjoined with God . . . are estranged from him . . . and reside in death . . . let them be united with him."[47]

Calvin employs spatial and architectural metaphors to express his convictions. Conversion is a *turning toward* God, a spiritual and spatial reorienting of the self. Calvin wants us to have a part of God, to take up a place within him: "He wants us to be *participants in* Him . . . we must therefore have *take up a place within* Him."[48] Calvin employs this synecdoche theologically to set in place a relationship not only between believer and God, but also between word and space. Shifting from a focus on empirical, external space to a concentration on inner space, he influenced a generation of Calvinist architects who represented this shift in designs of grottoes and subterranean alveolae,[49] rendering in concrete form Calvin's concern that religiosity, preoccupied with externals, must reorient itself within the inner man, the believer's heart. Calvin observes that Catholics, contrarily, leave no niches free of idolatrous statues in their churches ("they leave no angle unadorned"), an unwarranted accretion of structures in profaned space. Calvin finds that Catholics usurp space and overflow borders: "It becomes impossible for them to observe proper limits, when they leave no angle unadorned by effigy in their temples . . . They break boundaries . . . They do not heed frontiers . . . they've taken borders away . . . they go beyond their limits . . . they do not stay within the lines . . . and they dare reproach us with overstepping former boundaries."[50]

Only God may disregard boundaries and surpass limits: Calvin says that at the Ascension, Christ's "virtue was efficacious; it spread itself out beyond every limit of heaven and of earth."[51] Calvin distrusts artificial—which he defines as Catholic—constraints on Calvinism, but he readily steps into the well-defined space of Scripture, accepting the salubrious limitations imposed therein. Since Catholics do not attend properly to scriptural space, Calvin exhorts his faithful to observe the guidelines of Scripture: "we really must watch our tongues and our thoughts to see that they do not arrogantly push beyond the limits that God's Word has set for them. For how could the human spirit comprehend in its small self that infinite essence of God . . . Let us therefore remain within this enclosure, hold our spirits in leash, lest they overflow by an extreme and extravagant license."[52] He narrows the focus so that space may better be contained and utilized. The alternative is to wander frenziedly in a deceitful world: "After having conceived as it were on the fly some acquaintance with God, suddenly we return to our daydreaming, and we let ourselves be transported, corrupting thus by our vanity the truth of God . . . From this infinite swamp come so many errors, and the world has been covered with them, for every man's spirit is now like a labyrinth . . . which transports us only further in error."[53]

Calvin applies the labyrinth image to erring, to show it as a dangerous form of enlargement.[54] When he envisions space in which to articulate his religious beliefs, he means a certain judicious and scriptural space: "we will be as it were in a labyrinth, wrapped around on every side, if we do not find our sure way" [nostre adresse].[55] Cotgrave's Dictionarie of the French and English Tongues renders adresse as "a direct, sure route";[56] adresse is also "a place or a destination in His Word." Calvin reiterates this dialectic of tightness as opposed to looseness or flexibility in his theology: by observing the boundaries of Scripture, one achieves greater enlargement. He argues that because God reserves for us His full manifestation in the next life, nothing will be kept from us at the Last Judgment. Thus, as the Calvinist architects would learn, while worldly constraints frustrate, creativity may nonetheless ensue if scriptural limits are honored.

Calvin uses the language of the *Institution* both to discern structures and to spatialize their concepts. For Calvin, architectural space is not re-modeled; sacred and secular space will exist side by side until the invisible church is realized. However, inner, or *moral* space, *is* reconfigured. Thus, he refers to structures that render space theologically significant, among them the Ark of the Covenant and Solomon's temple. Calvin views Scripture as a network of sites that structure significance. Reading Scripture is not only an exegetical act, it is a move through space, described with all the muscularity of physical endeavor: "I will show them the *goal*, toward which they should *stretch and direct* their intentions . . . all the same, a person who is not well *exercised* in this task . . . in order not to lose his way, must *hold straight* to a certain *path* to arrive at the right *end*."[57]

The *Institution* arched a dramatic trajectory through space: along with the Bible, it was sent out into the world from Geneva on the backs of Calvinist peddlers and ministers heading into embattled France. Calvin considered these two books his best weapons; he claimed to shoot them like ammunition from a slingshot.[58] Their soteriologic path contrasts with the dangerous, unbridled move through space traced by papal promulgations: "The Pope extends his jurisdiction endlessly, and it in this he causes horrible damage."[59] Catholic tightening of the bounds in real space pushed Calvin into Geneva and pushed French Calvinists, even more constrained within the kingdom of Catholic France, into the only space remaining for them: the textual space of Scripture. Only there could they find the latitude necessary to worship fully. The experience of Calvinists in the world was one of forcible displacement. Spatial experience translated psychological and spiritual states: "because of our belief, some of us have been put in prisons . . . others have been banished . . . others have fled for their lives."[60] Scripture could effect its own reversal of displacement, however, a spatial change that translates into a spiritual homecoming: "Certainly the Gospel does not *limit* men's hearts to joy in this present life, but rather *lifts them up* to the hope of immortality, in no way *attaching* them to earthly delights, demonstrating instead that their hope which is laid up for them in heaven will *lift them on high* . . . to the eternal *kingdom* of God."[61]

Calvin expresses space through rhetorical concepts. Dialectics arrays pros and cons against each other in a diptychlike verbal structure, as in the Geneva/Rome combination. Calvin's ideal space occupies a middle ground between two poles of a dialectic linking the visible and the invisible church: "But [the Catholics] are far from the truth when they will recognize no church that cannot be seen by the naked eye, and want to enclose the true church within certain limits which are in no wise appropriate boundaries for her. This is why we take exception to them. First, they always require a visible and evident form of church. On the contrary, we assert that the Church can indeed exist without visible form and that, even should it have a visible form, that appearance is no guarantor of its truth-value."[62]

Prior to the sixteenth century, structures in the world were "invisible": they were not discernible to analysis because they were construed to be self-evident and self-sufficient in significance. John Calvin's opposition to some such institutions would make their structures visible, enabling revision and correction. The city-space of Geneva offered to Calvin a lens for the sort of scrutiny he would henceforth apply to structures and to space. Geneva acted as the pretext for theory and embodied the text of that theory's elaboration.

Calvin's Structuring Style: The Rhetoric of Reform

A textual dialectic always exists between prototype and derivative text. Such a dialectic determines the dialogue between Scripture and the *Institution*. Constructed as a sort of paraphrase of the Bible, the *Institution* is itself structurally a thoroughly spatial text. *Para-phrasis* means "to write around": Calvin writes around, in, and through Scripture in composing his own work. He both inserts Scripture into the space of his own text and adds faithfully to the space that Scripture already occupies, augmenting it with his writing. It is an intriguing corollary notion that the Geneva Bible was known for its marginalia, for the Reformers' comments surrounding the sacred text, establishing themselves upon it and amplifying its sense.[63] This stance of writing from, and in, the margins constitutes a strategy of spatial self-positioning symbolizing Calvinist experience in the world. The strategy shifts the power in the text so that the (literally) marginalized position now becomes central and normative for interpretation of the text on which it comments.

Calvin's new topology travels from city and church to the believer's heart; the invisible church is erected within the believer, and he is included in Christ: "being in his safe care, we are out of all danger . . . being incorporated within him we already partake of eternal life . . . it is necessary then that we be established upon this foundation, if we would be temples consecrated to God."[64] Such boundaries produce unitary belief. An outside/inside movement epitomizes how Calvin seeks faith in the individual believer, then turns toward the outside to establish the church: "Because it is so that two realms are established within man, and we've already spoken quite a bit about the former realm, which resides in the soul, or in the inner man and concerns eternal life, that inner space compels us to claim the second, which is the space to which external morals belong and should be well-ordered."[65]

The establishment of the church as Calvin envisions it will have a horizontal and a vertical axis.[66] It will measure itself vertically against God's rule or ruler, "la reigle de Dieu." Horizontally, Calvin will superimpose the church on God's *patron* or model: "let man's life conform itself to God's purety, as though following a pattern."[67] Calvin's church will be epitomized by what he calls *conionction*, as opposed to *coniuration*, characteristic of Catholicism: "Ezekiel was no gentler with them . . . 'the plotting (*coniuration*) of these prophets in her midst,' he said, 'is like a roaring lion ravishing his prey. They have devoured all life, and destroyed all that is precious. The prophets have built with poor cement.'" *Coniuration* fragments; its disconnected segments destroy sense: "each one [of the Catholics] wanted to add his own lump to it"; "they've sewn together bits and pieces."[68] Cotgrave defines *coniuration* as a gathering together to plot for evil.[69] In *coniuration*, centrifugal forces scatter original unity into senseless atoms: "[The Catholics] have a lot of ceremonies that no one can understand, they use these to amuse their audience as though they were a troupe of tumblers or comedians or a meeting of magicians"; "[t]hese vultures are like flim-flam shell tricksters . . . everything that they dream up in their heads distorts natural order."[70] *Conionction*, however, connotes a salubrious conjoining of the church with its prototype: "Let the conjoining that we should experience . . . be so established in the unity of faith, that faith will be its foundation, the end and the rule of conjoining . . . everything done outside the Word of God is an heretical undertaking."[71]

Calvin uses structuring vocabulary in his discussion of the sacraments: he calls them pillars of faith and equates them with buildings: "just as a building is built and established on its foundation, and every time that pillars are added, becomes still more solid . . . so our faith is built upon God's Word . . . when the sacraments are added, they act as pillars for our faith to make it stronger."[72] Contemporaries, not all of them sympathetic, recognized that Calvin was using language in a new way and was devising a lexicon peculiar to Protestant needs and aims. Pierre de Ronsard referred to him directly in his polemical pamphlet against the Calvinists:

You [Beza] have, in order to reinforce the error of your madness,
Taught your city of Geneva some old homily

Composed by Calvin, of which you here are preacher.
You have in your stomach some lexicon stuffed with
Injurious words that let it be known that,
Yourself a bad student, you've had a very bad teacher.[73]

Perpetuating the Program: On to a Second Generation

The *Institution* thereby metaphorically and linguistically enacts a textual displacement in order to define a Calvinist space within, yet distinct from and critical of, Catholic space. In constructing the *Institution* as a form of architecture, a textual edifice in which man and God may interact, Calvin envisions Geneva, the real space, as a textual—hence, reconfigurable and redeemable—space. Calvin's goal is to fill existing space with Scripture. Calvin still sees the edifice of the world as God's architectural creation, albeit distorted by Catholic deviance: "in this noble building composed of heaven and earth . . . God imprinted certain signs of his glory . . . We cannot contemplate artificial earthly building without becoming confused . . . [at best] it can serve as a mirror to contemplate God, who is otherwise invisible."[74] The Catholic mistake is to assert that all of God's glory can be contained by the terrestrial sphere. Calvin characterizes this as a sort of *squeezing* strategy: "in claiming that Christ is in the bread, they squeeze him in there as though into a hiding-place."[75] Instead, Calvin hopes for a doubling of space, an expansive vision in which the earth points above and beyond itself to God.

The generation of architects after him would convert Calvin's proto-architectural language and spatial concerns into an actual program for new space, reasoning that if Calvinism could not be injected into existing space, then somehow new space, however minimal, had to be created. The hostilities of the Wars of Religion and the ongoing persecution during the period of purported toleration forced them to rethink the notions of space and structure. Working within space that they were unable to alter, these architects managed, nonetheless, to change it—at least on a symbolic level. No longer able to hope for such expansiveness, they layered a biblical impasto over Catholic structure in order to label that structure as Calvinist. Extending Calvin's work as a self-described "architect of reconstruction," some of the second-generation architects reconfigured extant structures.

In order to alter space that cannot be changed, it is necessary to think of space in a new way. Calvin provided the prototype and vocabulary for such rethinking. Second-generation Calvinist architects literalized his abstract spatial concerns.[76] In his "Catechism," Calvin implies that, if the world is morally misshapen, believers must restructure it, as God structured the world initially. The Minister queries the Catechumen: "Then you do not suppose God's power to be inactive, but think it be such that his hand is always engaged in working . . . [as] maker of heaven and earth?"[77] These and other concerns show that Calvin viewed himself as "one of the . . . persons selected by God as architects to promote his work of pure doctrine . . . [His call] is to build up the Church now lying deformed among the ruins of Popery."[78]

Speaking a vocabulary of spatial jostling, in which Protestants and Catholics are portrayed as shouldering each other, shoving each other aside literally and metaphorically, Calvin asserts: "There was a time . . . when [Catholics] audaciously perverted certain passages of Scripture to confirm this palpable falsehood, but as soon as we *came to close quarters*, it was easy to *pluck out* of their hands the bits of lath to which, *at a distance*, they had given the appearance of words . . . they *flee* for aid to antiquity. But here also we *dislodge* them."[79] Calvin suggests a proxemics and a hermeneutics of confrontational space. Calvinist architects adapted some of their adversaries' techniques to their own ends. They inscribed on structures coded elements that seemed to mean one thing, but in fact signified something quite other. Calvin used the authority of Scripture to enable him to conceive of space in a dialectical way, while these architects, beginning where Calvin left off, used Scripture to furnish the code they would use in their reconceptualizing of structures. Because Calvin emphasized the invisible church and invisible or inner space, the second generation's structures could work much less monolithically in the real world. The Calvinist architects found in this emphasis on the invisible church their justification for the use of code.[80] Seeing could no longer be believing, because whole series of subtexts of invisible shifts in the structure now had to be deciphered.

Calvinist architects erected profoundly textual structures, which must be read by an alert and informed reader with an eye to understanding their meaning, rather than trusting to his view of them. Meaning is not immanent, but is generated by the tension between purported (and deceptive) immanence and the realization that truth lies elsewhere. Ultimately, the Calvinist architects were faithful to a metaphysical orientation that both worked in, yet rejected, real space. Usually, an architect is commissioned to erect a structure that conforms to a patron's wishes; he does so, and the patron is satisfied. The Calvinist architect proposed a structure that the patron may have seen as appropriate. However, the Calvinist architect reconfigured that structure internally, adding codes and pointers. Calvin used the term *enseignes* in a way that approximates how these architects applied coding strategies, noting that the "elect" are marked, but the damned also possess a label (which they do not see—a situation analogous to the difference between the Calvinist reader and the Catholic viewer of a structure): "It is necessary that we believe in the invisible church . . . just so the Lord has marked us with certain signs or *enseignes* . . . For he knows and has marked those who do not know him and who do not know themselves . . . he has marked us with certain signs, so that the Church appears clearly to us, as though we could see it with our eyes."[81] In this way, the Calvinist-created Catholic structure can become its opposite and thereby work to thwart the ambitions of the Catholic patron, establishing the religious perspective of the architect as the ultimate determinant of the structure's reception—at least to a select Calvinist literati.

Calvinists' use of code constituted a consummate strategy for tricking the king and employing trompe l'oeil in a metaphysical sense. Possessing only the Catholic-commissioned edifice they had erected on which to inscribe their theological belief, the Calvinist architects found a way to make this statement in code consisting chiefly of minute detail, marginalia, strategies of decentering, and fragmentation: an iconographic shorthand for a compulsorily curtailed theological statement. Many of the Calvinist architects' structures are surprisingly ornate, given that Calvin had enjoined a plain style. However, this very ornateness works against the Catholic-sponsored structures, because it both contains and conceals the coded elements that convey the critique.

It is a striking historical conjunction of circumstances that, framing in time Calvin's development of his theory about ecclesiastical and urban structuring, the popes in Rome, particularly Pope Sixtus V with his architect Domenico Fontana, undertook, in the 1530s and chiefly in 1585–90, an elaborate urban project of their own, reconfiguring their "holy city." The Calvinist architects of the second generation knew of this parallel, contradictory ideological structuring enterprise. In Geneva, the Calvinist cartographer and engraver Pierre Eskrich responded visually to the pope's urban renewal program. Eskrich's "Mappemonde papistique" (1580) revised Rome by spatially designing a Calvinist critique of it, superimposing the figures of the early church fathers (on whom Calvin greatly relied, since they symbolized the Calvinist claim to represent the pure, original church as opposed to Rome's latter-day distortions) over Roman space to both indict and appropriate the blasphemous city.[82] The city, a powerful image for both Protestants and Catholics, purported to be an exemplar of divine order. Consequently, the city's plan, spatial grids, and structures constituted the basic semiotic components of a revisionist theological narrative.

Thus, a rhetoric of structuring, design, planning, and approach to space as forms of text—whether scriptural or ideological—subtended the sixteenth and early seventeenth centuries in France. This rhetoric and its products found their textual and architectural prototype—for Calvinists, that which they implemented; for Catholics, that against which they reacted—in Calvin's theology.

3

Calvinist Recipes for Restructuring the World

Bernard Palissy's *Recepte Véritable*

BERNARD PALISSY (1510–89), Huguenot, founder of the Calvinist church at Saintes, geologist, collector of fossils, curator of his own museum of natural history, and designer of gardens, grottoes, military fortifications, palaces, and theaters, drew up plans for many structures during the period directly before and during the Wars of Religion.[1] He held the coveted appointment of *architecte du roi* for many years, working for royalty such as Catherine de Médicis, for whom he built the Tuileries, and Henri III. A contemporary of John Calvin's, he stands at the head of a line of Calvinist architects whose theology deeply informed their practice of their craft.

Palissy's buildings and gardens were much admired by his contemporaries. However, he is perhaps best known for two productions that are not explicitly architectural but which define crucial components of his architectural endeavors. Recognizing his innovations with ceramics, Catherine de Médicis created a special position and title, naming him "Ouvrier de la terre et Inventeur des rustiques figulines du Roy." Palissy's ceramics use impasto, swirling colors, distorted shapes, and reproductions of natural forms encrusted onto artificial surfaces to force an amalgam of nature with art. The tension of nature juxtaposed with art compels the viewer to reflect critically on their relationship.

The potentially antithetical coupling of nature and art, found in all of Palissy's structuring enterprises, is an artistic technique arising from his religious perspective. For Calvinists, nature is forever tainted by the Fall. Unlike Catholics, who read nature as God's Book, Calvinists can no longer discern in nature clear evidence of God's plan because of humanity's distortions. Palissy would rely on artistic creation to rectify this problem; since artifice typifies the world, he would use its artificiality to try to correct it and point out its ills. Distorted artistry indicts humanity's misshapenness. Palissy juxtaposed nature, formerly innocent, with the contaminated, or artificial, to urge a constructive critical meditation on their differences.

Palissy is also famous for a quirky, encyclopedic work entitled the *Recepte véritable* (1562). In this volume, and in other studies such as the *Discours admirables* or the *Discours sur la nature des eaux et fontaines*, Palissy offers his wish list for structures that he would erect if he were able. These structures sculpt a space to shelter Calvinists. These *en-texted* structures, idealized configurations that can only exist within the theoretical format of a text, are to real structures what Calvin's doctrine of the invisible church is to the visible church: future-oriented desiderata superimposed on an imperfect prototype.

The *Recepte* maintains a metatextual relationship with Palissy's real constructions by theorizing how his real structures should be interpreted. In the *Recepte*, the need to marry theory and practice is conveyed through dialogue; an interlocutor, Demande, represents theory, while Responce demonstrates practice. The conversation between theory and practice creates the appearance of room for discussion, something all too rare for a Calvinist, who was hampered by historical circumstances from making doctrinal statements. Nonetheless, Palissy remains trapped in the boomerang space between theory and praxis: their ultimately unproductive debate mirrors the Calvinist and Catholic inability to reconcile their differences. A dialectical space results, in which Palissy's Calvinist agenda is both continually present in the text and constantly denied by the context.

In the *Recepte*, Palissy recalls the dramatic nature/art struggle of his pottery. He describes nature exhaustively—detailing spiral shells, crustaceans, faults in the earth, erosion of river banks, types of trees—then revises these natural elements by including a selection in his projected constructions: his plan for a garden grotto includes encrusted shells, fossils, roots, and cracked cave walls. But these natural elements are now part of a metaphysical program, the task of restructuring the world, ultimately a soteriologic endeavor.[2] The authenticity of nature points out the artifice and pretension of the surface. Palissy's superscription of structure with ornament reminds the structure of what it should be, recalling it to its true purpose, that of glorifying God. "My advanced years . . . have made me remember that it is written: let no one abuse the gifts God has given him, or hide his talents in the earth . . . This is why I've decided to labor to bring to light here the things that it pleased God to enable me to under-

2. Palissy's invention of the *rustiques figulines*, as shown on this ornate ceramic platter, was aimed at conferring order on the chaos and fragmentation of the postlapsarian world. For him, shells, fossils, odd rock formations, all documented God's plan for humanity and history. This lead-glazed earthenware dish from his workshop in Paris, circa 1565, epitomizes Palissy's miniature animals, shells, snakes, lizards, ferns, and other elements of the natural world rendered in the creation colors of green, gray, brown, and blue. He encrusts these figures in collage fashion, covering all available surface. This art form symbolizes the return of artifice and nature to the original state of chaos, where lies a second chance for a fallen world. Bernard Palissy, *Assiette*. All rights reserved. The Metropolitan Museum of Art.

stand . . . I've scratched at the earth for forty years now, and delved within her bowels, so that I might know what she produces within her, and in this way I've found favor with the Lord."[3]

In an autobiographical comment in "De l'art de la terre," Palissy attests that his structuring projects are matters of life and death. He calls his efforts "persécutions et misères,"[4] attesting to a sense of martyrdom which is eerily consonant with the circumstances of his death: in 1589, Palissy died in the Bastille, tortured to death for his beliefs. Speaking of his craft in terms that recall the Resurrection, Palissy shows that his experiments with pottery are in fact a cipher for his desire for redemption: "All the imperfections in my pottery caused me such labor and distress that, as soon as I had melted my enamels to the same temperature, I believed myself to be at death's door; so it was that, while working on my pots, I felt so physically run-down that it seemed I had no arms or legs left."[5]

As Calvin viewed his spiritual architecture as scripturally derived and sanctioned, so Palissy viewed the occupation of potter as an appropriate Protestant profession. He conceived of pottery through the biblical legitimation provided by Jeremiah 18:1–11:

This is the word that came to Jeremiah from the Lord: "Go down to the potter's house and there I will give you my message": so I went down to the potter's house, and I saw him working at the wheel. But the pot he was shaping from clay was marred in his hands: so the potter formed it into another pot, shaping it as seemed best to him. Then the word of the Lord came to me: "O house of Israel, can I not do with you as this potter does?" declares the Lord. "Like clay in the hand of the potter, so are you in my hand, O house of Israel. If at any time I announce that a nation or kingdom is to be uprooted, torn down and destroyed, and if that nation I warned repents of its evil, I will relent and not inflict on it the disaster I had planned. And if a nation or kingdom is to be built up and planted and if it does evil in my sight and does not obey me, then I will reconsider the good I had intended to do for it."[6]

The potter's craft thus contained implicit biblical permission to act against ungodly regimes. In this light, it is significant that Palissy chose not to conform to ceramic conventions: "It was precisely Palissy's choice not to use the [potter's] wheel and not to model that enabled him to achieve his towering importance in ceramic art. That choice freed him from limitations that bound others . . . He did not have to fashion his own version of nature before he could do anything else. He could go to directly interpreting the world."[7]

It was precisely the feeling of constraint, of being marginal, that pushed Protestants to the pinnacle of their artistic creation and that impelled them to devise strategies for subverting the existing order. Constrained in his creations by official mandates and by his patrons' wishes, Palissy found his escape in technique: "Free of the inherent problem of the wheel and of modeling, Palissy never fell captive to concern solely with surface or to preoccupation with form . . . surface was always married to form . . . The relief was so high, its placement so complex, and its relationship to the ground . . . so intimate that distinction between surface and shape vanished . . . They were no longer plates and platters . . . They were creations unto themselves, each with its own integrity and its own being."[8]

This solution of fusing surface and content may translate Palissy's wish for integration and toleration. His artistic impulse responded to his theological quandary, as the violence that Palissy experienced was converted into a force for creation. His creations remained marked by their origin; "[his] pieces gave the feeling of having been forcibly subdued. Defiance . . . sullen resentment . . . [characterized them]. His cutwork pieces, for example, reflected a response of affront and anger coupled with helplessness." Palissy's style resulted from his reaction to the troubled climate in which he found himself: "Intellectually, Palissy began with accepted style and image, and deliberately violated almost all established canons governing their use. He attacked the norm at every turn. He thus waged his private war as a public battle. The making of each piece represented for Palissy a struggle. It was an *act of liberation*."[9] The hidden intent of Calvinist creations can be found in the detail applied to surface. Generally idiosyncratic, seemingly extraneous, deriving from another vocabulary, inappropriate or eccentrically placed, such "peculiarities [are] a part of every piece."[10]

Attention to minute detail, and an iconoclastic application of it, characterize Palissy's writings. For instance, in a tract on military fortifications, he obsessively describes the terrain. This concern for detail may document Palissy's desire to master or reclaim space.[11] This desire to abolish established order may explain why some of Palissy's structures have not survived.[12] Palissy's visual preempting of symbolic power amounts to a "counterfeit" representation.[13] Counterfeit creations subvert established order by circulating fraud at the center of the system of exchange. Discernible only through a virtually microscopic examination revealing slight discrepancies in detail, counterfeit survives by minimally altering sense or significance while appearing to conform. Did Palissy intentionally insert flaws in his structures? Do problems in the structure provide a symbol of his own desire to undermine the foundations of a hostile Catholic order? Did Palissy, who in the autobiographical sections of his writings identifies with his creations, see himself as the fault line in the system? The intriguing fact is that Calvinists, all creators commissioned by Catholics, persistently erected structures often no longer extant. In this way, they denied Catholic monumental expression, as the structure "goes the way of all flesh."

The memory and influence of these structures continued, however, prompting speculation on the odd alliance between Calvinist subversive techniques and the idiom of seventeenth-century classical French architecture. Calvinists may in fact have been the paradoxical originators of a French neoclassical style that found its apogee in the architectural exaltation of the Sun King, ironically the final persecutor and virtual eradicator of Calvinism. For instance, Palissy's grotto and grotto-inspired ceramics were the prototype for Versailles, which contemporaries called the "Trianon de porcelaine."[14] In both idiom and execution, these ceramics were the precursor of the grand classical style.[15] The marginal minority significantly contributed, however unconsciously, to in developing a state idiom. Frank Lestringant relates a French proverb in which a king and a potter change place, similar to the effect of Palissy's style and structures: "In France there was a custom: / A potter could become King; / A King could become potter."[16] Lestringant confirms Palissy's intent to subvert Catholic order through his creations: "it is indeed concerning a form of exchange of power and position by Prince and potter that the *Recepte* speaks to us."[17] The form of the *Recepte* cooperates in this project: the Demande/Responce format is reminiscent of the structure of Huguenot catechisms, thereby negating the Catholic catechism, a propagandizing instrument allied to the Catholic state.[18] Subterfuge and form, technique and tension coexist in Palissy's work, expressing a revisionist agenda. It is a neat irony of history that Louis XIV's predilection for Palissy's quirky pottery inspired him to create space for the very Calvinist style whose adherents he was persecuting, thereby perpetually inscribing these "heretics" at the heart of France's artistic self-conception.

The Plumb Line, Boundary Lines, and Crossing the Line

Psalm 145 should suffice, for the summary of what it tells us is so thorough that nothing is left out.

—Calvin, *Institution de la religion chrestienne* [19]

It is no small honor that God so loved us that he decorated the world magnificently so that we would not only view this beautiful theater but also be fulfilled by the diverse abundance and varieties of the riches that are displayed therein.

—Calvin, *Commentaire sur les pseaumes* [20]

This is why I wanted to structure my garden on Psalm 104, wherein the prophet describes the wondrous work of the Lord . . . I also want to erect this admirable garden so as to help men to once again become loving tillers of the soil.

—Palissy, *Recepte véritable* [21]

The above quotations illustrate the centrality of Calvin's writings as a pattern book, itself modeled on the Bible, for Calvinist architects. Time and again these architects articulate similar concerns and voice the same preoccupations as does Calvin. The first quotation establishes the Bible as norm for all writing; it is the rule by which all is to be measured, the line of excellence that may not be surpassed. The second quotation from Calvin attests to the sufficiency of God's creative work. The third quotation, from Palissy, recalls Calvin's comment and invokes the Bible as a model, extolling the cornucopia of God's world. Together, the quotations delineate a morphology of Calvinist aesthetics.

Order—a rationale for the structuring enterprise—is of primary concern to Palissy and other Calvinists who, during the Wars of Religion, incessantly tried to delineate their territory, both physically and spiritually marking themselves off from Catholics. Three sorts of lines are envisioned: reference to the biblical *plumb line*, standard of moral rectitude; *boundary lines*, real and imagined, to guard against aggression or infection; and *lines of transgression*, by means of which Calvinists surreptitiously overstep the imposition of Catholic containment. How do Palissy's structures subvert and supplant Catholic norms? How is his "ligne de transgression" drawn? [22] His garden structure epitomizes the boundaries, while his fortress represents a more hard-line definition of transgression. At the same time as he designs and builds structures, Palissy expresses his distrust of them. He instructs us to read his structures: they are more texts to be deciphered than buildings to be inhabited. Palissy makes literal what Calvin calls "the rule of faith," "reigle" referring both to rule and to law and to ruler, or measuring stick: "When St. Paul urged that all prophecy conform itself to faith, he put forth a sure rule for testing every interpretation of Scripture."[23] Following Calvin in his understanding of the "invisible church" of believers, Palissy also decenters, or unstructures, existing ecclesiastical edifices.[24]

"You stop too quickly at the walls, looking for God's church in the beauty of buildings, thinking there are found the true believers. How can we doubt that it's in fact the Antichrist who resides there? Mountains, woods, lakes, prisons, deserts and caves seem to me more certain and trustworthy places [for us]."[25] In this quotation, Calvin embeds an artificial construction, "prisons," in his litany of natural formations. Prisons sound odd there. Their deliberate inclusion suggests that Catholics' confinement of Calvinists somehow paradoxically liberates them, as do natural spaces (customary places of worship for Calvinists, who often had no other choice than to gather in the open air, in the mountains, at night to observe their faith). Paradoxically, sometimes creativity is most dynamic when constrained. Protestantism possesses a peculiarly privileged place in garden architecture: nearly all such garden structures subsequent to the death of Henri III were designed by Palissy or influenced explicitly by Calvinist designs. Protestants frequently wrote about and explicated their structures,[26] thereby creating a more full apprehension, a conjunction of word and image more consonant with a Protestant perspective than with the often exclusively image-oriented Catholic view.[27]

Thus, Palissy demonstrates, in these and other ways, an explicit affiliation with Calvin, both through a textual knowledge of him and through contact with him as a contemporary.

Un-Creating the Fallen World

The garden described in Palissy's *Recepte* must be examined from the standpoint of its creator's religious perspective and marginal confessional position. Catholic creators of gardens viewed the garden as the Book of Nature, an encyclopedia of God's creation, what John Prest terms "a re-creation of the earthly Paradise."[28] For Calvinists, however, the garden stood as sign of an absence, of the schism between man and God, a sign that Paradise was barred to humanity by two angels with flaming swords. Catholics believed that plants bore "signatures" written on them by God indicating the diseases for which they provided antidotes.[29] This perspective considered nature's use by humanity, a terrestrial focus. However, Palissy placed his own signature on Nature, redefining it to his own purpose, lifting nature beyond itself. He contended that nature was illegible unless read in reference to God's Word. "Throughout the sixteenth century, the changing forms of the gardens [nearly all designed by Calvinists] themselves reflect the growing absolutism of their owner's claims upon the world, a greater and greater domination of the natural terrain by a 'tectonic Spirit.'"[30]

"IN MY FATHER'S HOUSE, THERE ARE MANY MANSIONS"

The garden provided a propitious place for Palissy's reconfiguration of the world. Gardens began to exhibit architectural forms and vocabulary because so much of Europe had already been built; they offered an unsullied space for the free play of the imagination; they could "experiment with overall patterns and spatial order which architects and engineers, confronted with the built reality of old cities, could only project in the abstract."[31] Constrained in his options for artistic creation, Palissy fittingly chose to work with gardens. Guillaume Salluste Du Bartas, an intimate of Calvin's, described the Garden of Eden as a city, "a populous town or italianate garden."[32] Calvinists found gardens as new sorts of cities alluring because, like Calvin's *Institution*, this notion presupposed both a construction and a organizing principle for that arrangement: a literalized theory or blueprint for actualizing God's city. The garden functioned as a dramatic site of confrontation between two agendas, the patron's and the artist's. When the overwhelming preponderance of patrons was Catholic, and all the artists commissioned to do their bidding were Calvinist, the garden became a highly charged space, a multitexted arena to be decoded.[33]

Charles Estienne and Jean Liébault, both Huguenot landscape designers, published a text similar to Palissy's, although less theoretical. Oriented also to achieving an idealized reconfiguration of the fallen world and possessing a similar wealth of scriptural reference and structure, the *Maison rustique* (1582) was, however, more practical in conception. At least three-quarters of the book deals with technical considerations germane to husbandry, such as when to plant, where to sow, and how much seed is required. However, the first part of the book discusses how sacred and profane history have separated, and how the two might again become one. Published posthumously by Jean Liébault, Estienne's son-in-law, the *Maison rustique* thus owed its existence to a genealogical commitment to Calvinism similar to that found among the often intermarried and confessionally invariant second-generation Calvinist architectural families. This familial involvement and propagation both of the faith and of the text's endeavor can be seen in its epigraph:

> Charles Estienne of this champion house,
> As founder first it built,
> In part: but erst he coulde it ende,
> Sharpe, sudden death him spilt.
> To thee, then Liébault sonne in law,
> To famous, skilfull Steven . . .
> Is due to praise of second birth
> To halfe borne fruit, extended
> So that by hium, what was begunne,
> By thee, is fully ended.[34]

The quick reference to "second birth," easy to overlook, is also a Calvinist doctrinal statement of the need to be born again, in Christ.

The *Maison rustique* went into many printings over the following fifty years and enjoyed a great success in England, where it first appeared as *The Countrie Farm* in 1600. One of the reasons for its success in England was precisely the reason for the veiled language with which it was penned for publication in France.[35] Protestantism flourished in England during these years, and the *Maison rustique* clearly appealingly conceived of "husbandrie" in a pre-edenic sense: "Husbandrie . . . wherein we doe not only see with our eies and handle with our handes the works of nature: but (which is more) wee finde out thereby the incomprehensible power and greatness of God."[36] A list of biblical examples follows, attesting to the Calvinist desire to illustrate the parable of the talents, one also favored by Palissy: "It is my purpose (following the Proverbe, which saith that we must learne the manners of our ancient predecessors, and practice according to the present age) to lay out unto the waies, so to dwell upon, order and maintaine a[n] . . . *inheritance* in the fields as that it may keepe and maintaine with the *profit* and increase thereby" (2; my emphasis). "Inheritance," "profit," "increase" are all Calvinist code words that enjoin the enlightened reader not to store up treasures solely on earth but rather to be good stewards of God's creation so as to merit a spiritual reward. Estienne asserts that "the whole earth was once a Temp[l]e, an Eden . . . and the assigned possession and inheritance of man" (iii) lost through sin, now potentially retrievable through this do-it-yourself Huguenot husbandry manual. Estienne hopes to marry man's practical endeavor in the world to a spiritual search and striving: "This was the cause why our first parents did give themselves to the tilling of the earth . . . to the ende that he and his offspring might be stirred up and addicted to till the earth, the better to acknowledge the greatnesse of God" (i).

As is the case with Palissy, Estienne's gardening manual contains architectural considerations, and seems to envision all preparation of soil areas as a form of reformation: "And hereunto it came to passe, that all the yeere I have so carefully trimmed, so thoroughly examined from the ground worke to the verie top, and stone after stone, this our countrie Farme, as that I have in a manner made it all new" (ii). Scripture is upheld as the absolute standard of knowledge and wisdom, without which any reforming enterprise—be it theological or horticultural—cannot succeed: "[There are] so many new invented fashions of building, tilling, speaking or writing, [that I have written this] seeing, that by such means in seeking to reforme things without perfect knowledge . . . men have been brought oftentimes utterly to spill, spoile, and marre the same" (1). Similarly, Palissy's Calvinist aesthetics necessitates an informed, diligent, and well-disposed readership, one also disabused of the ability to repose confidence in things of this world.

Palissy himself acknowledges the impermanence of his structures, stressing their fragility, which makes it impossible to rely on earthly construction: "This breaks easily, and won't last long . . . There are certain layers of stone in which the stone is gelid, full of air and easily broken-up; similarly, there are sorts of earth which are very porous and spongy, which soak up any rain that falls on them. Once this water has been absorbed, if the temperature goes below freezing, the waters absorbed do violence to the earth in which they are found."[37] The friable construction materials suggest an analogy with Calvinism, which resides within the Catholic state and erects structures supposedly intended to glorify it, but which, in the long run, will undermine, at least symbolically, the body within which it lodges.

Palissy's garden, like Estienne's farm, requires a profound revision of the world and its meaning, a rereading of the world in a Calvinist sense.[38]

This revision occurs at all levels, among them the artistic, political, and theological. Palissy requires that his reader coproduce meaning within the symbolic, re-creative space of the garden. With the engraved maps of the period, "the description of the place is the incitement to a possible voyage."[39] However, the virtual voyage to which Palissy's garden points is a metaphysical itinerary.

THE NATURAL TEMPLE OF THE LORD

Palissy views nature, an unstructured region unlabeled by Catholic claims, as a fit venue for the preaching of God's Word. He follows Calvin in this: "*wherever* you see the Word of God purely preached and heard, and the sacraments administered according to Christ's institution there . . . a church of God exists."[40] In Calvin's *Commentary on the Romans* 10:14, Calvin notes that "[verses of] Holy Scripture . . . are oracles recorded on public tablets . . . setting forth the proper knowledge of God."[41]

Palissy's garden renders literal Calvin's conception of the invisible church of believers as a new Garden of Eden: "There is one church, which, by the increase of its faithfulness, spreads into a multitude, just as there are rays of the sun, but only one light, many branches in a tree, but one trunk, upheld by its tenacious root; and when many streams flow from one fountain, though from the copiousness of the supply, there seems a division into parts, still, in regard to the origin, unity is preserved."[42] This concern for division, appropriate distribution, and order is a hallmark of Palissy and other Calvinist architects. The world, unstable and disordered, must be restructured; the Calvinist architects will neutralize the threat of chaos. According to François Gebelin, the Calvinist architect Jacques Androuet du Cerceau expressed a similar concern for order: "All one needs to do is skim through *Les plus excellens bastiments* . . . by du Cerceau to find everywhere flowered parterres divided into orderly compartments surrounded by galleries."[43] English Protestant landscape architects also sought, in the cloistered space of the garden, to cultivate a disciplined world distinct from the wilderness, a metaphor for man's sin and depravity. In order to dramatize the proximity of wilderness to protected space, some English formal gardens included, as if to neutralize it, a small strip—usually a group of hedges, often composing a maze—near the edge of the garden which they called "the wilderness."[44]

The garden symbolized "the ultimate aim . . . to bring the wilderness under cultivation all over the world, and with this to bring the heathen to [Protestantism]."[45] The walled-in garden also symbolized the Reformed church; in *Grace Abounding to the Chief of Sinners*, John Bunyan recalled dreaming of the congregation as a walled-off group into which he had to batter his way. The garden metaphor—as with all biblical metaphors employed by Calvinists—was not merely an image or a construct; it was also a program for action. These gardens propose an interpretive grid, and posit a readership, for their structures. In 1706, roughly a century and a half after Palissy, John Evelyn, botanist and designer of gardens, stated that the purpose and the meaning of a garden was to *signify*: "the task [is] to comprehend . . . the whole of what the Earth has."[46]

"Des Choses Cachées Depuis la Fondation du Monde": Sequestered Secrets

Why so much space? And why space so assigned and punctuated? The theorizing of a garden is an ideal operation for a Calvinist, enabling his visionary rehearsal and reconfiguration of the world. He delineates acceptable from unacceptable, saved from damned, elect from unregenerate, distinguishing also between visible and invisible, above ground and below ground, that which can be displayed to view and that which can initially only be intuited: empirical reason as opposed to the certainty of faith. The process of the garden's construction traces a turn toward interior space, where truth may be found: Palissy states that in order to conceive of the garden: "I enter into myself, to delve into the secrets of my heart, and to enter into my conscience, to learn what there is within me."[47] The garden symbolizes the space of the self, in which the work of salvation is to transpire.

> For now, Reader, this grotto directs you to contemplate closely
>   . . . such a painstaking endeavor.
> Its vault seems like the highest heaven,
> And everything revolves variously around it . . .
> In truth, the grotto makes you think as you look here and there
>   at the animals climbing all around,
> That ingenious art has triumphed over nature.[48]

Palissy does not assert that the garden itself is "highest heaven." Nor does he assert that "ingenious art has triumphed over nature"; instead, he points to the garden's power to deceive: it "will make you *think* . . . that art has surmounted nature." Palissy's gardens and structures constitute subterfuges, traps for those unlettered in Calvinism. The more the reader believes in these constructions and accepts them for what they seem to be, the more suspect the reader. Palissy's structures act in this way as proof cases for right belief, focusing on the reader and on his interpretation or misconstruction of meaning. They recall the parables of the gospel: they have simple housings but dense interiors; they are never what they seem but require instruction to grasp their sense.[49] "I beg you to tell the workers, who cannot read, that they should study hard and learn natural philosophy. Following my advice, they will find to their surprise that the secrets about manuring and fertilizing that I've included in this book will become clear to them."[50] Palissy speaks here of day laborers and manure, referring in cipher to Calvinists who do the Lord's work in His fields.

Undoing Chaos: The Grotto as Space of Revelation

John Ruskin gave the name "grotesque" to what he also called "monotheistic art": art that takes many forms but nevertheless derives from only one source.[51] Grotesque art takes on a particular purpose and conveys a very specialized meaning for Calvinists. The Calvinist contribution to grotesque art infuses meaning into formerly purely visual forms. Randle Cotgrave provides the customary meaning of the term for the sixteenth century: " 'Grotesques': Pictures wherein (as please the Painter) all kinds of odde things are represented without anie peculiar sense, or meaning, but only to feed the eye."[52] For Palissy, however, more is there than meets the eye. Distortion now has a sense and a function: to recall the unreformed, perhaps unreformable, nature of the world. Further, such distortion has a utopian content, in that it forces the reader/viewer to push beyond boundaries, to imagine forms of existence not previously envisioned: "Artistic illusion is not only mere illusion, but a meaning that is cloaked in images and can only be described in images, of material that has been driven further, wherever the exaggeration and narrative structuring depict a significant anticipatory illumination, circulating in turbulent existence itself, of what is real."[53]

Thus, when Palissy describes his gardens, he offers elaborate detail, then stipulates that the garden possesses significance beyond its appearance: "Here is the meaning of the first of the four cabinets."[54] The actual meaning, however, is left to the reader to determine. The reader is obliged

3. This masonry archway displays cracks and apertures into which vegetation and weeds begin to insert themselves. The engraver represents the space between each arcade as a sort of lumpy, earthen texture, as though the earth were pushing back the walls of the structure to reclaim its space. Calvinist structures seek to reorder nature and to confer sense on a fallen world. Things hidden now emerge from the earth, as is predicted in the book of Revelation ("things hidden from the beginning of time"). Calvinists view themselves as of necessity having gone underground but their day of redemption will come. Philibert de l'Orme, *Architecture* (1626) 1: 46 verso. By permission of the Folger Shakespeare Library.

to participate in Palissy's reconfiguration of the world.[55] Palissy's reliance on the grotesque in a theologically determined blueprint demonstrates his conviction that the many debased variants of humanity ultimately have one origin, and he finds their only hope for redemption in a return to that source. Palissy uses artifice and exaggeration to dramatize the chasm between God and fallen humanity, a gap that Calvin expresses in this way: "Besides, this initial dignity only presents itself to us so that we, contrarily, should not always be obliged to contemplate the sad spectacle of our deformity and ignominy, inasmuch as we fall from our original state in the person of Adam."[56]

Grotto art (*grotesche*) undoes the created order in order to re-create it. Palissy's playfulness with new and different media and daring design are part of his experiment to reconstruct humanity in accordance with the divine blueprint. "Even the divine act of creation decomposes itself into two moments: an initial act of pure production . . . this is chaos, evoked at the beginning . . . 'This first world was a form without form.' The second moment of creation is that of modeling . . . the metamorphosis [of the first]."[57]

Certain of Palissy's structures are like Philibert de l'Orme's etchings that portray an ordered, artificial, and densely structured universe into which vegetation begins to insert itself, to reclaim the world for its original state. The porosity of these structures shows how strongly nature seeks to re-cohere derivative artifice—a sign of the Fall—to herself. Nature, imbued with the memory of her creator, strives always to regain what humanity has sought to wrench away: harmony, completion, the *imago Dei*. Grotesque art, epitomizing change, a passage from one state to another, even violence, creates evocative artistic renderings of this cosmic drama. Grotesque art is a fitting vehicle for Calvinists, outcasts within the kingdom, who retain a memory of a former organic, unified state while they are

des matieres, que d'autres defpenfes, foit pour ofter les terres, ou pour les façons, qui euffent coufté quafi la moitié d'auantage qu'il n'a faict, s'il y euft fallu proceder autrement. Vous pouuez iuger facilement du tout par la figure que i'en ay faicte deffous.

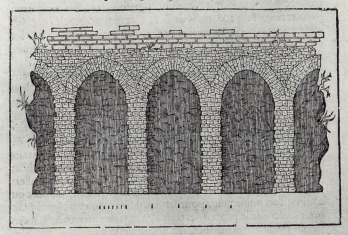

Belle inuention pour cognoiftre fi vn fondement fera meilleur eftant creufé & fouillé d'auantage.

CHAPITRE X.

Vandlon eft contrainct de beaucoup creufer & fouïller les fondements, pour autant qu'on doute qu'ils ne foient affez bons, & qu'on efpere de les trouuer meilleurs, ou bié que lon eft contraint d'aller plus bas qu'on ne voudroit, pour les caues & offices qu'on veut faire quelquefois dedans terre, on cognoiftra fi le fondement fera meilleur pour eftre creufé d'auantage en cefte forte. Il faut faire vn trou ainfi qu'vn puits, & non pas de grande profondeur: de quatre ou fix pieds il fuffira: en apres proceder comme quand on veut experimenter s'il y a fources d'eaux en quelques lieux & païs, qui fe pratique en cefte forte. Prenez deux cruches de terre cuitte, ou deux pots de quelque forme & capacité que vous voudrez, (il fera bon toutefois qu'ils tiennent enuiron vn feau d'eau) & les empliffez de laine, bourre, ou cotton, puis les couurez d'vne tuille ou aix, & regardez quelle eft la pefanteur & poids de tout enfemblément, lequel gardez à part. Cela faict mettez l'vn defdicts pots au plus bas du fondement & à vn coing, eftant bien couuert de quelque

Maniere de cognoiftre fi vn fondement fera meilleur pour eftre creufé d'auantage.

constantly reminded of their embattled minority status: it is art in turbulence and transition, art in tension with the times and context. In some of these engravings, natural elements and vegetation seem to foam up over the edges, seething through the interstices of a would-be impenetrable structure. The zone of assault and penetration gnawing at the structure's foundations undermines what the structure is intended to represent. Like ivy on bricks, Calvinist architecture offers lovely monuments to the eye while slowly and subtly nibbling tiny holes within, so that the structure eventually becomes aerated, porous, oblivious, and doomed.

Grottoes provide propitious theaters for Protestant art; they are places in which secrets reside, areas of potential waiting to be drawn above ground, just as Calvinist belief subtends Catholic domination. *Grotte* is derived from the Latin *crypta*: to hide. For Palissy, hiding his structures inside the earth figures a rebirth of the universe through a canny artifice.[58] The *Recepte* thus becomes a sort of textual tomb, one from which a resurrected form of Calvinism may emerge. In Palissy's work, gardens and grottoes serve three purposes. They provide an avenue for re-creation, they symbolically undo the fixity of official architecture, and they call for a rereading into a new sense.

It is instructive to compare the different treatment of gardens and grottoes by Catholics and Protestants. Pierre de Ronsard, contemporary of Palissy, Catholic poet and polemical writer, also elaborated textual structures.[59] In his constructions, Palissy valued content over form, while Ronsard emphasized formal perfection over statement. Their differences epitomize the emphasis Calvinists placed on the Word as well as the Catholic focus on rite or image. Ronsard criticized Palissy's work; in his "Chant pastoral sur les nopces de Msgr Charles duc de Lorraine," he described Palissy's structures as impertinent, disrespectful of their historical antecedents, impermanent, and displaying an unruly riot of rampant nature.[60] Ronsard's descriptions of palaces, however, attempted to merge structure with nature. He was not wholly successful; the structure remained outside its desired location, in "an incomplete metamorphosis . . . [in which] palace tends to become countryside, without ever wholly achieving that aim . . . there's a strange indeterminacy [to the structure]."[61] Palissy's program operates in reverse fashion: he does not seek to merge the structure with nature, but rather to have nature itself form that structure; there is an absolute absorption, an utter implosion of ordered form into undefined matter. Order, for a Calvinist, acts dialectically. Order must be disorder, since "order" is officially (oppressive) Catholicism.[62]

Thus, for Palissy and other Calvinists, "no structure more effectively illustrates the mockery of architecture—almost its very negation—than does the garden grotto." The grotto is the literal incarnation of the term sub-version, for it is beneath, and turns away from, established order. It is faithful to the apocalyptic vision of the world collapsing and crumbling as portrayed in Revelation, a preferred biblical book for Calvinists. Grottoes convey "the notion of chaos within the ordered scheme."[63] This chaos, however, is the source of great ferment, of a new life.

Calvinists are the ghosts in the machine; they are the trouble that looms for the Catholic establishment. Calvin describes the Calvinist church as being formless and hidden, yet nonetheless very real and strong. "What form do we think has shown in the church . . . How many times since the coming of Christ has the church been hidden without form? How often has it been so oppressed by wars, sedition, and heresy that she could be found nowhere?"[64]

Appropriately for the Protestant mentality, the grotto because of its customary association with reading matter emphasizes reading of Scripture rather than a visual or iconic apprehension of the sacred.[65] Palissy copies biblical quotations onto the ceiling spaces of grotto niches so that whoever enters the garden structure will be automatically enrolled in the text of salvation. This element most consistently differentiates Protestant from Catholic use of structures: spaces are no longer empty or filled in an unreflective or pictorial way; rather, they are discursive spaces, spaces marked by the speech or text that inhabits them. In Palissy's text, which requires a discerning kind of reading and which invites the participation of the reader, the expectation is that a reader will "walk" through the pages of its "garden." Palissy names this important character the *Promeneur*.[66] *Promeneur* is a code word, because Scripture refers to "walking" the path of Christian life, walking through the "strait gate," walking "by faith, not by sight." As Palissy conceives of his garden, the garden is pretext to a vast vista; it opens out upon utopian possibilities seemingly without limit, an opening from the margins onto a metaphysical journey. Other Protestant architects suggest similar permissions for "breathing room"; Philibert uses many engravings that show apertures, cracks, and interstices in an otherwise monolithic structure, allowing the eye to roam through and beyond the chinks in walls to envision a larger, idealized space.

Palissy's garden makes a large place for the biblical Book of Wisdom. The citations that circumscribe the niches in which a passerby is invited to rest are all taken from the Book of Wisdom. The *promeneur* thus how-

4. In this image of a utopian site populated with idealized structures, initial layers
of brick and stone crack open to reveal the vision of Calvinist architecture. Iconoclastic chinks let in light and create space for this new kind of architecture, a substratum of meaning formerly occulted by the other monument. Nature and artifice
join in this image, but artifice is used only as a means to an end, as a Calvinist tool:
nature prevails as vegetation reclaims its place, and the monumental structure on
the surface shows its impermanence, as the Calvinist inner structure remains, re-
splendent. Philibert de l'Orme, *Architecture* (1626), 1: 230 verso. By permission of
the Folger Shakespeare Library.

ever unwittingly inscribes himself within the space of Scripture, encrypt-
ing himself within its sense. Palissy in this way makes literal the biblical
warning "that men shall enter the caves of the rocks and the holes of
the ground, from before the terror of the Lord. (Isaiah 2:19)," such that,
as Calvin put it, "this word 'habitation' should be understood differently
from that of 'essence' . . . When Scripture mentions the eternal word of
God . . . 'word' means a wisdom residing in (inhabiting) God . . . the Word
is true God."[67] The garden constitutes a special space in which God's Word
may reside: driven away from Catholic-dominated space, Scripture here
finds audition. In the *Recepte*, biblical verses act as code: they inform and
inflect the structures, winnowing out qualified readers from readers who
are "code-illiterate." They operate by postulating a design or a description
available to everyone on the most superficial level. The sense of the pattern
or puzzle is not explicated; the reader must divine it by carefully listening
to clues in the coded anecdotes that Palissy recounts: "I will now tell you
about a wonderful, useful, beautiful commodity that is in my garden. And
when I've told you about it, you'll know that it's not without good reason
that I've made my garden abut onto rocks."[68]

Palissy represents what will happen to the reader of Scripture by including the architectural pillar figure of *termes* in his grotto. *Termes*, half
man, half pillar, support structures.[69] For Palissy, they symbolize the transition from one state of being to another. Palissy uses them in an eschatological sense: they enact the rehabilitation of humanity from its fallen
state, what Calvin calls "this unfortunate ruin into which we have fallen by
the fault of the first man."[70] These grotesque figures symbolize the conflict
between spiritual interiority and mundane or worldly appearance.[71] Christ
was interpreted as a grotesque figure: hideous upon the cross, it is that
very horror of his aspect, disfigured by the sins of humanity, that paradoxically produces our salvation.[72] The grotto is a model of metamorphosis;

LE HVITIESME

it describes the salvific process.[73] Palissy's grottoes emphasize interiority, typical of the Calvinist focus on the inner man and on the converted heart. Such inwardness distinguishes Palissy's work from Catholic designers of grottoes, for even the ornamentation of his interior structures recalls an inner location rather than mirroring the external landscape. "The grotto [as Palissy devises it] . . . [is] marked by a sort of mannerist inversion—i.e. a space designed for the outdoors is transferred to the indoors; in Palissy's gardens, "indoor" rooms are created outdoors, adding to the confusion of inside and outside."[74]

Grottoes, for this reason, are especially appropriate to the Calvinist recourse to code. They secrete meaning within themselves, hiding form within formlessness, structure underlying apparent chaos: "Grotesque . . . derives from the Greek 'to hide' . . . It gathers into itself suggestions of the underground . . . of secrecy."[75] Some grottoes reverse perspective, just as Calvinists wished to reverse the Catholic indictment of them back onto their persecutors. In a particular version of the grotto called *la grotte catopyrique*, in which views of the outside landscape are transferred by mirrors onto the walls of the inside,[76] the word "grotesque" signifies overcrowding or contradiction,[77] conveying the Calvinists' sense of being denied space for their theological expression while also contradicting this constraint by critically reflecting the world back to itself. Indeed, "the grotesque often arises in the clash between the 'virtuous' limitations of form and a rebellious content that refuses to be constrained."[78]

The Trompe l'Oeil Text

How do Reformed artists, and Bernard Palissy in particular, use the grotesque to disrupt or to undermine official standards and norms? How is their idiom distinct from that of Catholic creators? Iconographically, it may not in many cases be all that different.[79] However, once read back into the theological context within which it arose, the grotesque as applied by Calvinist artists aims at a different effect. First, the grotesque casts doubt on assumptions. That is the case for Catholics as well as for Calvinists, since the forms, and sometimes the amorphousness, of grotesque art always startle the viewer. But in the case of Catholic artists, such astonishment often seems purely gratuitous. In the case of Calvinists, however, a more tendentious element, a subtext, can be discerned. The grotesque is for them programmatic. By transgressing borders, altering perspective, shocking expectations, it first effects a disruption, then suggests a reformation, of official order. The grotesque is thus a profoundly *political* vehicle.

One of the grotesque's techniques is anamorphosis, in which that which one thinks one sees quickly alters, often into its opposite, something unpredictable, a mirror image critique of the first apprehension. In this way, the grotesque causes a decentering, which galvanizes the viewer/reader of Palissy's text to seek a new, better vantage point. "Anamorphosis intervenes first by making a fixed point both difficult to discern and essential to behold . . . Classical perspective, with a perpendicular point of view, always leaves relative freedom to the viewer to turn around an optimal point before the image comes undone or becomes seriously distorted . . . Anamorphosis requires that the viewer become the recipient of a code, seeking a point of view where the intended message of the game resides."[80] Anamorphosis is particularly useful to a Protestant because it replaces "the primacy of undistorted presence [with] the primacy of distorted appearance."[81] In the analogy, Catholicism fills the former role, while Calvinism adopts the latter as a ruse to criticize Catholic abuse. The reader is extracted from a rigid hierarchy of expectations to become co-creator of a Calvinist perspective within the plastic universe of the text.

With anamorphosis, Calvinist art enters the arena of plural meanings, not a customary venue for scriptural literalists. However, the plural meanings fostered by the discrepancy between initial viewing and ultimate deciphering are only multiple insofar as they represent the world's distortion.[82] Plurality ultimately resolves itself in unity, through a process whereby the unsettling character of the grotesque highlights awareness of the thing represented, requiring the viewer/reader to resituate it, create his own context for it, and make unaccustomed connections: the representation itself creates a new revelation. In this way, formerly unaccepted credos can achieve legitimacy.

Trompe l'oeil, another technique associated with the grotesque, works similarly in the *Recepte*, dramatizing the death of fallen nature and requiring a separation process to refine pure from impure, workable from unworkable: "Illusion . . . detaches pure form from impure content."[83] Thus, trompe l'oeil prompts the viewer to discern in artistic technique a theological function, wherein "the deliberate deformation of an image is an essential step in the process of reforming it."[84] The grotesque is a fitting medium for Calvinists, because it plays with its foundations in a way intended to invoke a realistic visual effect disassociated from the actual, concrete, material nature of the object. The grotesque thereby constitutes

5. De l'Orme's rusticated column incorporates natural and artificial elements. In his *Architecture*, Philibert says that "it is permitted . . . to invent . . . after Nature, as our predecessors have done. I mean by imitation, following the example of natural things that God has made" (1: 218–19). Philibert de l'Orme, *Architecture* (1626), 1: 213 verso. By permission of the Folger Shakespeare Library.

an abstraction, a spiritualized reflection on the base matter on which it builds and which it then dismantles.

In building his grottoes, Palissy artifices nature, sculpting trees so that they are at one and the same time real trees and signposts designating a higher meaning. This artificial process uses both geometrical and architectural remodeling. The process initially distorts nature, but such distortion is ultimately the vehicle to realign it with nature's original purpose: to stand as a directional arrow pointing to the Lord. "First I'll take some branches from the trees I've left standing, and having layered them as I did with the others, I'll create the form of a cornice, just as I made an architrave. I'll bring the branches together bit by bit, measuring them by geometry and architecture. In each housing formed by branches I'll place a well-proportioned antique letter . . . In the frieze will be inscribed a verse from Wisdom . . . so that men who reject wisdom, discipline and doctrine will be condemned by the testimonies even of vegetative, insensate souls."[85]

Philibert de l'Orme imitates this collage effect of nature and structure. Like Palissy's sign-bearing trees, his rusticated column incorporates a tree trunk, inclusive of foliage, as a primary structural support. Otherwise, the support is standard in form and style, suggesting that the tree may offer a rough-hewn Calvinist variation on a classical model. The column, because of the presence of the tree, appears alive: the organic heart of the Catholic nation-state, its central support is, perhaps, Calvinist.

An Entexted Re-Formation

Calvin's understanding of the invisible and the visible church was that the two may never absolutely coincide. The two realms may only conjoin in a metaphysical place (limned by the space of the text or by the coded shape of the Calvinist architect's structure, also something to be read). Protestant architects and artists dramatized these theological realizations. For

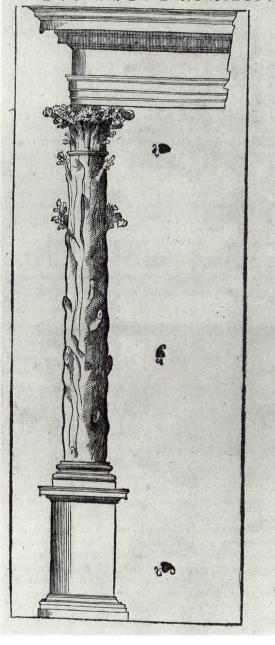

instance, a painting purporting to be the interior of a Protestant church constructed circa 1600 in the northern Netherlands displays a bizarre perspective cabinet: a Bible placed on a chair in the foreground creates a deceptive feeling of depth. This trompe l'oeil painting tells us that Scripture determines a space for itself into which it invites its reader/viewer.[86]

Similarly, Palissy would use strategies borrowed from the baroque, applying them idiosyncratically so that they became tools and not just techniques. In this, he is much like Philibert de l'Orme who, in his *Architecture*, describes the physical contact he expects his creations to make with their viewers, and the ensuing alteration this contact produces within the viewer. "When you want to use the triangle . . . cast your eye on the town, castle or square of which you want to take the measurement and make a preliminary mark on the paper to the best of your ability. Then go around the whole entity . . . In this way you'll represent accurately the forms of all angles and recesses of the city."[87] The physicality of the imperatives obliges the viewer/reader to assume a new posture: "cast your eye . . . take the form . . . go around it." Philibert tries to seize space by sight and to translate that space into his text, so that the text itself becomes the idealized structure. The reader is called to perform a similar operation. Just so, in the *Recepte véritable*, Palissy prepares the way for a re-vision of the world and a re-formation of the reader. If he can build a church through the hearing of the Word ("the only things involved were psalms, prayers, canticles and spiritual songs . . . that's how our church was built"),[88] perhaps he may bring about change through the reading of his word. His texts, and the structures they describe, are didactic events with a soteriologic orientation; he calls them *leçon[s]* and means them to have a spiritual effect upon the recipient. "In this troubled time, my friend Reader, searching for some honest human endeavor which along with meditation, would take away a part of my troubles . . . I decided to propose a small treatise . . . it concerns a grotto . . . you will realize that this work is in every geometrical component so ingeniously divided and composed, that the lesson it offers you will bring wonderment and pleasure to you."[89]

"Getting Back to the Garden"

The collector's cabinet, a phenomenon often associated with the Enlightenment, the burgeoning of science, and the development of museums, was in fact anticipated by a sixteenth-century, frequently Calvinist phenomenon: the "cabinet," a private space into which one inserted objects of perceived interest or value to compose a narrative reordering of the world in cogent form. Palissy is one of the first to discuss his chamber and collector's cabinet in detail. Like a grotto, a cabinet is a protected, secret space. Unlike the grotto, however, the cabinet is usually conceived for one individual alone. Thus, the cabinet structure makes literal the Calvinist belief that salvation was available to the believer, without the need for mediation by a priestly caste or intercession by a hierarchy of saints. For Palissy, the cabinet acts as a special preparatory site for the reception of Scripture or of the world in a scripturally conforming sense. He speaks of "the marvelous things that the author of this book has prepared and set in order in his cabinet, in order to prove all the things contained in this book, because some people didn't want to believe those things, in order to assure those who want to take the trouble to come see them in his cabinet, and having seen them, will be sure of all the things written down in this book."[90] This reordering occurs through the juxtaposition of text and specimen to create a relationship of complementarity. Palissy describes natural elements as forming the pages of a book: "You see therefore that stones of plaster, talcum or slate erect themselves then splinter off like the leaves of a book."[91] Clearly, Palissy intends a reading, not a mere viewing, of the objects in his cabinet. They are not disparate objects, but *semes* in a resolutely salvific narrative.

In addition, since the cabinet contains both natural and artificial components, the juxtaposition of the two prepares the contrast, especially salient for a contemporary Calvinist creator, between experimentation on humanity in brute form and the eventual relinquishing of the hope that humanity can be reconfigured. Palissy turns from the narrative, constructed within the cabinet through the assemblage of objects, to hypothetical alchemical experiments on the human body, intended to deal directly with human distortion. He approaches a new space: the human heart.

Many Calvinist creators rely on this technique of juxtaposition. Philibert de l'Orme uses it to signal irony or incongruity. Palissy uses his catalogue of the elements of nature to document the gap between man and God, as well as to recall their former union: "In order to encourage you to prepare your ears to hear and your eyes to see, I've placed here certain stones and minerals . . . to help you attend to a crucial point . . . [These are] obvious proofs."[92] The cabinet houses the process of inner structuring.

Palissy speaks a revealing vocabulary when exhibiting his collection to the reader. He repeats the verb *confesser*, conferring a theological tone on the proof case constituted by his argument and by the specimens adduced as evidence: "[Since you] hav[e] seen nothing more than my writing or flat figures . . . I've put this in place as evidence of a large number of stones, by which you may easily know to be true the reasons and proofs that I've adduced . . . And if you are not entirely crazy you will confess [God's truth] after having seen the stones' demonstration in my book . . . All those who see this will be obliged to confess the same."[93] The cabinet shapes the interior, validating the space of the self in which nature, reordered through narrative, attests to the human testimonial. Here, in a characteristic Calvinist reversal of terms, Palissy changes the customary negative valence of "constrained," making it positive. We are saved precisely because we are "constrained" to believe. Palissy's text is like the specimens in his cabinet. Extracted from natural sources, it must be brought to light and confirmed in its new function: "It is written that one should take care not to abuse God's gifts or to hide one's talents in the earth . . . This is why I've taken the trouble to bring to light those things that God has granted it to me to understand."[94] In addition, his text provides a companion commentary to the cabinet. Palissy speaks of two sorts of cabinets, his own and a cabinet of deception, warning "Mon ami lecteur" not to delude himself with the vain and speculative imaginings of writers who lack both real experience and a scriptural standard; these are the "choses vaines escrites aux cabinets."[95] He opposes unfounded conjecture and erroneous belief. His cabinet, however, offers a self-help space, in which the well-intentioned reader may instruct himself through the emblematic examination of the conjunction of word (the *Recepte véritable*) and image (the natural specimen). "Distrust any book composed only of imaginings, and of those that are impractical . . . take the trouble to come see my cabinet, in which you'll see marvelous things brought to prove what I have written; these things have signs so that every person can learn from them."[96]

John Dixon Hunt notes that "cabinet" can mean "garden."[97] Thus, Palissy repeatedly refers in his texts to varieties of like spaces, attempting to find a haven for the Calvinist faith and a venue for the free work of salvation. The cabinet helpfully summarizes the structures of both garden and grotto, detailing the theological technique for reading the created order.

A Mighty Fortress: Palissy and
Jacques Perret de Chambéry

A final example of similarities among Calvinist creators in their selection and revision of aesthetic vehicles for political and theological expression compares the idealized fortress structure of Bernard Palissy in the *Recepte* and the plans for fortresses devised by the crypto-Calvinist Jacques Perret de Chambéry in his work *Des fortifications et artifices d'architecture et perspective* (1601). Chambéry's work was a pattern book for the building of fortifications, and many of its structures were constructed during his lifetime. *Des fortifications* contained twenty-three engravings, accompanied by brief descriptions, of towns, temples, castles, and fortifications. The book at first seems straightforward and practical, accessible through a cursory viewing or a surface reading. However, closer attention to detail shows that the great majority of the designs for fortresses are circumscribed by biblical quotations or by Huguenot-sanctioned biblical paraphrases such as those taken from Clément Marot's translations of the Psalms. These biblical quotations, further, act subversively: they are ironic and may even directly contradict the purported effect of the image. The classic distinction between Catholic (image-reliant) and Calvinist (Word-attentive) obtains. The friction between the two apparently twinned but in fact warring systems of signification in the text generates multiple meanings and plural audiences. A Calvinist reader will find in this text the laying-low of his Catholic adversary, even when the forts described are commissioned for Catholic use. The power of the Word to undo the Catholic defense is stronger. Patricia O'Grady notes that "the series of engravings can best be characterized as a Huguenot statement in architectural terms. This characterization is not provided by the text which is strictly technical and descriptive. Indeed, Perret seems to have gone to some pains to produce a neutral text in the style of an architectural model book. . . . Under the terms of the Edict of Nantes defining the rights and privileges of the Huguenots, publications that were classified as having Huguenot content were restricted in their distribution. Perret could be trying to avoid this label as much as possible."[98]

The style of biblical citation, distinctly Protestant, quotes verses in full along with verse number, book, and chapter, which are incorporated seamlessly into the text. Other aspects identify the text as Calvinist, among them the inclusion of the coat of arms of the Huguenot duc de Rohan. Chambéry's artistic techniques recall those of Philibert de l'Orme. The framing device, in which word circumscribes and redetermines image, is one such technique. Another strategy is the decentering of an otherwise equilibrated image: for instance, a line may bisect a fortress, shifting it off center.[99] Chambéry, like Palissy, exalts auditory or intellectual phenomena over the visual through appeals to the imagination. He dismisses many details as unnecessary: "[I will here only] summarize the measurements that should be taken with the compass . . . [But] you'll find what you want [elsewhere]."[100] In addition, the Calvinist influence makes itself felt through the incorporation of numerous psalms into the format of the book. The Calvinists were known as psalm singers, singing in the vernacular while Catholic priests chanted in Latin. Those psalms selected, when examined as a unit, convey a very specific message, one that hopes for a safe place for Calvinists, "un fort lieu,"—a very different kind of fort from that purportedly displayed in the book, one located within the Word: "Psalm 91. He who into the safekeeping of God retires forever will be kept in good shade and a strong place forever. God is my safeguard, my high tower and the foundation on which I establish myself. This comes from Psalm 91."[101]

The repetition of Psalm 91 as source both at the beginning and at the end of the verse forms a frame, alerting the reader to heightened textual significance. Such repetition may also attest to a certain anxiety on the writer's part: he is grounding his word in Scripture, but continually seeks reassurance that such an establishing is allowed, that such an act is biblically ordained. The frame also recalls the strategy throughout the book, in which biblical quotes frame and determine the image they surround. The frame highlights the coded component of the text. In addition, architectural motifs are highlighted in the psalm verse chosen, as though to remind the reader that what matters is not the actual plan for the fort but a sort of interior consolidation, a standing firm on the Word. Thus, "garde," "fort lieu," "haulte tour," and "fondement" all are no longer empirical spaces, but rather spiritual spaces: the arena of conversion, of turning to the Lord for strength and structure.

Some of the citation/image relationships are particularly striking in that the Calvinist architect uses the biblical quotation to contain the image, to regularize it and, like Palissy, to shape it in a manner that conforms to Scripture. For instance, the following quotation surrounds the irregular, jagged-edged engraving of a fort with a clear, strong rectangular frame that the quote itself constitutes. The Word bounds, and redefines, image: "You will love the Lord your God with all your heart and all your soul and all your understanding; this is the first and greatest commandment.

And the second is like unto it: you will love your neighbor as yourself; from these two commandments hang all the law and the prophets. This is the summary of all law. Exodus 20 and Matthew 22nd chapter." [102] By amalgamating two authorities, the Old Testament and the New, the writer lends legitimacy to his structuring enterprise. This is an unusual citation with which to circumscribe a military fortress. The militant intent of the (Catholic) fortress is thereby in some measure neutralized as at odds with biblical mandates.

Sometimes the meaning of the structure is reappropriated from the patron. Thus, the label affixed to a fort designed for a Catholic nobleman undoes his prestige so that all honor will be rightfully redirected to God: "All you Princes and Lords filled with pride, Render — Fear God — Render unto the Lord all strength and honor. Psalm 29." [103] The phrase "Fear God" forms a solid block, spatially interrupting the caption's narrative flow, and stands as an admonitory cornerstone, reminding the reader that this structure serves not only a terrestrial but also a metaphysical purpose. A reminder that all are equal before God interrupts spatially the address to the nobleman. Three spatial blocks occupy the page. The first, to the left, says "en Dieu." The second, middle block has two tiers: above is "honorez le Roy," while "contentement en" inscribes the lower level. The final block, to the right, states "seul repos." In this way, the king receives brief mention, only to be circumscribed by verses oriented toward the Lord, a symbolic Calvinist leveling of a Catholic client. Further, this structure includes a fort and an entryway. The image depicts Henry IV taking the city of Paris, and the caption states that "the great city of Paris was besieged and taken by great King Henry IIII March 22 1594." [104] The skewed relationship between image and caption makes the phrase "le grand Roy" a mere minuscule point in the overall body of the citation; visually diminished, the king is instructed that he owes allegiance to a (Calvinist) God.

As with Palissy, many of these structures are more theoretical than actual. Their author intends, indeed hopes, that they will be undone. They stand more as exempla and reminders than as real forts. One fortress design, for example, bears this cautionary title: "it is all very well and good for someone to build his house; if the Lord doesn't help him, he only builds in vain. When seeking to assure the defense of the city, one can do everything without avail unless the Lord is involved." [105] The lack of punctuation and the repetition of "on a beau" emphasize the urgency of the message and its ineluctable consequences.

Of Spirals and Labyrinths: Palissy's Fortress
in a Fallen World

I hope that I may die a shameful death, if what I've included here does not contain truth . . . I take as my witness the Duke of Montpensier, who, having been brought to my lodgings in Saintonge, accompanied by several great lords, and having seen the grandeur of my work, or part of it, placed me in his safekeeping, me and all those of my house . . . and even if I were accused of being a believer in the new religion [R. P. R.], only he would judge of that . . . I also call [many others] to witness . . . And indeed the late King and Queen of Navarre saw my work, as did the Lord of Rohan.

—Palissy, *Recepte véritable* [106]

Palissy's letter justifying himself to his powerful patrons and seeking to indemnify him from future persecutions, even to secure his release from prison, demonstrates his need for structured strategies of self-protection. He envisions a fortress city that will protect him and fellow Calvinists: "Some time after I had thought about these horrible dangers of war from which God had so miraculously delivered me, I began to desire to design and sketch the plan for a City in which one could be safe in war-time."[107] This fortress is unique and noteworthy on several counts. Unlike Chambéry's, Palissy's fortress is *engagé*: while the former's fortresses seem intended for Catholic use (although, read in a new context, they contradict that purpose),[108] Palissy's fortress identifies itself as Calvinist (by referring to how it will protect the *esleus*) and mentions Scripture as its context. Palissy's fortress remains idealized. Unable (or unwilling) to find appropriate or adequate space in which to build it, Palissy defers its production, saying first that he will make a sketch of it, then that it must be accompanied by a text, next that a model will have to be made of it.[109] Representation and immanence are continually denied, as Palissy constructs a metaphysical, even an eschatological structure, whose lineaments are visible only in the mind's eye and which points to a time-out-of-time: one of peace and toleration.

Another distinguishing factor is that Palissy consciously seeks avatars for his design in unusual places: in nature, among the birds, the beasts, and the fish. He finds his prototype in the shellfish who makes its home in a spiral shell. Typically Calvinist, Palissy takes the model selected, then improvises to adapt it to his need, squaring the curves of the spiral to provide a more direct prospect for cannon fire.[110] In selecting the spiral shape, Palissy refers to Daedalus, the master mazemaker of the Greeks, who hid the secret of the Minotaur at the heart of his labyrinth.[111] What secrets do Palissy and the Calvinists hide in the kernel of their structures? Calvinists employed the trope of the labyrinth to represent the disorder of the post-lapsarian world. Here, that image is corrected: the world itself will now be structured to abet Calvinists and to remedy the sins of the Fall. Palissy's maze is protective and salubrious, soteriologic even. Just as the crustacean shelters in its shell, so Palissy's work protects him.[112]

Palissy tries to shape a space for peace, not merely defensive war, stating that most fortress cities function for aggression or defense, but his offers a solid structure favorable to a peaceable way of life.[113] All its parts are imbricated (*concathenez*) each within the other; thus, as in Scripture, all are members of one body, rather than isolated, potentially schismatic units: "It's a pretty sorry city, one in which the members are unable to consolidate and help each other . . . It is very easy to beat the body when the body parts cannot come to its aid."[114] The negative reference to the kingdom of France and its treatment of Calvinists not as subjects of one state body but rather as deviant units can be heard.[115] Such rebuke of the king's failure to observe the Calvinist model of the patriarchal household constitutes a Calvinist commonplace. Palissy's structure seeks to move beyond politics, to obey the biblical mandate of "one body in Christ."

Finally, Palissy's fortress-text contains a significant theoretical component: it is itself an apologia for the subject's right to self-defense, an issue which *Des fortifications* does not raise: "From a military standpoint, Palissy's project is interesting but hardly useful. It is on the personal level that the city represents something much more important for him. He seems to believe that his inspiration for the undertaking comes to him from God and that, despite his ignorance of things military . . . God is sufficiently powerful to grant adequate ability to him . . . The art of self-defense is innate; this explains why Palissy, as a creature of God, looks to see how other creatures defend themselves."[116] Like Calvin's *Institution*, Palissy's text conforms closely to its model by discussing both real space and wished-for space. Chambéry's text, written some twenty years later, seems to assert that this is a utopian hope; all realistic space is Catholic-determined and can only be subverted through inscriptions redirecting the sense in which their structures are received.

In Chambéry's endeavor, a certain complicity with the reader is assumed, a certain familiarity with the project anticipated, creating a privileged readership much like that at which Palissy's soteriologic, participatory text aims. The primary task of the text, despite its description of fortresses, is oriented toward the interior rather than the exterior. Like Calvin's focus on the believer's heart, like Palissy's decision to go into hiding in order to delineate the space of salvation, Chambéry's method is to display many pages showing large buildings complete with detailed blueprints, but then to add the rather unusual feature of a cutaway revealing the entire interior of the structure. On one such image a scriptural paraphrase forms a square textual frame: "Making one happy is my one great pleasure; let us all do unto one another as we wish to have done unto us."[117] Other Calvinist architects demonstrate such an interior turn. Salomon de Brosse, for example, interprets the injunctions of the Edict of Nantes, which banned outward Protestant monuments, in such a way that his temple at Charenton is monumental only through the two-tiered columns concealed in its interior.

Calvinism constitutes the "other" for Catholics, something that is both within them and strange to them. Calvinism thus labels itself multifarious; it offers an opposing position to the state religion. As such, while it, too, aims at singularity and unity of doctrine, it can commend diversity. Thus, in Chambéry's caption that follows, the multiple possibilities proffered by the text might appear to convey the Calvinists' plea for tolerance and their decision to speak as "other": "This figure is composed of diverse plans for fortifications, and it has a variety of advantages that will satisfy many tastes. But its great importance and expenditure should be resolved through a consultation of capable people, and one alone should be designated to lead them."[118] Diversity is initially upheld, but ultimately resolved, after "une bonne consultation" (a code phrase for Calvinist attentiveness to the Word) with "un seul pour commander" (one true God). The fortress forms the prototype for a firm foundation and a sure guard in Christ.

Another blueprint turns image into word, assuring a normative Calvinist focus on the divine, in two ways. First, a label "Christians, children of God, are themselves the true temple"[119] on a big building which "could actually serve as a large temple" effectively undoes the concrete blueprint, since the verse makes real structure unnecessary. The aim seems to be to reassure dispossessed Calvinists that, while they might lack their own structures for religious observance, their faith is no less valid. Second, while they might lack their own space for theological expression, they may theorize and eventually realize it, as the reality of the Huguenot community of the period includes the concept of the *ville-refuge*; which is an entirely new town built to harbor displaced Huguenots fleeing intolerance in France to Protestant strongholds in the same country.[120]

Like Philibert de l'Orme and Palissy, Chambéry finds a way to inscribe himself into his work, wedding his trade to his confessional stance. His device, I.P.E.R.R.E.T. above a doubled circle containing architectural instruments, proclaims boldly: "An inventor who fears God fears nothing else."[121] He may be creating structures for Catholic kings, but he is not about to imperil his faith.

Conclusion: Structuring Salvation

Palissy's *Recepte véritable* postulates a paradigm for theorizing spiritual space. It offers the assurance that the Calvinist believer, despite his imperiled status, may indeed continue to affirm his God. The *Recepte* suggests the resources of a subversive strategy for undermining the official state it appears to uphold, and it reorients nature, marked by the Fall, so that debased humanity, a natural element, may be recuperated. Most particularly, the *Recepte véritable* devises a glossary of Calvinist aesthetic devices—trompe l'oeil, grotesque, truncation, juxtaposition, decentering, framing, bisecting, imaged contradiction, verbal literal rendering—that enables the success of this recuperative program.

Palissy puns on the term "recepte" in his title, for not only does he prescribe (a recipe for) how nature may be realigned with God (by eliminating Catholic practices), but he also indicates his certainty that his wishes will, indeed, be realized: "recepte" is also a receipt of payment due, a token or assurance of salvation.

Philibert de l'Orme and the "Peculiar Problems" of Protestant Architecture

Evangelicals and Proto-Protestants

Philibert de l'Orme was one of the most influential yet controversial architects of his time. A man of great arrogance and contentiousness, he was also a provocative, ambitious architectural theorist. Convinced that others were jealous of him and conspiring to sabotage his efforts, Philibert brought calumny on his own head through his pridefulness and bitterness. "People have done so much damage to me, and accused me of so many crimes of which I've since been found innocent, and they've taken away from me anything I've ever earned . . . I believe that God has punished me because I care more to serve men than to serve Him. So, instead of studying how to build castles and houses, I'll learn how to edify [build up] men."[1] Architectural historians have documented the difficulties and vagaries of this prominent and controversial personality and puzzled over the factors motivating Philibert's often irate response to events and people in his life. Philibert was also an evangelical during the tense political and religious period just prior to, and during the early years of, the Wars of Religion.

An evangelical stance in the first few decades of sixteenth-century France signified a desire to reform the Catholic church from within. Evangelicals were much influenced by the work and writings of Martin Luther, as was Calvin. Marguerite de Navarre, a noted evangelical and protectress of Protestants—indeed, of Calvin himself—translated many of Luther's tracts into French. As evangelicals gathered in *cercles*, such as the famous Cercle de Meaux headed by Lefèvre d'Etaples and Guillaume Briçonnet, their faith often became more high-profile and less covert. After the Affaire des Placards, however, many resorted to more veiled criticisms of the Catholic church.[2] This was the case with Marguerite de Navarre's courtier, Clément Marot, poet and translator of the psalms, who experienced persecution at the time of the Affaire des Placards, was imprisoned for breaking Lenten tradition and "avoir mangé le lard," and eventually left France for Calvin's Geneva.

Many evangelicals published with evangelical presses—often with the same press, that of Jean de Tournes.[3] Reluctant to break with the Catholic church, yet aware of its need for reform, convinced of man's depravity and God's grace, reliant on Scripture and distrustful of "works righteousness," evangelicals greatly influenced France during the late 1520s and early 1530s. At the time of the Affaire des Placards, however, they were obliged to resort to strategies of nicodemism in order to protect themselves and their beliefs. Although clearly resembling Protestants in their religious and ecclesiastical preferences, many evangelicals never actually broke with the church.

Philibert de l'Orme may have been one of their number. One telling factor is the influence of another evangelical, the Italian Sebastiano Serlio, who practiced and published in Paris contemporaneously with Philibert. Serlio published his architectural manuals—one of which, the *Extraordinario libro*, was dedicated to Marguerite de Navarre, with whom he maintained a lengthy correspondence—in a format carefully imitated by Philibert. Serlio emphasized a pragmatic, utilitarian focus, the use of many engravings and plates, and certain thematic preoccupations—most notably, that of the difference between a simple, plain style and the more ornate (what Serlio viewed as abusive) idiom of the other major influence on architecture of the period, Vitruvius. Serlio's architectural manuals contain ideological position papers. As an evangelical, Serlio practiced strategies of nicodemism and subversion.[4] His *Extraordinario libro* models how to subvert a theological as well as an artistic purpose.[5] Like Philibert, Serlio demonstrates ambivalence toward architecture. Who is it intended to monumentalize? Are they worthy of being commemorated? What sort of structuring activity is the most significant? For Serlio, the true temple is established within the human heart (Revelation 21–22): "indeed, material [constructed] temples are really not needed for worship of God."[6] Serlio's distinction between the visible and the invisible church is a crucial point in Calvin's theology, as well. Thus, for Serlio, Philibert, and the second-generation Calvinist architects, structures are equivalent to *adiaphora*: accommodations to a fallen world.[7]

6. Philibert de l'Orme's self-portrait, of a stern, thoughtful, fairly prosperous man, interestingly angled obliquely away from the viewer, offering no real purchase on the subject's thoughts, thus providing a form of artistic self-protection. In the same vein, Philibert hid the entryway to his private house through an oblique side stairway. Philibert de l'Orme, *Architecture*, (1626), 1: 5 verso. By permission of the Folger Shakespeare Library.

Serlio's Protestant perspective can also be discerned in his choice of scriptural passages. Serlio, like Philibert, Palissy, Bullant, Boyceau, and most Calvinist architects and writers of the period, favored the parable of the talents. Serlio also referred to the parable of casting pearls before swine to rationalize what Calvin would have called his nicodemism, much as Philibert hinted at his Protestant sympathies. This strategy of dissimulation requires an elite group of interpreters: "It's not possible to share the truth with everyone. Only the elect will know how to find [the truth]. The reprobate, predestined to damnation, will in no way be able to understand [truth]. Why, then, try to convince them [of it]? . . . The topos of the interiority of faith, of the church as the [invisible] assembly of the elect, [makes it useless to try] to explain things to swine . . . As for all humans, so it is for architects, too: there are the elect, and there are the damned. Thus in architecture, too, there exists a truth, almost a revealed truth . . . except, this truth is not for everyone."[8]

Philibert quotes Serlio in his writings. He was particularly influenced by Serlio's ambivalence toward ornamentation, an ambivalence that Philibert, too, turns against his patrons. In the *Settimo libro*, Serlio speaks "of how to distinguish, with [his] small intellect, a sober, simple . . . architecture from one that is weak, facile, affected, obscure and confused."[9] Philibert's use of detail and ornamentation, as with the second-generation Calvinist architects, is one of the most telling ways in which his evangelical sympathies are encoded on his constructions.

While Philibert has never been identified explicitly as a Calvinist, and while some aspects of his later life suggest that he remained nominally Catholic until the end of his days,[10] other characteristics of his career and writings indicate a strongly evangelical stance and perhaps Calvinist sympathies. The trait that most affiliates him with other Calvinist architects is his tendency to cite Scripture, particularly books of the Bible more favored by Protestants. In addition, all the other Calvinist architects who would succeed him hailed him as their great progenitor. His troubled relationships with his more militant Catholic clients also hint that his confessional

perspective proved problematic for his career. It is not surprising, then, that Philibert's sympathies were not declared openly. They did, nonetheless, inform his work.

Playing with Contradiction: The Personal History of Philibert de l'Orme

Born in Lyons around 1510, Philibert de l'Orme was the son of a master mason. Philibert seemed destined for an architectural career from his early years. During adolescence, fascinated by the idiom in which ancient cultures erected structures, he took part in archaeological excavations. While traveling through Rome (1533–36), Philibert worked as Cardinal Du Bellay's archaeological secretary in 1535, then returned to Lyons in 1536, where his first work, the house of Antoine Bullioud, is located. For Guillaume Du Bellay, Philibert engineered fortifications, and he built the château at St.-Maur near Paris from 1541 to 1544. St.-Maur was Philibert's first experience of having to build a structure in conformity with a predetermined site rather than on leveled ground. He commented that "its underlayer had been deeply mined by quarries and by the coursing of water,"[11] rationalizing his inability to implement fully his architectural vision there. During work on this project, Philibert articulated his resistance to incorporating preexisting work by other architects on a site.[12] St.-Maur was also an occasion of constraint for Philibert on ideological grounds; Catherine de Médicis eventually compelled him to revise alterations he had already made in the plan and demoted Philibert to Primatice's subordinate.

In 1547, Philibert directed the construction of François I's tomb. He describes this endeavor in his *Instruction de Monsieur d'Ivry*. Shortly thereafter, Philibert was awarded the benefice of the Abbey of Geneston. Under Henri II, who also named him superintendent of buildings, Philibert rebuilt Anet for Diane de Poitiers. In this enterprise, he was given more latitude for personal expression; as long as he worked around the Château of Brézé at Anet, he was able to rework the structure from its foundations. At Anet, he strove "for a way to grab hold of space, through the use of forms recalling heavenly forms,"[13] as though seeking to compensate for the constrained spatial circumstances under which he had performed at St.-Maur. While large parts of Anet are no longer extant, we know from engravings in Philibert's *Architecture* that Anet was unusual in possessing three differing sides to its court; Anet epitomized difference and asymmetry and rejected uniformity. Anet was extremely innovative: "de l'Orme's design does not go back . . . to . . . any model."[14] For Henri II, Philibert also worked on alterations at Fontainebleau and constructed a bridge at Charenton. Subsequently, he received the abbeys of Noyon and Ivry. He completed the chapel at Vincennes 1551–53.

In 1557, Philibert erected the unusual freestanding symmetrical Château-Neuf at St. Germain, iconoclastic in its deviation from the traditional model of a court enclosed by four wings. This bold architectural statement created its own Protestant lineage; it was adopted as a prototype by the militant Calvinist architect Salomon de Brosse at Blérancourt some years later.[15] Such borrowing by other Calvinist architects would become increasingly frequent, with Philibert's stylistic idiosyncrasies composing the architectural vocabulary of later Calvinist architects.[16] The construction of Château-Neuf inaugurates the second phase of Philibert's work, a period in which he exercised considerable architectural power.[17] This is also the approximate date (1560) during which his evangelical sympathies become more pronounced. His architectural style now having received royal imprimatur, Philibert may have felt emboldened to align himself implicitly with the theology of an unpopular minority to whom he appears to have been sympathetic for years.

Philibert's interest in Protestantism appears in his prefaces and texts, bestrewn with scriptural references,[18] a large component of which is specifically Calvinist in his citation of authorities: Paul, for instance, is given preference over James, a book more favored by Catholics at the time. While it was customary for both Catholics and Protestants to quote from the Gospels of Matthew and John, pre-Reformation Catholics did not extensively quote the Pauline letters to the Romans and Corinthians. In addition, "one quarter of all references used by pre-Reformation French preachers [were composed of] other, non-biblical sources,"[19] while Philibert relies either on architectural predecessors or on the Bible, to the exclusion of other sources. In *Des scandales*, John Calvin makes frequent reference to biblical books. His selection of quotations is important, both because it differs from Catholic citation choices and because it establishes a model for scriptural quotation, one which Philibert emulates.[20] The book from which Calvin quotes most is the Gospel of Matthew (eighty-three references), followed by Corinthians (at least fifty references), Romans (more than thirty-nine references), then Acts. There are also numerous quotations from 1 and 2 Timothy, but only six from James. Calvin refers very infrequently to the Old Testament, except when explicit structuring is

7. The frontispiece to Philibert de l'Orme's *Nouvelles inventions pour bien bastir et a petits frais* (1561). The tree wrapped with a scroll recalls Palissy's sign-bearing trees, is characteristically Calvinist in its marriage of natural and fabricated elements, and recalls the caduceus form—prescriptively medicinal to right the world's ills, also emblematic of eternal life—that the Good Architect holds in an architectural allegory by Philibert, discussed later in this chapter. By permission of the Folger Shakespeare Library.

concerned (as is the case with his *Institution*). Similarly, Philibert cites the Old Testament only in reference to his project of erecting a structure using the measurements of Solomon's temple.[21] Philibert's project is consonant with Calvinism: building should further God's kingdom, rather than simply supply intellectual or artistic satisfaction.[22] Philibert, like Calvin, uses Scripture as the textual template for his building activity in general.

Personal unpopularity and political changes led to Philibert's fall from favor. Dismissed as superintendent of buildings after Henri II's demise, in the *Nouvelles inventions pour bien bastir et a petits frais* (1561), written during this period of disgrace,[23] Philibert lamented: "Please, God, grant me a more free spirit; shield me from the fears and worries that I've experienced since the death of King Henry."[24] He did continue to build, although to a lesser degree. Around 1564, Catherine commissioned Philibert to design the Tuileries. Here, too, he inaugurated a Protestant genealogy, for Jean Bullant later closely imitated Philibert's architectural innovation in the use of detail on the elevation of the Tuileries palace.[25] This period forms the third and final stage of Philibert's architectural activity, one typified by fear of persecution until his death in 1570. During this later period, he published his most audacious architectural writings. The *Nouvelles inventions* subverts classical expectations, addressing an audience of (Calvinist) craftsmen rather than an elite corps of architects. Philibert also turned away from the standard legitimators of power.

Philibert's most important writings on architecture were composed and published in a period of increased Catholic-Calvinist polarization. His *Nouvelles inventions* (1561) was in draft form at the time of the Conjuration of Amboise (1560), contemporary with the Massacre of Wassy in 1562. In 1567, he published nine books of his *Architecture*. Philibert's constructions, both those actually erected and those described in manuals, are idiosyncratic and often startling. The *Architecture* "combines the theoretical and practical aspects of architecture in a remarkable manner. The main reason for this seems to be that the author writes from his own personal

NOVVELLES

INVENTIONS POVR BIEN

BASTIR ET A PETITS FRAIZ, TROVVEES

n'agueres par Philibert de L'orme
Lyonnois, Architecte, Conseiller & Aulmonier ordi-
naire du feu Roy. Henry,
& Abbé de S. Eloy
lez Noyon.

A PARIS,

De l'Imprimerie de Federic Morel, rue S. Iean
de Beauuais au franc Meurier.

M. D. LXI.

Auec priuilege du Roy.

experience . . . [and] gives priority to the practical side of architecture."[26]
One key to the unusual tenor of that experience is the Calvinist content
that informed his later structures and texts. Philibert's will left instructions
to bury him as a canon in Notre-Dame, and he was interred in the nave as
requested. His Calvinism remained always a crypto-Calvinism; symbolically, this Calvinist sympathizer asked to be buried at the base of a Catholic
structure, a fitting emblem for his architectural subversion.[27]

Philibert and the Peculiar Protestant Prototype

Philibert de l'Orme was the most inventive mind to appear in French architecture
in the sixteenth century, and a detailed study of his work may . . . help to throw
some light on the peculiar problems of [this architecture].
                                                  —Blunt, *Philibert de l'Orme*[28]

Philibert de l'Orme puzzles art historians. His architectural manuals
and erected structures display apparently contradictory impulses, causing
perplexity as to the sources of his idiosyncratic architectural vocabulary and
forms. Anthony Blunt speaks of the "peculiar problems" of French architecture during Philibert's period and briefly acknowledges his Protestant
adherence, suggesting that Philibert's Calvinist confessional stance was a
significant factor in the development of his style. Blunt does not directly
equate religious perspective with the development of a unique architectural idiom or body of structures. However, Philibert himself hints at such
a relationship in his prefaces, where he indicates that his role as Calvinist
architect commissioned to monumentalize Catholic nobility profoundly
determines the nature of his work. Philibert situates himself within a Calvinist scriptural tradition when describing his architectural aims, deploying
a particular iconography and architectural vocabulary aimed at circumventing or subverting Catholic power. Some of his structures are so encoded or visually skewed that the apparent glory they confer on a Catholic
patron is contradicted by the code or superscription. A minority Calvinist
readership, familiar with Calvinist exegesis and conversant in vernacular
Scripture, could decipher the vocabulary of Philibert's structures in a different way from the uninitiated's approach to the structure as mere visual
surface. Alerted to the scriptural components on which the structure was
based, these Calvinists would then interpret the propagandistically Catho-

lic structure in a way consonant with their theology. They could read the structure back into their own sense.[29]

Playing Hide-and-Seek with Philibert's Writings and Works

In sum, there's really no need to go to such great lengths to understand how he means those words.

— Calvin, *Institution* [30]

[It's] as though it were sewn together piecemeal.

— Calvin, *Institution* [31]

The beams having been extended from the centers, and assembled with such joints as I've described, are found to be incredibly solid when constructed . . . such joints and assemblies cannot be discerned without the aid of ornamentation.

— Philibert, *Nouvelles inventions* [32]

The hidden core of Philibert's work and structures is Calvinist. His conception of buildings is Calvinist in character and displayed in code. This Calvinist confession creates a kernel of hidden strength within the citation system of his work, demonstrating a refusal to sacrifice belief to constraint.[33] Philibert applies a Calvinist coating to his structures. The first epigraph, taken from Calvin, epitomizes the gap between meaning and expression. Calvin decried allegories, asserting that their opacity fostered misinterpretation. Nonetheless, when portraying his marginal stance, Philibert often uses allegories, perhaps because allegories and parable-like stories require interpretation on a different level than that on which they are first received. As Philibert uses them, they camouflage the Calvinist content of his thought and structures. The components of his structure can then be assigned various meanings within an allegorical reading that obfuscates their true significance, thereby protecting—by obscuring—Philibert's implicit cultural critique. In the second and third epigraphs, Calvin's concern over a patchwork approach to interpretation is transformed into Philibert's decision to implement such an approach as a subterfuge.

Philibert relates an occasion on which he had to compose a structural support out of "diverse pieces." He covers those disparate fragments over with a trompe l'oeil veneer that creates an impression of uniformity. Yet he knows, and tells his readers, that what lies beneath possesses only an illusory unity. This structure, commissioned by a Catholic patron, is riddled with cracks. Similarly unsound, this clever representation suggests, is the power base of the patron. Philibert deliberately deceives the patron as to the substantiality of his structure. "When all these beams are assembled as I described to you above, if they are to form a hall or room, no one will want to see the [places for pegs] hollowed out in the middle of the beams. They would think such a spectacle a heap of garbage, a spider's nest, which may in fact be the case. So, to avoid this unsightliness, these beams must be adorned with gilded pieces or other ornaments, as sumptuous as possible . . . to hide the disparity underneath."[34]

In this passage, Philibert plays hide-and-seek (in French, *cache-cache*, or the act of remaining doubly, or jointly, hidden) through a doubled trompe l'oeil. He not only mentions the strategy of hiding disparate fragments beneath a uniform surface, one cobbled together out of ersatz materials; he recommends "lambris dorez," gilding rather than real gold. Ornament deceives the eye into perceiving an integral substance rather than a motley "amas d'ordures." Similarly, Philibert's self-protective space, described by—and, to some extent, formed by—his text, arises from the actual dissimilarity, but apparent harmony, between ornament and underlying structure. Philibert counteracts constraint with an impasto of detail that functions subversively, in contradistinction to the structure on which it is found. The detail is the parasite on the host, and it saps the strength on which it feeds. Philibert both metaphorically and structurally hollows out ("therefore hollow in the middle of the beam") the support system of his patron, undermining it through the very structure commissioned to perpetuate it. Disparity hides beneath the surface of many of Philibert's buildings. Similarly, in his texts lurks "something more" that "others won't find beautiful to see." Philibert's strategy has the same intent as that used by Serlio in revising Vitruvius, but is its mirror opposite. Serlio opposes excess ornamentation and criticizes overadornment on Vitruvius's structures.[35] For Serlio, ornament has a negative ideological dimension. Philibert, who also prefers the biblical *stylus rudus* for his architectural statements, distrusts ornament and amply expresses this distrust in his texts. Yet, when building, he may use excessive ornament to represent that which threatens his Protestant perspective. Through the overweening *copia* of ornament, he indirectly criticizes the system that produces ornateness, deception, and ritual.

In a textual demonstration of his subversive program, Philibert asks his reader to envision a situation resulting from a noble's inheritance of a castle that he deems inadequate: "Let's suppose that some great lord inherits or in some manner acquires a castle or house built by his grandfather . . . and the heir . . . doesn't really like what he's got . . . so he wants to redo the building in a wholly new way."[36] Reluctant to destroy the original structure, the patron decides to commission alterations. However, he is compelled to tailor his expectations to the already-occupied site, which requires the architect to have great sensitivity to spatial concerns that inevitably inhibit the realization of all the client's desiderata. "The heir, insomuch as he has become a rather great lord . . . also wants to have . . . a larger building wherein he may lodge his friends . . . even so, he doesn't really want to tear down the former dwelling of his predecessors . . . this all causes the space to be unconformable to his wishes."[37] Philibert tells a story about this patron's predicament. When Philibert wants to describe a tactic for subversion, he typically narrates or allegorizes it. Through repetition, he not only accentuates the client's feeling of constriction but also hints at a more personal dynamic. Philibert has made similar statements about his own feelings of constraint elsewhere in his prefaces. Under the guise of the patron, he may be recalling his own experiences of constraint: "In such ill-favored conditions, subjection and constraint, the Architect must have good understanding, and take care not to speak as do the ignorant . . . He must carefully research the site, and know where each thing should be placed, according to the needs of the structure."[38]

The requirements of place ("selon qu'elle le requiert") are enumerated in a language common to Calvinist architects, who are aware of spatial limitations curtailing their confessional statements. Philibert counsels the fictional architect to circumspection and canniness. The psychological sensitivity of the portraits ("he doesn't really have"; "he wants") in Philibert's micronarrative also attest to his very acute awareness of how others are thinking, of what they want, of his willingness—or refusal—to meet those needs, and of the effects that his response may engender. Such an exquisite awareness of the other characterizes one who feels endangered, rather than a member of the majority. Several aspects of this story bear out such an interpretation. The parable-like quality of Philibert's statements, the considerable detail of the image, are significant in themselves; the story is not a mere accessory to the larger structure but rather requires decoding, not a naive reading.[39] The scriptural reminiscences of the passage further situate it within the Calvinist tradition of the "close reading" of Scripture: "l'héritier" is often used in the Gospels in reference to the Kingdom of Heaven.

When Philibert applies an impasto of detail, he speaks in code, imitating—in order to denigrate—Catholicism, of which excessive ornamentation is typical. Philibert says that "A good architect, wanting to represent a building in its 'natural state,' should never, as I've said, make a gilded model or one enriched with painting . . . as those who want to deceive people ordinarily do."[40] The way Catholic ornamentation functions, Philibert says, is by causing a misreading or a distorted apprehension: "They apply cosmetics to their works in order to deceive men . . . They try to draw the eyes of viewers to them in order to pull their judgment away from a true consideration of the work."[41] Philibert's Protestant perspective can be found in the detail, and especially in the idiosyncratic placement, the unaccustomed or excessive use, of the detail. He thus reconfigures a Catholic technique, hollowing the detail out internally to fill it with his own meaning. In this way, he deceives the Catholic audience while communicating with the Calvinist audience.

Philibert crafts new terms for his enterprise in order to approximate the essence of his multilayered endeavor. "I beg the readers not to find it strange if I sometimes use in these treatises other sorts of words. Because to tell the truth, our French language, in the expounding of so many things, is so poor and sterile that we do not have enough words that are adequately representational, unless we use a foreign vocabulary or resort to lengthy circumlocution."[42] Philibert instructs his reader in the novelty of his lexicon, but without defining his terms. Such circumspection suggests a strategy of concealment or of self-revelation only to the privileged, trusted few: "In this matter [I don't want to leave out anything except for the majority of] those words that are understood by men in this kingdom."[43] In this era, during which national identity was being forged, when men such as Du Bellay, Ronsard, Sebillet, and others struggled to formulate a national idiom, Philibert's striking rejection of that language as inadequate seems ideologically motivated, tantamount to a rejection of the Catholic-determined nation-state. His reference to "Royaume" hints that the "plusieurs" who are able to understand his new language exist in the kingdom in a differentiated state of being: they are the persecuted Protestant readership toward whom Philibert's work is directed. As the Gospels call Christians to be both in the world yet not of it, this enlightened group who shares in Philibert's self-constructed language is both in the kingdom yet spoken of as distinct from it, since the majority of those in the kingdom are incapable of comprehending Philibert's new terms.

In one of the prefatory pieces to the *Architecture*, Philibert describes his feelings of oppression. Feeling "surchargé," he creates works with a weighty application of detail. Philibert's embattled self-portrayal as architect subject to criticism and censure is emblematic of the Calvinist creator at bay: "The Architect will be sure to anger no one, similarly not to be irritated by anyone, insomuch as working for someone else, he can never order things to be as he would wish. He really couldn't complain to the patron every time something was wrong. I know myself how many irritants must be endured in such undertakings . . . And yet they always want to lay the fault at the Architect's feet."[44] Philibert portrays the architect as a scapegoat, unprotected by the power structure, who must appear to conform to the circumstances of constraint in which he creates. This "overladen" aspect of his structures symbolically castigates the source of persecution. "Being wrongly laden down and overloaded with calumny, problems, ills and displeasure, I nevertheless manfully sustained them and bore them always without flinching."[45]

Philibert describes his work as inevitably truncated; while he aims at perfection and completion, his enemies limit his creation to a mere fragment. His architectural dilemma parallels the Protestant predicament as marginal members prejudicially disjoined from the body. "But, in truth, someone seeing me begin to write in this way about Architecture will say that I resemble the man who has a beautiful statue of gold or silver, and because of his love for the Republic, he only gives the statue one arm, an imperfection for the whole body, which nevertheless does not totally lack for harmony in all its members and parts. Considering all this, I decided not to write this book you now have before you, without at first perfecting everything necessary for the full realization of said Architecture, and not merely one part alone . . . I would have done all this, had it not been for several lords, who [required] me to bring this part to light."[46]

This micronarrative of the one-armed statue allegorizes Philibert's predicament as a Protestant creator of Catholic-commissioned structures. He is not part of the "corps universel," nor does he desire to be. Philibert inscribes an appropriately Calvinist reference to iconoclasm in his description of the truncated statue. During the Wars of Religion, Calvinists vented their anger against what they deemed blasphemous representations of the divine found in Catholic statuary. Here, on the eve of those troubles, Philibert speaks of the statue as representing his text. That text has been fragmented at Catholic behest ("several noblemen pressured me . . . to publish this part separately"). Iconoclastically fractured, Philibert must now struggle in a hostile world to confer unity and completion on his writing and works.

Philibert stocks an arsenal of strategies. He asserts the authority and truth-bearing nature of his text; it is not merely a virtuoso performance. "But what do I hear? The listeners and the audience, having heard of nothing so novel or new, suddenly recoil from what I've said, as though I wanted to lie to the King! But I've always had a great horror of lying."[47] Philibert's statement suggests how Calvinist code functions: he characterizes anything developed within circumstances of constraint as potentially false.

Truth-value, therefore, may still inhere in a Calvinist structure or statement because, even though the truth that the structure wants to express—at odds with its commission—has been distorted through compulsion, truth still exists in a dialectical sense. "I've thought a lot about how this could be remedied and still satisfy his Majesty's desires: it may be necessary to find some way to put to use diverse sorts of wood, and again employ a disparity of small pieces, and do without the entire trees that were formerly used."[48] The glory of the Catholic monarch to whom Philibert erects structures is not be the full tale the structure tells, for underneath appearances lies another reality, one composed of all sorts of wood and all sorts of small pieces, a subterranean story of response to constraint.

Philibert's responses to feelings of persecution and marginality represent themselves iconographically, often in a building's substructure, through a detail freighted with a second layer of meaning or in anecdotal asides conveying his text's concern over religious and political issues. For instance, he says that his architectural works will achieve completion, "God willing, with some good and sufficient reasons, if great happenings do not oblige us to abandon them,"[49] and he requests the new king, Charles IX, to maintain the true religion.[50] The meaning of the term "vraye" is unambiguous. Is Philibert speaking here still as a Catholic, upholding the "vraye religion," or is he rewriting the pejorative Catholic script, claiming Calvinism as "vraye"? At this time, Pierre de Ronsard, a staunch Catholic polemical writer, wrote vehemently against Philibert, while devout Calvinists such as Bernard Palissy praised him.[51] Philibert's Calvinist sympathies speak through the adjective "vraye," an adjective counteracting the pejorative "religion *prétendue* réformée."

Philibert also works with the allocation of space and distribution of weight, as in this meditation on a Tuscan column: "In order solidly to support that column, we must recall that in those places where it bears the most weight, it must be made thicker and larger, in order that the column may resist the ponderous weight to be placed on it."[52] Tension and weight to be borne are customary architectural considerations. However, when interpreted in reference to Philibert's fears of persecution, such concerns may encode a Calvinist agenda.

Similarly, when Philibert uses trompe l'oeil to describe structures typified by dissimilarity, even contradiction, between inside and outside, he often follows such descriptions with protestations of loyalty to the Catholic monarch. "And in order to know when a tree is diseased, within its very heart, [even when it appears healthy,] when, after cutting its ends you take a hammer and strike one end, and someone putting his ear against the other end, a hollow heavy sound will be produced, and that will be a sign that the trunk of the tree is rotten within . . . as such things can help us to better understand our undertakings, I will not forget to mention them. For the greatest desire that I could have is to do things pleasing to my sovereign lord."[53] Philibert alerts us in this way that outward appearances are deceiving and that he dissembles for purposes of self-protection.[54]

Philibert's biographer notes, "No one has understood Philibert de l'Orme well. This man made it difficult for people to love him: he lied, he did not reveal who his masters were, he attributed influences to others which they could not have realistically had on him." And he asks, "In order to live and build, was it really necessary that he lie?"[55] The resolution to the enigma of Philibert's problematic personality resides, at least in part, in his Calvinist adherence. His contemporaries called him a "reformer of buildings," voicing, perhaps, greater truth than they knew. Philibert's Reformed perspective communicates through details such as the *charpentes* of some of his structures, which recall early Christian churches[56] and which, like the Calvinist theological system, demonstrate a desire to circumvent Catholicism in order to return to the true, primitive church.

The Calvinist Inheritance: Calvin's Influence
on Philibert de l'Orme

Therefore, before beginning to build, you must consider also these things, and
then you must not be deluded but rather certain of gaining profit and honor all
the days of your life and even after your death from the good order that you have
established and maintained in all your endeavors.

—Philibert, *Architecture* [57]

All who have added something to the edifice of the church that does not correspond to its foundation will have labored in vain.

—Calvin, *Institution* [58]

The two epigraphs have to do with appropriate ordering and with the
correct establishment of structures. Philibert's quote sounds like a Calvinist program for an upright, moral existence, while Calvin's statement roots
both moral life and structures in theology. Construction for a Calvinist not
only occurs externally, it must first occur internally. If correctly aligned and
consonant with the confessional norm, the theoretical edifice is approved;
it may then be actualized. Buildings that are not first visualized in theory
and then made conform to doctrine are unregenerate, epitomizing man's
sinful nature: "many beautiful buildings . . . have been built to accommodate other older buildings, but after the new buildings were built, their
errors, inconvenience and poor structure were recognized . . . that's why
they had to be demolished or held in contempt . . . but no one thought to
think about their problems ahead of time." [59] The term "erreur" resonates
theologically and recurs in Philibert's writing, characterizing an unregenerate structure as well as the wayward heart. "Erreur" also recalls Calvin's
image of the labyrinth of the world through which humans wander, lost
without the compass of Scripture.

Situated within such a network of references to Scripture, Philibert
conceives of his architectural project as a form of scriptural structuring:
"For the establishment of the building is of such great importance, that
if the initial foundation is not laid straight and squared, the rest of the
building will never be free of deformity, and such a fault will cause others.
It is true that not everyone will have the judgment to recognize this." [60]
The vocabulary echoes Calvin's. It postulates a privileged Protestant audience, a special literacy ("fondation" and "faute" possess both architectural
and theological meanings here) enabling the structure to signify differently

than it would to a scripturally uninformed Catholic: "il est vray que tous n'ont pas le iugement de le bien cognoistre."

Philibert continually yokes theological statement with architectural structure. The juxtaposition of the two lexicons in his texts underscores their relationship. "So to imagine life and salvation, we must expect men to remember the death of their one sole mediator Jesus Christ . . . But we'll leave such subjects to theologians, and we'll take up our geometrical considerations as appropriate to architects."[61] Philibert's theological perspective, here uncompromisingly Protestant, tellingly identifies Christ as the "*seul* médiateur" rather than placing faith in Mary or the saints. He camouflages the extent of his interest in theological matters, but although he demurs that such topics are not the province of architects, he nevertheless returns again and again to a theological grid through which he validates his concepts and structures.

Stylistically, the idiom of Philibert's structures either anticipates his conversion to Calvinism, as is the case with St.-Maur, or directly correlates with adoption of the Reformed perspective. At St.-Maur, Philibert implemented in his schema of fenestration an approach that art historians have deemed unusual for the time period: "It is in the design for the windows that the mixture of advanced and traditional methods appears . . . The window let in plenty of light and enabled anyone inside to lean out and enjoy the whole view, which . . . was impossible [formerly]."[62] Protestants sought to abolish representational and even decorative motifs, so that the clear light of God might stream through unimpeded. Philibert places the same emphasis on clarity here.

A similar alliance between Reformed *culte* and architectural considerations is found in Philibert's *Architecture* when he refers to psalm singing, a specifically Protestant practice. The psalms were translated early in Reformed history by Clément Marot and integrated immediately into church services; they remained the preferred content of singing—as opposed to Catholic chanting and plainsong—of the Calvinist church. Loud singing of psalms, deemed "defiant" by the Catholic hierarchy, was directly responsible for the massacre of Calvinists by Catholics in the episode at Pré-aux-Clercs in Paris in 1558. Consequently, when Philibert urges, in a text contemporary with this incident, that acoustic spaces for the audition of psalm singing be constructed, he implicitly construes worship space as paradigmatically Calvinist. "It's necessary to know how to represent an echo, and how to cause words and voices to resonate and be heard well, from near and from far. This is required in temples and churches where psalms are sung."[63] Philibert's texts, like his structures, attest to varying stages in his evangelical formation. Both Calvin and Philibert trace a movement from pre-text to text to space which, at least in theory, the text will revise.

Philibert distinguishes two parts in his texts. The first he labels "orthographies." These are the plans for his buildings. "Orthography" demonstrates a kind of prescriptive writing, a texted structure, just as Calvin's *Institution* is a textual blueprint. The second part, "scenographies," concerns the elevations and façades of buildings. It is writing as a form of *mise en scène*, a theater of spatial preoccupations.[64] Philibert revises architectural models, reworks conventions, subverts expectations, and also, like Calvin, constantly refers to Scripture as the prescriptive book for his building activity. It contains "certain precepts and teachings that will lead Architects and others to choose a more propitious time to begin to build all sorts of structures. We'll resume our discussion of this in the book I plan to write on divine proportions."[65]

Philibert is also similar to Calvin in his rhetoric. For one thing, he uses the disclaimer frequently. The *disclamatio* is a rhetorical ploy designed to make one's position seem self-evident or to suggest the existence of proof for one's position without ever providing such documentation. "I won't write any more to you about it, so as to eschew prolixity, which is usually boring. If any one wants to know more about it, let him seek me out, and I'll reveal to them that for which they are searching."[66] He creates a private space, within the public realm yet insulated from it, to which he invites a privileged reader.

Another similarity between Calvin and Philibert is their shared concern for the reclamation of order from disorder and their attempts to describe a method whereby this may be achieved.[67] A preoccupation with method is typical of late sixteenth-century Protestants, most notably Pierre Ramus. Philibert states that he wants to "assemble and sew back together properly the pieces that are now in disarray and that cry out for reorganization . . . All that is needed is to display the principles and method of this restructuring."[68]

The Biblical Intertext: Philibert as/to
the Protestant Reader

I don't employ the measure of the King's foot nor that of the classical foot and
certainly not that of the Romans, nor any other measurement other than those
proportions that I've discovered in Holy Scripture, the Old Testament, and I'll say
this without bragging, I am the first to have used these measurements. . . . My second book on architecture will be entitled "Concerning Divine Proportions."
—Philibert, *Architecture*[69]

Philibert identifies the Bible as the primary template for his productions. His comment is both theological and ideological: he rejects several
standard measurements, including that of the king's foot. The second book
that he plans to write, "Concerning Divine Proportions,"[70] is problematic; like a good Calvinist, Philibert recognizes the blasphemy inherent in
trying to replicate attributes of the divine. To feature himself in any concrete way as continuing God's endeavor would imply that God's work was
unfinished or imperfect. The first component of Philibert's project, the
Architecture, thus remains forever incomplete.[71] One half of an unrealized
diptych, theologically consistent with Calvinism's emphasis on human imperfection, the first book seeks to mold itself to Scripture ("conform to
the measurement and proportions found in the Holy Bible") but does not
claim to fulfill it.[72] Philibert employs another Protestant rhetorical tactic,
that of "proof texts," or bolstering one's argument by adducing Scripture
as authoritative. Concerning his blueprints, he says, "I could cite many
other found in Holy Scripture."[73] He describes himself as constantly resorting to Scripture for inspiration: "Truly, such proportions are so divine,
so admirable, that I can never cease from reading them, rereading them,
contemplating . . . and . . . adoring them."[74] Philibert is a reader not only
of biblical passages but also of proportions, the lineaments of structures,
within the scriptural text. For him, a blueprint is a text; a building is also
a text. Like the framework of Calvin's *Institution*, that of Philibert's *Architecture* rises from the textual foundation of Scripture as though from an
architectural plan.

The biblical books that Philibert favors are the same chosen by Calvin
and other Calvinist writers and preachers of the period, thus constituting
a sort of privileged frame of reference, an imbricated book-within-a-book:
the point of departure for a code on which the Calvinist architects all appear to have drawn for inspiration, authority, and illustration. Calvinists
decried preaching that rested on authorities other than Scripture. While

8. This page of Philibert de l'Orme's *Nouvelles inventions* displays several interesting iconographic features. The band of stylized imagery at the top of the page shows the Calvinist reliance on grotesqueries to convey their world-view. Here, a Neptune figure coils around the far left and right edges; he wears a crown shape on his head. Two dogs scowl defensively back at him, while two muses or angelic figures display an artistic product on a pedestal. Most important is the historiated initial that begins the first word on the first page of the first book of the *Nouvelles inventions*: it is the only such initial to incorporate a human figure, and it is a Philibert signature piece, in that he inaugurates his architectural and textual enterprise with his own initial, the letter *P*. The human figure recalls Palissy's use of grotesque *termes*, or human figures in a state of incompleteness, marred by the Fall. Yet this figure, holding an overflowing cornucopia on its head, represents Philibert's artistic plenitude; it offers a microallegory of Calvinist architectural abundance and textual *copia*. The figure's arms continue out into scrolling volutes, as Philibert writes his own identity and existence into the fate of the buildings he erects: iconography and identity conjoin. Philibert de l'Orme, *Nouvelles inventions* (1561), 1. By permission of the Folger Shakespeare Library.

both Catholic and Protestant preachers quoted from the Bible, Protestants, like Philibert, distinguished themselves in several ways: citations from the New Testament far outnumbered those from the Old and when reference was made to the Old Testament by Protestants they favored the historical and prophetic books, which Catholics tended to disregard.[75] The Protestant emphasis on historical and prophetic writings may be explained by their need to find some biblical indication that their lives and confessional perspective could have an enduring meaning as part of God's plan working itself out, however unfathomably, in history.[76] In his conception of the *Architecture*, Philibert also follows the Protestant trend toward simplicity for the sake of clarity; on the practical level, he aims at an audience of artisans and designers. Consequently, he simplifies so that his theories may be easily adapted and applied. Similarly, Protestant preachers used significantly fewer scriptural citations than did Catholics, and those they did use were generally brief, clearly explained, to-the-point applications.[77] Calvinist legalism, logical development of thought structures, Ramist concern for orderly exposition, and interest in practical, everyday morality led them to rely often on the books of Numbers and Deuteronomy;[78] Philibert, too, frequently refers to the Book of Numbers. Finally, "the most dramatic and obvious change made by the Reformation was the omission of secondary authorities."[79] Here, too, Philibert conforms to the Calvinist model: he and his own experience and expertise ultimately constitute the

LE PREMIER LIVRE DES
NOVVELLES INVENTIONS POVR
BIEN BASTIR ET A PETITZ FRAIS,

trouuees n'a gueres par M. PHILIBERT
DE LORME Lyonnois, Architecte,
Conseiller & Aulmonier ordinai-
re du feu Roy HENRY, &
Abbé de Sainct Eloy
lez Noyon.

PLVSIEVRS ont accoustumé d'user au commencement de leurs liures de quelque preface, contenant les louanges, excelléce & co-
moditez de l'art ou sciéce de laquelle ilz de-
liberent escrire. Ce que ie ferois icy tresuolõ-
tiers, selon la petite capacité de mon esprit,
n'estoit que ie pretend, auecques l'aide de
Dieu (duquel toutes graces procedent) mettre de brief en lumiere une œuure qui com-
prendra tout ce qui est necessaire pour la perfection d'Architecture. Ou ie n'oblieray chose , de laquelle ie me
pourray souuenir, qui serue & soit propre pour illustrer ladicte Archi
tecture : la poursuiuant d'un bout en autre de grande gayeté de cueur,
pourueu que i'aperçoiue ce premier vol de mes escripts auoir trouué
lieu aggreable enuers les doctes, & vertueux. Qui sera cause, qu'icy re-
trenchant tous preambules accoustumez, i'entreray de droict fil en
matiere, & deuant toutes choses escriray le plus brieuement & facilement qu'il me sera possible, comme il fault cognoistre & choisir les
bons arbres pour s'en sçauoir aider aux nouuelles inuentiõs, lesquelles
ie delibere icy familierement descouurir, & proprement enseigner,
comme plusieurs autres choses, Dieu aidant.

Prologues
accoustumez
aux commé-
cemens des
liures.

Brieueté a-
uec facilité
estre aggrea
ble aux le-
cteurs.

B

final authority. He writes himself into his architectural manuals in a way that graphically demonstrates this stance; the frontispiece for the *Nouvelles inventions* displays an inaugural rubricated initial, the letter *P*. This first letter of the text is the only one in the entire book to contain a human figure. Philibert points to himself as the creator of a new way of envisioning the world. The figure is, in fact, a *terme*—instead of feet, it culminates in a volute mirroring the cornucopia that it holds on its head. Philibert, as architect, is the source of invention; he possesses an artistic *corne d'abondance* but avoids the sin of pridefulness because his self-depiction is incomplete.

Architecture/Architexture as Reading Strategy

Right reading, correct understanding—both Calvinist emphases—are essential to the comprehension of Philibert's plans in the *Architecture* and the *Nouvelles inventions*. Those who learn how to decipher his structures, that which constitutes the "vray, universel, Architecture," will benefit greatly from it ("en tireront un profit inestimable"). He asserts, "I will soon add even more [to my text so as to] have the perfection of Architecture illustrated and accompanied by all its constituent parts. In this way, all who want to be true architects . . . will draw inestimable profit from my works."[80] "Profit," derived by the well-informed spectator and created by the "surplus" of meaning which Philibert will add, is a code word that deciphers as "salvation," recalling the passage in Matthew, "For what does it profit a man if he gains a kingdom but loses his soul?" Philibert devises a hermeneutic strategy that functions both literarily and theologically upon an architectural field. This strategy is aimed at an elect audience: "I hope that good, virtuous, peace-loving men, those who know how to ascertain and value that which is good, will find equally good my intention and my invention: and to such men I address my writings, and not to those who would criticize me."[81]

Philibert uses the term "witness" to describe the purpose of his structures and texts. "These witnesses will leave ample testimony to my capabilities, knowledge and skill . . . therefore, even more so will glory and honor be rendered to God, author of all good things."[82] Likening himself to Jesus, a prophet unappreciated in his own country, Philibert describes himself as in, but not a part of, the world, a biblical paraphrase that resonates with his marginal position as a Calvinist architect in Catholic France: "I do not want to forget here that my work and study have always aimed at this goal and end . . . and gave service to . . . my country . . . Just so, one generally is not valued or esteemed in his own country, as Jesus Christ himself can attest."[83] He again uses the verb "to witness," to describe both Jesus' and his own works, identifying his plight with that of the persecuted Christ. He shifts himself out of the embattled space of France to secure himself, through his meditations on structure and architecture, in another space, the scriptural space of the gospel: "In his Gospel, I have never ceased from desiring to live."[84]

As Philibert reads himself into the protective space of the gospel, he obliges his reader to make a choice, to either accept or reject such spatial redetermination. The text serves as a catechesis, requiring one to choose sides. Defining himself against an opposing view, Philibert resorts to a New Testament parable, one most frequently used by Calvinists, the parable of the talents, to describe how he produces in hiding that which has the most merit, then makes it available only to a few cognoscenti: "I praise God, author of all blessings, and thank him humbly for the good talents and favor that He has shown me in allowing me to share with other men a part of that talent which it pleases His holy Goodness to give to me in order that men of good will should take from [these gifts of mine] some profit and fruit."[85] The biblical lens clarifies to the viewer things formerly hidden or foreshadows things to be revealed in Philibert's structures, encouraging complicity between Philibert and his Calvinist reader. Speaking of himself, Philibert subtly shifts his pronoun usage to make his book not his own but something shared with the reader, a joint production of meaning: "just wait until I shall write for you *our* book about Divine Proportions, the book that I have earnestly promised to you."[86] Witnessing involves developing something in secret which is then disclosed, tentatively and selectively.

Something to Build On: *Architecture* (1567, 1626, and 1648) and *Nouvelles inventions* (1561)

Why did Philibert include such detailed discussions of buildings that he knew would never be built? Why are the plans for such idealized structures so technically and aesthetically eccentric? Why include such improbabilia at all? "Throughout the *Architecture* the author constantly refers to buildings which he himself has erected, but he also publishes certain designs which seem never to have been carried out . . . De l'Orme rightly says that these 'inventions' may appear incredible to many."[87] When historical circumstances conspire to render impossible the building of a structure conforming to one's belief system, then the text becomes the safe place in which such structures may be dreamed about, hypothesized, and described. In the process of displaying fanciful invention in an abstract realm, the real tensions curtailing actual construction appear. The abstract textual structure offers a venue for theorizing about such problems. The textual structure is itself a theory, however impossible to implement in the real world, of how avoidance of constraint might proceed, as well as of how iconography might programmatically contradict such constraints.

Philibert therefore needed to present his books as appeals to well-intentioned, informed readers: "hommes de bonne volunté" or "bon esprit."[88] Philibert tried to present his books as persuasive; if the reader will just try it Philibert's way, he will be convinced of the wisdom of the approach: "this small discourse seems to be enough to me to let you understand the rest of this illustration of a proposed arch: therefore I won't write you any more about it, assuring you instead that if it so pleases you to take up your compass, and to look on the blueprint and on the site that I've suggested, you will find it to be just as I have said."[89] The suggestion resembles the biblical injunction "seek ("chercher") and ye shall find" ("trouverez ainsi"). This rhetoric creates a climate of complicity between Protestant reader and Philibert, one that leaves the uninformed Catholic reader in the dark: "I will beg those who have some judgment to please note this line [I've drawn here]: for if they understand it, they will understand many more like it."[90] The Calvinist reader coproduces meaning, an intellectual and theological structure scaffolded on the blueprint of Philibert's text: "the explanation that I could give [for these things] would not only be laborious, but also would bore those of good will, those men who can easily conceive of and understand the descriptions and figures that one proposes to them without the need for words [of explanation]. For this reason, I think you should be content with the little I have written, and imagine my meaning as much as you can."[91]

Philibert implicitly asks his reader, "Can you see it my way?" This sort of seeing requires a complicity of the imagination, a spiritualized understanding. Quoting St. Paul, Philibert requires that his reader be specially trained: "Such people ought always to have before their eyes the saying of St. Paul, which is: SI QUIS SE EXISTIMAT, SCIRE ALIQUID, NONDUM COGNOUIT QUEMANDMODUM OPORTEAT EUM SCIRE. This means: 'if any one believes that he knows something, he does not yet know what he ought to know' . . . I exhort them to ask for guidance and help from God, before they begin any undertaking."[92] Philibert translates the biblical passage from Latin into French, consistent with the Reformed program of rendering into the vernacular so as to be relevant to ordinary life. Translation also acts as a metaphor for the process necessary to comprehend Philibert's text: the Calvinist reader must translate it out of its protective, ciphered form so as to grasp its hidden meaning.

The spatial limitations imposed on the actual production of the book refer symbolically to the spatial constraints and menace that Philibert himself experiences. "If the size of the paper makes it possible to put on it everything that one would like to put on it and draw together all the parts and ornaments of the plan . . . in order that the drawings be of adequate size to convey their measurements, I would willingly set them down on paper . . . but the size of the paper would be too small, given the paper that our book is made of, so that the reader would only with great difficulty profit from such drawings."[93] Just as Protestants do not have adequate space in which to express their theological beliefs, so the site for Philibert's abstract structures, the paper, cannot accommodate the grandeur of his conception. Philibert points out this constraint but also works within it, playing with the concepts of large and small, to compose a trompe l'oeil text. "Therefore, it seemed better to me . . . to show these drawings and to teach their parts by pieces one after the other . . . accompanying all this with smaller figures, sometimes with figures as large as the sheet of paper in the book will permit."[94] Trompe l'oeil unsettles certainties. The fragmentary rendering that Philibert employs ("par pièces") demonstrates his intention to disrupt expectations.

In addition, because available space is already determined by Catholic occupation, the idiosyncratic detail or ornament becomes the small space in which Philibert may express a personal perspective: "for I will act as it pleases Her Majesty to order me, except in the matters of ornament, symmetry and measurements, which Her Majesty will leave to my discretion."[95] Ornament overlays a preexisting foundation and may reconfigure the meaning of that foundation. When the all-important detail, freighted with the responsibility of signaling the presence of textual code, is somehow omitted from his text or accompanying illustrations, Philibert agonizes. This causes "complaint and grief by the author, that his illustrations ["figures"] are not well and truly engraved . . . I took great pains to design them and to portray them, but the engraver did not do his job as well . . . as I would have liked."[96] Thus, a gap exists in Philibert's book between representation (image, engraving, written description) and intention as

9. Pierre Reymond's (1513–84; probably Protestant) cup with cover, or *tazza*, depicts scenes from the historical Old Testament Book of Joseph. These include Joseph's prophetic dreams, which eventually led to his reversal of fortune and influence over Pharaoh, a story with which oppressed Protestants identified. Enamel, partly gilded, on copper, with a gilded metal finial of a later date, and probably fabricated in Limoges, the *tazza* provides an example of collusion among Protestant artisans of various sorts: it is adapted from biblical illustrations engraved in a book by Bernard Salomon (1506–61), published in Lyons by the evangelical printer, Jean de Tournes. Protestantism establishes its own artistic affiliations, and relies on biblical literacy to convey its message. Such canny ornamentation is similar to Philibert's revisionist use of detail. The Metropolitan Museum of Art.

expressed by the text. Philibert expresses "great regret and displeasure, because I had wanted by them to give profit and pleasure to those who wanted to learn from them."[97] The text thus must produce a corrective re-reading, a reformation of the representation. This new hermeneutic slant is provided by detail or ornament.

The space between representation and intention epitomizes the gap

between Protestant desire for theological expression and Catholic spatial domination. One of the ways in which Philibert deals with this gap, and with the misrepresentation by others of his intention, is by producing a multiplicity of engravings. "And because I see that the engravers of my illustrations and stories did not do their job as clearly as I would have wished, I hoped to repair their inaccuracies by the multitude of designs and drawings that I have caused [now] to be engraved."[98] If he cannot take up real space, he aims to take up *textual* space.

Philibert discusses and portrays two sorts of architectural developments in his texts. The first is the sort of structure one erects when one is required to alter an already standing building: this situation imposes a variety of limitations and expectations. The second is the sort of structure one erects when one has a virgin site with which to work. However, even in the second scenario Philibert does not have a situation in which to create free from ideological determination. That possibility obtains only in his text, and even there does not amount to complete permission for personal expression.

10. This illustration shows how to construct a supporting beam from disparate pieces, joined by a system of locking pins. While the curve of a supporting arch is made possible through this technical innovation, one is left to wonder whether the composite composition of the support offers sufficient stability. Philibert suggests that such supports, while facilitating clients' requests, may actually enfeeble the structure. In the *Nouvelles inventions*, Philibert actually admits to such a possibility, stating that "it may happen that some such pieces may rot from age or other reasons" (II, 39). The dichotomy and tension between inside and outside, surface and inner support, Catholic expectations and Calvinist codes, is a major theme in all of Philibert's texts. Philibert de l'Orme, *Nouvelles inventions* (1561), 40. By permission of the Folger Shakespeare Library.

CREATING FROM CONSTRAINT: REWORKING PREEXISTING STRUCTURES

To tell the truth, one should fear greatly to fail in such an undertaking, and especially where buildings that will be seen all throughout one's life are concerned.[99]

Let one choose an expert Architect, fully in possession of all his craft's wisdom, and let his freedom be utterly without constraint or subjection of spirit.[100]

Sometimes one is constrained to do things against reason in order to obey the will of the lord who ordered the building to be built.[101]

In these quotations from the *Architecture*, Philibert rehearses one of his obsessions: the surveillance and control exercised by the client over the architect. He views the client-creator relationship as frequently adversarial and counterproductive. Philibert describes the test of character to which a patron initially subjects an architect as one in which personal qualities such as moral stature (or correct religious adherence) seem more important than professional expertise.[102] However, Philibert then suggests a way in which this power relationship could be altered. He notes that an architect has power over the client in a revisionist sense: he builds the structure by which the client is judged. The architect thus has the power to inflect the client's reputation negatively.[103] By describing a sloppily built house that threatens to topple at any moment, Philibert portrays the menace that the architect may thereby pose to the client, suggesting the paradoxical power of the commissioned architect. Philibert's example, that of the king's house, effectively dramatizes his ambivalence over his status as a Protestant in a Catholic kingdom: "I know one of the King's houses where the beams are worthless, and across them are such large locks going across

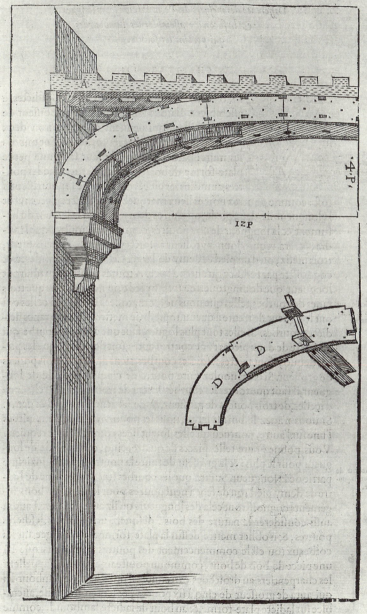

11. Philibert's famous *trompe*, an airy structural innovation designed to create space where no more exists, accretes itself to the exterior of a structure, both embellishing it and acting as a parasite. This *trompe* plays with surfaces and textures, its winding staircase and fluted base possessing no apparent relationship with the rather subdued building from which it emerges. In the writings and works of the Calvinist architects, their "plain style" message is often ironically communicated through a similar subversive strategy of ornamentation. Philibert de l'Orme, *Architecture* (1626), 1: 89. By permission of the Folger Shakespeare Library.

the walls, used to hold up the portals and galleries on the sides, that if it were necessary to put other beams up, the galleries would be in peril of falling . . . and if he who has the upkeep of this dwelling is not vigilant, and doesn't know his trade, who knows what will happen [to this building]?"[104] The locks are there to hold the joined pieces of wood in place, but they also point to the fragmentary nature of the support system.

The Calvinist architect possesses resources enabling him to reconfigure a situation of constraint:[105] he may elect to describe or represent the constraint within the structure itself; he may revise the constraint by pointing out its negative aspects through iconography; or he may devise a phantasmagorical structure, one so loose and free that it defies constraint. Such is the case for Philibert's use of the *trompe* at Anet. The *trompe*, a bulbous overhang projecting from a flat wall, ingeniously constructs an aerial space where no space exists within the structure proper. The *trompe* is for Philibert a liberated construction paradoxically occasioned by a condition of spatial constriction. Rather than bow to constraint, Philibert forces it to work for him: "this *trompe* resulted from constraint . . . in order to accommodate a cabinet in the room of late King Henri . . . The constraint was because there was no space or place to add on to the body of the house which was being built, nor to the old structure . . . Seeing, therefore, such constraint and narrowness of the space, I was in great perplexity."[106]

Philibert's response to the lack of space is at first to interiorize and theorize it ("je fus redigee en grande perplexité"), then to envision from that circumscribed position a new spatial solution. His revision entails getting a new angle on the situation: "I was greatly perplexed . . . I gazed at an angle near the King's chamber . . . [f]rom one side of the garden . . . and it seemed to me a good idea to construct a vault suspended in the air, so as to create more space there."[107] In theory, then, a Calvinist could displace the responsibility for his potentially subversive work onto the Catholic patron: the structure arose merely in response to the latter's request.

Another way in which Philibert creates from constraint is through his ornamental complexity and the marriage of apparent architectural contraries. The cryptoporticus at Anet is far more intricate than any others surviving from the sixteenth century.[108] Philibert's cryptoporticus emerges from an existing structure, but so radically revises its base as virtually to deny its original conception: "[Its] staircase . . . instead of being circular, is oval . . . Philibert appears as a fully conscious Mannerist, taking . . . a classical feature and altering it so that its essential character, in this case its complete symmetry, is destroyed."[109] Constrained on site, Philibert revises the existing faults of the structure, a reformation tactic: "This place seemed favorable to me to accommodate the old building with the new structure . . . as was necessary for the perfecting, beauty and decoration of it. For in this way not only the faults of the existing building are obviated, and the constraint and subjection of its components mitigated, but also both buildings will be more admirable, strong and pleasing to the sight."[110]

Philibert aesthetically allies old and new. The new structure—often synonymous with Calvinism—inhabits, at least in theory, a newly legitimated space. He makes the old structure cooperate in the establishment of the new: "It'll be a thrifty thing to employ old materials, those chosen by the architect, together with the new."[111] Philibert, therefore, acts like a Reformer: he selects from an old, distorted, or flawed structure requiring rectification those elements that can be redeemed and reused ("desquelles on se veut ayder"), rejecting those that cannot be saved.

The reformation is foundational; as with the Reformation, it rebuilds from the ground up. Philibert entitles this chapter, essentially a meditation on working within conditions of constraint, "The Ways in Which a Foundation Can Be Strengthened When One Has Found Solid Ground on Which to Establish It."[112] Faults in the building, always blamed on the previous architect, are treated like sins; surveillance of the structure in process suggests an analogy with the Protestant mandate of examination of conscience: "Truly, when I think about building projects that have been taken on heedlessly, and about others' work done in haste and poorly, I don't know what to think or say, considering that if such great faults can occur in architecture, I'll show how one should proceed to avoid such faults."[113] Philibert's text oscillates between considerations of real space and discussions of scriptural space: "For if one building holds up, but the other doesn't, the edifice on top will crack and break in many places, and could lean or fall . . . If the architect is forced to build in such a place, he must show his wits by devising ways to ameliorate the site . . . the truest and most sure foundations are on rock, as everyone knows."[114]

The reference is to the Gospels, where Jesus speaks of building one's house on a rock, a firm foundation. When Philibert adds "comme chacun sçait," he refers ironically ("everyone" does *not* know!) to the select, scripturally literate Calvinist readership, underscoring the gnomic quality—to Catholics—of some of his writings and structures. When Philibert refers to his patron as the "seigneur," another "Seigneur" is invoked, in contrast: "But to avoid such problems, the architect should choose a good and wise Lord who will uphold him and protect him from ill wishers, and who will love and preserve him."[115] Philibert inscribes an idealized patron, God, within his text, thereby ensuring the scriptural legitimacy of his work.

DISGUISING DISPLACEMENT: CODES AND IMPROVISATIONS IN PHILIBERT'S NEW EDIFICES

When Philibert devises his own constructions, as opposed to modifying an already existing structure, his anxiety over personal expression intensifies. Now he can no longer disguise, or redetermine, a format already in place; rather, he is responsible for every inch of the new building. "Blame and praise, honor and dishonor, customarily accompany great buildings and great works, especially those that are public."[116] In developing new structures, Philibert wagers heavily on the inability of an ill-disposed viewer to comprehend the message of the structure, thereby protecting himself in public space: "We have a multitude of beautiful styles in France, which no one ever takes into consideration for lack of understanding. What's even worse, no one ever tries to discern the excellence and beauty ["beaux traicts"] of these structures."[117] *Beaux traicts* mean features of a building. However, Randle Cotgrave's *Dictionarie of the French and English Tongues* lists "lines of writing" as a second meaning of *traicts*; these are forms of rewriting or overwriting.

Philibert dramatizes this Calvinist strategy of self-concealment in the following micronarrative concerning an exposed structure and a passerby's defacement of it. "[It was] as though it were a Tuscan column, possessing very little adornment in the exposed location where it was found. Indiscreet and malicious pages and lackeys customarily break everything they

12. Here is Philibert's "signature." This figure, a form of gratuitous doodling not even necessarily related to the structure on which it stands, might seek legitimacy as a stand-in for a classical statue. However, its cocky pose presents a stylistic *clin d'oeil* to the viewer. The figure deftly holds his spear as though he could easily become erect and vigilant, but his little smile shows that he is somewhat amused. He is off-center on his pediment, a technique typical of the Calvinist architects. The engraving truncates the second figure before we can see his full form, yet he bends his neck to peer back down into the frame, jauntily greeting the viewer with his gaze. Such a marginal, off-angle perspective also translates a Calvinist architectural technique. These apparently carefree and confident figures stand atop the monument, redetermining it in a new way, so that they dominate, rather than rely on, the monument. Philibert de l'Orme, *Architecture*, (1626), 214. By permission of the Folger Shakespeare Library.

touch or at least scribble on it and deface it, so it seems to me that when you have such columnar bases, you should put on them the least amount of detail possible." [118]

While purportedly protecting the structure, Philibert in fact is equating himself with the graffiti scribbler. His reasoning that such bases should be unadorned, or minimally adorned, in fact only leaves greater room for the comments of the graffiti artist. On the structures he erects in Catholic-dominated public space, he will fill the space they occupy with his own meaning. This is either a signifying void—the empty base—or his own statement, redetermining graffiti crayoned onto a structure through detail that somehow contradicts that structure. By recommending that such structures possess the minimum amount of ornamentation possible, he actually creates space for his, and for the Calvinist, reassignment of meaning. Philibert equates Catholicism with the void, refusing in this way to identify with the institutional structures of power that he has been commissioned to construct. This is how Calvinist architects can rationalize creating for Catholic monarchs: by "underscor[ing] that Christian liberty is an interior, spiritual fact, one that could perhaps appear reconciled to an external [notion of] liberty—without being enslaved to it—but one that could never identify itself with that exterior phenomenon." [119] Like the pages and lackeys who amuse themselves by doodling, in his own application of ornament to his structures Philibert overlays bases with massive doses of detail. Calvinism becomes a literate structure, a writing strategy that invests the blank space, conferring on it either scriptural or worldly conformity. Philibert will not allow the Catholic void to remain unoccupied. The graffiti writers thus constitute an emblem of Philibert's desire to

13. Philibert deliberately placed an off-center stag at the entrance to Anet. The situation of the stag on the façade seems almost humorous, perhaps even an imaged insult: the stag is hardly turned at an advantageous angle. This chapter on doors and entryway seems to open an unexpected interpretive door, one perhaps critical or dismissive of the power of the structure's patroness, Diane de Poitiers. Philibert de l'Orme, *Architecture* (1626), 1: 247. By permission of the Folger Shakespeare Library.

write over existing (Catholic) space. He hides behind the subversion constituted by graffiti cipher.

Philibert's sense of humor is sometimes expressed in his doodling, in his jaunty way of signing his work. For instance, in one engraving he portrays a vigilant watcher atop a monument. This is no statue; rather, it is a statue come to life, as in the children's game of statues. The cocky stance of the figure, hand on outthrust hip, his half-smile, his disproportionately large pike, and a caduceus-like shape on his breastplate (the caduceus reappears in other of Philibert's engravings, notably his allegorical renderings, as a symbol for the enlightened Calvinist architect) constitute a personal and Calvinist emblem for Philibert.

Taking transgression as the hallmark of the graffiti writers' endeavor and of Philibert's own program, we may examine aspects of this boundary violation in order to establish a morphology of the Protestant subversion of Catholic space and structure. For instance, in Philibert's construction of Antoine Bullioud's dwelling, "symmetry is ignored to a degree which would have scandalized any Italian architect, and Philibert's method of continuing the entabulature below the gallery, though the rest of the Doric order is interrupted, is the kind of irregularity which is often described as mannerist, but is more probably due to a lack of respect for . . . the use of the orders." [120]

Asymmetry, irregularity, and intermittence constitute intrinsic structural iconoclasm, a negative force undermining the structure from within. The Protestant aesthetic rereads excessive detail, skimming it for hidden significance. It also disrupts perspective, thereby undoing patterns of predictability within the economy of the Catholic control of the work. Irregularities in erected structures include the asymmetry of the composition of Anet, where the left-hand wing has no loggia, the central corps de logis features a colonnade of twinned Doric columns, and the right-hand wing displays an arcade on single piers. Anet demonstrates other irregular alternations: "the subtle variation of rhythm produce[s] an effect otherwise

Des portes du dedans des logis, pour entrer aux salles, chambres,
gardcrobbes, galleries & autres lieux.

CHAPITRE XIII.

Es portes qu'on faict pour entrer dans les salles,
doiuent estre differentes selon les grandeurs des-
dictes salles, & lieux ausquels on les veut faire
seruir. Car la porte d'vne grande salle de bal pour
vn Roy, où vn Prince, ou quelque grãd Seigneur,
doit estre plus large & plus haute, que celle que

Les portes des
salles denoir e-
stre differentes.

unsought-for by French architects of the period," including unusual Corinthian columns (while such columns occur fairly often in tombs, they were "very rare" in nontombal structures or on "such a large-scale.") [121] These columns have a trompe l'oeil quality; apparent unity is unmasked as merely a façade plastered over disparate pieces: "Unable to find large enough stones to sculpt columns out of one stone alone, or at least columns made of only a few large stones, he accepted pieces of small height. Some say that he hid the joints of these many small pieces with decoration." [122] At St.-Maur, several fragmentary pieces, hidden under an overhang, constitute the architrave. This recessive space recalls Philibert's plight: himself forced to "give ground" before critics and ill-wishers, Philibert designed a structure that mimicked his own *affaissement de terrain*.[123]

Other architectural oddities include the large-scale mythological clock mechanism in the third bay. This clock is architecturally unusual because of its plastic, sculptural handling of the masses. Philibert's treatment of the sarcophagus at Anet is also an original conception: it features a cruciform coffin, which deepens the three-dimensionality of the structure due to the two projecting arms, which rest on fluted supports. Appearances here construct deception—the illusion of depth—consistent with Philibert's Calvinist program of code and complication. Anthony Blunt notes that one of the characteristics of Philibert's mature work is a "tendency towards using variations on clear basic forms so subtle that they are not immediately noticeable." [124] Philibert may also give greater importance to exterior appearance than to the use value of a structure, which also correlates with his signature use of detail, in which its unexpected application or placement redefines the character of a structure.

Complexity and ingenuity, de l'Orme's hallmark, attest to a plan to complicate the picture, to insert interfering factors into a work's legibility.[125] Such interference is expressed iconographically as episodes of interruption. "One feature of the east end of the Anet chapel remains puzzling. The entablature which forms the lower line of the lower and broader pediment is broken by the central window, but the mouldings are simply cut off and do not follow round the side of the window itself." [126]

Intentional asymmetry works to the same effect. At St.-Maur, "there is a deliberate dis-symmetry between the windows and the opposing walls." [127] Philibert's tendency to push limits, to construct works that surprise or are not initially easily interpreted because they do not employ conventional vocabulary, is associated with versions of architectural interference. At François I's tomb, "the disposition of the Ionic capitals is a revealing example of de l'Orme's mode of thought. In a sense he may be said to have followed the classical ideal of symmetry with complete logic, and yet by pushing it so far he has arrived at a result which is totally unclassical. By ruthlessly pushing logical methods he has reached a result which is bizarre and in a sense illogical."[128]

Philibert's own house, which he constructed on the rue de la Cerisaie in Paris around 1558, huddles behind a self-protective façade, from which a front doorway is conspicuously absent. A compromise between a bourgeois house (dimensionally) and an aristocratic *hôtel particulier* (in layout), the house favors the wing furthest removed from the street. In this way, Philibert again disrupts expectations aesthetically. An angled route (aesthetically enacting the Calvinist perception of being pushed into a corner)[129] is necessary to gain admission: under the arcade on the left-hand side, a hidden flight of stairs leads to a concealed entryway. Not surprisingly, Philibert built his house during the wave of persecution of Protestants under Henri II.[130] Philibert's model for his house relates closely to blueprints for private dwellings contained in Serlio's *Il sesto libro serliano, delle abitazioni per tutti i gradi degli uomini*.[131] This repertory of private dwellings constitutes a pattern book for Philibert, just as others of his "inventions" have scriptural models. During this period, Philibert's tastes and idiom altered, becoming more ornate, fanciful, and richly detailed. Such a change accords, at least in part, with a concern for self-concealment in a progressively more hostile cultural climate, only two years before the Conjuration d'Amboise. Self-protection and dissimulation characterize "the [great] variety of Philibert's style, mak[ing] it hard to find any formula for his style during this period."[132] At this time, the Catholic monarchy, consolidating its presence in Paris though an architectural program, compelled Philibert to redefine his position vis-à-vis his Catholic patrons. His already evangelical stance can be discerned in the increasingly biblical tenor of his pronouncements. On being named Abbé de St.-Serge, an honorary benefice, he announced in his correspondence that he would devote himself entirely to the reading of the gospel, hardly a customary interest for contemporary Catholic benefice holders.[133] His progressively Protestant perspective inevitably affected his professional self-perception. Particularly in the later years of his career, when his work "gives evidence of an extreme refinement and subtlety,"[134] such as is the case with the staircase at the Tuileries, or when he adorns Chenonceau chiefly with ornaments, masks, picturesque detail, and fanciful traits, Philibert seems to play architectural and theological hide-and-seek.

14. Philibert de l'Orme built his own house in the rue de la Cerisaie in Paris during a particularly troubled, almost paranoid period in his life. The design is striking in that it has no evident entryway. Rather, to enter one must proceed around the side of the house, where an angled staircase is hidden beneath an overhang. In this image, Philibert tries out different possibilities for constructing houses without pillars or columns and includes an apparently intentionally destablized right corner section that is significantly smaller than, and awkwardly turned away from, the rest of the façade. The central arcades are windows and ornamental structures rather than functional entryways, a form of camouflage. Philibert de l'Orme, *Architecture* (1626), 1: 252 verso. By permission of the Folger Shakespeare Library.

In building the columns for the chapel at Villier-lès-Rets, Philibert constructed another amalgam, composing its columns of disparate pieces. He claims this procedure is unavoidable, due to constraints both on his latitude for architectural development and on the availability of materials. The beauty of the column dissimulates its fragmentary substructure. Here, ornament or surface covers a structure in which the façade and the interior are not in harmony or of like kind; ornament hides and redefines something, makes something appear other than it is. "It is true that, because of the straits in which I found myself, unable to get quickly and for little expense columns made all of one piece, I caused them to be built of 4 or 5 pieces, with beautiful ornament and moldings so as to hide where the pieces joined: so that in seeing them they seem all of one piece, appearing beautiful and graceful."[135]

What does it mean to fashion supporting columns for the Queen Mother's palace from fragments? While they seemed to supply firm support, the reality is that several of Philibert's structures constructed in this manner did not survive the century because of faults in the buildings.[136] Structurally, they were mined from within. Philibert scrupulously covered over the surface, so that the flawed nature of the internal construction was concealed, by devising deceptive surfaces and creating an illusion of unity.

In Philibert's structures, something more than readily meets the eye goes on beneath the surface. Structure and significance struggle at counter purposes in his work. Architectural historians describe his work with terms like "concealment," "subterfuge," and "camouflage."

*Autre face de maison monstrant comme lon y peut appliquer
des fenestres & portes, sans aucunes colomnes, & piliers,
ou bien leurs corniches & ornements.*

CHAPITRE XVII.

*L'Auteur respõd
& satisfaict à
l'opinion & per-
semét d'aucuns.*

AVCVNS pourront penser, apres auoir leu ce que
i'ay escrit des faces des bastiments, pour monstrer
la disposition des fenestres, que ie les voudrois cõ-
traindre, ou bien assuiectir, de mettre des colomnes & piliers aux faces des maisons, ce que ie ne
pretens aucunement : car tous ceux qui veulent
faire petites despenses, n'ont besoing de si grande curiosité &
enrichissement de face de maison, pour autant que leurs facul-
tez ne pourroient soustenir si grands frais : mais il est bien vray
que ie voudrois, que la constitution & ordre des fenestres qui
doiuent

Philibert's Allegories: Iconographic Refigurations

Two illustrated allegories in the *Architecture* display the repertoire of Philibert's stylistic traits. Allegory appropriately represents Philibert's voice, not least because it presents objects in isolation from their surroundings, uses oblique form and disconnected imagery,[137] and disrupts expectations. It requires interpretation, often on multiple levels. George Puttenham's sixteenth-century definition of allegory refers to its quality of dissimulation, in which "every speech [is] wrested from his owne naturall signification to another."[138] Because of the implicit violence of the conditions of its articulation, allegory often expresses an ambivalent relationship to power. Consequently, Philibert's decision to include allegories indicates that they are guides to the interpretation of his personal, architectural, and theological constraints. Because allegory does not straightforwardly represent, it effectively illustrates a shift in Philibert's stylistic treatment from early emphasis on explicit image to reliance on narrative network in decoding a structure. For example, at Saint-Léger, "the absence of any central frontispiece [usually adorned] for the dwelling is significant. At a time when the courtyard at Ecouen was being transformed and enriched with monumental frontispieces, at a time when, after having designed the frontispieces for St.-Maur, Delorme was working on Anet's, it is no accident that he created the considerable, vast, neutral space of St.-Léger . . . The austere exterior cannot be understood and has no meaning except in comparison with the interior treatment of the *mur-écran*; there can be found grouped and magnified some of the elements used on the entryway."[139]

Philibert's structure can only be fully understood in literary fashion, creating significance by interrelating its components.[140] The textual nature of the architectonic structure is thus constituted by its relationships, its many levels of meaning, and its desire to convey a message rather than merely to display an image. Similarly, allegory is composed of elements that play roles in an interlocking narrative; these can be decoded through their reference to a metanarrative framework.

At three points in his *Architecture*, Philibert interrupts the detailed exposition of the technique for the building of an edifice from its foundations to the roof. These interruptions are not digressions; rather, they are three lengthy allegories designed to function as metanarratives indicating the appropriate reception of the text. They prescribe an interpretive path for right reading, a quintessentially Calvinist concern.

The first allegory is exclusively textual, while illustrations accompany the other two. The lack of images in the first allegory indicates that the allegorical text relates to its "host" text (the *Architecture*) as a commentary or interpretive schema. The two imaged allegories are the only nonarchitectural drawings in the book. Philibert explains them at length, showing that they comment in an important way on the larger text.

The art critic Anthony Blunt labeled the two illustrated allegories "The Good Architect" and the "The Bad Architect." However, Philibert provided no such designation, leaving the interpretation of the allegories open. Blunt's labels distort the meaning of the allegories. As Philibert's accompanying narrative states, one of the images does not represent a "bad *architect*" but rather denigrates any *critic* of Philibert's architecture. According to Philibert's correspondence, such critics were manifold. This illustrated allegory symbolically silences the Critic through an iconoclastic strategy that defaces and distorts the body of the Critic.

By misinterpreting these two allegories, Blunt inadvertently dramatizes how allegory functions for Philibert. Blunt's misreading of Philibert equates with the Catholic distortion of Philibert's structures, showing the Catholics' inability to perceive hidden significance. Paradoxically, such incomprehension works to Philibert's advantage, enabling him to communicate his agenda in code to those Calvinists able to decipher it. Philibert intensifies his subterfuge, implying parallelism between the two allegories, while in fact unmooring the image from its textual description. Separately, the image of the "bad architect" tells one story, while the addition of (authoritative, for Calvinists) text alters its interpretation. Reading requires attention to detail as the privileged vehicle for meaning in the allegory. Allegorical detail contradicts the message derived from a cursory viewing. Because the significance of the allegory is not readily accessible, Philibert can employ allegory as a system of self-defense, "[w]hich nevertheless I will show some day, with several other fine inventions that I've made, if it please God to make my spirit more free, and to put me where I will be safe from harm such as I've experienced since the death of King Henry."[141] Distance ensures obfuscation. Therefore, Philibert allows considerable space to exist in the allegory, room for misinterpretation created by the allegory's multivalent components. He who misinterprets chooses thereby the wrong subsets of meaning and reveals himself as subscribing to a different belief system. Philibert separates himself from misreaders. "[You must] protect yourself from people who don't know how to do things right, nor should you frequent those who do not know what is good to do, nor should you listen to those who hear bad things, or have no sense of what is good and useful."[142]

The phenomenon of accurate interpretation highlights Philibert's crypto-Calvinist stance. Philibert finds two specific uses for allegory. First, allegory defends his personal being and official role from jealousy, slander, and attack. He describes himself as being in a deliberate and dangerous misinterpretation: "The architect is quite likely to hear and receive many calumnies and false reports saying bad things about him. This is why he must know that, however virtuous and wise he may be, even more will he be criticized and envied by the ill reports of ignorant or malicious people, and the more his building increases in beauty, the more will he be spoken ill of and dismissed . . . with an infinity of lies, as I myself have often experienced, to my great sorrow; indeed, people have even rendered me suspect."[143]

Second, allegory surreptitiously inserts Calvinist language and concerns into the public, seemingly acceptable structures that he was commissioned to erect. Allegory supplies a veiled critique of the hierarchy, a denunciation of contemporary cultural norms, and a camouflage for his private self. Allegory constitutes the subversive mode par excellence because "it says one thing and means another. It destroys the normal expectations about language, that our words mean what they say."[144]

Allegory is therefore a mechanism for the symbolic wresting of control away from oppressive authority because it is a subversive improvisation on that oppressive order's techniques. "[Allegory is] a new language of deployments and manoeuvers, with sly sallies that have an implied weighting far in excess of their surface meaning . . . No political structure, if continued long enough for people to master its ways, is capable of preventing forms of expression that tug at the limits of patronage."[145] The dense iconography of Philibert's three allegories, their place in the text, their commentary on the text, and their symbolic encapsulation of his extratextual concerns express the constrained "room for maneuver" Philibert experiences in his architectural expression and as a Calvinist.[146]

For Calvin himself, however, allegory caused a gap between intention and reception.[147] Allegory, jumbled and piecemeal, "as though sewn together from many pieces,"[148] disrupted meaning by separating signifier from signified.[149] Calvin decried allegory as "deceptive, distorting and papistical."[150] Calvinists customarily avoided allegorical writing. Philibert, slyly, found a fitting tool in allegory precisely because of its slippery, disparate qualities. By employing allegory, Philibert symbolically reversed Catholic techniques against their Catholic authors. The deformation of meaning, a thoroughly *un*-Calvinist approach, indicted Catholicism as responsible for requiring such distortion.[151] In addition, by adopting a technique used by Catholic writers and eschewed by Calvinists, Philibert disguised his confessional perspective. Parodying what Calvinists labeled the Catholic preference for gloss over reading and reliance on surface semblance rather than an extraction of meaning, Philibert's allegories camouflaged him from persecution by appearing to praise Catholic structures while simultaneously criticizing them in code. Allegories act as mirrors for ideology. They iconographically reversed the constraint exercised on Philibert, enabling him to take power symbolically and to occupy space subversively.

The *Architecture* is a two-layered text. One level of narrative, a builders' manual, incorporates an allegorical subtext, which comments ironically on the first narrative. Here, allegory shows how a powerful patron compels a gifted architect to build in ways contrary to his creativity and expertise. Through allegory, Philibert describes this pressure: "being wrongly charged, charged yet again, and overladen with calumny, crossings at every turn, mistreatment and displeasures, I have bravely sustained them and, unburned, constantly withstood the same."[152]

The Allegorical System in Philibert's Architecture: The First Allegory

Philibert's first allegory, textual and unillustrated, concludes the prologue to the third book of the *Architecture*. This allegory emphasizes the spatial quality of structures, as well as offering an interpretive grid for the text. The allegory illustrates how the *Architecture* constitutes a liminal space of deviance between dominant discourse and marginal expression, Catholic imposition and Calvinist resistance. Philibert envisions a situation in which "the liberty of the Architect must be free from all constraint and subjection of creative spirit."[153] Spatial stricture ("such constraint and narrowness of place")[154] causes him vexation and "great perplexity."[155]

The first allegory envisions an ambiguous audience: "all those who profess to be, or who want to be, Architects, and *to others* also."[156] "Others," apparently referring to nonarchitects who do not seek to master the art, indicates a program surpassing straightforward instruction in the builder's craft. Those "autres" receive "singulier plaisir & prouffit" from the text. The motif of pleasure and profit derives from Horace and was popular in French humanist writings. However, its presence in what claims to be a technical and, hence, nonliterary manual is surprising, suggesting a textual agenda unavailable to the uninformed reader.

Other components of the allegory demonstrate the need for an initiated reader. Philibert situates the personae of his allegory in spatial coordinates ("in the first place I show an Architect . . . as though coming out of a cave or hidden place"),[157] a reference to Plato's *Republic*. Here, however, the architect is not content to look at shadows on a wall, but rather exits his confinement in order to look at the real thing. Analogously, Calvinists emerge from Catholic-dominated situations to see clearly or, in a larger theological reading, come out of death into life. Alternatively "a place of contemplation, solitude and study,"[158] the cave could function as a privileged place *à part* representing the desire for a haven. The cave is an intellectualized, abstract space ("contemplation"; "estude"), not part of reality. Blank frames such as the cave provide for the Architect's emerging figure; they represent a "process of shifting inclusion and exclusion,"[159] a technique that architectural parlance calls *subalternation*. In this way, Philibert displays tension between public and personal domain and demonstrates the need for spatial redetermination.

Philibert's other goal is truth: "[in order] to arrive at the true knowledge and perfection of his craft."[160] The allegory thus assumes the status of an ontological or metaphysical narrative. Viewed in this light, the instability of the signifying components of the monuments included in the allegory, structures built for Catholic patrons and intended to represent them, is a sign of the patrons' eschatologically suspect status.

Similarly, the figure of the Architect is not a portrait, but rather yet another symbol that points beyond itself: "he pulls up the hem of his robe with one hand, wanting to show . . ."[161] Significance shifts incessantly in this allegory, just as Philibert's works, both text and structures, are characterized by motion, transition, change, and subversion. The components of the Architect's figure are equally protean: the Architect holds a "compass wrapped around by a serpent"; elsewhere, Mercury holds a caduceus. This iconography seems a stock humanist reference,[162] but when the repeated image of the serpent is juxtaposed with a description of the serpent in Calvin's *Institution*, another meaning seems possible: "Moses . . . shows how the invincible power of God is on his side, so that he is able to swallow up everyone else's rod with his own . . . This transformation occurs before their very eyes . . . and then a little later the rod resumes its first shape . . . God made a serpent from a rod, then immediately after, a rod from a serpent."[163] Philibert's allegory thus develops when joined to a Calvinist scriptural reference. Calvin's textual image of the serpent becomes a symbol for Calvinist architectural resistance to the imposition of Catholic norms. Philibert equates himself with the serpent: the serpent has God on his side and metamorphoses into unexpected shapes to defy attempts to control him. As such, he is the privileged medium for God's display of omnipotence. The serpent is a loaded symbol, who here represents the transforming transgression of power inherent in Calvinist architecture.

The Calvinist hermeneutics of the allegory is strengthened by Philibert's citations from Paul, who exhorts Christians to adopt strategies of self-protection: "Be ye wise therefore like serpents."[164] Interestingly, the evangelical Sebastiano Serlio published with the Reformed editor Jean de Tournes who, from 1547 to 1563, was associated with the Lyons printer Guillaume Gazeau. The motto on Gazeau's printer's *devise* was "estote prudentes sicut serpentes."[165] Philibert's incorporation of Scripture into his allegory highlights the scriptural tenor of the *Architecture*, studded with biblical allusions and scaffolded on biblical models. Much of his architectural writing reads like a new version of scriptural exegesis.[166]

Philibert's Architect picks a path around obstacles (the "scandals" or stumbling blocks of the gospel), following a narrow path ("with prudence and wise deliberation, in order to be sure of the path to which he should keep among men"),[167] which recalls the biblical "strait gate." The path passes by a palm tree, symbolic of Christ in contemporary genre painting and, here, emblematic of Calvinism: the tree's resilience symbolizes an opposition stance.

Not only symbols, but also theologically coded terms, enrich the allegory: "perte" denotes a loss of time and money but also connotes a sense of sin: "he who does not possess this wonderful virtue of prudence will not know how to remedy this failing" ("perte").[168] Philibert asserts that the only recourse in a fallen world is to reform that world. He gives a theological dimension to the term rather than limiting it to the architectural meaning of historical restoration. Similarly, if read allegorically, the blueprints of Philibert's *Architecture* limn plans for the reformation and renewal of the human heart. Required by Catholic patrons to bend his inspiration for new structures to accommodate preexisting buildings, Philibert views the latter as "bastiments imparfaicts."[169] His task is to redeem the structures, completing them by bringing them into line with Scripture, a prototype for the appropriate assignment of space: "by means of these things, not only are existing faults removed from the structure, . . . but also the dwelling is rendered admirable . . . old materials can be made to serve the purposes of the new." [170]

Philibert not only creates a theologically correct standard but also sculpts a protective personal space; he reverses the judgment critics make of his work and of his theology. "I want our Architect to have a clean soul, not deceitful, abusive or malicious. He will be nevertheless calumniated for his imitation of the serpent, that is, for being prudent and wise in order to keep himself safe from the malice and deception of evil men. His virtues . . . will be such that the name of Wisdom will substitute for the name of Ruse (just as most men call Virtue, Vice)." [171]

The scriptural interpretive framework prohibits a mere humanist reading of the caduceus, which now symbolizes a Calvinist program to overwrite existing space and structure, so that both may be redetermined scripturally. In encoding "ruse" as "wisdom," and in deploying different uses for the serpent image, Philibert employs what architectural theory calls *field reversals*, which occur when the symbols of a dominant group are subverted by their use in a different space and sense. The first allegory thus offers a paradigm of how Philibert proposes to defend his private self from slander, his architectural constructions from derision, and his Calvinist adherence from detection. This allegory describes the panoply of defensive recourses employed by a text that beneath the surface, hiding like the joints of Philibert's columns behind papier-mâché ornamentation, makes some very bold assertions.

Critical Iconoclasms: An Allegory of Misreading

The second allegory, illustrated, is found in the conclusion to the ninth book of Philibert's *Architecture*. A mutilated man lacking eyes, nose, ears, and hands stumbles along a path littered with skulls and pocked with crevasses. Another twisting path leads to a turbulent river bridged by a trestle abutting a fine fortress onto which rain is falling. In the background, a small town nestles around a church spire, while in the central plan, straight trees sketch a vertical line dividing the picture into two planes, separating town from fortress. The man's figure, stooped and crooked, contrasts with the trees' erectness, deviating from the vertical line. Another vertical line, a straight line emerging from one of the fortress's turrets and reaching to the clouds, echoes the trees and church spire, evoking, to a Calvinist reader, the biblical plumb line, symbol of spiritual alignment with God's plan. The structures in the engraving are proportionate and harmonious. The only deformed structure is physiological: the man's twisted body, his mutilated face and hands. Anthony Blunt, focusing on details for his interpretation of this allegory, erred as Philibert knew that Catholics would misread, being seduced by image rather than performing an overall reading to situate those images in context. Blunt assumed the allegory portrayed a "bad architect," one who could not see to convey his vision and who lacked hands to manipulate materials. As Philibert describes it, "in any great building project . . . There is never a dearth of men and servants, but usually they are unfaithful . . . They understand nothing about the project . . . Those men resemble this figure."[172] Allegories are misread when readers do not know the proper code. Philibert's allegories thus act as tests of right readership and right religious adherence. He requires that his allegorical structure be interpreted in reference to biblical parables. Beginning the companion text to the allegory in parable-like fashion, "Truly, truly I say to you,"[173] he demonstrates that Scripture is the intertext for his work.

Philibert's deciphering of this dense image assumes that the entire *Architecture* will be taken into account; he works into the allegorical frame details from elsewhere in the text, thus establishing the set of allegories as interpretive paradigms. Concern over criticism, jostling for political power, denigration by unsympathetic viewers, and theological condemnation of such misinterpreters are the allegory's message. The dried oxen skulls cluttering the critic's path repeat the visual motif beginning Philibert's chapters. Philibert thus installs the staring head of the critic symbolically at the head of each part of his endeavor.[174] These heads reappear, cast before the man's figure in this allegory, along with stumbling blocks in his path: "Several dried oxen skulls are in his way, along with several stones to make him stumble."[175] The Critic's criticism will trip him up, Philibert's iconographically phrased assertion makes clear. Criticism, lurking everywhere, is defused in this allegory: the skulls now topple from their accusatory position to lie trampled beneath the representation of the originator of their *own* negative discourse: the Critic. Philibert's allegory is not that of a "bad architect," but rather the archetype of the evil-wishing Critic. The skulls and stones with which he vilified the Architect now become the instruments of the Critic's self-mutilation, as when, in the image, thorny bushes "catch at and tear his clothing."[176] Applying the field reversal of symbols, Philibert's allegory disarms the Critic's weapons, effecting a Calvinist iconoclasm, truncating the Critic by removing his hands ("to show

15. Philibert's allegorical illustration, dubbed by the art critic Anthony Blunt "The Allegory of the Bad Architect" and renamed by the argument of the present study "The Allegory of the Critic." The architecture here is of an inferior, fortresslike, medieval sort and contrasts strongly with the lovely and elaborate buildings found in its companion allegory. The allegory is discussed in detail in the text. These allegories are especially noteworthy in that we have no similar allegorical illustration of architectural issues from the period. They demonstrate the combination of a highly visual with a determinedly textual treatment, an enriching innovation for the genre of the architectural manual. Philibert de l'Orme, *Architecture* (1626), I, 329. By permission of the Folger Shakespeare Library.

that they don't know how ["ne sçauroient"] to do anything").[177] Similarly, Calvinist iconoclasts mutilated religious images to deny their pretensions to represent the divine. The verb "sçauroient" is ambiguous, proposing, first, the ignorance of the Critic: he knows not how to do anything; second, it implies that he is henceforth powerless: the French interprets "ils ne sçauroient" as "they are not able" to do anything.

Philibert thereby projects onto the Critic the very constraint that he experiences. If Philibert's hands have been figuratively tied by patrons, if his confessional stance must be covert, the allegory of the Critic recalls Philibert's situation, then reverses its effects onto the Critic himself, neutralizing and silencing him. The Critic is not one individual alone; Philibert evokes him in the third person plural, indicting a multiplicity of critical distortion. Philibert's critics now lack eyes ("to see and discern good building"), ears ("nor ears, to hear and understand wise men"), and noses ("not even a nose . . . so as not to experience any good thing").[178] These latter deprivations are especially significant, for while the removal of the Critic's hands eliminates the ability to act, the removal of eyes, ears, and nose is associated biblically with a *moral* distinguishing capacity. Here, too, Philibert labels those who lack the capacities of distinction and comprehension as "damned"; Serlio had indicated that "only the elect will be able to seek truth, which will be found beneath appearances."[179] Critics are thereby labeled unregenerate; they cannot judge the Calvinist elect: "such people hate . . . because of who they are, . . . not only wise architects, but every virtuous man, and even virtue itself."[180] A Calvinist reading of this allegory ranks critics among the unreformable: they are damned if they do not "have ears to hear" the Word of God. Philibert excoriates their sinfulness, employing the same term he had applied to defective building structures, that of *faultes*: "the sins they commit/the defects they produce."[181] Phili-

bert includes the Critic in his text in order to neutralize him, turning his presence to Philibert's advantage, "assuring myself that no further harm could come to me from him."[182] Similarly, Philibert erects structures for Catholic patrons, but he finds a way to contain those patrons' aspirations by framing the structures within his Calvinist reinterpretation.

This allegory also acts as a decoding device for the informed reader by displaying the strategy that Philibert uses against his critics. The camouflage of the allegory dupes the Critic, deflecting criticism of the architect by apparently incorporating it into the text itself so that there seems no need for further criticism. The choice of genre represents Philibert's sense of constraint, foisting it back on its source: "whatever inhibits the reader's freedom is *something in the work* . . . the lack of freedom [is] inherent in the work. Whether by form or by some limitation of content [or crowding of it], the [allegory] makes a constricted work of art, which in turn imposes its own constraint upon the reader."[183]

In the Allegory of the Critic, the allegorical system breaks down—as it is intended to. For, finally, Philibert deflects the power of interpretation from the Critic, ascribing it to God alone. "But let's leave off such topics, and put everything into God's hands, who will cause the truth of all things to be known in a fitting time and place. Let's resume, therefore, talking about our Architect, who I desire to be so wise, that he will learn to know himself and to recognize his own merit, abilities and strengths: and if he knows of any lack in himself, I advise him to ask quickly that the Lord remedy it."[184] The architect's self-knowledge is described in Calvinist terms, consistent with Calvin's doctrine of the knowledge of God, a dialectical relationship in which man's self-knowledge and his knowledge of the Lord interpenetrate: when he learns to know himself, he will receive knowledge from God. Philibert inserts himself into the privileged, protective space occupied by God, just as in the allegory the fortress provided a shelter from the storm clouds of criticism.

"The Allegory of the Good Architect": Protected Space

The architecture in Philibert's third and final allegory recalls that of the classical golden age. The illustration portrays a *locus amoenus* of temples, basilicas, and historiated triumphal arches framed by abundant fruits and flowers, signs of a benign natural order. While in the allegory of the Critic a stern, upright tree established the standard of rectitude, here a graceful, vine-covered tree drips with foliage and ripe grapes, epitomizing flexibility of form. A stream trickles from a rocky outcropping to the right, symbolizing the living waters of the Gospels, Philibert's source of inspiration.

The Allegory of the Critic was situated in an unprotected space open to menacing elements, but here ornate structures crowd out external space; only a bit of tranquil sky shows at the top. In this Calvinist re-vision, space is reclaimed. Together, the two allegories also demonstrate the passage, and eventual redemption, of time. The Allegory of the Critic displays structures more medieval in form, while the Allegory of the Good Architect represents Renaissance architecture. The Critic, linked with Catholicism, is thus associated with the abuses and corruption of the medieval Catholic church (as decried in Calvin's *Institution*) and the deformities, as Renaissance architects viewed it, of medieval architecture. The Allegory of the Good Architect revives pure and harmonious structure in a humanist context. Thus, time, too, is redeemed by the association of the Calvinist program with humanist techniques.

Certain iconographic elements of this last allegory rework components of the first one. The first allegory featured a winged Mercury with caduceus, and Mercury symbolized wisdom in the pursuit of Architecture: "the Architect must . . . be quick to know and understand useful knowledge and disciplines, over which Mercury presides."[185] However, Mercury posed a problem: in interpreting instructions or in implementing "divine proportions," would the Architect be able to emulate Mercury without becoming "mercurial, that is to say, changeable and babbling, sometimes frequenting one [man or opinion], sometimes the other[?] . . . I would rather have it that he follow and imitate good [men], so as to himself be good."[186] This final allegory provides a solution by eliminating the potential for slippage between scriptural model and human reproduction: now the Architect himself is a Calvinist Mercury, wearing wings on his feet, God's messenger.[187] Mercury's model juxtaposes with the Architect's structures: a statue of Mercury adorns the temple, addressing the Architect in a mirroring relationship.

In contrast with the handless Critic, the Architect possesses many hands, emphasizing his capabilities. He holds his hands in the opened, finger-separated posture characteristic of the evangelists' position preparatory to speaking, demonstrating that his utterance will be "gospel truth."[188] He holds a scroll, representing both the knowledge of his craft and the Scripture from which it derives,[189] and offers the scroll to another figure, whom Philibert labels "Ieunesse" (Youth). "Youth" stands in the central

16. Philibert's allegorical illustration, called "The Allegory of the Good Architect" and interpreted in the scope of the present study as a representation of Calvinist architecture. This allegory also supplies an imaged history of the development of architecture in France, including classical, medieval, and Renaissance features. The allegory is discussed in detail in the text, and is rich in symbolism; note the Mercury-like winged feet on the older figure, the doubled sets of hands, the detail of the statuary, and the reappearance (from the frontispiece of the *Nouvelles inventions*) of several varieties of Philibert's representative cornucopia. Philibert de l'Orme, *Architecture* 1:341 [*sic*: correct pagination is 331]. By permission of the Folger Shakespeare Library.

space formerly occupied by the Critic in the second allegory. The Youth is the ultimate recipient of Philibert's interlocking allegories, as well as the privileged reader of the *Architecture*. Philibert recalls, like Calvin, Matthew's Gospel, where Jesus declares that "the Kingdom of heaven . . . will be inherited by the children . . . only those whom God has adopted as his children will profit from this inheritance."[190] The transmission of his knowledge to the Youth indicates the presence of a Calvinist readership capable of interpreting the Architect's work correctly. "Ieunesse" may also represent Christ coming to speak approvingly to the Architect of his projects; he is described situated like the young Jesus sitting in the temple with rabbis and scholars, "representing Youth, who must seek out wise and learned men, to be instructed as much verbally as by memoirs, writings, drawings and models."[191] The Youth inherits the Architect's wisdom. He in some manner thus also becomes Philibert himself, ensuring that Philibert is one of the elect, heir to Christ's kingdom.

The use of detail weds architecture and theology. The intricate structures of this final allegory compose a near-complete catalogue of the techniques for design and ornament in Philibert's text, from frames to pilasters, cornices, volutes, and arcades. Each technique is a part of architectural practice that has been turned to a different use. The Allegory of the Good Architect, as a concluding summary of Philibert's repertoire of coded structures, encapsulates the text's message.[192] It confirms the merit of Philibert's endeavor and ensconces him in an unassailable position, impervious to criticism. Protected from calumny, assured of salvation, Philibert situates himself in a personal and private space: "After having ordered all that is necessary to execute his commissions, let [the Architect] retire and keep himself solitarily in his study, cabinet, room, library, or garden, as he may have available to him."[193]

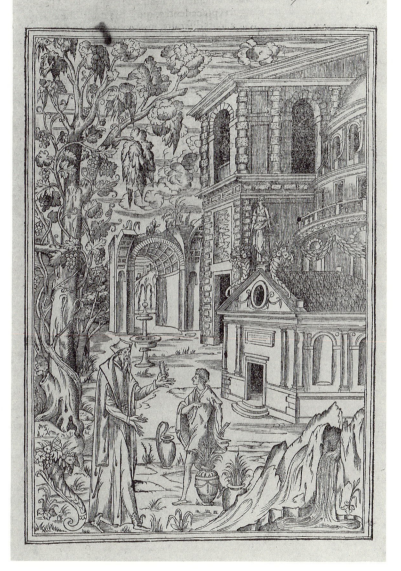

While producing in an inhospitable public sphere, where critics abound and Catholics reign, Philibert nonetheless finds spaces that sustain him in which he may assert his own meaning for the structures that he has built. Significantly, the allegory portrays the architect "devant le temple d'oraison." Churches—particularly the Calvinist *temples*,[194]—offer protection from persecution. The Architect possesses keys, one of which functions defensively "to foresee the future and time to come . . . in order to protect and arm himself against so many attacks, injuries, calamities and miseries in this miserable world in which one is so often derided."[195] The other two keys designate him as one of the elect. His predestined status further exalts the Architect over the Critic: where the Critic was mutilated and deprived of senses, the Architect is amply supplied, in fact possesses a surplus—for example, the text stipulates that he has four ears, "showing that one should listen more than speak" and emphasizing his access to Scripture (and in fact responding to Philibert's reading of a verse from St. James).[196] The spatial situation of the Architect in the text defines him theologically: Philibert's description weaves him into a web of scriptural citations proving the Architect's conformity to the Word, in contrast to the dearth of scriptural material in the allegory of the Critic.[197]

By guaranteeing his status through scriptural confirmation and by aligning his textual structures with biblical architecture, Philibert equates his text with the Bible. In contrast to such lay fragmentation ("being in this world, we have no knowledge of the arts and sciences, if only by little bits and pieces"),[198] Philibert's Architect gathers fruits spilling from the cornucopia, the riches of God's Word: "I show the Architect having a plethora of four hands . . . from everyone who comes to visit or see him in his garden, he doesn't hide his beautiful stores of virtue, his cornucopias filled with beautiful fruit, his vases full of great riches and secrets, his springs and fountains of wisdom."[199] Through his text, Philibert offers a way to "get back to the garden," a new paradise built on the blueprint of scriptural structures.

Iconographic Subversions

Philibert intentionally does not explain all aspects of the last two allegories. These areas of imprecision camouflage his countercultural stance, as well as entrap the ill-intentioned reader or viewer. Elsewhere in the *Architecture*, other techniques implement Philibert's program: fragments, the overflowing of borders, marginalia, trompe l'oeil ornamentation, skewed perspective, and "misquotation" of the customary architectural vocabulary comprise the tactical lexicon in which Philibert rearticulates his structures.

The first allegory depends solely on textual transmission; unpaired with any image, it alerts us to search beneath ornamentation for meaning, under the surface for significance. The two illustrated allegories dialectically conclude the *Architecture*. The Allegory of the Critic represents the misapplication of the hermeneutic process suggested in the first allegory and describes the tension between the intersection of public and private space, between institutionalized Catholicism and resistant Calvinism. The final allegory summarizes the strategies implemented throughout the *Architecture*, indicts critics, and describes the Architect as he who erects structures of salvation, thereby fulfilling Scripture. Unable in the real world to create buildings reflective of his Calvinist beliefs, Philibert places his faith in the future kingdom of God which, he argues, his text realizes.

Reading Philibert's allegories allegorically, noting their location, their ambiguity, the narrative they develop, and their similarities and differences, demonstrates that they constitute interpretive signposts in a work that ostensibly conforms, and limits itself, to existing standards of architectural expression as obedient representations of power structures. Philibert's substratum of significance, however, empowers the Calvinist program for scriptural conformity and sculpts a space for Calvinist expression within the text. Philibert's series of allegories, taken as a whole, eliminates the possibility of "bad" architecture, if architects will only pattern their craft on his text's precepts. Such patterning will effect a reformation both of them and of their work. His allegories, themselves "structures" composed of architectural components, perform a corrective reading of all structuring enterprises. In so doing, they realize, within the space of Philibert's text, the architecture for which Scripture calls. They do so by rehearsing the varieties of human imperfection found in (mis)constructions of buildings and (mis)interpretations of meaning.

Conclusion: (A)mazing the World

Now I'd like to show you how to build a two-storied building with a Corinthian order, which is to say, I'll show you how to do the opposite of what people usually do.

—Philibert, Architecture[200]

Even in terms of the genre of the architectural manual, Philibert subverts expectations and denies conventions within his use of convention itself. He alerts his reader to a second, coded meaning contained in the structures he erects. He forces a reevaluation of the ornamentation of his structures by comparing them with their divine prototype. Philibert sees the world as a confused and hostile space, a sphere rife with potential critics and persecutors. Calvin called the fallen world a maze or labyrinth,[201] while Philibert compares himself to a master maze builder, a mystifier who possesses the art to outwit his opponent through his structures. Calling himself a new Daedalus, averring also that he surpasses him,[202] Philibert describes Daedalus through an architectural reference, as "[he who] is said to have been the author and inventor of the very first houses and dwellings."[203] Daedalus is actually best known as the architect of the labyrinth that housed the Minotaur. In this way Philibert deceptively minimizes, in order to camouflage, Daedalus's potency. Similarly, Philibert portrays himself as creating structures to disguise his strength, the menace that, like the monster, lurks at the heart of the maze.

Philibert's recommendations to his reader as to how to read his text are similarly veiled. He suggests that his text is not self-sufficient, that the reader must move beyond it to complete the text for himself: "I will add that written things never give so much pleasure and instruction as do those that are practical, pointed out at fingertip . . . this material is very difficult to work with . . . which is the reason why it is so difficult to teach it in writing, in a book."[204] However, he then lists the merits of his text: "you'll find in it other pleasing things from which you will greatly profit as you will see for yourself . . . when you've carefully read and reread this volume."[205] Philibert's ambivalence arises more from the question of the *process* of interpretation than the text itself: the reading act is freighted with significance, and any favorable reading of the *Architecture* necessitates a corresponding ideological sympathy, inherently dangerous both for Philibert and for the sympathetic reader. Consequently, Philibert chooses his words carefully and uses code. Philibert's reader cannot remain neutral. Having penetrated to the substratum of meaning, the reader is formed as Calvinist.

The Calvinist program documents how the architect is vilified, contains strategies for defending the architect, attempts to open a space for an interpretation more favorable to the architect, and tries to coopt the reader's sympathy. Blamed and persecuted, Calvinists seek a space in which to express their religious beliefs. Constraint generates a creative response, resulting in the redetermination of the persons exercising the constraint by the person constrained.[206] The *Architecture* not only lists the principles for building well, it describes how to restructure the human heart.

5

The Second-Generation
Calvinist Architects

Encoding Constraint

> By the 1550s a new generation of architects had come
> to maturity in France, and their style, which as time
> went on became increasingly disturbed and exaggerated,
> reflects the tensions produced by the religious and social
> upheavals of the period.

> From the mid-1580s until peace was achieved under Henri
> IV, almost nothing was built . . . By the second decade of
> the new century, growing confidence in the social order
> began to be reflected in increased building activity among
> civic and religious authorities.
> —Rosalys Coope, *Salomon de Brosse*

THE ABOVE QUOTATIONS purport to trace an evolution from a troubled
time marked by minimal building activity to one of peace, harmony, and
expansion. The underlying reality, however, is more nuanced. During the
second period described, despite the nominal restoration of order and
the toleration purportedly extended to Calvinists, Calvinist architects continued to write of being outsiders, being distrusted, and of themselves
distrusting the very authority and institutions that their structures were
commissioned to glorify.[1] It is a striking fact that, during the period of explicit persecution of Protestants, the two most influential architects were
Calvinists: Jean Bullant and Jacques Androuet du Cerceau. The inevitable
tension between this second-generation Calvinists' religious beliefs and
political opposition was translated through stylistic similarities common
to all Calvinist architects of this period,[2] constituting a cohesive, conscious
cell of countercultural creativity. While art historians consistently group

them in this way, the significance of their theology has not been explored. Yet, the Protestant architects referred to their endeavors in biblical terms, stating that they were "building up Jerusalem" or "tearing down Babylon [Rome]." Such a biblical metaphor is "a program in shorthand . . . In principle, biblical metaphor, provided we interpret it correctly, both states a problem and provides a programme for solving it."[3] Labeling this an intermediary period between the distinct Renaissance style and the formalized classical style, architectural historians have failed to account adequately for the oddity of the period because they have overlooked religion as a major factor. "The generation of men that Henri IV had working for him as painters, sculptors and architects has tended to be neglected, with attention directed instead to its precursors and successors; none of the names of that generation really became famous. This is especially the case as concerns the architects, because the era was spent trying to work on the buildings begun previously . . . The works of this generation are thus only fragments of a whole that belongs to others."[4]

It is, nonetheless, incontestable that a theological perspective informed and inflected the Calvinist architects' artistic production. The characteristic of fragmentation mentioned above labels this generation as Calvinist; their works were fragmentary because of their imperiled status.[5] This fragmentation links them to first-generation Calvinist architects such as Philibert de l'Orme who employed detail, fragment, and trompe l'oeil subversively to contradict oppositional ideology. The first generation had already demonstrated marked affinities among themselves. Bernard Palissy's *Recepte véritable*, for example, explicitly refers to the "new French order," a decorated series of bands around shafts of columns, devised by Philibert. Citing his predecessor, Palissy used tree trunks, historiated and ornamented as structured columns. Palissy achieved the effect at which Philibert had aimed, which was to bulge outward, breaking the lines of the columns,[6] disrupting symmetry, to force an acknowledgment of the world's deformity. This pattern of fulfilling a contemporary's program continued with the second-generation architects, who also enriched their precursors' architectural resources. Salomon de Caus, for instance, borrowed widely from de l'Orme.[7] This circuit of Calvinist citation has been termed a "Huguenot statement in architectural terms."[8]

If the second architectural generation advanced the program of the previous generation of Calvinist architectural exemplars, it was also indebted to them. For instance, in implementing Henri IV's urban reforms and building programs, the architects of what is now the Place des Vosges took as their model for the individual units the blueprint for Philibert de L'Orme's private house in Paris.[9] This in itself may not seem so surprising. However, when we examine the quirky structure of de l'Orme's house, in which a camouflaged front entryway hid under a flight of stairs leading around to the side of the house, we find a form of trompe l'oeil stagefront, an apt emblem for Philibert's perceived need for privacy and protection. The code, as used by the second-generation architects, consists in the paradoxical emphasis on the very feature that Philibert had tried to hide: "Delorme privileged the wing, removed from the street, while Henri's architects emphasized the front pavilion . . . for the view of the square."[10] The structural decision suggests that royal authority is surface and sham, mere show based on something that evades the view, a deceptive and concealing façade. In addition, the pavilions of the Place Royale did not incorporate classical motifs but were unrepresentational, in keeping with Calvinist iconoclasm, as though to remind the king, at the heart of his display of royal dominance, of the Calvinist faith he had forsaken. The simplicity of their building materials (red brick, cream stone, and black slate) and their rudimentary ornamental motif stressed the foundation of the structure rather than any message it might convey.[11] Such visual or structural techniques partake of a Calvinist world-view which "used the Bible as a code understood among themselves but whose meaning was not immediately obvious to others."[12] One factor that hints at a Protestant perspective is a tendency to biblical citation. In his work on English Protestant subversive activity and production of "coded" works during the seventeenth century, Christopher Hill speculates: "one great advantage of quoting the Bible is to avoid responsibility for specific assertions and personal attitudes . . . [they used] Aesopian languages, in order to say what they wanted without falling foul of the censor."[13]

Several noted Calvinist architects exemplify this observation about coded statements. Salomon de Brosse, a militant Calvinist, worked on the second Protestant temple at Charenton and other Huguenot churches, as well as on Catholic structures. Other architects were more reluctant to have their beliefs known. Jacques Androuet du Cerceau tells in his prefatory remarks to his publications of the persecutions that his family endured: because of their Calvinist beliefs, many were killed and several had to flee France. This narration is very terse and strained, as though he wanted to say more even than he did disclose. His religious stance can also be discerned in the delineation of his buildings. But most striking of all are those occasions on which he consciously revised existing structures or plans: the areas of dissimilarity between du Cerceau's drawings of de l'Orme's structures and the original structures themselves (designed in a somewhat less imperiled theological climate and therefore substantially freer in scope) show the increasing constraints under which du Cerceau labored. Some Calvinist architects never acknowledged their beliefs publicly; only their personal papers, or an event in their lives such as exile to Geneva, permit conjecture, as is the case with the artisan Jean Richier, a convert to Protestantism who left France and later died in Geneva.[14] A tendency to quote from certain books of the Bible more favored by Calvinists can also provide clues to the architect's beliefs; this is the case with Jacques Perret de Chambéry's blueprints for fortresses: all the images are circumscribed by Bible verses.[15] The verses, however, contradict the grandeur of the monarch who commissioned the structure, reminding him that power resides not in his hands but with the Lord.

Thus, the Calvinist citation strategy was employed against Catholics (as a form of misquoting) and in favor of Calvinists (models were quoted in order to be reworked). This citation strategy constitutes a meta-architecture, one that theorizes its own principles of construction.[16] The illusory monumental statement actually points beyond itself to a message it both disguises and reveals. One clue to the existence of a coded message in a Calvinist structure is nearly always a certain resistance to interpretation, an element of ambiguity resident in the structure itself: "A nicodemite discourse transmits an occluded message, something difficult to grasp: a variety of techniques, more or less sophisticated, permit the creation of an ambiguous or ambivalent thesis."[17]

Jean Bullant: *La Reigle Générale de l'Architecture* (1564)

My lords, in order to render a more clear understanding to the laborers of my second printing, I've done everything possible to explain anything in my work that might have seemed obscure or hidden. Also, to tell the truth, when any building is made, it is easy to discern its faults, but there are very few who can rectify them! I've applied myself to this aim, using that small skill which God has seen fit to give me.
—Bullant, *Reigle générale*[18]

Jean Bullant was born between 1520 and 1525 in Ecouen and died in 1578. He trained as a mason, was an architect of the second generation, and authored treatises on agriculture, geometry, sundials (1561), and architectural orders (1564–68).[19] He imitated an architect of the first generation,

17. Jean Bullant's La Fère-en-Tardenois in Aisne, 1552–62, is a monolithic structure with smaller, ill-assorted decorative chunks. The dentellated pattern formed by the bricks on the top of the lower arcades seems incongruously miniaturized in comparison to the larger, blocky structure. Photograph by Randall Balmer.

Philibert de l'Orme. Bullant was the architect for Catherine de Médicis at Chenonceau, succeeding Philibert as architect to the Queen Mother in 1570.[20] Like Philibert, Bullant studied architecture in Italy. Philibert introduced the colossal order to France; Bullant learned it from him and gave it its first complete manifestation at Ecouen (1545–56). At Ecouen, Bullant distinguished himself through the monumental quality of the orders he used there, as well as through their bold vertical lines (in Calvinist church building, vertical lines are employed to lead the eye — and the aspirations — upward to God). In addition, in typical Calvinist fashion, he included contrary tendencies in a single structure, compelling the viewer to reconcile them.[21] Another example of contradiction, Bullant's Petit Château at Chantilly (circa 1547), displays continued tension between two different forms, with the two small storys playing against the single large orders there. He translated architecturally the Calvinist program to represent an alternative theological perspective for the French nation.

While Bullant's early style closely followed Philibert's early idiom, particularly in his use of detail, he found his own style in his later work. This latter period had a major influence on another Calvinist architect of the second generation, Jacques I du Cerceau, prompting the latter's stylistic exaggerations.[22] Du Cerceau's engraving of Bullant's Chenonceau, for example, incorporates many distortions and alterations. Bullant's structure possesses its own unusual qualities, especially the large, empty spaces under the arcades, which seem almost to mine it from below rather than support it. Du Cerceau's version adds a drawbridge to the tower at the far left and incorporates the tower to the rest of the structure by adding a walled extension; he also utterly omits the roof and building that the arcades purportedly support. Du Cerceau in this way used his Calvinist predecessor, built upon and revised him, to make his own Calvinist architectural statement in a slightly changed time and context. Such Calvinist architectural cross-pollination, with many influences intersecting and reinforcing each other within the Calvinist community, is characteristic of the context in which the second-generation Calvinist architects worked. The Calvinist subversive style is a hybrid of strong, revisionist signatures.

18. Bullant's south wing of the château of Ecouen displays another series of irregularities in scale, alternating between a massive, monolithic surface and smaller, almost precious ornamental schemes. The arcaded doors toward the foreground seem crushed beneath the weight of the overhanging structure.

In his later work, Bullant was an iconoclast "consciously breaking rules governing the use of orders." In addition, the scope of his projected architectural ambition surpassed available space for structures: "his desire for the colossal [grew] greater; [at St.-Maur] it could not be happily harmonized with the existing building."[23] The south wing of his château at Ecouen seems to weigh disproportionately heavily on the bottom third of the structure, and the arcaded, partly recessed doors at the bottom center of the building seem about to implode, as though the château were about to crash forward. At Chenonceau, the pediments covering the windows overlap the panels filling the intervening spaces. The bridge arcade at La Fère-en-Tardenois, which he built between 1552 and 1562, is structured on massive pillars, while the superstructure of the arcade seems inordinately petite, in contrast. He gives an apparently contradictory directive in the *Reigle générale de l'architecture*: "in no matter what building, one must be very careful that there be no disharmony. This applies also to ornament; it should always correspond to the main structure."[24] The statement raises the suspicion that such contradictions are intentional, meant to illustrate that no space exists in France for Calvinist expression, theological or architectural.[25]

Bullant's *Reigle* is rich in such codes and complexities. His emblem for the text consists of a quatrain framed by architectural implements. The emblem is found on the last page of the *Reigle*, an unusual and belated location for a personal *devise*.[26] Placing the *devise* at the beginning of the text composes a directive statement to the reader about how to understand the author and, consequently, the work. Placing the *devise* at the end, however, calls into question what has gone before, requiring the reader to rehearse all that has been said in the text in order to determine whether or not its assertions are consistent with the hermeneutic pattern now suggested by the emblematic statement. As befits a Calvinist architect of the second generation, the cryptic quality of Bullant's textual exposition of the emblem disrupts expectations:

Age and time will expose to view
All that in the earth now is hidden

19. Bullant's Chenonceau, which was significantly revised and altered by Jacques Androuet du Cerceau. The clustered masses of the main structure toward the left contrast with the more open blocks of masonry in the center and to the right of the structure.

> And will hide beneath a dark blanket
> That which we've seen, held, and done.[27]

The book of Revelation was much read by Calvinists, who found in its evocation of the disruption of the world during the "end times" paradoxical hope for change and rectification. It speaks of things hidden in the earth ("tout ce qui est en la terre cachée") that will be revealed later. The intertext of the *devise* is thus both apocalyptic and revisionist. All things of this life come under a subversive scrutiny and a revolutionary reinterpretation. Bullant's other *devise*, the phrase "Mors in me / In me vita," bears out a similar theme of dichotomous reversal of appearances, of something hidden within an outer shell that contradicts that exterior frame. Its chiastic construction, "MORS- in me / In-me-VITA," with MORS and VITA framing the mirrored repetition of the self ("in me"), heightens the feeling of intense subjectivity and, in typical Calvinist fashion, revises life as death and death as life. It is also significant that the image shows a pelican tearing its own flesh in order to nourish its young, an image customarily associated with Christ sacrificing himself for the faithful. Bullant, named in the motto following the image, thus affiliates himself with Christ. In addition, Bullant's architectural tools—mason's square, ruler, plumb line—frame the pelican, advertising a Calvinist conception of architecture.[28]

The "advertissement aux lecteurs" of the *Reigle* creates a dual scene of reception, that of the Good Reader and that of the Bad Reader, recalling de l'Orme's distinction between the Architect and the Critic as symbols for reading and misreading:[29] "My intention was never other than this: to make known (to the best of my ability) things that are well or poorly understood . . . I beg you forgive me if I have not clearly explained the text." The Calvinist mandate is always to explicate the text clearly, so something more than a modest demurral is involved in Bullant's disclaimer. The possibility that clarity may not have been achieved, coupled with the option of "bien ou mal," postulates misinterpretation of the text, alerting us that Bullant may be creating in code.

The vocabulary with which Bullant describes his structures also makes

coded references. Reacting against the charge leveled at Calvinists that they were "new," a heresy deviant from tradition,[30] Calvinists responded that their form of ecclesiology recalled the Early Christian Church and counter-charged that Catholicism was the "new," deviant version. Similarly, Bullant defends his structures against charges of novelty meant to render them suspect. Bullant defends his "opinion"[31] that no one should "either add to nor detract from" his structures in any way.[32] In his *Institution*, Calvin uses the same phrase to legislate that nothing should be added to, or taken away from, Scripture.[33] Bullant's reiteration of Calvin's terminology raises the issue of right interpretation and biblical fidelity, underwriting the ar-chitectural manual with a subtext on Calvinist scriptural explication.

Olivier de Serres's *Théâtre d'Agriculture* (1600): Tilling the Soil, and Talents

For what good does it do a man to be discontented with the place where he must spend his life? Can he change the mountains into plains, and the plains into moun-tains? Let him console himself, therefore, in the providence of God.
—Olivier de Serres, *Théâtre d'agriculture*[34]

Olivier de Serres (1539–1619) is best known as an ardent Calvinist and as a strong advocate, as Henri IV's agronomist, of sericulture, the raising of silkworms. His *Théâtre d'agriculture* (1600) sought to bolster the king-dom of France agriculturally and economically. This text was widely read; Henri IV had portions read to him every night before retiring, and paid to have several of its chapters printed in pamphlet form prior to the publica-tion of the completed manuscript.

De Serres's treatise, like those of Philibert and Jean Bullant, speaks the Calvinist language of construction and revision. Just as for Palissy the parable of the talents had a broader significance than that of agriculture alone, but rather represented the appropriate cultivation of France as God's earth,[35] so Olivier de Serres identifies himself as a Huguenot concerned to establish the kingdom rightly.[36] In his preface he states that "both my incli-nations, and the state of my finances, kept me in my own house and fields, and caused me to spend a considerable part of my best years there, during the civil wars of this kingdom, cultivating the earth with my servants, to the extent that that was possible in those troubled times. In this God so blessed me with his grace as to preserve me safe from all the calamities."[37]

De Serres makes an architectural distinction: certain structures are appropriate for peace, others for wartime. He describes a privileged position, his house, "more a house of peace than of war," requiring reconfiguration in order to be a protective redoubt against the evils of the century. At the same time, he indicts a situation of constraint, the common experience of Calvinists: he is obliged to stay in his house to avoid persecution. "During this miserable time, to what work could I more profitably turn my spirit than to find something of interest? . . . The war by its many vicissitudes imposed on me the need to stay in my house."[38] Significantly, he describes his psychic and spiritual malaise through reference to a *structure*.

He reads the world similarly, interpreting space theologically as formerly uncorrupted, now suspect, but potentially retrievable in some future time. In true Calvinist spirit, his *text* will provide the nostrum for situational and contextual ills: "My intention is to show, if I can, briefly and clearly everything that one should know and must do in order that the earth may be well cultivated, and that, in consequence, one may live in harmony with one's family, according to the nature of the place in which one lives."[39]

Space determines life experience, liberty or impediment, prosperity or persecution. But acknowledging the very real curtailments imposed by the wars and recognizing the corruption of political space ("who can imagine such a Paradise, since the great states of the world are wrapped round with such thorny difficulties?"),[40] de Serres switches to an eschatological space, stating that "it is easier to hope for, than to find, a place where heaven and earth would be as one."[41] Like Palissy, de Serres proposes to measure out such an ideal space by speaking of Wisdom in an architectural way: "Wisdom is the recourse to good usage, the ruler and compass of how to do things well."[42] For de Serres, the idealized space will be attained only once humanity has been reconfigured and reinstated. The vehicle for this recuperative process is agriculture, de Serres's analogue to Calvinist architectural programs: "So, wherever you turn, your final resort must always be agriculture . . . the most holy and natural occupation of mankind . . . Agriculture is not just for people in the fields; those who live in the cities and towns must take part in it too."[43]

De Serres expands the definition of agriculture, showing that it is a process of rehabilitation, of the restoration of natural order. Agriculture has a metaphysical meaning: the cultivation of the human heart. To develop this metaphor, de Serres refers to the Wars of Religion, the negative for his positive image: "Every good householder should be slow to build,

quick to plant . . . he should have no quarrel with anyone, if possible . . .
[un]like the excesses of the civil wars."[44] To strengthen the parallel, de
Serres adds autobiographical details, confiding that during the Wars he
raised peacocks because their raucous cry guarded the house by alerting
him to intruders: "during the civil wars they gave me many proofs of their
loyalty: having several times, while perched on low bushes, [screeched
to] let me know of the secret approach of the enemy during the dead
of night."[45]

To shift from a description of war to the discussion of a peaceable
kingdom, de Serres uses the symbol of the farmer, who embodies an ideal
society governed by a paterfamilias on the Calvinist household model.
The Protestant patriarch gathers his family together, holds evening prayer
meetings in his home, advises his wife, instructs his children, and brings
his family up in the true Christian faith. He is the repository of absolute
authority, and his morals and demeanor are irreproachable. Other Calvinists made similar assertions: " 'The man should know that it is God's will
that he should rule [his wife] and the whole house in Christian earnestness
and by good example, raise them in all discipline and respectability, and
keep wife and child.' . . . In this new understanding of the proper relation
which ought to hold between husbands and wives, the work patterns and
civic moralism of [the Protestant model] . . . became the touchstone for an
entire society."[46]

De Serres uses the *père de famille* as a cipher for the king, thereby
offering the Calvinist household prescriptively to the kingdom as a whole.
In the space of de Serres's ideal *mesnage*, "we will learn to police our own
house, and especially to instruct our children in the fear of the Lord, our
servants likewise . . . so that each may live righteously, wisely dealing
with his neighbors."[47] De Serres concentrates pragmatically on the private
realm, a quintessentially Calvinist domain, knowing that there is not much
sympathy for them in public space. The goal is to proceed from this private
realm to its public extension, taking, like Palissy in the *Recepte véritable*, a
revisionist promenade beyond the garden walls.

De Serres bravely mandates—thinly veiled *lèse majesté*—that the *père
de famille* "will also love his subjects, cherishing them as his children, protecting them if need be . . . even during wars . . . keeping them safe from
violence."[48] The good *père de famille* is described as "someone who will
strive to make himself worthy of his charge, in order that knowing how to
lead those beneath him, he'll earn their obedience."[49] Further, he will be a
peacemaker, not a war wager: "he will try to settle differences and quarrels

among his subjects amicably so that peace may reign among them;[50] . . . what more ugly thing is there in the world than that dissension and hatred reign between those who eat the same bread, live in the same house, like children of the same father? . . . And so that only good shall come of this, . . . the *père de famille* must never cease from maintaining all his children in a fraternal bond."[51]

This is a striking metaphor for the civil strife between Catholics and Calvinists, sons of one father, partakers of the same bread. De Serres further underscores the point (and perhaps betrays some Gallican political leanings), asserting that "the poet sings of rustic happiness / In which the honest home seems a republic."[52] This happy *mesnage* and harmonious kingdom will be realized, de Serres advises, if the pursuit of agriculture is observed. "Let him add to his household some honest trade, whereby, along with the cultivating of the earth, he will enrich his harvest . . . and be able to exercise every good office of honesty, charity and liberality . . . Thus, in this way he will become the *père de famille* that Cato called for: that is, more a seller than a buyer."[53]

The image of Christian charity meshes with the capitalist ideal of a favorable balance of trade to demonstrate that the Protestant patriarch is also the model for the king's most productive economic manifestation. If the King does not emulate the model of the patriarch, he will "devour himself, wasting his inheritance . . . by eating one piece after another." "Heir" and "inherit" are terms often associated with Christ, while the anthropophagic king figure recalls that of the mother turned wolf who cannibalizes her infant in Agrippa d'Aubigné's *Les tragiques*, a series of Calvinist tableaux dramatizing the horrors of civil war.[54] The figures of household and harvest conjoin in de Serres's plan for the "reformation . . . of the household."[55] Indeed, "maison" is the architectural prototype of a metaphysical yearning, a space in which harmony and peace may reign: "By such a correspondence [if you follow my model] peace and concord will be nourished in your house . . . and will do honor to you . . . and by this sign your house will be known as God's house; God will live in it, as Scripture has promised."[56]

Finally, de Serres calls for a structural representation, a sort of architectural mock-up, of this new order: "Enough talking; let's do something about this, so that we may reap the benefits of our agriculture. And, since the blueprint for a building is only painted paper, without stone, chalk, sand, wood or other materials, to erect this building, we will have striven in vain to depict the household . . . if we do not begin to work . . . to build."[57]

Henri IV took de Serres's advice seriously on a practical level. The Place Royale was established specifically to facilitate sericulture, at de Serres's suggestion, in 1605, forming the city's first planned square.[58]

Jacques Boyceau and the *Traité du Jardinage*

Men's ambition and greed have . . . left the care of the soil to those who are hard in body and in spirit. That's why so many are ignorant about the art of gardening, because they learn it from those already ignorant . . . never understanding the reason why things are done.

—Jacques Boyceau, *Traité du jardinage*[59]

Jacques Boyceau, a Calvinist landscape designer, worked for Henri IV in Paris, at Fontainebleau and St.-Germain, as well as shaping many other gardens and structures. Boyceau wanted to write a book that would describe the best use of the earth, viewing this ambition and his profession as a religious vocation deriving from Abel, who tilled the soil because of Adam's sin.[60] Boyceau associates gardening with a form of latter-day innocence ("for this reason, those who [garden] seem to lead a more blameless life"); the typically Calvinist-held post of *jardinier du roy* attests to theological merit. Boyceau writes himself into his book by placing his portrait (and two *devises*) at its beginning. Interestingly, however, his nephew, Menours, who later edited the work and added engravings of his own, claims that appearance and reality do not perfectly conjoin where Boyceau is concerned: there's more to him than meets the eye. As is the case with other Calvinist creators, the full and true story is found in their texts, rather than in image alone. The nephew explains, "I've represented his Visage according to my art and abilities, but his spirit and his knowledge are better depicted in his work."[61] Boyceau's text itself is painstakingly exact. One of its more striking features is the inclusion of marginalia reminiscent of the Geneva Bible. These marginalia serve a different purpose, however: rather than act expositorily, they provide definitions (as befits the Calvinist emphasis on the plain style), elucidating unfamiliar vocabulary so that the reader will be fully instructed. "Marcottes," for example, is defined in the margin as "shoots from the first growth: branches du premier iet,"[62] recalling Christ's parable of the well-pruned vine and its branches.

Boyceau's preface to *Traité du jardinage selon les raisons de la nature et de l'art* (1638) combines a concern to restructure the world with the need to acknowledge appropriately a godly heritage. Boyceau asks, "Will we speak about the wonders of our Lord without admiring His grandeur? Will we possess our inheritance without rendering homage to Him? . . . Will we rejoice in these things without singing hymns of praise to Him?"[63] However, an awareness of persecution and menace tempers the gardener's glory in the manifold marvels of the world; a prayer follows close upon the above quotation, voicing the imperiled Calvinist's concerns: "O God . . . With a strong saving hand / lend support to us in our sorrows."[64]

Reference to the Lord is a touchstone throughout the *Traité*, and biblical quotations abound; Boyceau's treatise on gardening is strewn with them. Minerals in the soil are discussed in light of their biblically assigned role; for instance, Boyceau says that Christ compared the apostles to salt, "saying to them, 'you are the salt of the earth, and without it nothing can have flavor.'"[65] The *Traité* acts like a biblical *summum*: it recalls Genesis, the creation story and the Garden of Eden. The biblical references work to reinscribe the fallen world within the biblical system, so that nothing eludes the determining force of the Word. For example, Boyceau asserts that one of the roles of the Holy Spirit is to teach man how to garden.[66] Boyceau maintains that if the earth is properly cultivated, man will be in harmony with God. Gardening is also the prototype for any construction; Boyceau notes, following Calvin, that nature is the avatar of all rightly ordered constructions.[67] Gardening and landscape design encourage interaction between man and nature, foster a nostalgia for the Garden of Eden, and promote realignment with scriptural standards. The intimacy of the man-nature relationship in a productive, soteric relationship is expressed in injunctions such as the following: "Dig down two feet, then put a handful of the earth that you find there into a glass. Moisten it with rain water or some other pure water, then let it settle. Drink the water that separates out from the sediment of earth at the bottom of the glass . . . If it tastes good, this earth will produce a rich harvest."[68]

The good harvest (from *le bon grain*) contrasts in Scripture with the failure of the crops due to the bad seed (*l'ivraie*). Since Calvinists call themselves true Christians and deny that Catholics are faithful to biblical mandates, Calvinists equate themselves with the good harvest. As with Palissy's grotto, for Boyceau the garden epitomizes that privileged, protected site for the Calvinist faithful. The designation of the appropriate garden site is of the utmost importance. Its selection corresponds with the Calvinist perception of election: "Thus, it is our responsibility to choose the right place for the Garden . . . and from this choice will come for us the greatest benefits."[69] The choice of gardener is equally important. Boyceau maintains that only a special few can do the job, and those must be formed rather than found. Boyceau's assertions echo the format of the Calvinist examination of conscience, in which the believer exercises a rigorous self-surveillance in order to ascertain his worthiness: "Shall we hire, for this great undertaking, the first man to come along, without getting to know him well so as to make a good choice? Even if we look very carefully, it will be very hard to find a man who possesses the requisite knowledge . . . It's for this reason that I think that we'll have to *make* the man we need, rather than be able to *find* such a one."[70]

Landscape gardeners are made, not born: they must be cultivated and cultivate themselves. They must have the right disposition of spirit.[71] The landscape gardener chosen will have qualities that fit the profile of the Calvinist architect: he will excel in portraiture, geometry, the mechanical arts, and architectural training, "so that," Boyceau tells us, "he may not fall into error."[72] He will be a young man, like Philibert's youthful heir to the kingdom in the *Architecture*.[73] In addition, this gardener will be a good and charismatic preacher. Proselytizing will be expected of him, so he can impart his wisdom and delegate his tasks to others: "the Gardener will have to know how to make his people work and how to teach them, because so many things can never be done by one man alone."[74]

Because nature is marked by the Fall, the Gardener must correct its failings and supplement its shortcomings, prefiguring the work of salvation. "This will be the secret of the sort of agriculture that we do: we will use our intelligence to apply things in order to help nature . . . knowing that nature is rich in many things from which we can take and choose to realize our needs . . . We will avoid vain curiosity, and limit ourselves to correcting nature's faults and defects."[75]

Like Palissy, Boyceau's gardener relies on artifice to perfect nature's shortcomings.[76] Nature is a tool or a material for soteric reconfiguration, not an autonomous force. The theoretical thrust of the Calvinist program places a grid over the world, so that its deviation from the ideal pattern may be discerned and remedied. "Gardens . . . shall be composed of alleyways, halls and cabinets in straight lines . . . your design should be made this way, and well-drawn-up. To do so, you must trace it on the ground, and follow those markings . . . to make the earth conform itself to the design . . . and thus evaporate the ills that can be found in it ordinarily."[77] Boyceau insists that these designs are individual to each designer, thereby obviating the need for artistic mediation from a third party. "If the Gardener is ignorant about design, he won't have any inventiveness or judgement . . . if he tries to borrow these from someone else, how will he ever be able to trace them onto the earth?"[78] He demonstrates the characteristic Calvinist distrust of intercessory figures such as priests or saints.

This ability to possess knowledge and assert one's point of view was something Calvinists were denied theologically. Consequently, one of the strategies that Calvinist architects employed against Catholic patrons involved playing with the perspective, or the position of the interpreter, of the structure they erected. Boyceau disjoins what is seen from the ground from what is perceived by looking down onto a garden surface. The point of view is crucial to accurate perception: a stance on the moral high ground is the best vantage from which to view the harmonious disposition of the garden's components. "Great pleasure can be gained from viewing the gardens from up high . . . You really can't see their design from below. The disposition and divisions of the Garden being viewed from on high, to a quick glance it appears as a unified entity, of which can then be discerned the diverse ornaments. You may judge how a perfect correspondence is established among the parts. This unity gives more pleasure than the isolated segments of the Garden."[79] The details of the Garden must be suited to the Garden itself. However, Calvinist architects superinscribed their structures with details not always in keeping with the structure, translating in code the Calvinists' feeling of being out of place. Boyceau implies a similar disjunctive use of detail: "other forms will find their place in Gardens, if these forms are arranged according to the nature of the place."[80] If such is not the case, something may be going on beneath the surface.

Boyceau completes his textual exposition of gardens with a series of stylized engravings intended to function as "patterns" for garden layouts. Nearly all these designs, however ornate, possess a common simple spine: they are cruciform and radiate out from a central point. For instance, the "Parterre des costes de la fontaine du Mercure a St. Germain en Laye" is circumscribed within the letters of alpha and omega, along a cruciform plan. This reduction of variety to a uniform format is consonant with Boyceau's Calvinism. Itself perceived as aberrant, Calvinism, particularly in the more rigid, standardized form that the *epigoni* (such as Theodore Beza, Boyceau's contemporary) developed, aimed at regularizing religious practice, paring it to its essential elements. In his concern for order Boyceau not only describes his sentiment of being out of order as a Calvinist in Catholic France but also prescribes a salubrious order that he would wish on the world, via garden layouts that resemble systematic Ramist diagrams of relationships.[81] This concern for correct ordering causes Boyceau to state that garden structures will work best "when they are well and architecturally-ordered";[82] that structural idioms should not be mixed ("I don't expect you to mingle them together confusedly");[83] and that grotesque burgeoning of visual metaphors in grottoes is to be subordinated to a strict underlying schema of order (one should "arrange them in a good architectural order").[84] This concern for ordering, and the space devoted to identifying it, paradoxically designate a prevailing state of disorder, one that must be distrusted and corrected.

Jacques Androuet du Cerceau: The Architectural Writings

[to Catherine de Médicis:]
Madame, if [only] the dangerous times and troubles now taking place had not prevented me from visiting the châteaux and houses that your Majesty wants included in the books that she has commissioned me to compile and design . . .
    —Jacques Androuet du Cerceau, *Perspective* (1576)[85]

Jacques I Androuet du Cerceau (1520–1608?) wrote several manuals and many books theorizing architecture. He also designed furniture, created wall hangings, and designed and engraved many architectural books of blueprints and actual structures.[86] Du Cerceau was the only son of a wine merchant in Paris. After his father's death he traveled around the Loire Valley, working in Tours and Orléans; he eventually married Jeanne Vannier. In 1545, he secured letters of patent and royal *droits d'auteur* for his design books, having been named by Marguerite d'Angoulême to the important post of *architecte désigné*, an honorary pension and title. In 1551, he collaborated on Henri II's entrée into Orléans, helping to design and construct triumphal corteges and trompe l'oeil scenery. In 1559, he published the first of three *Livres d'architecture*. Book 1 dealt with practical architectural considerations, while Books 2 and 3, following Calvinist norms, discussed the detail found on structures: doors, windows, and miscellany, like fountains. Around 1561, he was awarded the title *architecte du roi*. In general, he did more design and engraving work than actual work on construction. His sketches of views of St.-Germain-en-Laye, the Tuileries palace, the church of La Madeleine in Montargis, and many others astound contemporary art historians with their "extravagances" and "irregularities." He seemed to feel entitled to revise existing structures as he pleased: on many of the engravings, additions, subtractions, details, even entire floor-plans, simply are not rendered accurately.[87] While effecting all these unauthorized changes, du Cerceau justified his "corrections," making his version the definitive architectural text: "Moreover, having well studied this little book, you will have the knowledge not only of all books ever written about this, but, even more, when you look at sketches of masonry work, you'll be able to judge for yourself whether the masters or the laborers made them."[88]

Du Cerceau characterizes his texts as truthful "mirrors" of how things *really* are.[89] He is concerned with truth telling, rectifying distortion, continuing (or exacerbating) his predecessors' vision: an architectural plain style, if somewhat convoluted in the way he conceives it. The author of many books on various aspects of architecture and construction—including studies of specific aspects, such as the use of grotesques in ornamentation or how perspective works—du Cerceau was an innovator who made significant contributions to the genre of the architectural manual through his insistence on the frequent inclusion of personal anecdotes, a tendency we have also witnessed, to a somewhat lesser degree, in the architectural manuals of Philibert de l'Orme. While Philibert was the first French author to pen an architectural manual (following Serlio), du Cerceau was the first French architect to use Philibert and Serlio's "formula" to produce and edit "des livres des modèles," or pattern books.[90]

Du Cerceau's emphasis on personal experience may derive from the highly individualized Calvinist tradition of "witnessing," offering a public *confession de foy* of the power of God in one's life. In the *Plus excellens bastiments*, for example, du Cerceau recounts a conversation consisting of "paroles ironiques": "whenever he chanced upon a well-maintained building in his travels, the King would wisecrack: 'This one's not one of mine.'"[91] Prior to 1560, architectural manuals usually maintained a neutral tone, letting readers make their own decisions. However, as a Protestant partisan, du Cerceau adopted a theologically directive stance toward architecture. Another way in which he added his own stamp to the genre of the architectural manual was by using copperplate engraving: Serlio, Philibert, and other predecessors had all used illustrations rendered by the less precise *gravure sur bois*.[92]

Du Cerceau is uncompromising about his Calvinist beliefs and the persecution he experienced because of them. After the Edict of Amboise, which only permitted Protestant nobility the freedom to worship in curtailed areas, du Cerceau, a self-avowed Calvinist, "had no choice but to flee."[93] Many of du Cerceau's family, all Calvinists, were killed during the

War of 1563.[94] His house, which he had built for himself in Orléans in 1535, was twice sacked, and he states that he was "forced to resign his post as architect to the King because of [his] religion."[95] He found shelter at the court of Renée de France, in Montargis. In the *Premier recueil d'ornements et arabesques grotesques* (1566), he speaks frankly of this troubled time. Du Cerceau remained with Renée from 1565 to 1575 and was retained, upon her death, by her daughter Anne d'Este (who, although not Protestant, honored her mother's Calvinist sympathies). Du Cerceau raised his three sons, Baptiste, Jacques, and Charles, in the trade and in the faith. They eventually received his architectural *fonctions*, which were transmitted hereditarily.[96] In the preface to his *Premier recueil*, he talks about the effect of religion on his career: "I set off to visit those private dwellings formerly mentioned, and to begin my work on them. But the miserable troubles [of the Wars of Religion] started in this kingdom, which caused me so much harm and loss, and similarly to all my family, that since then I've had no means or ability to fulfill my intentions."[97]

Historians have noted that it is odd that even after the St. Bartholomew's Day Massacre, du Cerceau dedicated three of his works to Catherine de Médicis, whom, along with her son Charles IX, Protestants held responsible for the bloodshed: "What are we to make of this [choice of dedicatee]? Should we see in it a sign of religious indifference, or a testimonial of such poverty that [du Cerceau] was utterly dependent on the Court?"[98] Du Cerceau's Calvinism is beyond question, but it was inconceivable in this hostile religious climate that he not seek to mollify the Court, out of a very real need for self-preservation. During this period, other Calvinist architects were frequently denied commissions and thus inevitably experienced a dwindling clientele. To Charles IX, to whom du Cerceau dedicated the *Livre pour bastir aux champs*, he complains, "Sire, I had no way . . . to transport myself to those sites so that I could make the drawings of them that you asked of me."[99] Du Cerceau reacts against any constraint on his projects and expresses this in spatial terms.[100] His architectural renderings also react to spatial curtailment through a very personalized approach to the drawing, which results in revision, invention, and extravagant departures from the model.[101] His designs are remarkable for their "imaginative qualities, their freedom of execution, and emphasis on detail."[102] In his *Leçons de perspective positive* (1576), conceived to accompany the first volume of *Les plus excellens bastiments*, the "variety of methods of illustration and the flexible use of perspective are among the most striking characteristics of the collection."[103] His spirit of improvisation, the multiple possibilities for application of his designs, and their innovative conception all attest to a heuristic focus and an insistence on attaining some latitude for Calvinist expression.[104]

When the hostilities—at least in military form—ceased, du Cerceau finally published the book to which he refers above; this is the *Les plus excellens bastiments de France*, a collection of engravings of already-existing structures. In the preface to this collection, du Cerceau relentlessly rehearses the devastation that Catholics have wreaked on France. The *Livre* is a monument to what has managed, nevertheless, to survive the holocaust: it is a testimony to the salvaging act he performs as a Calvinist. "After it pleased God to send to us through your agency the peace that everyone had so desired, I thought that I could do nothing better than to bring to light the first book of the exquisite Buildings of this kingdom, hoping that we poor Frenchmen (whose eyes and minds are filled these days with nothing but desolation, ruins, and the sack of cities brought about by the former Wars), will take some pleasure and comfort in contemplating herein a part of these beautiful and excellent structures which still do remain in France today."[105]

On a similar note, in the preface to the *Livre des edifices antiques romains*, he asserts, "I've always been of the opinion that . . . the mother of all arts and all wisdom is peace . . . long wars and sedition kill the arts . . . this can be seen especially clearly in architecture . . . civil wars . . . make it so that great marvels can no longer easily be seen around us . . . these buildings are buried."[106] However, the *Livre* has another function for du Cerceau. "Leafing through its pages, Catherine de Médicis could not help but be aware, with a mixture of pleasure and ruefulness, especially with the second volume, that over half of the buildings remained at the project phase, and had progressed very little towards realization, or not at all."[107] The Calvinist architect boldly indicts the failure of the Catholic project of self-monumentalizing.

When du Cerceau is able to resume his official architectural functions, he makes a revealing plea to the king, in which anti-Spanish sentiment is directed toward foreign architects, but in which can also be discerned a Calvinist assertion that Huguenots, unlike imported Spanish architects, are not "estrangers": they are part of the realm and should be treated as such, given commissions for work, allowed latitude in their architectural expression, and preferred over foreign architects. "I've designed, drawn and engraved . . . [these things] to the glory and adornment of your kingdom, which can be seen daily to increase with sumptuous and beautiful buildings, so that henceforth your subjects shall have no need to travel to foreign countries to see any better. And now, besides, it will please Your Majesty excellently to upkeep your good workers who are of this nation, and no longer to hire strangers . . . Your very obedient subject and servant." [108]

Another way in which du Cerceau's Calvinism informs his architectural projects is by causing him to express concerns that simply are not found in contemporary Catholic-authored architectural manuals such as those of La Primatice. In his statement "Au lecteur" in *Les plus excellens*, du Cerceau describes his occupation in biblical and theological terms. [109] He identifies himself as one of the elect, asserting that God has chosen him to be an architect, and expresses the need to transmit his craft to an heir who will witness to God's bounty. "Divine Providence wanted to establish order among rational creatures, so that each, according to the gifts and grace which God has given to him, would leave for his descendants some testimony of his vocation." [110]

Du Cerceau's statement recalls the similar iconographic representation of a biblical inheritance passed on by Philibert de l'Orme to a youthful recipient, showing the similarity of Calvinist concerns and a like manner of illustrating these issues. [111] Echoing Philibert's and Palissy's reference to the parable of the talents, du Cerceau sets himself the task of analyzing "in depth distortions of construction and faults in architecture, scorning those who build only in order to glorify themselves ostentatiously." [112] This latter group, of course, is composed of Catholics, criticized by du Cerceau. [113] Like other Protestant architectural manuals, too, du Cerceau's possesses a pedagogical, pragmatic thrust: "even the title of his book attests to the reader that one is in the presence of an intelligible and highly practical demonstration rather than that of a theoretical work; one is in the presence of a sort of technical prospectus." [114] Stylistically and thematically, as well, du Cerceau clearly associates himself with other Calvinist architects. In his third *Livre d'architecture*, for example, he follows the divisions and stratification of land assignment recommended by Charles Estienne in *La maison rustique* twenty years earlier. [115]

Many Calvinist architects were related to one another by marriage. [116] The others knew one another very well and probably saw each other on a daily basis. For example, the Calvinist architect Salomon de Brosse attended the Reformed church in Verneuil, where the du Cerceau family lived. [117] Further, Salomon de Brosse was much influenced in his design work by Jacques II Androuet du Cerceau, copying from him the lines for the Palais de Luxembourg from the Château de Verneuil. [118] Later, Francis

Hotman, one of the Calvinist *tyrannomach* writers, married into the du Cerceau–de Brosse family, taking Madeleine du Cerceau as wife in 1634.[119]

Where they were not genealogically or geographically related, they were stylistically related. For instance, du Cerceau engraved the plates for books made by Jacques Besson, a Genevan naturalized Protestant and maker of *ingenia*, or automata, who fled to England in 1572.[120] In a poetic epigraph penned for Hugues de Sambin's work, *De la diversité des termes* (1572), the Dijonnais poet Estienne Tabourot Des Accords suggests a link between Sambin, a Calvinist architect from Dijon, and du Cerceau. Here, Des Accords alludes to a similarity between the two architects, stressing the elaborate ornamentation and detail of their "termes," truncated human figures employed as pillars or buttresses. "This gratuitous accumulation of detail . . . results largely from imitation in Sambin's works . . . in particular, borrowings from Jacques du Cerceau are incontestable. The extravagance of the majority of the compositions engraved by this Dijonnais artist surpass the bounds of verisimilitude and render them impossible to realize."[121]

Calvinists are also concerned with the architectural assignment of space. Du Cerceau, like other Calvinist architects, customarily represents buildings "in the middle of a vast space, while contemporary geometers and mathematicians who, fascinated by the *camera oscura* in France and Italy of the sixteenth century as in Holland of the seventeenth century, choose rather to show interiors, or landscapes, in order to illustrate issues of perspective."[122] The same concern to enlarge and redefine space appears in the Protestant plans for urban restructuring designed by Sully and Henri IV. Finally, du Cerceau's work "always demonstrates his conscience and his disdain for conventions."[123] Rather than aim at precision in his depictions, his goal is always a useful and informed interpretation of the structure: his personalized, Protestant, interpretation.[124] In *De la perspective*, for example, each engraving requires a different sort of viewing, one that draws the viewer's eyes directively along certain lines representing the right gaze, the appropriate way to view and construe. One plate (*leçon lx*) uses triangulated perspectival lines as metaphysical directional arrows that draw the eye upward. The buildings at the top of the engraving seem to float in another space. A line traces an itinerary through a street, through trees, over a bridge, then follows the perspective indicators, ending at the top right of the sheet, appearing lost in the clouds. The movement is in and through terrestrial structures, ultimately leaving them behind, to inhabit a celestial structure that resembles a temple. Just so, Calvinists move through, and out of, the maze of the world, to God.

20. A plate from Jacques Androuet du Cerceau's studies on perspective. Du Cerceau played with different renderings of perspective in order to set up juxtapositions between metaphysical and terrestrial realms. Du Cerceau, *Leçons de perspective positive* (1576), lx. By permission of the Avery Architectural and Fine Arts Library, Columbia University in the City of New York.

A Protestant intertextuality links these second-generation Calvinist structures. This sort of intertextuality is implied, for instance, by one architectural historian who refers to du Cerceau's engravings as "thèmes et variations,"[125] terms that recall the literary process of translation from mother tongue to second language and back again. Calvinism is thus perceived to constitute its own architectural lexicon. Du Cerceau also perceives architecture as text; throughout the *Architecture* (1559), he states what he means by structures and how he wants them interpreted. This is a form of exposition, a technique typical of Calvinist sermons, which through exegesis strove always to relate the biblical message to present-day circumstances. Du Cerceau thoroughly describes it in an annotated table of contents, listing "architecture" as an entry separate from his compendium of images, as something deserving of interpretation in its own right.

Thus, in his prefatory and dedicatory materials, in autobiographical digressions, and in his conception and execution of design, du Cerceau represents himself not only as a skilled architect but also as a committed Huguenot, one for whom Calvinism and architecture compose inextricable forms of theological expression. His commitment to his religious beliefs often directly accounts for apparent "errors" in his designs of existing monuments. In the case of Vincennes, for example, du Cerceau puzzles critics by omitting in his engraving the chapel that had actually been erected there.[126] This is not an error but rather a tendentious omission with Calvinist significance: the refusal to represent something unacceptable to du Cerceau's creed.

Du Cerceau is perhaps best known for his engravings of the celebrated monuments of France, most of which were constructed by Philibert de l'Orme and Jean Bullant.[127] Du Cerceau's revisions of those models, especially when the building is still standing, are strikingly idiosyncratic: he invariably redesigns the building through his illustration, often significantly altering the structure, "insert[ing] in this book designs embodying ideas which he himself would have liked to have been carried out rather than those of the actual designer of the building in question."[128] Sometimes repetitions of his vision for a structure proliferate, insisting on an

alternative vision for the construction; for example, he repeats the plan of Philibert de l'Orme's chapel at Anet at least three times in three different ways, none of which are accurate. "Du Cerceau is often unreliable in completing unfinished buildings according to his own fancy and in adding ornaments of his own invention to existing structures."[129] His engravings act as revisions, contradictions, corrections, exaggerations, or politicizations of the actual structure. Some of the changes that du Cerceau visualizes directly contradict his models' goals—as when, at St.-Léger, he revised Philibert's concept by flanking the seventeen arcades with two full *travées* of unequal height, amplifying the dimensions of the chapel and decentering its door so that it opens onto a gallery pillar. This change amounts to a metaphor for constraint: the door dead-ends by opening on to an obstruction. Many of du Cerceau's engraved revisions of structures were uniformly characterized by a waste of space,[130] as though the space he lacked in reality he sought to compensate for by spending it profligately in his idealized drawings. In addition, sometimes he fabulated structures, attempting to pass them off as real.[131] These constructions have been characterized by art historians as "dream buildings," "anti-classical," "anti-architectural," and "essentially decorative and fantastic."[132] Such productions suggest the desire to circumvent constraint, to compensate for some lack in a predecessor's building, or to imagine an unprecedented response to a specific need.

Generally, du Cerceau's revisions were intentional and systematic; he methodically transformed his models.[133] Such reworking is ideologically and theologically tendentious. The puzzling technique of portraying a structure as other than it was represents a quintessentially Protestant perspective: all earthly structures or beings stand in need of reformation—be it architectural or theological—and all appearance is subject to the critique engendered by its juxtaposition with true meaning. The revision of existing spatial assignment, drawing, or structure was practiced by many Calvinist architects, invariably with a theological agenda.

Because so many of the alternative versions that du Cerceau tries to pass off as accurate and representative are skewed, they enact visually an encoding of their models. He criticizes the circumstances of the structures' conception and the compromises entailed: "many of these combinations and variants have such glaring faults of proportion that they stand out . . . many of them could be conceived as the result of experiments that du Cerceau was conducting precisely to throw into higher relief some of their components . . . the incompatibility of certain elements and the need to, in this case, have recourse to another sort of combination is evident."[134]

One of the results of such experimentation can be an increased symmetry aimed at establishing concentric protective circles. This has the effect of extending an illusion of interiority to the external structure itself, establishing a double line of defense: "The concept of symmetry . . . takes as its corollary an attempt at systematizing the allocation of enclosures. The internal organization projects itself outward to a complementary encircling wall."[135] Such a defensive "masking strategy" was employed by Calvinist theologians, architects, artists, editors, and publishers, as a nicodemite strategy of dissimulation and revision.[136]

Clearly, many factors could account for the way in which du Cerceau appropriated these structures and reworked them, as it were, without permission, audaciously asserting their authenticity despite proof to the contrary. "Far from copying in slavish fashion the model before him, he feels its potential so strongly that he reconceives it, as it were, from the ground floor up, as he would have started out fresh for one of his own creations."[137] Some of the reasons are strictly architectural. However, something about du Cerceau's structures—and those of other Calvinist architects—persistently defies easy explanation. "[Look at] all the ornamentation . . . the archivaults, the garlands, the masks . . . We know that much of this detail work was common to other architects; nevertheless, much of this is attributable to the personal accents of the artist . . . [and] a fantastical imagination so bizarre."[138] Given the similarities among the Calvinist architects, it is possible to infer a feeling of belonging to an oppressed minority. This perception leads du Cerceau to treat his predecessors' works, themselves originating equally from within that marginal community and from those conditions of external constraint, as if they were his own. In revising them, he was simply better equipping a structure to function for the good of the Calvinist community, by facilitating the expression of the Calvinist agenda and the subversion of Catholic dominance. In addition, by essentially publishing a catalogue of how *not* to do things, accompanied by revisions that rectify the original error, du Cerceau recalls the pair of allegories that summarize Philibert's thesis in the *Architecture*. A compendium of models not to imitate is a tip-off that the author aims at some other, unavowed end: a critique of the century, perhaps, and a restitution of a metatextual criterion of rightness (or a metaphysical standard of righteousness).[139]

One way to highlight the difference between appearance and reality, an effective way to criticize a dominant order, is through tricks of perspective. In this, du Cerceau follows Calvinist designers such as Palissy who used trompe l'oeil for similar reasons. In *Leçons de perspective positive*, he develops a theory of how perspective works, distinguishing between baseline (*ligne-terre*) and *points accidentaux*, those perceived by looking at a structure on a slant (*de biais*) rather than straight-on. The viewer is required to shift or alter his stance in order to perceive accurately the real, presumably occulted significance of a structure. The logical consequence of this flexible, movable perspective is that the monolithic viewpoint assumed by a member of the dominant group will not allow meaning to be grasped but will instead convey only a superficial impression. The *terre-ligne* is the lowest point of a structure, and it never moves. Everything appears to be established upon it, but more is there than meets the eye: "In my conception of 'positive perspective,' the more that the stages of a drawing come near our visual line, the shorter they become. This is why you can't see on them what is figured on them so largely in drawings."[140] An optical illusion ensues, demonstrating that designs and structures must be approached with suspicion because they require decoding. The eye has many choices for constructing interpretive patterns: "from each of the four views one can consider three main locations, upper, middle and lower, so named for the position of the eye that is doing the looking."[141] This plethora of possibilities simply further facilitates the Calvinist architect's options for playing with, and parodying, normative structures by slightly skewing or reorienting them. Depending on who is doing the looking, and on his point of view, the visual line will differ: "your visual line is situated in the second plane . . . this slant causes specific accidental points to develop . . . You will view things from this angle."[142]

The theological implication that can be drawn from this architectural discussion is that Calvinists have a different ideological "visual line" than do Catholics.[143] Calvinists, therefore, starting from a different standpoint, will necessarily conceive of things differently, just as the viewer in one of du Cerceau's demonstrations of perspective will create his own visual line and, from the accidental points that arise, will begin to structure the building anew, for himself, based on his own perceptions: "you'll find other aspects that will lead you to want to draw them for yourself on the design."[144] Interestingly, these shifts in visual approach culminate in a process of "drawing-on," a hands-on reconceptualizing of the structure reminiscent of Philibert's allusion to graffiti scribbling.

Several of du Cerceau's engravings of structures illustrate the results produced by the different combinations ensuing from the distinction between *ligne-terre* and *points accidentaux*. One plate (*planche lvii*) of the *Ar-*

chitecture represents a temple's columns as slightly off-kilter on their bases, suggesting an instability in the structure. Another engraving (*planche lviii*) playfully speculates about the dynamic quality that structures possess: one of the statues walks off and away from his pediment, while Neptune and another figure to the left turn to stare incredulously. The statue has his back to the viewer as he stalks away. He refuses to be included in the illustration, to be framed or labeled by it. In turning his back on the viewer, defying deciphering, he mimes the Calvinist strategy of sealing significance from all but the eyes of the informed. In another illustration (*planche lxxxvi*), du Cerceau offers a series of façades pulled back sequentially, as if in an anatomy, to reveal the front all the way to the inner chamber. The "flaying" technique of the diagram implies that reality is serial, never unitarily grasped. Onion-like layers lead the viewer away from a first apprehension of the image, ever receding, to a hidden reality.

Another clue to du Cerceau's Calvinist-informed architecture is the utopian character of much of his work; it has been noted that *Les plus excellens*'s "chief importance . . . lies in recording sixteenth century buildings which were . . . altered or never built."[145] This decision to display those structures despite their state of imperfection was not reached thoughtlessly. The curtailment of space results in a halt being called to a building project; alterations are the consequence of a patron's dissatisfaction with an existing structure. The analogy with Calvinism's lot in France is evident. Another example of du Cerceau's Calvinist architectural idiom is his frequent incorporation of irregularities;[146] yet another characteristic is architectural iconoclasm. Du Cerceau's rendering of Verneuil is in some measure a destructive act: he shatters architectural canons, destroying its classical potential through the disruption of minor architectural features; he also slathers the exterior with exuberant ornament.[147] It looks as though he has populated Bullant's structure with his own buildings in the blueprint *Planum veteris*; the incorporation of a partly cloud-shrouded building in the upper right-hand corner of the engraving *Designatio orthographiae* of Verneuil acts like a revisionist signature, recalling du Cerceau's playing with perspective in *Leçon lx* of *Perspective*. Sometimes iconoclasm operates, as it were, in reverse: rather than eliminating features, du Cerceau includes details that simply are, in reality, nonexistent: the *Facies exterior* of Verneuil, as du Cerceau himself admits in his notation, "was not completed," yet here he displays an ornate and sufficient version.[148]

At Gaillon, he lowers the roofs excessively, making an intentionally distorted design; at Charleval, the elevation of the front courtyard has

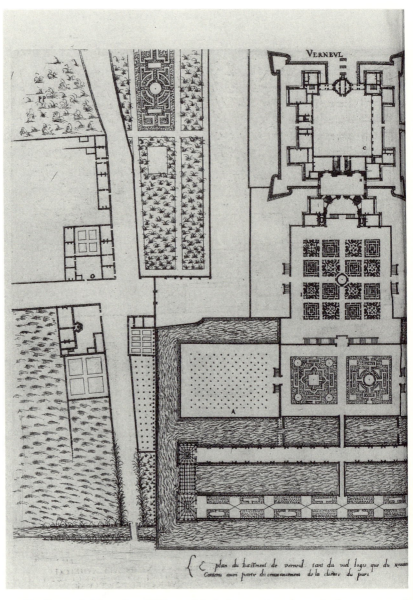

VERNEVL

{ C plan du bastiment de verneul tant du vies logis que du nouuau
Contens aum partie du commencement de la clature du parc

21. Du Cerceau's blueprint of Verneuil includes portions from the former, as well
as the newly built structure, and creates architectural inconsistencies where they
were not present before. There is an intriguing hint of unruliness in his quickly
sketched thatch marks and loopy lines indicating vegetation, especially where these

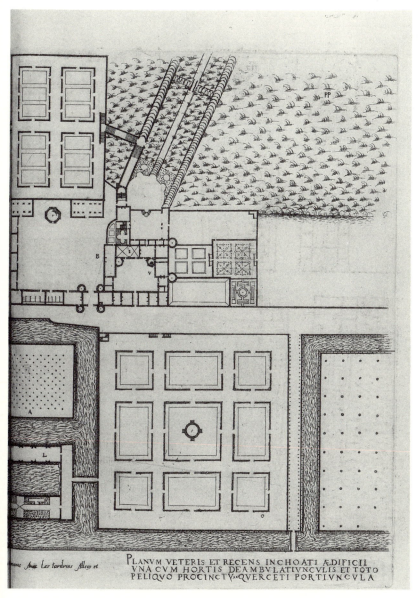

PLANVM VETERIS ET RECENS INCHOATI ÆDIFICII
VNA CVM HORTIS DEAMBVLATIVNCVLIS ET TOTO
PELIQVO PROCINCTV QVERCETI PORTIVNCVLA

extend over the orderly paths they are supposed to demarcate, as in the far left of the image and in the upper right-hand corner, as though defying the fledgling absolutist nation-state. Du Cerceau, "Planum veteris," *Les plus excellens bastiments de France* (1576), 45. By permission of the Folger Shakespeare Library.

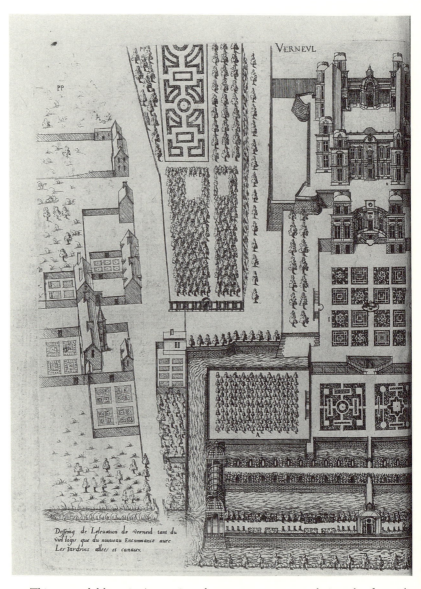

Desseing de Lelcumion de Verneul tant du
viel logis que du nouueau Encommance auec
Les Iardrins allees et canaux

22. This second blueprint/engraving shows structures populating the formerly
blank spaces, but not all the structures conform to the initial specifications. The
gate opening onto an *allée* at the top far right, for instance, no longer retains the
empty lozenge shape of the "Planum veteris," but is now bisected by a transverse
structure and terminated by a curved gate. Other, unplanned structures have been
added, such as the continuation of the roofed structure across the alleyway between
the two groups of buildings originally planned at the far left. Note du Cerceau's

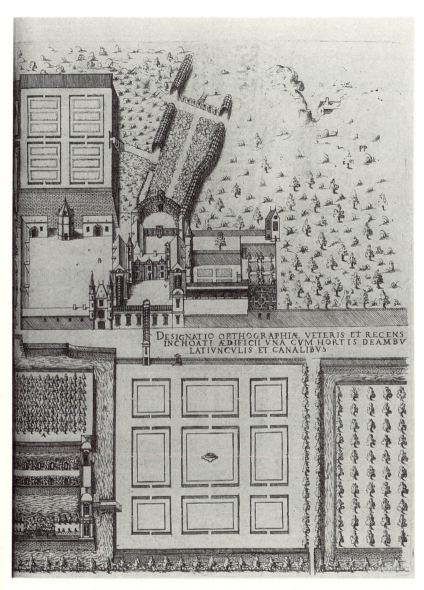

DESIGNATIO ORTHOGRAPHIÆ VETERIS ET RECENS
INCHOATI ÆDIFICII VNA CVM HORTIS DEAMBV
LATIVNCVLIS ET CANALIBVS

"signature," the half-sketched building floating in a cloudlike ornament at the top far right. As in his plate from the *leçons* in perspective, du Cerceau seems to have doodled this structure in as a sort of metaphysical marker—it may be a church, or *temple*—that stands in tension with the rest of the layout. Du Cerceau, "Designatio orthographiae," *Les plus excellens bastiments de France* (1576), 46. By permission of the Folger Shakespeare Library.

23. This is the chapel at Anet as Philibert de l'Orme designed and built it. It contrasts sharply with the next illustration, a revision by du Cerceau. Photograph by Randall Balmer.

no relationship to the rest of the drawing and is unrealistically placed; at Anet, du Cerceau omits the chapel in his orthogonal view and takes the rest of the drawing out of context, even turning the sculptured stag's head in the wrong direction.[149] In fact, du Cerceau's revisions of Anet amount to actual iconoclasm, especially obvious when his and Philibert's drawings are juxtaposed: light streams in unhindered through the central window as he knocks out Philibert's stained glass window; he minimizes the eucharistic table so that it is now a lectern; takes saints' statues out of their niches — and, just as blatantly, leaves the niches empty. His cross-sectional engraving, *Desseing du dedans de la chappelle*, leads relentlessly upward, nearly eliminating the minuscule space for human performance of religiosity. Its "flaying" technique seems to indict the emptiness of ritual. At Amboise, du Cerceau depicts the Hurtault tower as an open amphitheater, an astonishing distortion that has led critics to speculate that such exaggeration can only be a *clin d'oeil*, although they still wonder why. And, finally, for the Louvre, "the monumental incarnation of the hegemonic ambitions held by the French monarch," du Cerceau provides a "disappointing," almost schematic rendering, criticizing the monarchy's arrogance.[150]

In addition, *impossibilia* often mark his renderings; at Verneuil, for example, the front entryway simply cannot work, because he leaves the stairs incomplete.[151] At St. Germain, du Cerceau alters Philibert's structure by blocking the windows (*Scenographia*), and his revision of Philibert's chapel there (*La Chappelle*) reduces the structure to a lacy confection of fanciful arabesques, hardly a serious enough structure for religious worship — a form of Calvinist iconoclasm through overornamentation. Thus, du Cerceau batters standards and uses ornament and unusual or excessive detail to convey an ulterior meaning.[152] This ornamentation is often improbable or exaggerated; du Cerceau tends toward monstrous mixtures, such as human busts, dogs' legs, and butterfly wings, and, like Jean Duvet, another Calvinist architect,[153] his human figures are frequently abnormally elongated, or figures of conflicting scale are contained in the same elevation. As though exploring all his options — a utopian menu of possibilities, which the Calvinist architect did not in reality possess — du Cerceau "attempt[ed] to exhaust the variations of which a theme was capable."[154] He could only do so in theory, however, or in the space of a text. This proliferation of

24. Du Cerceau's revision of Philibert's constructed reality at Anet is very different. The juxtaposition of the two images shows how second-generation Calvinists
radicalized many predecessor structures. Du Cerceau has acted like an iconoclastic
Calvinist, bashing out the stained glass window, removing saints' statues from their
niches, and, even more defiantly, retaining the niches, empty, as a way of showing that such representations are devoid of sacred power. The eucharistic table has
been minimized to resemble a lectern, the cross is reduced to miniature display, and
the revisionist du Cerceau has knocked out the confining side walls of the chapel,
moving toward a very Protestant, auditorium-like space such as that erected by
Salomon de Brosse at Charenton. Photograph from a slide by Randall Balmer.

weird forms and odd positioning suggests a virtuoso playing with space,
a space that can only exist in the mind's eye: plastic manipulation of real
space is not possible for the Calvinist, to whom space is denied, so he resorts to textual modeling. Significantly, du Cerceau was poorly regarded
during the apogee of French absolutism, probably because he was a known
Calvinist. On 12 May 1672, the Royal Academy of Architecture stated that
his works "are more dangerous than useful, because of the unwarranted
liberties that he takes in his inventions."[155] By this date, of course, Protestantism had been virtually eradicated from France.

Spatial and structural considerations in a peculiar Calvinist vein were
transmitted genealogically: du Cerceau had a son, Jacques II Androuet,
who worked as an architect under Henri IV and who, unlike his king, remained Protestant. In many ways, Jacques II perpetuated the program and
preoccupations of his Calvinist father. He reprinted the two volumes of
his father's *Les plus excellens bastiments de France* in exactly the same format
in 1607. He imitated not only his father's style but also that of Philibert de
l'Orme and Salomon de Brosse. Jacques II left Tours and went to Paris in
1594 with Henri IV. There, he began work on the new building program
at the Tuileries, for which "his design goes back . . . to his father's drawings . . . and to Bullant."[156] Jacques II was responsible for the alterations
and additions to the Château of Montceaux-en-Brie, modifications which
Philibert de l'Orme had begun. Like his father, Jacques II emphasized irregularity and disproportion.[157] However, he differed from his father when
he turned to Jean Bullant as a source, choosing from the work of this Calvinist predecessor "more architectonic designs . . . [and] a more mannerist
vocabulary,"[158] as can be seen at Chantilly and the Tuileries pavilion. Not
surprisingly, he received much contemporary criticism of his work from
Catholic audiences.[159] Jacques II embodies the genealogical continuation

25. Du Cerceau's third engraving of Verneuil lifts all structures fully from their foundations, realizing the indications on the blueprint and revising many of those. The representation is not fully faithful to Bullant's constructed product. Du Cerceau, "Facies exterior," *Les plus excellens bastiments de France* (1576), 48. By permission of the Folger Shakespeare Library.

of the Huguenot architectural concern and idiom. The du Cerceau family is one of the best examples of this phenomenon: Jacques I drew and engraved the elevations for the court façades of the Louvre in 1576, but it was his son, Baptiste, who finally finished the building for Henri III in 1580.

Salomon and Isaac de Caus were also Calvinist creators, landscape designers famed for their commitment to their faith and renowned for the extravagance and audacity of their design work. Originally from northern France, the *pays* de Caux, Salomon had worked under the Italian architect Bernardo Buontalenti on the gorgeous gardens at Pratolino. While the de Caus family was Protestant, their works were nonetheless commissioned by Catholics throughout Europe, such as the Hapsburg archduke Albert. Such commissions continued, despite religious tensions, because "men as gifted as de Caus were in short supply."[160] Salomon's endeavors were continued and perpetuated by his son Isaac, who reprinted his writings and edited them in England as part of an introduction to his own work. The Calvinist architectural lineage thus stretched through the generations. In fact, the two great architectural families during the reigns of Henri IV

26. In "Scenographia interioris," du Cerceau shows St. Germain from the interior, as befits the Calvinist emphasis on interiority. He has oddly skewed the bottom central right portion so as to show the interior of the arcades; they are torqued in a structurally impossible way that is also dissonant with the presentation of the remainder of the structural section. The building is thus viewed from a plurality of viewpoints, as though inscribing different perspectives in a single construction. Du Cerceau is known for such *impossibilia*. In "Aedificium novum," however, he seems to revert to stressing symmetry; he represents the front part of the structure as fluid and harmonious, from a frontal and unified perspective. Du Cerceau, *Les plus excellens bastiments de France* (1576), 37. By permission of the Folger Shakespeare Library.

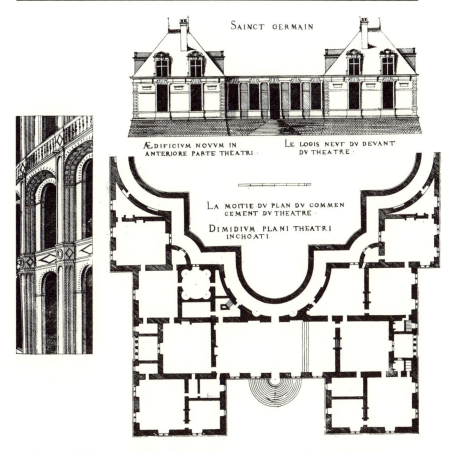

SAINCT GERMAIN

ÆDIFICIVM NOVVM IN
ANTERIORE PARTE THEATRI ·

LE LOGIS NEVF DV DEVANT
DV THEATRE ·

LA MOITIE DV PLAN DV COMMEN
CEMENT DV THEATRE ·

DIMIDIVM PLANI THEATRI
INCHOATI

and Louis XIII were solidly Huguenot: two were du Cerceau's grandsons, Jean du Cerceau (1590–1649), son of Baptiste du Cerceau, and Salomon de Brosse, son of du Cerceau's daughter Julienne and her husband, Jehan de Brosse.[161]

Salomon de Brosse and the Temple at Charenton

Salomon de Brosse was born into a Protestant family, of which many members were Reformed pastors. Julienne, his mother, was the daughter of Jacques I Androuet du Cerceau. He was born in Verneuil, where the château constituted the center of the architectural activity of the du Cerceau workshop. Verneuil was also a Protestant town.[162] During the Wars of Religion, the de Brosse family endured much persecution. In his autobiography, en-

27. Du Cerceau's engraved version of the chapel at St. Germain offers an isolated structure adrift on an ornamental ground fashioned of fanciful arabesques, volutes, and puffy, shrubbery-like forms. His interest seems to lie more in the composition of the background, which requires at least one-half of the space of the engraving, than in the structure itself. The quirky, quickly drawn lines at the top of the engraving suggest glyphs. Du Cerceau, "La Chappelle," at St. Germain. Photograph from a slide by Randall Balmer.

crypting his concerns by writing in the third person singular of himself, de Brosse states, "as was the case with so many Huguenots . . . persecution being severe . . . his family fled . . . taking various routes and changing location frequently."[163] Persecution resumed in 1584 after the Edict of Nemours, and from 1588 to 1592 de Brosse's name featured on a governmental list designed to monitor Protestant activity within the kingdom. After the promulgation of the Edict of Nantes, he and his family moved to Paris, where they took up residence in the Quartier St.-Germain, at that time known as "petite Genève" because of its extensive Huguenot population. Here, de Brosse raised his seven children in the Huguenot faith.[164]

As an exponent of second-generation Calvinist architecture, Salomon de Brosse continued the pattern of building on precursors—a form of architectural intertextuality. Jacques II Androuet du Cerceau "assumed responsibility for training the young Salomon de Brosse . . . [who] by 1608 [was] very well established."[165] In 1615, de Brosse succeeded du Cerceau as *architecte des bâtiments du roi*. De Brosse's architectural signature-piece was the rebuilding of the Reformed temple at Charenton in 1623. In 1606, when he began work, Protestants were barely tolerated by Catholics at Charenton, and Catholics inveighed against the impending construction of a *temple*.[166] Salomon de Brosse devised a structure symbolic of Huguenot religious expression in his design for Charenton: "Protestants themselves at this time in France really were undecided as to what appearance their religious structure should have. Salomon de Brosse here, more than anywhere else, was called on to be creative."[167]

In 1621 the first building, designed by his uncle Jacques II in 1606, burned down. In 1623 de Brosse devised a similar structure but of far vaster proportions, seeking to accommodate as large a crowd as possible around the preacher's *chaire*, since the Word of God composed the focal and auditory center of Calvinist worship. Rebuilt in 1624, the temple accommodated three thousand people. It is instructive to contrast de Brosse's case

La Chappelle

with that of Inigo Jones, architect of what he called "the biggest barn," at Covent Garden, for Anglican worship in all of England. Jones had the space, and official tolerance, in which to construct such an amphitheater; de Brosse did not have such leeway, and as such his work is especially heroic and important. Because the Edict of Nantes placed strict limitations on the number of places available for Calvinist worship, any architect of a Protestant church had to anticipate an enormous multitude of listeners who would agglomerate in the few structures allotted them and prepare space accordingly.[168] Consequently, the temple at Charenton, possessing doubled rows of galleries on three sides, resembles more a conference hall than a church as conventionally defined. De Brosse also inserts large vertical windows into the temple's walls; this choice is consistent with Calvinists' iconoclastic belief that stained glass windows impeded the free flow of God's light. In some respects, the temple's style harked back to early Christianity, because it was modeled on a Roman basilica. In addition, de Brosse creates new forms of structural expression, consciously resisting conformity to Catholic norms of ecclesiastical construction: "we must indeed recognize the extraordinary effort that Salomon de Brosse made to free himself from his age's traditions concerning the interior arrangement of a Christian church."[169]

In rebuilding the temple, Salomon de Brosse both perpetuated and significantly altered his predecessor's plans, which had included "a centralized plan . . . [on] a grand rectangular design."[170] This design recalls structurally the designs for fortifications popular with Protestant architects, attesting to a self-protective Protestant architectural agenda. De Brosse modifies and intensifies the plan. He moves away from the "fortress mentality," in which one shelters one's vision of ideal space from the world, to the space of Scripture as the only safe place (scriptural passages are called *loci*, or "places"). By adding interior columns rising up through two storys, a side space for an upper gallery, and a side entrance with doors that break the symmetry of the structure, he stresses the vertical movement of Calvinism, oriented toward God and away from earth—the sole remaining hope was to be found in heavenly space rather than terrestrial. His technique, typical of second-generation Calvinist architects, decenters in order to dramatize their marginal stance. In addition, he locates the pulpit in a central position in order to create an unobstructed auditorium for the reception of the Word, supplanting architecturally the Catholic norm of the altar backed up against the wall for the celebration of Mass. Finally, he places a belfry on the roof. This last addition is significant—tantamount to a symbolic subversion through acceptance of constraint—for under the Edict of Nantes, one of the few things *not* restricted regarding Calvinist worship was the ringing of bells to summon worshipers to service. De Brosse's prominent belfry took defiant advantage of its permission to exist. Ironically, bell ringing had earlier enraged local Catholic faithful and had been responsible for numerous acts of violence against Calvinists, similar to Calvinist psalm singing, which had been judged inflammatory at Pré-aux-clercs, outside Paris. The belfry is thus a fraught space, the sign of the only shred of freedom of worship left to the Calvinists as well as the concrete form of a catalyst for potential violence against them. The belfry points to the need for a coded reception of the structure. After this church, too, was destroyed by a mob, Calvinist church building was forbidden in France.[171] However, Salomon de Brosse's model at Charenton was extremely influential throughout the Continent.

De Brosse also designed and built his own parish's church at Saint-Gervais-de Brosse, "a novelty in ecclesiastical architecture, for it [applied] to a church façade . . . the three superimposed orders regularly used for the entrance to a château,"[172] perhaps a Calvinist statement that ecclesiastical worship and everyday life should conjoin.[173] The desire to render a building more utilitarian, and the attempt to make a building designed for purposes of worship less ornamental, show a refusal to insinuate that any sacral aspect might inhere in a structure—something Catholics, with their reliquaries and shrines, took as an article of faith. Like the other du Cerceau and de Brosse family members, Salomon worshiped near Senlis. Much influenced, like Jean Bullant's work, by Philibert de l'Orme, de Brosse's structures at Blérancourt (the Château Neuf, 1614) and the second St.-Maur at Luxembourg (1615–24) recall their model, particularly in their use of clean architectural masses. The dramatic skyline of the Luxembourg palace and its intense verticality are innovative[174] and recall the Calvinist desire to orient the focus upward from terrestrial to metaphysical. Calvinist architects endured dwindling commissions and tardy payments of monies owed them; for instance, Salomon de Brosse received "peu de chose" financially after he finished building the Palais du Luxembourg: "he suffered many times from long, unconscionable delays in payments which should have been made to him by his noble clients."[175] In 1624, the date of the completion of the Palais du Luxembourg, Salomon de Brosse was in disgrace, embroiled in several legal processes, in which his Calvinism was an issue.

Earlier, however, as architect for Henri IV, Louis XIII, and Marie de Médicis, "he was entrusted with the building of several of the most im-

28. Salomon de Brosse constructed St. Gervais in Paris. Unlike the vertical direction of Charenton, this Catholic-commissioned church short-circuits a metaphysical movement: its lines move horizontally following the curve of the upper structure, and the pillars terminate in large horizontal cubes that arrest potential vertical movement. Photograph by Randall Balmer.

portant monuments of his time."[176] Appointed *architecte général* in 1616, de Brosse earned 2,400 livres a year. He was the architect of the aqueduct of Arcueil, the Hôtel de Bouillon, Coulommier (1613), the façade of St.-Gervais (1616–21), the Grande salle of the Palais de justice in Paris (1618), the Petit château of Louis XIII at Versailles, and the Palais du parlement in Rennes. On the whole, however—and this is typical of seventeenth-century French architectural careers—de Brosse devoted most of his endeavors to the completion of structures begun by his predecessors (itself no small factor in contributing to the development of an explicitly Calvinist architectural style, since enormous disparities with others' original structures would have been ill received).[177] Others of his structures were interrupted, never to be completed, by the "troubles":[178] this was the fate of the aqueduct at Arceuil. Hence the recourse to code: otherwise, structures, as well as texts, would be censured, as Salomon de Brosse experienced with Catherine de Médicis. "Salomon de Brosse was commissioned by his coreligionists in the Reformed church in Paris to build their temple at Charenton; this coincidence explains very plausibly the Queen Mother's bad faith toward Salomon de Brosse concerning Luxembourg . . . The Queen, obeying her confessor's instructions, could not be favorable to the architect charged with erecting, at the very gates of the capital city, the main monument wherein heresy was going to reside."[179]

This theological tension would be encoded on a series of structures: the temple, the "monument," and the gates of Paris. Text and structure experience the same treatment. Individual emphases in treatment, rather than absolute conformity to the Calvinist paradigm, can also be discerned in de Brosse's work. His structures tend to be heavy and brooding: "the excess of moldings on the walls and columns, the persistent use of small roofs over too-steep profiles, confers a weighty, crushing aspect to these buildings."[180] De Brosse's manipulation of space, however, continues the typical Calvinist preoccupation with the availability (or lack) of space for expression and construction.[181] As is the case with other Calvinist architects, art historians find in his work idiosyncracies and foibles;[182] they criticize him

29. Salomon de Brosse's Palais du Luxembourg in Paris. Photograph by Randall Balmer.

for his flippant use of detail[183] and judge that he "led himself into certain complications."[184] What some architectural historians have deemed to be a stylistic and structural weakness may in fact devolve, in a positive way, from de Brosse's Calvinist idiom and his propensity for disequilibrium between detail and surface.[185]

De Brosse also maintained a textual relationship with other Calvinists; most notably, he reedited Jean Bullant's *Reigle* in 1619. Given the puzzles that de Brosse has posed for art historians, it should not come as a surprise that he chose to edit a man who stated that distortion was—perhaps even should be—a rule in building: "That's why I beg those workers who have good judgment, and all others who enjoy practicing this craft, to look out especially for the way [in which they build] when that time comes; for the work [the building] will always deviate [do other than] from what the blueprint calls for."[186] The *ouvriers de bon iugement*, contrasted with *autres*, recalls Philibert's distinction between those "who have ears to hear" the gospel and those who do not, thereby setting up a split between a literate Calvinist audience for the structure as opposed to a less thoroughly biblically instructed Catholic spectator.

De Brosse's work and his relationships with other Calvinists attest to the predominantly Huguenot character of French architecture in the late sixteenth and early seventeenth centuries: "often from father to son, one might be at the same time mason, director of the work yard and architect . . . like so many other craftsmen and artists who became Protestant."[187] Upon de Brosse's death in 1626, the inventory of his household listed a Geneva Bible and a New Testament. He was buried in a Protestant cemetery on the Rue des Sts.-Pères. His influence, however, continued. Pierre Le Muet (1591–1669), a follower of De Brosse and a Calvinist, worked under him at the Luxembourg palace and at the château of Ponts et Chauvigny. Also influenced by de Brosse was François Mansart (1598–1666), believed to have conducted the work at St. Gervais under his direction.

In this way, de Brosse's Huguenot metaphor directly affected the architecture of French classicism. Calvinist strategies of subversion, and their architectural realizations, thus subtended the very nation-state that actively sought the elimination of their religious stance.

6

Conclusion

Constrained Creations

Understanding Calvinist Architecture

NO STRUCTURE IS MEANINGLESS. A structure has meaning—in and of
itself; in context; through opposition, apposition, and juxtaposition; in
germ ("entexted") and actualized; in its inflection of present form(s), revision of past shapes, and suggestions for future spaces. The erection of a
Calvinist structure is the metaphor for a theological stance.

In this book I have described a Calvinist treatment of structure originating during the hostilities prior to the Wars of Religion in France and
ending with the virtual eradication of Huguenots from France in the
seventeenth century. My focus has been aesthetic and metaphysical, architectural and theological, word- and Word-oriented. I have interpreted
Protestant structures as potentially subversive agents lobbying for an un-
achievable space that would allow for the free expression of Calvinist
faith. These structures form a nexus of dialogue and polemic, generating
forms of rewriting or revising Catholic-commissioned structures through
a panoply of architectural techniques that, employed in an ex-centric way,
contradict through iconography the structure itself.

Some concluding examples of how these Calvinist architects for
Catholic kings created monuments possessing a coded element, form, or
function demonstrate how a Protestant theory of textual structure worked
against the solely visual awareness of a monument. After converting to
Catholicism in 1598, Henri IV embarked with his minister Sully on an extensive building program intended to consolidate his power and display his
presence in Paris.[1] Several of the structures that he commissioned display
unusual aspects, puzzling many contemporary observers. The incomprehensible features can be deciphered if read in relation to, and as resulting

from, the architect's Calvinist stance and the resulting tension between his belief and his commission. These structures include the Pont Neuf, begun under Henri III, which took twelve years to complete, the statue of Henri IV, the Place Dauphine, and the Place Royale. Henri IV also began the Place de France (1610), created the Hôpital St. Louis, and laid the foundations of the Collège Royal in 1607. Henri's plans generally contained highly symbolic components, which reassigned the space in a new way, consistent with the Calvinist architects' tendency to redefine the space allotted them through iconography and code. For instance, the Place de France "consisted of a semi-circular space enclosed along the diameter of the walls of Paris . . . Round the diameter were seven buildings for markets and other public services, separated by roads leading radially away from the Place . . . These roads were cut by an outer ring of streets . . . each street bore the name of a French province."[2] This place's design is uncannily reminiscent of the concentric, geometric shapes structuring Palissy's "crustacean model" fortress city: "First I make the shape of a large square . . . around that I draw the outline of a number of houses . . . there will only be one street, and one other . . . [proceeding] by straight lines, turning at each angle, leading up to the square."[3] The Calvinist architectural idiom existed, and was continued, even in purportedly Catholic space. Calvinist town planning, like Calvinist architecture, sought to find space for itself. "It is characteristic of . . . Henri IV that, whereas his predecessors had planned a single block of such building, he should have extended the idea to a whole square which in its turn was part of a larger scheme of town planning."[4]

Two examples illustrate the context, the constraints, and the solutions. No records have survived of the identity of the architect of the Place Royale, the first planned square in Paris; however, most likely one or both of the royal architects, Jacques II Androuet du Cerceau (1550–1614) and Louis Métézeau (1559–1615), worked on the project.[5] Salomon de Brosse (1591–1626) may also have collaborated in its design. De Brosse and du Cerceau both probably also worked on the Louvre. Du Cerceau's work continued the Calvinist structural idiom; his models were Jean Bullant's work at Chantilly and the Tuileries pavilion.[6] The sources of inspiration for all the Calvinist architects were other Calvinist precursors or contemporaries; together they created a specific Calvinist style. The Place Royale "was unique in that it had no monument to justify the opening of public space."[7] Rather than superscribe Catholic monuments to redetermine them, Calvinist architects dispensed with them here.

The Place Royale also had a different function from previous public squares: documents from silkworm workshops attest that it was conceived as a commercial square, befitting the practical Calvinist focus. Urging the revival of France's war-torn economy, encouraging domestic commerce through the initiatives of Calvinist traders such as Barthélemy Laffemas (1545–1611), Henri IV sought to create spaces favorable to trade, and thereby stem the leaching of capital. Many Protestants were involved with the introduction of sericulture into the realm, among them Olivier de Serres (1539–1619), the Protestant agronomist and author of *Le théâtre d'agriculture*, which went into four editions between 1600 and 1610; the royal gardener Claude Mollet (probably Protestant), who wrote two treatises on silkworms; the royal architect Etienne Dupérac, who designed a nursery for the incubation of silkworms; and the author Pierre le Muet, who wrote the *Manière de bien bastir pour toutes sortes de personnes* (1623). Many Calvinists took up lodging in the new Place Royale: among others, Charles Du Ry, who often acted as contractor for his brother-in-law Salomon de Brosse, le Duc de Chastillon, le Sieur de Sancy, and the Protestant Etienne Gillot.[8] Calvinist architects required to carve out a public, officially Catholic space may have chosen to eliminate the customary spatial justification (a monument) as witness to their hope that Catholic domination would not last, thus creating a symbolic aporia of power. When it is no longer centralized and concentrated in a monument, power becomes symbolically diffuse and weakened, without a focal point. The concern then becomes space and vista, rather than monumental punctuation points.[9]

In 1607, Henri IV commissioned the construction of the Place Dauphine, to complete the Pont Neuf. There was to be a bridge without houses, without a royal equestrian statue on a bridge platform, so as not to hinder appreciation of the view. "The decision to complete the Pont Neuf without any encumbering buildings . . . was calculated to exploit the view of the Louvre [the King's residence], which Henri IV was in the process of enlarging. The bridge unleashed the eye to roam the city at large . . . as . . . spectacle. It was a new way of seeing Paris [that] . . . encouraged an aesthetic perception of the city."[10]

This new way of seeing was predicated on a Calvinist world-view and theological formation. The *Prévôt des marchands* (1601) implicitly equated the very Calvinist nature of Henri IV's program with Calvin's use of Augustine's *civitas homini/civitas dei* distinction, observing, in a declaration to the municipal government, that Henri IV "wishes to make this city an entire world and a miracle on earth, which certainly shows us a love that is more than paternal."[11] The Calvinist architects of the public square chose to represent the city as an abstract ideal, rather than to endorse the conventional understanding of urban architecture as a network of relationally significant buildings studding a space. In this way, the architects dramatized space's inadequacy: it cannot capture or resume a concept; the eye can take in the city at a glance but possesses no privileged focal points to mark or maintain its visual conquest. Further, the Place Dauphine, a deliberately asymmetrical square, featured the statue of the Vert-Galant, which only obliquely regarded its center, offering only a partial view of itself from the square. These last factors were especially criticized later by Catholic architectural critics Henri Sauval and Jean-Baptiste Jaillot. Sauval's comments demonstrate his incomprehension of what the Calvinist architects were doing. He says, "both the sculptor and the mason unquestionably had very little skill to have so poorly positioned the pedestal and the statue . . . [marked by] irregularity . . . It would have been easy for them to establish its center where they wanted." [12]

Another assessment, that of Jaillot in his *Recherches critiques, historiques, et topographiques sur la ville de Paris* (1772–74), frankly attests to the critic's puzzlement: "One would have expected [or preferred] that those who inspected the plans for this statue had placed it facing the opening onto the Place Dauphine and the gate of the Palais." [13] Architectural research, however, shows that "the misalignment did not result from ineptitude or carelessness, but from conscious choice. The axial relation between the square and the statue was simply not the paramount concern of Henri IV's architects . . . [who] focused on other formal priorities . . . [such as] the particular features of the site [and] on the experience of the passerby." [14] Sauval's criticism is the result of the customary assessment of a square from a central point, a visual crystallizing of power. Here, the Calvinist architects mandated an angled perspective, a view from their margins. The Place Dauphine, "a distinctly irregular triangle," requires a new, irregular or ex-centric apprehension. The architects skewed the eyesight of all spectators in the direction in which they wanted to take it. In addition, "at the Place Dauphine, form was allowed to unfold through movement . . . a fluid sequence of possibilities," [15] as the architects "accepted the inequality of the *quais*, knowing that it could only be perceived in plan, in order to structure an urban experience . . . of viewing the royal statue *as one moved.*" [16] The movement becomes lived experience rather than an immutable imposition in stone.

In the works of the second-generation Calvinist architects, du Cerceau in particular, with his free-form revisions of predecessors' structures, the creation of the illusion of movement to loosen spatial constraint was a characteristic strategy. The Calvinist architects' theory of structural treatment and spatial reorientation arose from their reliance on aesthetic manipulation as a tool to ironize. In addition, as with other Calvinist architectural trompe l'oeil, a façade effect is present: "it was only within the square that the irregular geometry of the Place Dauphine was visible . . . The architects shaped the Place Dauphine from the outside in."[17] Given the earlier discussion of Philibert de l'Orme's indebtedness to the evangelical architect Serlio, and given the existence of a unique Calvinist structural idiom, it is not surprising that the closest model for the façades of the pavilions lining the Place Royale comes from Serlio's sixth book, on domestic architecture.[18] A Protestant theological perspective underlies the irregular style of the square and its structures. In so many respects, Henri IV's architectural commissions continued to reflect his Calvinist ideology, even though he had abjured it. His royal topographer (1591) and royal engineer (1595) le Duc de Chastillon (1559–1616), a Protestant and a member of Henri de Navarre's army, wrote a compendium recording the king's battles and building campaigns. His text, copiously illustrated, was conceived as a complementary tract to du Cerceau's encyclopedic project, *Les plus excellens bastiments*, the two together composing a Calvinist image of the shadow Calvinism of the now-Catholic Henri IV.

Along with new public squares, monuments, and other structures, Henri IV's adviser, superintendent of finance (1598), fortifications (1599), and buildings (1602), captain of the artillery and *Grand Voyer*, Maximilien de Béthune, duke of Sully (1559–1641), also undertook a program of urban planning, proposing an ideal town that he called Henrichemont. He founded it in 1606, renovated his residence by remodeling it on the Arsenal model, and rebuilt the châteaux of Rosny, Sully-sur-Loire, and Villebon. He commissioned Salomon de Brosse to do the work. The site chosen was the former town of Bourges, essentially a tabula rasa because the Protestants had captured it in 1562 and razed it.[19] This unencumbered space—the Calvinist ideal—allowed for the theorizing of a Calvinist architectural program in which a town is like a narrative or text, of which each building composes one *seme* in a network of structural significance. Sully intended the town to be settled by his fellow Protestants, for "freedom of worship [in the town] was ensured by the provision of "une église et . . . ung Temple."[20]

The stipulated goal for the town was never actualized, however, because although the town was constructed, the desideratum of a Protestant haven existed only in the ideal space of de Brosse's blueprints. In his desire to protect fellow Calvinists through urban planning, Sully inaugurated—or perhaps continued, if we recall the idealized and defensive fortress towns of Palissy and Chambéry—a tradition parallel and counter to that of the Catholic emphasis on the monumentalizing of power: that of the Protestant *ville-refuge*, an anti-institutional space subtracted from the dominant sphere of power, not itself a monument but rather a series of lived relationships that evolve in contradiction to monumental impositions. "It has generally been assumed that the ideology of monarchy centered on the deified king translated into programs of city-planning devoted to self-glorification . . . this misconstrues the interrelated social and architectural concerns that animated [Henri IV's] urbanism."[21] The theological stance of the king, newly converted to Catholicism but still bound by emotional ties to Calvinism, played a role in differentiating his building program from that of other French kings.

There was much interest in town planning during the period, with Charles de Gonzague building Charleville in 1608 and with the construction of Montauban, a planned town, in 1616. It is instructive to contrast Henrichemont with town planning some years later. Richelieuville, constructed in 1632 by Jacques Lemercier,[22] was the urban space envisioned by one of the chief persecutors of Huguenots, Cardinal Richelieu. Richelieu's plan exemplifies the classical nation-state, emphasizing the centralizing tendencies inaugurated by Louis XIII and culminating with Louis XIV. "The city conceived by the Cardinal . . . was characterized by checkerboard streets, identical houses signifying a new, geometrical order . . . Now everyone would know that 'all things are subordinate to authority,' and that the State is a force defined in terms of power and command, a visible force."[23] This city-space, which speaks volumes about Richelieu's ideology, imposed uniformity. There was absolutely no space for difference (for "difference," read "Calvinism"). Standardization was Richelieuville's hallmark: "The village of Richelieu would be enlarged to a township planned and executed according to the most rational principles. This project . . . still stands today as one of the most consistent examples of town-planning on a small scale. The town forms a rectangular grid with a main street forming the long axis and connecting the two squares, and the houses are of uniform design, built of brick with stone quoins." Ironically, it appears that the town built by the Catholic minister "is in fact an extension of [the formerly Calvinist] Henri IV's ideas for the Paris *place*."[24] Just as Palissy's ceramic conceptions paradoxically produced the dominant Versailles Sun King style, so an erstwhile Calvinist king's projects for urban planning were absorbed into an absolutist, Catholic project.

Calvinist Cryptography

The legibility of architecture is dependent on the act of deciphering. To claim that it must be deciphered is to admit that its language of ornament reads like a cryptogram: that is, a set of effects and conventions whose meaning does not lie clearly on the surface and whose meanings do not correspond in an unambiguous and permanent relation, to its appearances.
                        —Daniel Barbiero, "Rereading the Classics"

The architectural object (taken in the largest sense of the term: city, garden, house, machine, monument, furnishing) seems endowed with a complex semantic status. First of all, it can be conceived as a hermeneutic object . . . in which an inside (always more or less hidden) is necessarily distinct from an outside . . . [creating] strategies for interpretation . . . Any architectural object can be understood by literary analysis as an object of discrimination, a differentiating factor, analyzing space by compartments and contiguity. Finally, every architectural object can be understood . . . as an object in a hierarchy, as a system of constraints.
                        —Philippe Hamon, "Texte et architecture"[25]

The preceding quotations highlight several of the issues that I have explored concerning Calvinist architectural creation. Arising in a climate of constraint levied on their belief system, their Calvinist architectural idiom anatomized those conditions. Calvinists overlaid with iconography the oppressive system: with code (Philibert); hidden spaces for dissent (Palissy's grottoes; Philibert's architect's cave); trompe l'oeil (Philibert and Palissy); eccentric or fantastical deviations (du Cerceau); parable-like microstructures offered as countercultural correctives to the nation-state (de Serres and Boyceau); scriptural undermining of Catholic defenses (Palissy and Chambéry); excessive ornamentation (Philibert and Bullant); or new paradigms (de Brosse). Perceiving themselves as a people of textuality and interiority (following Calvin's emphasis on biblical literacy, the priesthood of all believers, recourse to the Bible as authoritative in all things, and the conversion of the heart), the Calvinist architects played on the dissimilarity between interior and exterior, surface and ornament, "message" and meaning, of their constructions.[26]

Catholic structures constitute *representations of space*, while Calvinist structures display *representational space*. Representations of space are tied to the relations of production and to the "order" that those relations impose. Representational space, on the other hand, embodies complex symbolisms, sometimes coded, and linked to the underground side of life. Thus, if "all architecture is a kind of rhetoric of power,"[27] representations of space model and reinforce that power, while representational space exercises linguistic strategies of play, containment, contradiction, and concealment against that power.

Protestant architects had a different logic of visualization, which they directed against the Catholic order. This visualization required examination in conjunction with Scripture in order that the Calvinist viewer comprehend the true sense of the architectural endeavor. It may seem odd, or counterproductive, to a present-day reader that an architect should write a "manual" (itself a generic term connoting a practical application) in which what is taught is *not* what is stated, or of which the ultimate message contradicts both the text's, and the naive reader's, presuppositions. But one way of winnowing the sympathetic, elect audience out from a hostile readership is through such a strategy of obfuscation; as Serlio stated: "it's useless to try to teach to one who cannot understand."[28] Calvinists relied for the success of this strategy on the Catholic tendency to venerate images and statues and to accept other forms of outward appearance, iconolatry, as seamless manifestations of spiritual reality. They also tended to weight tradition more heavily than Scripture in ecclesiological matters. Thus, Protestant structures erected structured meaning, which the Catholics were deluded into accepting as self-sufficient structure. Calvinists look to Scripture for confirmation that the world order is flawed; they consult the Bible for signs of its disorder. They use Scripture in a disruptive way. This is a profoundly ironic recourse for Calvinists, for, while looking to Scripture in an attempt to pin meaning to its words, in Catholic France, where they had to subvert from within, it was nevertheless necessary for them to introduce slippage between word and meaning, such that Calvinist significance destabilized the dominant discourse. Unable to possess power, these architects adopted the role of witness. Theirs is not a witness to weakness but a witness of sophistication (after all, they were the artists commissioned by the state), enabling them to criticize in code and to "reproduce the [prevailing] reality in ways that . . . empower[ed] them to act."[29] Ultimately, the interpretive perspective for which both their writings and their structures call is theological, rather than architectural—and relentlessly Protestant.[30]

Investing Space with Something Beyond

For Calvinist architects contemporary with John Calvin (Palissy and Philibert), and for the second-generation Calvinist architects, I have detailed the ideological program that Calvinists represented on structures erected in response to Catholic commissions or for predominantly Catholic public use. I have also catalogued the components of the Calvinist hidden agenda and described how its iconography differed from the Catholic world-view. These Calvinist architects constituted an architecturally significant subculture: they shared religious beliefs; stylistic similarities in architectural treatment; and a role as *"hommes de récit,"*[31] or storytellers through structures. They related both their own story and that of other Calvinists, but also rehearsed, in order to revise, the cultural master narrative. The spaces, places, and constructions that they produced are forms of *"lieux-récits,"*[32] historiated structures that tell something about the architect's self-perception and his reading of the age. The significance of the role of narrative in these structures is consistent with the Calvinist emphasis on literacy, textuality, and textual interpretation, and constitutes a counternarrative.

Calvinism created a religion and a mentality apart. The embattled Huguenot poet Agrippa d'Aubigné emblazoned this difference on everything that he wrote: "We are those who are separated from [others], not by distinction of birth, by face color or by lineage, but by our earnest belief in purity of doctrine, in a way of life, and an adherence to standards of justice, such that we disdain both worldly goods and even our lives for the service of the Lord."[33]

John Calvin devised theories about space hinged on his understanding of what the visible church should be in relation to the invisible church. He assayed and implemented these theories within the bounded city-space of Geneva. Bernard Palissy employed similar spatial perceptions, manifesting them in ceramic craft and architectural projects. He described a utopian space for Protestants, one enwombed within Catholic public space. His attempt remained in large part theoretical and idealistic: while appearing to offer hope for a Calvinist protected domain, the parameters of his city, seemingly infinitely extensible, in fact opened on to no real thing or place. They came up short, confronted with the same empirical constraints that hampered the full actualization of Palissy's Calvinist expression. Philibert de l'Orme's structures displayed the problem of how a Calvinist, whose personal stance was necessarily in some measure oppositional to that of his Catholic patron, might encode structures in such a way as to articulate symbolically his forbidden statement. Philibert deployed a variety of revisionist techniques to ironize the apparent meanings of his structures. His allegories of the Architect and the Critic catalogue these techniques, summarizing Philibert's program to recuperate the dignity and merit of the Calvinist architect. Jacques Androuet du Cerceau revised many of Philibert's structures, as well as those of Jean Bullant and other Calvinist architects, extending their agenda to enhance its potential for social and theological critique, as well as attempting to undermine further the visual image of Catholic dominance. Salomon de Brosse's architectural endeavors at times baldly asserted Calvinist worth; his *temple* at Charenton, among other structures, effected a paradigm shift for European architecture at the beginning of the seventeenth century. His career displays many of the tensions attendant upon, and compromises necessitated by, adherence to the Calvinist faith in a Catholic world.[34]

These men found it impossible to restructure the world in a sweepingly programmatic way. Instead, they implemented their ideal of restructuring in a quintessentially *Calvinist* way. Calvin called for religion to return to its roots, to actualize its linguistic root: "the word *religion* . . . derives from the word *to re-read* . . . God's faithful have always reread and diligently meditated on what they should do . . . for true piety develops within the confines of the Word."[35] The Calvinist architects reread the world into their own sense. As a result, their architecture is a predominantly written architecture, an *archi-te(x)ture*.

Consequently, we read these Calvinist architectural texts not as stories that express a praxis but rather as stories that craft a praxis. Within the structured space of the text, they produce antitexts, allow avenues for dissimulation or escape, possibilities of moving into other landscapes. These are stories that diversify. The Calvinist stories about space exhibit the operations that constrain their own developments. The result is a new sort of Calvinist iconoclasm, which does not mean destroying art works but rather intruding into them. Through the means of monument, structure, and building, Calvinist architects adopted an incarnational component more characteristic of Catholicism. They did so in order to give concrete form to their own version of things: the monument provided a base on which they can write, rather than an image of total meaning. The Catholic monument thus embodied the Calvinist critique and represented its own undoing.

The Aftermath: Spatial Substitutions

In 1685, Guy-Louis Vernansel engraved an illustration to commemorate Louis XIV's extirpation of Calvinism. Entitled "Louis as Defender of the Faith" and allegorizing the Revocation of the Edict of Nantes, it portrayed Louis, richly clad, implacably grinding a stack of Calvinist books and tracts beneath his heel. This last detail is particularly telling, given that Calvinism and its consequent resources and responses were preeminently textual in tenor.[36] A few Protestant voices, mostly in exile in the Netherlands, bemoaned Louis XIV's promulgation of the Edict of Fontainebleau in 1685, which revoked the Edict of Nantes. Their exiled status underscores their position of speaking from the margins, their perpetual spatial displacement and lack of space for self-determination.[37] Typically, they revised a preexisting text in order to convey their complaint. Bossuet had praised Louis XIV, saying, "the entire State is resumed in his person." The Protestant author of the tract *Soupirs* reworked this statement, decrying the king's strategy of usurpation in this way: "the King has taken the place of the State."[38] This new version, a Calvinist countercultural statement, prefigures Jean-Jacques Rousseau's preoccupations in the *Social Contract* a mere century later, in which Rousseau voiced the fear that the citizenry, the true constituents of the state, would not be heard by a tyrant. Thus, the Calvinist concern for appropriate spatial distribution continued well beyond the days of Calvinism's virtual disappearance from France.

In the nineteenth century, Baron Georges Eugène Haussmann was commissioned to widen and reconfigure the streets of Paris so that protests against the government by barricading alleys and narrow streets would no longer be possible. No one until Haussmann (himself a Protestant), two hundred years after Henri IV, was to match the scope and brilliance of the former Calvinist king's building activity.[39] At the time, the "state architect," representative of "the grand tradition," was Félix Duban. Oddly, in 1828, when Duban, his career still developing, was attempting to make a case for his structural idiom, he presented a proposal for a Calvinist *temple* to make his plea.[40] In other words, Duban used a Protestant symbol to shake his fist at the establishment: "Duban's *envoi* was . . . an attack on the academic conventions expanded into an historical resuscitation of the age of Protestantism . . . Duban was thus reintroducing the Charenton church type back into France, making good the cultural break brought about by the revocation of the Edict of Nantes."[41] This expedient having succeeded, he himself became the "establishment," embodying in his structures "government" and "tradition," thereby necessarily forsaking the Protestant symbol that he had used to arrive.

Baron Haussmann, later Duban's rival, was from a German Calvinist tradition. He competed with Duban, each architect offering different proposals for how the space in front of the Louvre should be assigned. Haussmann, who eventually won the commission, chose to highlight the scale of the church of St.-Germain rather than to make it more ornate; he scaled it up by doubling it and he placed its bell tower in charge of its central space. This last decision was ironic, for it was from the bell tower of this very church of St.-Germain l'Auxerrois that Catholic queen Catherine de Médicis had ordered the tocsin to be sounded so that the St. Bartholomew's Day massacre of the Huguenots might begin. Haussmann, as a member of the Reformed faith, stated in his *Mémoires* that his work on the project troubled him precisely because of this problematic role of the bell tower and the tension that it engendered with his beliefs. He coped with his historically and theologically motivated unease by making the bell tower something that was no longer chiefly religious in function: he reconfigured it to fulfill the purpose of public amusement, adding to it a carillon solely for musical appreciation at public concerts. The former explicitly Catholic (more militantly Catholic) function of the bell tower was thus redetermined, through a Reformed subversion of form and function. In addition, Baron Haussmann faced down the *goût du roi* by framing the church with two architectural blocks, not even pilasters, so uncompromisingly unadorned as to refuse to mirror the accepted "grand style." In this way, he situated the church that had in some measure been responsible for the massacre of the Huguenots between structural embodiments of the Calvinist "plain style," redetermining the structure through its new frame. Further, Hausmann portrayed the area as representationally afloat in a world of little bits and pieces, mimicking the fragmentation and dismemberment of Calvinist bodies on the day of the massacre. The space of Catholic domination was thus undermined visually.[42] In this way, the history of urban architecture before, during, and after Haussmann would always be, in some measure, and however unconsciously, Calvinist.

Protestant architecture persisted in other odd ways. Ironically, Jacques Androuet du Cerceau, denigrated by absolutist architects for his "dangerous designs," had to wait over two centuries for one of his own structures to be constructed: in 1870, working on a commission from the Rothschild family, the architect Eugène Destailleur erected a formerly unrealized design by du Cerceau.[43]

30. It is wonderfully fitting that Philibert de l'Orme, consummate graffiti artist, in the sense of subversive architectural technique, should have his own publication inscribed with another's (probably seventeenth-century) graffiti. This copy of the *Architecture* contains only one page on which anything is scribbled: this penciled imitation of the curve of the top of Philibert's engraved column. Like the Calvinist revisions that du Cerceau effected of Philibert's and others' work, this rendition is not exact: the second row of lines projects out beyond the top row of two lines, altering the gradual whittling down of the line on Philibert's column. A decorative component of the central portion has been omitted, as well. The artistically playful aspect of Calvinist architecture, as well as its appeal to many and its continuance by imitators, is well illustrated textually here. Philibert de l'Orme, *Architecture* (1626), 1: 219 verso. By permission of the Folger Shakespeare Library.

The full story of Calvinism's subterranean mining of state architecture in France is an unacknowledged substructure, an unaccounted-for ghost. Its lineaments exist in germ in Calvin's *Institution* and would be implemented by the first and second generation of Calvinist architects, forming the blueprint for an alternate vision and a new world to come. We who read their structures can reactivate the compelling strength of their oppositional theology, unravel the complex encoding that disguises their polemic, and bear witness to the paradoxical persistence of a talented minority that the state paradoxically sought both to subvent and to silence. In building "to code," Calvinist architects found ways to build codes that, once deciphered, narrate the secret story of Calvinist creation from constraint.

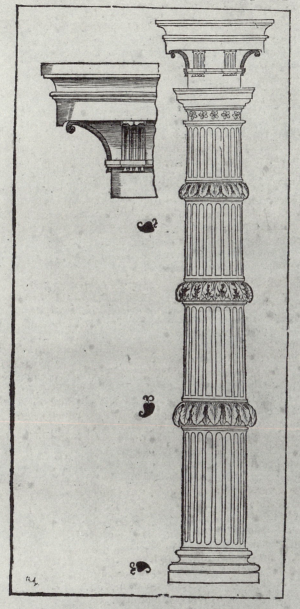

J'ay

Notes

Introduction

1. "Confort[e] des fidèles apeurés par des risques accrus de persécution." Calvin, *Des scandales*, 1. All translations into English that appear in the text are mine unless otherwise noted.

2. Ibid., intro., 8.

3. Kelley, *Ideology*, vi.

4. Marin, *Portrait*, foreword, xv.

5. "Ideology, because it is unconscious, pervades all symbolic activity." Ibid., ix.

6. Kelley, *Ideology*, vii.

7. "Si je ne pensais qu'à ma vie et à mes intérêts privés, je m'en irais aussitôt autre part. Mais quand je pense à l'importance de ce coin de terre pour la propagation du royaume de Christ, c'est avec raison que je me préoccupe de le défendre." Calvin, letter cited in *Des scandales*, 22.

8. Mario Carpo offers a similar characteristic lexicon for Sebastiano Serlio, the evangelical architect: "modestia, semplicità, pudenze, ragione, licenza, capriccio, ardire, mescolanza, novità, vizio, cose inusitate, bizarrie, confusione, errore." Carpo, *La maschera*, 21–22.

9. Or, again, they acted like the Calvinist *tyrannomach* theorists (such as Francis Hotman), who found very occasional suggestions in Calvin's writings that tyrannicide might be justifiable were the monarch disobedient to the Lord's mandates (such suggestions being much less frequent than Calvin's upholding of the authority of kingship) and developed these into a full-blown permission for regicide.

10. "Parce qu'ils cachaient par opportunisme leurs croyances religieuses de tendance évangélique sous des pratiques externes catholiques-romaines." Calvin, *Das scandales*, 15.

11. "Clandestinità e simulazione facevano parte della vita quotidiana delle *élites* riformata urbane." Carpo, *La maschera*, 105.

12. Ibid., 100.

13. "L'indifferenza all'esteriorità era un principio ideologico e teologico." Ibid., 105.

14. "L'interiorità della fede . . . esprime un atteggiamento spirituale comune a varie correnti dell'evangelismo, ma può anche alludere alla necessità, ed alla legittimità della simulazione religiosa." Ibid., 111.

15. Nicodemism thus permitted "the production of ciphered messages, all meaning of which was only accessible to an elect group"; there is "an elite public,

and a reprobate public: each group will find what they seek . . . a good architecture and a bad architecture." Ibid., 109–11.

16. "Il registro dell'architettura 'giudiziosa' . . . dipende ancora una volta della moderazione nell'ornamento, in particolare dalla scarcità degli 'intagli' . . . Serlio invoca piuttusto rigore ed austerità nel trattamento delle superficie (56) . . . La stravaganza e le incongruenza delle storie avrebbero spinto il lettore a scoprire l'inganno, a smascherare le verità dissimulate . . . (7) questa regole . . . sans tutte [nell' *Extraordinario libro*] deliberatamente violate, o contradette (8)." Ibid.

17. "Il progetto editoriale delle' *Extraordinario libro* . . . matura in un contesto cultural ed ideologico particolare." Ibid., 18.

18. "L'autore sembra prediligere l'ambiguità, o la reticenza, ad una presa di posizione precisa; molte contraddizioni . . . l'autore si trovava in compagnia . . . di besti feroci." Ibid., 65.

19. This is also the case with Philibert de l'Orme's almost obsessive enumeration and attempted rectification of "faultes."

20. Bourdieu, *Field*, 218.

21. "Vitruvio è un 'autorità' a cui sì deve prestare 'piena e indubitata fede'; I suoi scritti 'sacrosanti e inviolabili . . . sì che tutti quegli architetti . . . saranno eretici nell' architettura." Carpo, *La maschera*, 39.

22. Regarding Serlio, Carpo avers, "the text was to be interpreted, but its authority was not negotiable." [Il testo dev'essere interpretato, ma la sua autorità non è negoziabile.] Ibid., 39.

23. "This order is the only order possible [the configuration of places as hierarchized optic] . . . that of absolute visibility through the perfect legibility of the gaze." Marin, *Portrait*, 191.

Chapter 1. A Context for Code

1. "Elle tourna la face à la ruelle vers Marguerite, sa femme de chambre, qu'elle avoit laissée vivre à la religion Reformée; à celle-là qui lui disoit: *Tournez les yeux vers Dieu, qui vous relevera*, elle respondit ces mots: *Je suis accablée des ruines de la maison*. Pour l'explication de cela faut savoir que les devins luy ayans prédit dès sa jeunesse qu'elle seroit accablée des ruines d'un édifice, sur cette crainte, elle faisoit appuyer les maisons et planchez où elle logeoit." D'Aubigné, *Histoire universelle*, 7: 335.

2. "L'infidelle . . . Perd bien le jugement, n'ayant pas conoissance / Que cette maison n'est que la maison de France, / La maison qu'elle sape; et c'est aussi pourquoi / Elle fait tresbucher son ouvrage sur soi . . . / Elle ne l'entend pas, quand de mille posteaux / Elle fait appuyer ses logis, ses chasteaux: / Tu ne peux empescher par arc-boutant ni fulcre / Que Dieu de ta maison ne fasse ton sepulchre." D'Aubigné, *Oeuvres, Les tragiques*, "Misères," vv. 861–78, p. 41.

3. "L'architecte mondain n'a rien qui tienne lieu / Contre les coups du ciel et le doigt du grand Dieu." Ibid., vv. 878–80, p. 41.

4. Thus, "the elaborate framework of the sixteenth century garden, with its

growing luxury and profusion of symbolic devices, pseudo-classical settings, grottoes, statuary . . . was directed gradually toward aesthetic, intellectual, and political
ends." W. H. Adams, *French Garden*, 21.

5. Hunt, citing Addison, in *Garden and Grove*, 96.

6. The first-generation Calvinist architect Philibert de l'Orme offers numerous examples of such confessions of faith associated with, or articulated indirectly
through, architecture. "[Les architectes] qui disent que la figure de deux lignes
qui s'entrecouppent par le milieu à angles droicts, & représentent le charactère de
la croix, (c'est la figure architecturale privilégiée) . . . Mais laissons à part [which
he does not do; he explicitly includes it] l'honneur & révérence que nous devons
tous avoir en général pour la croix, pour la satisfaction qui a esté faicte pour nous
en icelle, par la mort de Iesus Christ nostre seul justificateur, & la prenons et
considérons comme une des premières & parfaictes figures de Géométrie." [Some
architects . . . say that the figure of two straight lines which intersect at the middle
in right angles . . . describes a cross (the privileged architectural form) . . . But let's
leave aside the honor and veneration that we should all have for this cross, because
on it, by his death, Jesus Christ accomplished our salvation, as our only justifier,
and let us take and consider as one of the first and best forms of geometry, that
same cross.] Philibert de l'Orme, *Traité d'Architecture* (1567), II, ii, 32. Here, Philibert, through phrases such as "our only justifier," reveals his Calvinist theology. By
dealing with the cross as a geometrical construct, he attempts to cloak his Calvinism under a universally acceptable—and nonideological—mathematical form. It is
striking how many Protestants are early geometricians in the sixteenth century. See
on this Perez-Gomez, *Architecture*.

7. The quotation is from Psalms 51:18. The same phrase is used repeatedly
by Protestants throughout Europe. We find it, for example, in "Unlock my lipps,"
by Margaret Hannay. Cited in Maryanne Horowitz, ed., *Privileging Gender*, 34.

8. See, for example, Babelon, *Paris au XVIᵉ siècle*, Carpentier, *Histoire de
France*, and Greengrass, *Age of Henri IV*.

9. "[Le] contenu [de l'Edit] renferme, en germe, bien des menaces pour la
minorité religieuse que, par ailleurs, elle met en exergue . . . le mérite douteux de ce
texte législatif est d'avoir mis noir sur blanc l'antagonisme de deux communautés,
et donc de le justifier." Garrison, *L'Edit de Nantes*, 21–26.

10. "Le fait qu'Henri IV ait jugé nécessaire d'octroyer à ses anciens coreligionnaires le droit de tenir des assemblées et de conserver cent cinquante et une
places fortes pour leur permettre d'imposer éventuellement leurs droits montre
bien que l'édit de Nantes est un acte de réalisme politique de la part du roi et non pas
la traduction d'un véritable climat de tolérance. La violente opposition des parle-
ments à l'enregistrement de l'édit, les résistances acharnées des milieux catholiques
les plus divers . . . témoignent dans le même sens." Carpentier, *Histoire de France*, 28.

11. A complicating factor in this picture is that archival research has documented a substantial amount of Protestant resistance to Catherine de Médicis'—
and other nobles'—extensive building programs (deemed profligate by many).
Were Protestant architects, then, in conflict with other members of the Protestant community, and not only with Catholics, over their participation in Catholic
building endeavors? If so, they were doubly defensive—first, to keep the goodwill

of the patron, and second, not to be rejected as pariahs by fellow believers. We need to untangle these two tensions and see how they would play themselves out in different ways in the work of these architects. In this way, Calvinists, people of the Word and of the Book, adopted tactics to articulate their confessional beliefs in a period that did not favor their theological expression.

12. The Camisard rebellion in the Cévennes a century later gives the lie to this latter assertion, at least for that area.

13. "Beaucoup de protestants craignaient pour l'avenir de leur foi. En effet, l'Eglise catholique dans les premières décennies du XVIIe siècle bénéficiait d'un puissant élan résultant notamment de la mise en oeuvre dans la plupart des pays romains des réformes voulues par le clergé de Trente . . . la paix issue de l'édit de Nantes permettait au clergé de lancer des missions, des prédications . . . dans des places fortes du calvinisme." Carpentier, *Histoire de France*, 88.

14. "Ils perdaient les moyens de peser sur le destin politique." Bercé, *La naissance dramatique*, 95.

15. See Moussiegt, *Hotman and Du Plessis*.

16. "Tost passa ce changement particulier du Roy envers monsieur du Plessis, . . . envers la Religion mesmes, car le Roy prenoit peine et plaisir de destourner de la profession d'icelle ceux qui estoient près de luy, leur déclarant que, persévérans, il ne pouvoit rien faire pour leur avencement . . . Se plaisoit aussy S. M. [Sa Majesté] à magnifier envers tous l'obligation qu'Elle avoit au Pape et l'obéissance qu'Elle luy vouloit rendre, à dénigrer au contraire l'Eglise réformée et les ministres d'icelle." Charlotte Arbaleste, Madame de Mornay, *Mémoires de Madame de Mornay*, 2 vols., ed. Catherine de Witt (Paris: Jules Renouard, 1869), vol. 1, 235. The *Mémoires* are edited, but the letters remained unedited to this day. To the best of my knowledge, no scholar has remarked on the extensive—and frustratingly difficult—code used in the letters, nor has anyone speculated on the significance of such a coding strategy. It is known that Protestants used a form of symbolic identification—a sort of code—to manifest themselves to other Calvinists when they were traveling in unknown, potentially hostile territory: in the Bibliothèque du protestantisme at La Rochelle, as well as in the Musée du Désert in the Cévennes, can be found a large collection of these symbolic tokens, or *méreaux*, coin-shaped objects which one Protestant would place in the palm of another. An appropriate response would then presumably be made. This response was probably Scripture-based, as the iconography of the *méreaux* tended to be biblical (Jesus as shepherd, for example). It therefore seems logical to assume that, if such symbolic forms of identification were required, why not the use of code in other forms, as well?

17. Ibid., 368.

18. Ibid., 381–82, for instance.

19. Ibid. This information is gleaned from a close reading of the unnumbered letters contained on 127–249 in the edition of Charlotte d'Arbaleste's *Mémoires*.

20. "Les amours de Madame et Monsieur le Comte de Soysons se reschauffent, et y qui les veulent persuader à l'emploier comme utiles à l'Estat."

21. Note the following example: "Messieurs de la court de Parlement pressent le roy pour 5.1. a dit à 160. 28. 101. 40. à propos de ma lettre qui 12. ne 30. u. ra. 118. 87. 12. Il y a eu de la brouillerie à Béziers." [The parliamentary judges urged

the king to . . . [this man] said . . . concerning my letter that . . . then a great tumult occurred in Béziers.]

22. Les Elseviers, *Histoire de la vie de Philippe de Mornay* (Leyden: Bonaventure & Elsevier, 1647), 712–15, cites these statements in full.

23. Marin, "The Utopic Rabelaisian Body," in *Food for Thought*, 105 and 109.

24. "Ce n'est de maintenant que les gens reduictz à la créance évangélique sont persécutez; mais bien heureux est celluy qui ne sera pas scandalizé et qui toujours tendra au but au blanc que Dieu, par son cher Filz, nous a préfix, sans par ses affections charnelles estre distraict ny diverty." François Rabelais, cited in Marin, *Food*, 185.

25. Ibid., 178–85.

26. Ibid., 88. It is utopian, because, as Marin points out, the *act* of constructing the Abbaye is elided. The Abbaye, in reality, remains *un*constructed: "the story of the construction is, properly speaking, absent: there is not a trace of the building itself yet the process is described at great length."

27. I am tempted to use the adjective "virtual" to describe the Abbaye. It strikes me that many of Rabelais's projects are forerunners of our postmodern concept of virtual reality, just as the *paroles gelées* could be construed as the symbolic representation of postmodern sign theory.

28. "Thus, Vitruvius' architectural text allows humanity and the world to be reconciled by a system of analogies and . . . a geometric system . . . guarantees . . . reconciliation." Marin, *Food*, 97.

29. Blunt, *Art*, 27.

30. Ibid., 72.

31. "È la traduzione in scultura di quegli studi teorici a cui si stanno dedicando gli architetti del tempo, a cominciare dal Serlio . . . Nel frattempo Goujon subisce qualche noia di carattere privato; nel 1552 viene imprigionato per un breve periodo e la stessa cosa gli accadrà nel 1554, molto probabilmente per motivi religiosi: come tutte le persone colte e progredite del suo tempo, Goujon è in fatto protestante . . . al 1562, a quest'epoca lascia con ogni probabilità la Francia (i motivi più plausibili sono ancora quelli religosi." Vitzhum, "Jean Goujon," 1–15.

32. Ibid., 27.

33. Cerceau, *Les plus excellens*, 21.

34. Blunt, *Art*, 127.

35. Ibid., 141.

36. "Il lettore dovrà ripristinare da solo le 'belle forme' che l'autore ha volutamente nascosto sotto sembianze monstruose . . . per riscattare la virtù bisogna cercare al di là delle apparenze . . . la verità qualche volta si nasconde, ed è un premio per chi vuole cercerla. Non tutti vogliono." Carpo, *La maschera*, 80. This is the case with Sebastiano Serlio, also working in a tense religious and political climate: "in order to find the true virtue, or meaning, of the work, you must look far beneath its surface semblance . . . the truth sometimes is buried; it's a prize for whoever perseveres in seeking it."

37. "Ogni modello è una trappola." Ibid., 82.

38. Here again, there are parallels with Serlio: "Ma quest strategia pedagogica ma non è un'invenszione serliana. Non, è né innocente, né ingenua partecipia

di un atteggiamento spirituale generala, di une sorta di spirito del tempo, comme agli ambienti culturali ed editoriali, che Serlio frequentava in guegli anni." [But this pedagogical strategy is not Serlio's invention . . . it is part of a general spiritual attitude . . . common to the cultural and publishing house circles which Serlio frequented at the time.] (83).

39. "Ainsi qu'à un Poète il ne suffist pas de scavoir bien teistre un beau vers: Ny à un maçon de tailler proprement une pierre: il les faut après arranger pour la structure d'un Poeme, ou d'un edifice; dont les membres viegnent à se correspondre, et les parties deuement se rapporter à leur tout, comme si ce n'estoit qu'une seule pièce." Blaise de Vigenère, *Images* (1578), 12–13.

40. "Je te veux bastir une Ode, / La maçonnant à la mode / De tes palais honorez, / Qui pour parade ont l'entree / Et de marbres acoustree, / Et de hauts piliers dorez, / Afin que le front de l'oeuvre / Du premier égard décoeuvre / Tout le riche bastiment: / Ainsi Prince, je veux mettre / Au premier front de mon metre / Tes vertus premièrement." Pierre de Ronsard, *Odes* (Paris, 1550), 430–32.

41. McGowan, *Ideal Forms*, 123.

42. "L'ordonnance à Blois reste étroitement attachée à la structure . . . A Chambord, au contraire, l'union disparaît entre l'ossature et le décor. Ce dernier . . . acquiert une existence propre . . . les croisées ont ensuite été perceues sans liaison aucune avec ce décor." Gebelin, *Châteaux*, 14.

43. Such distrust of fictional invention [*fingere*] as a form of lying is uniform throughout the early Renaissance, but becomes heightened by the emphasis on plain saying and truthfulness during the Reformation.

44. "Or, la création n'est point une transfusion, comme si on tiroit le vin d'un vaisseau en une bouteille; mais c'est donner origine à quelque chose qui n'estoit point." Calvin, *Institution* (1552) I, xv, 214.

45. "J'ai veu tant de fortes villes / Dont les clochers orgueilleux / Percent la nue et les cieux / De piramides subtiles, / . . . Superbes d'artillerie . . . / Mais toy, cité bien heureuse / Dont le palais favory / A la justice chéri, / Tu règne victorieuse: / Par toy ceux là sont domptez / Qui en l'impudique guerre." Ronsard, *Odes*, ed. Charles Guérin (Paris: Les éditions du Cèdre, 1952), 519.

46. "Le mimétisme de *La Sepmaine* . . . est fondé sur l'organisation même du signifiant textuel. Il érige donc le discours poétique en objet de mémoire, en monument." Miernowski, *Du Bartas*, 211.

47. "L'éparpillement de cette liste laisse apparaître des plages textuelles, des lieux qui, à ce stade de structuration, restent vides et qui attendent d'être remplis, organisés." Ibid., 50.

48. "Son contenu, privé de continuité . . . de dessein compositionnel, s'éparpille en une multitude anarchique de sujets [et] . . . désordre." Ibid., 11.

49. "L'auteur de *La Sepmaine* distribue des signes apparents de sa conformité au code idéologique et artistique du protestantisme . . . le message reste soumis au premier et serait absolument incompréhensible sans l'aide de la Bible. La lecture du monde passe obligatoirement par la lecture de la Parole qui commande tout le processus de cryptage de l'univers." Ibid., 93.

50. See chapter 1 in Catharine Randall Coats, *Subverting the System: d'Aubigné and Calvinism* (Kirksville, Mo.: Sixteenth Century Studies Publishers, 1991).

51. "En employant une métaphore spatiale . . . se propose d'étaler l'univers dans l'univers de son poème . . . la verticalité de la description, l'horizontalité de la narration." Miernowski, *Du Bartas*, 41.

52. Ibid., 316–17.

53. "Les uns bronchans contre le premier feuillet de ce bastiment, trouvant son titre bien estrange . . . Je les renvoye au dernier chapitre de la Cité de Dieu de S. Augustin, duquel j'ay pris et le tiltre, [et] l'argument, et la division de ce livre. Et ne doute pas que l'authorité de son texte ne me serve pas de sauve-garde . . . Mais dites-moy où vous avez appris de juger de tout un Palais par son seul frontispice? Je n'ay point encore jetté les fondemens des deux tiers de mon bastiment: vous ne voyez que certaines murailles imparfaictes et qui monstrent le dehors, et les pierres d'attentes pour se lier avec le reste de l'édifice." Du Bartas, *La Sepmaine*, 1: 344–45.

54. "La mer . . . / Verse dessus les flots de montagnes bornez / Le pouvoir de ses cornes . . . / Mais voy comme la mer / Me jette en mille mers . . . / Voy comme son desbord me desborde en paroles!" Ibid., vv. 195–217, pp. 106–7.

55. "Ce premier monde estoit une forme sans forme, / Une pile confuse, un meslange difforme, / D'abismes un abisme, un corps mal compassé, / Un Chaos de Chaos, un tas mal tassé." Ibid., vv. 223–27, pp. 12–13.

56. See Carpo, *La maschera*, 55.

Chapter 2. Spatial Situations

Note to epigraph: "Il y a une correspondance de la foy avec la parolle, dont elle ne peut estre séparée ne distraite. Icelle mesme parolle est le fondement dont elle est soustenue et appuyée; duquel, si elle est retirée, incontinent elle tresbusche." *Institution* (1969), III, ii, 20–21.

1. Torrance, *Space*.

2. Ozment, *The Age of Reform*, chapter 1.

3. E.g., Zwingli's notion of theology infusing the public, civic sphere. See Ozment, *Age of Reform*, 325–28.

4. This is the term coined by Patricia O'Grady, an architectural historian at the University of Toronto, in her manuscript entitled "A Huguenot Statement in Architectural Terms," on a Calvinist designer of fortifications (Jacques Perret de Chambéry, circa 1603).

5. Calvin, *Institution*, I, vi, 90; my emphasis.

6. "En s'amusant aux syllabes, ils ne regardent pas en quel sens et avec quelle liayson ces mots se doyvent prendre." Ibid., III, iii, 66.

7. "Parquoy il nous marque double peuple: l'un est tout le lignage d'Abraham, l'autre une partie qui en est extraicte, laquelle Dieu se réserve comme un thrésor caché, tellement qu'elle n'est point exposée à la veue des hommes." Ibid., III, xxii, 425; my emphasis.

8. Upon observing this close link between thought and space, we may attempt a working definition of city-space. City-space is a designed, and designing (both in the sense that it creates something, as well as demonstrates an intention),

narrative that explores all the potentials, tensions, distortions, and revisions of empirical space. These nuances are then compared to the aspirations and necessities of abstract space. The juxtaposition of real and abstract space produces city-space. Because the two templates can never wholly conjoin, they can only, ultimately, be found in textual form: we must theorize city-space.

9. "Au contraire, si le diable a gagné la place, comme un mauvais chevaucheur et estourdy il l'égare à travers champs, il la fait tomber dans les fosses, il la fait trébuscher et revirer par les vallées, il l'accoustume à rébellion et désobéissance." Calvin, *Institution* (1969), II, iv, 75.

10. Ibid., Epistre, I, 40; my emphasis.

11. Ezekiel 48:15, cited in ibid., I, xiiii, 156.

12. Ibid., IV, vii, 124. Here Calvin paraphrases Jerome: "S'il est question d'authorité, dit-il, le monde est plus grand qu'une ville. Qu'est-ce que tu m'allègues la coustume d'une ville seule? Est-ce que tu assuiettis l'ordre de l'Eglise à peu de gens, dequoy vient la présomption?"

13. He uses similar spatializing techniques throughout the text. For instance, he divides the human into two parts: "Puisqu'ainsi est que nous avons constitué deux régimes en l'homme, et qu'avons desia assez parlé du premier, qui réside en l'âme, ou en l'homme intérieur, et concerne la vie éternelle, ce lieu cy requiert que nous déclairions aussi bien le second, lequel appartient à ordonner . . . les moeurs extérieurs." Ibid., IV, xx, 505. "Et de là il descend à mettre en avant deux Iérusalem opposites l'une à l'autre, pour ce que comme la Loy a esté publiée en la montagne de Sinaï et l'Evangile est sorti de Jérusalem, aussi plusieurs . . . se vantent d'estre enfans de Dieu et de l'Eglise; mesme n'estans que semence bastarde, mesprisent les vrais enfans de Dieu." Ibid., IV, ii, 43.

14. "Touchant ce que le Pape estend ainsi sa Jurisdiction sans fin, en cela il fait une grosse iniure et outrageuse . . . à toutes les autres Eglises, lesquelles il descrire par pièces, pour édifier son siège des ruines d'icelle . . . Il faut qu'ils me confessent que Rome ne peut autrement estre mère des Eglises, sinon qu'elle soit ainsi Eglise, et que nul ne peut estre Prince des Evesques, qu'il ne soit Evesque. Veulent-ils donc avoir à Rome le siège Apostolique? . . . Or comment me monstreront-ils aucune face ny apparence d'Eglise? . . . je dy pour replique qu'une Eglise a ses marques pour estre cogneue . . . il est question . . . du régime qui doit tousiours apparoistre en l'Eglise." Ibid., IV, vii, 144.

15. "En Jérusalem . . . il donna une certaine arre . . . arre de nostre héritage [et il] a habité en eux." Ibid., II, x, 215.

16. "Je susciteray, dit-il, le pavillon de David, lequel est decheu; ie muniray toutes ses brèches et répareray ses ruines. (Amos 9:1) En quoy il monstre qu'il n'y avoit autre signe de salut, sinon que gloire et maiesté royale fust derechef redressée en la maison de David; ce qui a esté accompli en Christ." Ibid., II, vi, 110.

17. McGrath, *Life of Calvin*, 79.

18. Monter, *Calvin's Geneva*, 3–4; also 187.

19. On this, see Agrippa d'Aubigné's description of his later involvement in a similar project, recounted in *Sa vie à ses enfants*, in *Oeuvres*.

20. Roger Stauffenegger uses this term throughout in his magisterial, two-volume, amply documented study of the city of Geneva. *Eglise et société: Genève*

au XVIIe siècle. His thesis is that, for Calvin, Geneva was "un champ expéri-mental" (xi).

21. Wallace, *Calvin*, 134.

22. Höpfl, *Christian Polity*, 108.

23. Calvin quoted in the English in Wallace, *Calvin*, 106.

24. "Ils attendoyent une cité bien fondée, de laquelle Dieu est le maistre ouvrier. Ils sont tous morts en ceste foy, sans avoir receu les promesses, mais les re-gardans de loin, et sachans et confessans qu'ils estoyent estrangers sur la terre. En quoy ils signifient qu'ils cherchent un autre pays." Calvin, *Institution* (1969), II, x, 207. See also Du Four, "Mythe," 78 and passim.

25. Du Four, "Mythe," 78.

26. Whittingham, incipit to his translation of the New Testament, quoted in ibid., 78. Tagaut is paraphrased in ibid., 79: "une ville saincte," "le témoin triom-phant . . . de la même vérité évangélique."

27. Battles, *Analysis*, xi.

28. Quotation from Alistair McGrath, *Calvin*, 108. We know, for example, from an examination of blueprints that Calvinist architectural style had an extraor-dinarily widespread influence on the churches built by the Marian exiles.

29. "Posons le cas . . . des Papes . . . tout le siège avec ses principales jambes estoit renversé et decheut." Calvin, *Institution* (1969), IV, vii, 48.

30. Ibid., II, viii, 167 and ix, 191; my emphasis. "Ils sont insérez en Christ" (II, viii, 186).

31. "Christ . . . est la longueur, hautesse, largeur et profondeur . . . il bar-roit noz esprits des treillis, pour les empescher de décliner tant peu que ce soit ça ne là, quand il est fait mention de Christ, mais les exhorter à se tenir à la grâce de réconciliation." Ibid., II, xii, 239.

32. "Nous sommes comme eslognez de Dieu, estans pèlerins au monde, Iesus Christ est entre deux, pour nous mener petit à petit à une pleine conionc-tion." Ibid., II, xv, 273.

33. "Dieu le Père nous élargit son esprit . . . en a mis en luy . . . dispensateur de sa libéralité envers nous . . . ses mesmes dons luy ont esté commis en dépost pour en élargir . . . l'Esprit est distribué à chacun . . . selon la mesure de la donation de Christ . . . est conionct." Ibid., III, i, 9.

34. "Il est besoin d'eslevez nos pensées aux promesses de Dieu qui nous sont données, et aux choses intérieures et spirituelles qui nous sont démonstrées." Ibid., IV, xvi, 339; my emphasis.

35. "Iesus Christ nous est comme oisif, iusqu'à ce que nous le conioignions avec son Esprit . . . pource sans ce bien nous ne faisons que regarder Iesus Christ de loin et hors nous . . . il s'unit avec nous . . . pour nous retenir à soy et pour estre mutuellement possédé de nous." Ibid., III, ii, 11.

36. "Iesus Christ par le Baptesme nous a fait participans de sa mort, afin que nous soyons entez en elle." Ibid., xv, 321; my emphasis.

37. "Le nom d'Ascension si souvent réitéré ne signifie-t-il pas que Iesus Christ soit bougé d'un lieu à l'autre? Ils le nient . . . Mais ie leur demande dere-chef: Quelle a esté sa façon de monter? N-a-il pas esté eslevé en haut à veue d'oeil? Les Evangélistes ne récitent-ils pas clairement qu'il a esté receu au ciel?" Ibid., IV,

xvii, 410–11. Some of the terms in Calvin's spatial vocabulary found throughout his text, include: *attouichast*; *tiré*; *tresbusché*; *envelopper*; *réside*; *espancher*; *desvoyant*; *comprins*; *vuide*; *destituée*; *occupé*; *entré iusques au profond*; *diverty*; *distrait*; *se jette hors des gons*; *perdu en*; *unis*; *reietté*; *tenir son lieu*; *tout enclos sous*; *se desborderoyent*; *liez sous son joug*. They are frequently repeated, along with other such terms.

38. Ibid., IV, xvii, 380.

39. "La chair de Iesus Christ estant esloignée de nous par si longue distance parvienne jusqu'à nous . . . c'est que l'Esprit unit vrayement les choses qui sont séparées de lieu." Ibid., IV, xvii.

40. "Canal ou conduit." Ibid., IV, xvii, 384.

41. "Abraham . . . a esté père des fidèles circonciz; quand la muraille a esté rompue, comme dit l'Apostre, pour donner entrée au royaume de Dieu à ceux qui en estoit forcloz, il a esté fait aussi leur père, ia soit qu'ils ne fussent circonciz. Car le Baptesme leur est pour Circoncision." Ibid., IV, xvi, 350.

42. "À son serviteur Abraham, il luy adiouste la promesse de la terre de Chanaan, pour luy déclairer sa grâce et faveur sur luy. En telle sorte il faut prendre toutes les choses terriennes qu'il a promises au peuple Iudaïque, tellement que la promesse spirituelle procède tousiours comme fondement et chef, auquel tout le reste se rapporte . . . de luy sortiroit la semence dont toutes les nations de la terre seroyent bénites." Ibid., IV, xvi, 349; my emphasis.

43. "En lisant l'Escriture, nous rencontrons beaucoup de passages obscurs, qui nous arguent et conveinquent d'ignorance; et par ceste bride, Dieu nous retient en modestie, c'est d'assigner à chacun certaine mesure et portion de foy." Ibid., III, ii, 16.

44. "Bien est vray que le Temple estoit anciennement dédié par le commandement de Dieu pour offrir prières et sacrifices; mais cela estoit pour le temps que la vérité estoit figurée sous telles ombres, laquelle, nous estant désclairée maintenant au vif, ne permet point que nous nous arrestions à aucun temple matériel. Et mesme le Temple n'estoit pas recommandé aux Juifs à ceste condition qu'ils deussent enclorre la présence de Dieu dedans les murailles d'iceluy, mais pour les exercer à contempler l'effigie et image du vray Temple. Parquoy ceux qui estimoyent que Dieu habitast aux Temples construits de mains d'hommes furent grièvement reprins." Ibid., III, xx, 373–74.

45. Ibid., IV, xvii, 380, 377, 378, 380; "J'admoneste les lecteurs de ne contenir point leur sens entre si estroites bornes et limites, mais qu'ils s'efforcent de monter plus haut que ie ne les puis conduire" (381).

46. "Cependant que nous sommes hors de Christ et séparez d'avec luy . . . nous sommes entez en luy . . . et le vestons . . . jusques à ce que nous soyons faits un avec luy." Ibid., III, i, 8; my emphasis.

47. "De là se fait qu'il habite en noz coeurs, et néantmoins nous sommes eslongnez de luy" (ibid., II, ix, 192); "Il est nostre Dieu à telle condition qu'il habite au milieu de nous . . . une telle présence . . . or les âmes, si elles ne sont coniontes avec Dieu . . . estans estrangères de luy . . . demeurent en mort . . . qu'elles ayent sa conionction, et elle leur apportera la vie permanente" (II, x, 202).

48. "Il les veut donc faire participans de soy . . . Il nous faut donc avoir part en luy." Ibid., IV, xvi, 354; my emphasis.

49. Among which Philibert de l'Orme's *crypto porticus* can be included.

50. "Il s'en faut beaucoup qu'ils ne gardent ces limites, quand ils ne laissent anglet vuide de simulachre en tous leurs temples . . . ils rompent ces limites . . . ils ne regardent point ceste borne." Calvin, *Institution* (1969), I, 37–39.

51. "Ainsi la vertu et efficace s'est espandue outre toutes les limites du ciel et de la terre." Ibid., II, xvi, 297.

52. "Il nous faut bien estre sur nos gardes que nos pensées ou nos langues ne s'avancent point plus loin que les limites de la parolle de Dieu ne s'estendent, car comment l'esprit humain restreindra-il à sa petite capacité l'essence infinie de Dieu . . . Demeurons donc entre ces barres, auxquelles Dieu nous a voulu enclorre, et quasi tenir noz esprits enserrez, afin qu'ils ne descoulent point par une licence trop grande d'extravaguer." Ibid., I, xiv, 179–85.

53. "Après avoir conceu à la volée quelque sentiment de Dieu, incontinent nous retournons à nos resveries et nous en laissons transporter, corrompans par nostre vanité propre la vérité de Dieu . . . De là est sorti de ce bourbier infini d'erreurs, duquel tout le monde a esté rempli et couvert; car l'esprit d'un chacun y est comme un labyrinthe . . . phantosme au lieu de Dieu . . . nous transporter plus loin en erreur." Ibid., I, v, 81.

54. "*Labyrinth* suggested the anxiety implicit in the powerlessness of human beings to extricate themselves from a self-centered alienation from God . . . He used the notion of entrapment in a labyrinth to convey the sensations accompanying acute uncertainty and indecision in the face of the future . . . [and] his terrible sense of urgency for bringing [the world] into conformity with God's will and the cosmological model for its reform." Bouwsma, *John Calvin*, 82.

55. "Nous sera comme un labyrinthe pour nous entortiller de tous costez, si nous n'avons nostre adresse en la Parole." Calvin, *Institution* (1969), I, vi, 89.

56. Cotgrave, *Dictionarie*, s.v. "adresse."

57. "Je leur monstreray le but, auquel ilz devront tendre et diriger leur intention, en le lisant. Combien que la saincte Escriture contienne une doctrine parfaicte, à laquelle on ne peut rien adiouster . . . toutesfois, une personne qui n'y sera pas fort exercitée à bon mestier de quelque conduite et addresse, pour sçavoir ce qu'elle y doibt cercher: à fin de ne s'esgarer point, ça et là, mais de tenir une certaine voye pour attaindre tousiours à la fin où le Sainct Esprit l'appelle." Calvin, *Institution*, "Argument du present livre," 1552, p. 26; my emphasis.

58. Kingdon, *Geneva and the Wars of Religion*, 129. Kingdon makes the point concerning the significance of the two books, and paraphrases Calvin to this effect. He also observes the significance of scriptural structuring in the development and perpetuation of Calvinism: "When the revolution came, Geneva, the central authority of Calvinism, though in theory a nonbelligerent, in practice still served as the fountainhead. It was the prime source of ecclesiastical leaders and the outpouring of printer propaganda; it was a staging-base for conspiracies, a negotiating point for loans, and a producer and distributor of armament. Much of this was determined by the structure of an institution based on a few biblical verses."

59. "Touchant ce que le Pape estend ainsi sa jurisdiction sans fin, en cela il fait une grosse iniure et outrageuse." Calvin, *Institution* (1969), IV, vii, 142.

60. "A cause de ceste espérance aucuns de nous sont détenus en prisons, les

autres fouettez, les autres menez à faire amendes honorables, les autres bannis, les autres cruellement affligez, les autres eschappent par fuite." Ibid., "Epistre," I, 32.

61. "Certes l'Evangile ne retient point les cœurs des hommes en une joye de la vie presente, mais les eslève à l'espérance d'immortalité, et ne les attache point aux délices terriennes, mais démonstrant l'espérance, laquelle leur est préparée au ciel, les transporte en hault. Car à cela nous meine la définition qu'il en met en un autre lieu . . . le royaume éternelle de Dieu." Ibid., III, 91; my emphasis.

62. "Mais eux, ils sont bien loin de la vérité, quand ils ne recognoissent point d'Eglise, si elle ne se voit présentement à l'œil, et la veulent enclorre en certains limites, ausquels elle n'est nullement comprinse. C'est en ces poincts que gist nostre controversie. Premierement, qu'ils requièrent tousiours une forme d'Eglise visible et apparente. Nous, au contraire, affermons que l'Eglise peut consister sans apparence visible, et mesme que son apparence n'est à estimer de ceste braveté." Ibid., "Epistre," I, 41.

63. Hill, *English Bible*, 49, 35, 52, 57, 64 and passim. Hill also notes that the Bible was a storehouse of information and reference in code: "We must distinguish between the way in which men felt able to express themselves, their conventionally loyal language, on the one hand, and their actions on the other. Their language was often Aesopian, conveying messages different from what appears on the surface . . . The Bible facilitated this double-talk. Men knew their Bible very well in the seventeenth century, and could convey messages through allusions to it which are lost on a godless age," 49.

64. Calvin, *Institution* (1969), III, xv, 270. Similar passages are found in I, vi, 90: "la doctrine qui est pour establir sa principauté spéciale," and 91: "La beauté de ton temple est sainctété permanente."

65. "Puisqu'ainsi est que nous avons constitué deux régimes en l'homme, et qu'avons desia assez parlé du premier, qui réside en l'âme, ou en l'homme intérieur, et concerne la vie éternelle, ce lieu cy requiert que nous déclairions aussi bien le second, lequel appartient à ordonner . . . les mœurs extérieurs." Ibid., IV, x, 505.

66. He conceives of the structure of his text, one so preoccupied with spatial issues, appropriately in spatial terms: "even so I here *interlace* this point with the next." III, iii, 73; my emphasis.

67. Ibid., II, viii, 181. "Que la vie de l'homme soit conformée à la pureté de Dieu comme à un patron . . . que lors nostre vie sera bien ordonnée à la volonté de Dieu nous le propose pour reigle et patron (183) . . . l'homme a esté créé à l'image de Dieu, d'autant qu'il a esté formé au patron du Christ (xii, 239) . . . pour constituer l'ordre que nous devons tenir en terre, il ne nous faut suyvre autre patron que le Seigneur mesmes nous a baillé" (IV, vi, 115).

68. "Ezechiel les traitoit bien aussi asprement . . . 'la coniuration, dit-il, de ses Prophètes au milieu d'elle, est comme un lion rugissant, et qui ravist sa proie. Ils ont dévoré la vie, et ont ravi ce qui estoit précieux . . . les Prophètes ont édifié de mauvais ciment'" ibid., IV, ix, 173; "y ont voulu adiouster chacun son loppin après l'autre . . . coudre pièce sur pièce" (IV, x, 205).

69. Cotgrave, *Dictionarie*, s.v. "coniuration."

70. "Davantage, n'est-ce pas un vice digne de grande repréhension, qu'ils usent beaucoup de cérémonies non entendues, pour amuser le monde comme à

une bastellerie et ieu de farce ou à quelque coniuration d'enchanteurs? . . . toutes les cérémonies dont on use en la Papauté n'ont ne doctrine ne signification" (ibid., IV, x, 200); "Mais ces vauteurs, semblables à joueurs de passe-passe, n'estiment pas qu'il y ait nulle puissance de Dieu, sinon que par le monstre qu'ils forgent en leur cerveau tout ordre de nature soyent renversé. Ce qui est plustost borner Dieu et luy assigner ses rayes, à ce qu'il soit contraint d'obéir à nos fantaisies" (IV, xvii, 408).

71. "Que la conionction que nous devons avoir . . . dépend tellement de l'unité de foy, que ceste-cy en est le fondement, la fin et la reigle d'icelle . . . tout ce qui se fait hors de la parolle de Dieu est une faction d'infidèles." Ibid., IV, ii, 46.

72. "Nous pouvons user d'autres similitudes pour pleinement désigner les Sacremens, comme en les appellant pilliers de nostre foy; car ainsi qu'un édifice se porte et se soustient sur son fondement, et toutesfois quand on y adiouste par dessus les pilliers, il en est rendu plus seur et plus ferme, en ceste manière aussi-nostre foy se repose et soustient sur la parolle de Dieu comme sur son fondement, mais quand les sacremens y sont adioustez, ils luy servent ainsi que de pilliers, sur lesquels elle s'appuye plus fort, et s'y conferme encore mieux." Ibid., IV, xiii, 271.

73. Pierre de Ronsard, *Response aux injures et calomnies. Oeuvres complètes.* ed. Paul Laumonier. Hachette: Droz, 1914–1975. 20 vols., 35. "Tu as, pour renforcer l'erreur de ta folye, / A ton Genève apris quelque vieille homelie / De Calvin, que par cueur tu racontes icy, / Tu as en l'estomac un lexicon farcy / De mots injurieux qui donnent à cognoistre / Que mechant escolier tu as eu mechant maistre."

74. Ibid., I, v, 68–69.

75. Ibid., IV, xvii, 393.

76. Many second-generation Calvinist architects knew Calvin personally, as did Bernard Palissy. Others were formed in their faith by his teaching, preaching, commentaries and catechism.

77. Calvin, "Catechism of the Church of Geneva," 93. Quoted in the English.

78. Wallace, *Calvin*, 134, referring to Calvin's letter of October 1541.

79. Calvin, *Necessity*, 18. Quoted in the English. Emphasis added.

80. As Christopher Hill has noted, this was also a phenomenon that obtained during the English Reformation. The coding process was complex and multivalent, to the extent that one Protestant denomination might not grasp the inner layer of meaning derived from Scripture by another Protestant denomination.

81. Calvin, *Institution*, IV, 1, 19.

82. See Frank Lestringant, "Une cartographie iconoclaste: 'La Mappe-Monde Nouvelle Papistique' de Pierre Eskrich et Jean-Baptiste Trento," in Lestringant and Szykula, *Géographie du monde*, 99–120. Lestringant's argument reinforces my contention that the Calvinists used a subversive strategy in employing their opponents' techniques but in turning them to their own purposes. "Tout en condamnant, au nom de la pureté de l'Evangile, l'idolâtrie prétendue des catholiques, [la Réforme] a su recueillir, pour l'employer à des fins polémiques, tout un imaginaire fabuleux qu'elle a retourné ironiquement contre ses tenants les plus obstinés. Ce mécanisme de dénégation ambiguë touche également le domaine de la cartographie, dans son avatar allégorique et religieux. Dans ses *Disputations chrestiennes touchant l'estat des trespassez* (1552), le pasteur Pierre Viret, compagnon de Calvin à Genève, imagine le dessin d'une 'cosmographie infernale,' afin de ruiner, au moyen

d'une démonstration par l'absurde, les prétensions de la théologie scolastique à lé-
giférer sur le mystère divin de la vie éternelle. Retournant la fable cartographique
contre ses inventeurs, mais la prolongeant par là même, Viret se plaît à arpenter des
contrées aveugles de l'au-delà qui offrent paradoxalement au touriste théologien
une complexité topographique sans égale. Le même détournement sarcastique . . .
est à l'oeuvre dans la *Mappe-Monde Nouvelle Papistique.*"

Chapter 3. Calvinist Recipes for Restructuring the World

1. It is possible to make unprecedented links between this early Calvinist
interest in automata, technology, and protoscience and the later discourse of the
encyclopédistes of the eighteenth century. The *encyclopédistes'* incorporation of the
mechanical arts in the detailed, fully illustrated 2,285 planches of the *Encyclopédie*
was an attempt at enacting a socially leveling discourse, one that valorized artisanal
endeavor, incorporating it within the format of what remained, admittedly, an elitist document. The Calvinist plain style, aimed at eliminating five-tiered medieval
exegesis and at attaining clarity in explicating the divine Word, was also a highly
pragmatic and practical vehicle for the exposition of protoscientific thought, technology, and rational ways of ordering, describing and explaining the world. Calvinist architects were perhaps the first to exalt the trades, artisans, the mechanical arts,
and early forms of technological innovation such as the tinkering with automata
and robotlike constructions that so occupied much of the early seventeenth century. Frontispieces and quasi-emblematic illustrations found at the beginning of
their publications often incorporated tools of the artisan's trade and may be interpreted as prefiguring such a focus in Enlightenment thought. Bernard Palissy's
Recepte véritable displays a device showing a figure digging in the earth with a spade
and holding aloft a pair of calipers. Another example is the Calvinist architect
Jean Bullant, who commences his *Reigle générale de l'architecture* with an illustration of an astrolabe, a compass and ruler, and a mason's square. The notion that
the world can be retooled derives from the Calvinists: their reordering schemas,
such as Palissy's postlapsarian garden intended to realign humanity with God, are
similar—if not in intent, in method—to Enlightenment tactics for shedding the
light of reason on humanity. How far a step is it really from Palissy's or Bullant's
artisan emblems to the *Encyclopédie's planches*? One *planche* from Diderot's encyclopedia displays the interior of a printer's workshop. Each implement, letter case,
piece of type, is carefully delineated, and men stand at various stations around the
workshop, performing their functions—choosing type, inserting it, rolling sheets
of paper, inking the cases—with a precision and machinelike unitary effect of effort
that can be compared to the manifold moving pieces of an automaton. Many
Calvinists worked on automata, among them Palissy, who created them to show
how, if nature was irremediably marked by the Fall, artificial constructions could
offer a corrective expedient, mechanistically programming a machined re-creation
of humanity. Similarly, the human figures interacting with the tools of their trade
form a machined unit, an ordering and producing complex. Like the various com-

ponents of an automaton, the human figures function as *semes* in a new mechanical discourse, one that produces a rational sense immediately comprehended by all viewers. For Calvinists, since nature was reprobate, no metaphysics could inhere there. The Calvinists' denial of a Catholic belief in immanence leads logically, then, to a more rational discourse such as that of the *philosophes*.

2. "Palissy worked in two broad styles. On many of his plates, platters, and pitchers he encrusted high relief leaves, insects, and sea life, so naturalistically molded that their exact species are identifiable. And on other pieces he used elements from the store of classical motifs common to Renaissance architects. The latter formed for Palissy a ready allegorical vocabulary. Often he combined the two." Johnson, "Palissy," 403.

3. "Le nombre de mes ans . . . m'a fait souvenir qu'il est escrit: que l'on se donne garde d'abuser dons de Dieu, et de cacher le talent en terre . . . Parquoy je me suis efforcé de mettre en lumière les choses qu'il a pleu à Dieu me faire entendre . . . [ja'i gratté l'espace de quarante ans, et fouillé les entrailles d'icelle, à fin de cognoistre les choses qu'elle produit dans soy, et par tel moyen j'ai trouvé grace devant Dieu." Palissy, *Discours*, 130.

4. Palissy, "De l'art de la terre," in *Oeuvres complètes*, 217.

5. "Toutes ces fautes [en poterie] m'ont causé un tel labeur et tristesse qu'auparavant que j'aye eu rendu mes esmaux fusibles à un mesme degré de feu, j'ay *cuidé entrer jusques à la porte du sépulchre*; aussi en me travaillant à tels [sic] affaires, je me suis trouvé si fort escoulé en ma personne qu'il n'y avait aucune forme ny apparence de bosse aux bras ny aux jambes" (my emphasis). Ibid., 218. The phrase "si fort escoulé" structures Palissy's broken body as very much like that of the battered, truncated, architectural "Terme" in his garden grotto, a "forme martelée" that incarnates debased humanity.

6. Ibid., 210.

7. Johnson, "Palissy," 405.

8. Ibid., 404.

9. Ibid., 409.

10. Ibid., 410.

11. "La terre des combats subit la même évocation . . . 'le chemin . . . la forêt . . . les lieux inaccessibles . . . la rade . . . le ruisseau . . . les marais' . . . On pourrait parler d'une influence littéraire sur les textes gouvernementaux . . . [Tout ceci] n'est pas la preuve d'une prise de possession, mais seulement le figure d'un désir." Méchoulan, *L'état baroque*, 344–45.

12. Ibid., 404. Such is also the case with many of Philibert de l'Orme's constructions. "The grotto, like most of Palissy's works, did not last—the waterlogged bodies of its porous clay creatures almost immediately flaked and cracked with winter freezes."

13. "Contrefacteur." Lestringant, "Palissy à Saintes," 643.

14. Ibid., 405.

15. Paper and text of a talk by architectural historian at the University of Toronto, Patricia O'Grady, entitled "A Huguenot Statement in Architectural Terms," 4. O'Grady ascertains the architect's Calvinist stance from other of his engravings and writings, all issued under the same ciphered name. Other visual pre-

cursors of the epitome of French classical style can be found in the works of other Calvinist architects and designers. An engraving by "J. P. de C.," a protectively self-disguising yet self-avowed Calvinist, portrays a royal pavilion, "the most futuristic [of his] designs . . . proposing to house 900 people [and stylistically] a precursor of Versailles."

16. "La France avoit mestier / Que ce potier fut Roy, que ce / Roy fut potier." Lestringant, "Palissy à Saintes," 644.

17. "C'est bien d'un échange de souveraineté entre le prince et l'artiste, que nous entretient . . . la *Recepte véritable*." Lestringant, "Prince et potier," 5.

18. Ibid., 7.

19. "Pour le présent un Psaume nous suffira (Psaume 145), auquel toute la somme de ses propriétez est si diligemment récitée qu'il n'y a rien laissé derrière." (1552), I, x, 118.

20. "Car ce n'est pas un petit honneur, que Dieu en faveur de nous a si magnifiquement orné le monde, afin que nous n'ayons point seulement la veue de ce beau théâtre, mais aussi que nous ayons la fruition de la diverse abondance et variété des biens qui nous sont exposez en iceluy." (Geneva, 1561), p. 3.

21. "Voilà pourquoy je veux ériger mon jardin sur le Pseaume cent quatre, là où le prophète descri les oeuvres excellentes, et merveilleuses de Dieu . . . Je veux aussi édifier ce jardin admirable, à fin de donner aux hommes de se rendre amateurs du cultivement de la terre." 126.

22. Ibid., 22.

23. "Quand S. Paul a voulu que toute prophétie fut conforme à l'analogie et similitude de la foy, il a mis une très certaine reigle pour esprouver toute interprétation de l'Escriture." Calvin, "Epistre au Roy," *Institution* (1552), V, i, 31.

24. At the time Palissy was writing, Calvinists had no churches in which to celebrate; they could only hope to appropriate a barn, such as the "grange" at Wassy, and consecrate it, or to occupy and redefine a Catholic church.

25. Calvin, *Institution* (1552), I, 42. "Vous vous arrestez trop aux murailles, cerchans l'Eglise de Dieu en la beauté des édifices, pensans que l'union des fidèles soit là contenue. Doutons-nous que l'Antechrist doive là avoir son siège? Les montagnes, et bois, et lacs, et prisons, et deserts, et caves me sont plus seurs et de meilleure fiance."

26. Ibid., 254.

27. "Parquoy combien que les hommes doivent dresser les yeux pour contempler les oeuvres de Dieu, d'autant qu'ils en sont ordonnez spectateurs, et que le monde leur est dressé comme un théâtre à cest effect, toutesfois le principal est, pour mieux profiter, d'avoir les oreilles dressés à la Parole, pour s'y rendre attentifs." Calvin, *Institution* (1552), I, vi, 88–89.

28. "The value of a Botanic Garden was that it conveyed a direct knowledge of God. Since each plant was a created thing, and God had revealed a part of himself in each thing that he created, a complete collection of all the things created by God must reveal God completely." Prest, *Garden of Eden*, 8.

29. Ibid., 62.

30. Comito, *Idea*, 14.

31. Ibid.

32. Lestringant, "L'art imite la nature," 167.

33. "Comme le rappelaient Charles Estienne et Jean Liébault dans leur *Agriculture et maison rustique*, le dessein d'un jardin d'agrément suppose la rencontre de deux désirs à la fois complémentaires et concurrents: celui du jardinier-géometre qui invente et trace les compartiments du parterre, et celui du 'maistre et seigneur à qui appartient le parterre.'" Ibid., 137.

34. Charles Estienne, *Maison rustique, or the countrie farme*, b2.

35. Its interiority and hiddenness are revealed in its description: "beautiful with inward rooms, secrets . . ." (Ii) like Palissy's grottoes; and also in the book's concern that what it has to say might not be for all to hear: "and now . . . this my countrie house . . . beseecheth [that it] may dare to shew itself openly." (Ii)

36. Estienne and Liébault, *Maison*, 1. Succeeding citations to page numbers appear in parentheses in the text.

37. "Cela est dangereuse à rompre, et de petite durée . . . il y a certaines mines de pierre desquelles la pierre en est gelice, venteuse, & dissolutive, en cas pareil, il y a aussi des terres qui sont si poreuses & spongieuses, lesquelles s'abreuvent des pluyes qui tombent dessus. Et estant imbibées s'il vient à geler, ladicte imbibition fera violence au corps où elle sera enfermée." *Recepte véritable*, 254–55; hereafter cited as *RV*.

38. "Du Bartas, as had Palissy, reworked classical architectural modes. If it is true that, since Vitruvius, 'ancient inventors of great buildings took their models from columns, trees and human forms,' the conclusion that Du Bartas draws from this in building his 'Eden' is that the trunks of plane trees and palms are the living pillars of God's church . . . Already in Book VII of his first volume of the *Architecture*, Philibert . . . like Bramante, added to classical columnar orders stones resembling trees . . . to such highly effective trompe-l'oeil pieces was added a spirit of insistent geometry . . . In order to depict the work of 'simple peasants' in his book *Misères* d'Aubigné used the same metaphors . . . the 'parquets and mosaics' of the architect Androuet du Cerceau could also serve as models for the representation of a deliberately Euclidean Eden." Lestringant, "L'art imite la nature," 169.

39. Marin, *Portrait*, 185.

40. H. B. Taylor, "Historical Study," 101, citing Calvin. Emphasis added.

41. Ibid.

42. Calvin, quoting Cyprian, *De unitate ecclesiae*, in *The Necessity of Reforming the Church*, 146–47.

43. Gebelin, *Châteaux*, 39.

44. Hill, *English Bible*, 128.

45. Ibid., 143.

46. John Evelyn, cited in Hunt, *Garden and Grove*, 81.

47. "J'entray en moy-mesme, pour fouiller les secrets de mon coeur, et entrer en ma conscience, pour savoir [ce qu'il y avoit] en moy." Palissy, *RV*, 46.

48.
"Car maintenant Lecteur, cette Grotte te range
A contempler de près un oeuvre sourcilleux,
En sa voulte semblant au grand tout des haultz cieux,
En diverses façons qui tout autour se change.

. . . Au vray te feront dire, en voyant ça et la,
Les animaux rampens à l'entour de cela,
Que l'art ingénieux surmonte la nature." *RV*, 259.

49. See Origen's *Commentary on Song of Songs*, cited in Fletcher, *Allegory*, 329. "The word pro-verb denotes that one thing is openly said, and another is inwardly meant."

50. "Je te prie instruire les laboureurs, qui ne sont litérez, à ce qu'ils ayent songneusement à s'estudier en la philosophie naturelle, suivant mon conseil: et singulièrement, que ce secret et enseignement des fumiers que j'ai mis en ce livre, leur soit divulgué et manifesté." *RV*, 52.

51. John Ruskin quoted in Harpham, *Grotesque*, 66.

52. Cotgrave, *Dictionarie*, s.v. "Grotesques."

53. Bloch, *Utopian Function of Art*, xxxiii.

54. "Voilà toute l'édification du premier des quatre cabinets verds." Palissy, *RV*, 142.

55. "Si tu es homme de bon jugement, tu pourras assez aisément entendre, combien la chose sera plaisante, estant érigée en la forme que je t'ay dit: venons à présent au cabinet, qui sera au milieu du jardin." Ibid., 152.

56. "Au reste, cette première dignité ne nous peut venir au devant, qu'à l'opposite nous ne soyons contreins de voir un triste spectacle de nostre deformité et ignominie, d'autant que nous sommes decheuz de nostre origine en la personne d'Adam." Calvin, *Institution* (1552), II, i, 8.

57. "Même divin, l'acte de créer se décompose donc en deux temps: un acte initial de production pure . . . c'est alors le Chaos, évoqué au début . . . 'Ce premier monde estoit une forme sans forme.' Le deuxième temps de la création est le modelage . . . sa métamorphose." Bellenger, "La métamorphose," in *La métamorphose*, 103.

58. "To focus on the garden grotto is to focus on the artificial cavern—the creation of a cosmos in miniature, a nature that is cultivated and controlled. Art imitating and surpassing nature; the theme is constant . . . [in] Palissy." Miller, *Heavenly Caves*, 10.

59. See Fenoaltea, *Du palais*.

60. "Ils furent esbahis de voir le partiment, / en un lieu si désert, d'un si beau bastiment: / le plan, le frontispice et les pilliers rustiques, / Qui effacent l'honneur de ces colonnes antiques / De voir que la nature avoit portrait les murs / De crotesque . . ." Vv. 45–46, cited in ibid., 109.

61. Ibid.

62. D'Aubigné, *Oeuvres*, 429.

63. Miller, *Heavenly Caves*, 44, 53.

64. "Quelle forme pensons-nous avoir reluy en l'Eglise . . . combien de fois depuis l'advènement de Christ a-elle esté cachée sans forme? Combien souvent a-elle esté tellement opprimée par guerres, par séditions, par hérésies, qu'elle ne se monstroit en nulle partie?" Calvin, *Institution* (1552), "Epistre," I, 42, 5.

65. Hunt, "Ut pictura poesis," 104. Hunt notes a precedent for reading material being used to fill empty spaces in grottoes.

66. The deist descendant of Palissy's personage is Rousseau's *Promeneur solitaire*.

67. "Ce mot de résidence doit estre pris en autre sense que celuy d'Essence... Quand l'Escriture fait mention de la Parolle éternelle de Dieu . . . Parole signifie une sagesse résidente en Dieu . . . la Parole est vray Dieu." Calvin, *Institution* (1552), I, xiii, 152–53.

68. "J'ay à présent à te faire le discours d'une commodité, qu'il y aura en mon jardin merveilleusement utile, belle, et plaisante. Et quand je te l'auray contée, tu cognoistras que ce n'est pas sans cause, que j'ay cherché de faire mon jardin joignant les rochers." *RV*, 148.

69. Miller, *Fountains*, 244. See in this regard the *Oeuvre* of the Calvinist Dijonais architect Hugues Sambin, famous for his *termes*.

70. "Ceste mal'heureuse ruine en laquelle nous sommes tresbuschez par la révolte du premier homme." Calvin, *Institution* (1552), I, 1, 51.

71. "Sileni [o grotteschi] simbolizzano il conflitto fra interiorità spirituale ed apparenze mondane." Carpo, *La maschera*, 123–25.

72. "Erasmo [come Rabelais] tornerà sovente sul terme dei sileni di Alcibiade . . . I sileni erano geni, o demoni, di natura equina, con orecchie e code di cavallo . . . I sileni persero la forma equina e divennero demoni scherzosi e ridicoli, grotteschi . . . In ogni caso, la comparazione era ben nota agli umanisti. La citazione veniva riferita a tutto ciò che dissiumlava, sotto un'apparenza ridicola o vile, un fondo serio o prezioso." Ibid., 123.

73. "In any form, the [grotto] signified a transformation, a metamorphosis from one sphere into that of another." Miller, *Fountains*, 244.

74. Ibid., 266.

75. Harpham, *Grotesque*, 27.

76. "Les vues de l'extérieur sont transférées sur les murs à l'intérieur de par des miroirs." Baltrusaitis, *Aberrations*, 20.

77. Harpham, *Grotesque*, 3.

78. Ibid., 7.

79. "The word *grottesche* was applied to certain ornamental designs modeled on recently excavated Roman frescoes. These designs were primarily decorative in character but they differed from most traditional ornament in that not only were they capable of filling a space all by themselves, with no help from any central subject, but they also incorporated interpretable, frequently human, elements into the design, and so they were ambivalently meaning-bearing as well as decorative." Ibid., xxi.

80. "L'anamorphose intervient d'abord en rendant à la fois problématique et nécessaire la découverte d'un point fixe donné. La perspective classique, à point de vue perpendiculaire, laisse toujours au spectateur une relative liberté de déplacement autour du point optimal avant que l'image ne se defasse ou ne se déforme sérieusement . . . L'anamorphose requiert que le destinateur entre entièrement dans le jeu du code, à la recherche du point de vue ou du mode de vision qui délivre le sens 'intenté.'" Ferdinand Hallyn, "Le thème de la métamorphose," in Bellenger, *La métamorphose*, 122.

81. Perez-Gomez, *Architecture*, 178.

82. "Stunning reversals of natural patterns and human conventions betrayed a loss of direction that often led artists to look at the world upside down . . . Ideological losses were contemplated by a multitude of styles . . . the language of the world no longer aimed at unity . . . Instead, it engaged in mannerist contemplation." Maiorino, *Portrait*, 5.

83. Lefebvre, *Production of Space*, 97.

84. Harpham, *Grotesque*, 97.

85. "Je prendray premièrement certaines branches de celles que j'auray laissé debout, et les ayans couchées en la manière des autres, j'en feray la forme de la corniche, en telle sorte que je t'ay dit de l'architrave: car je feray avancer les branches par degrez, mesurées par art de Géometrie et Architecture . . . Je feray tenir à une chacune gitte, ou branche, une forme de lettre antique bien proportionnée . . . Il y aura escrit en ladite frise une authorité prinse au livre de Sapience . . . afin que les hommes qui rejetteront Sapience, discipline et doctrine, soyent mesme condamnez par les tesmoignages des âmes végétatives et insensibles." Palissy, *RV*, 141–42.

86. Leeman and Schuyt, *Hidden Images*, 90–92.

87. "Quand vous voudrez ayder du triangle, vous regarderez par un des costez tel qu'il vous plaira . . . cela faict vous jecterez votre veue sur la ville, chasteau ou place, de laquelle vous voulez prendre la forme & figure, & en ferez premièrement un esquiche marqué sur du papier grossement ainsi que votre jugement le peult comprendre. Puis vous ferez le destour du tout. Si vous voulez il ne fault que tenir en mémoire ou par escrit une chacune face . . . Et ainsi continuant vous représenteray iustement la forme de tous les angles & destours de la ville." De l'Orme, *Architecture*, II, v, 42–43.

88. "Il n'estoit question que de Pseaumes, Prières, Cantiques et Chansons spirituelles . . . Voilà comment nostre Eglise a esté érigée." Palissy, *RV*, 200.

89. "En ce temps si trouble, & calamiteux, amy Lecteur, cherchant quelque honneste exercice humain, lequel avec autres meilleures méditations, m'osterait d'une partie de tant d'ennuy, où je me voy enveloppé, avec plusieurs, je me suis advisé de mettre en avant un petit discours . . . C'est d'un Grotte . . . Tu cognoistras que l'oeuvre en toutes parties géometriques est si ingénieusement divisé & conduict, que la leçon qu'icy je te propose, t'apportera plaisir & admiration." Ibid., 235.

90. "Qui sont mis au dessouz des choses merveilleuses que l'auteur de ce livre a préparé et *mis par ordre* en son cabinet, pour prouver toutes les choses contenues en ce livre, par ce qu'aucuns ne voudroyent croire, afin d'asseurer ceux qui voudront prendre la peine de les venir voir en son cabinet, et, les ayant veus, s'en iront *certains de toutes choses escrites* dans ce livre." Palissy, "Coppie des Escrits," in *Oeuvres complètes*, 2: 258.

91. "Tu vois aussi que les pierres de plâtre, de talque et d'ardoise s'eslevent et se desassemblent par fueillets en la forme d'un livre." Ibid., 260.

92. "Et pour bien t'inciter à préparer tes aureilles pour ouyr et tes yeux pour regarder, j'ay mis icy certaines pierres et mineraux . . . pour te faire entendre un point singulier et de grand poix . . . ces preuves évidentes." Ibid., 262.

93. "N'ayant veu autre chose que mes escrits et plattes figures . . . ay mis en ce lieu en évidence un grand nombre de pierres, par lesquelles tu pourras aisément

connoistre estre véritable les raisons et preuves que j'ay mises . . . Et si tu n'es du tout aliéné des sens tu le confesseras après avoir eu la démonstration des pierres naturelles lesquelles j'ay figuré en mon livre . . . ceux qui les verront . . . seront contrains de confesser." Ibid., 258.

94. "Il est escrit qu'on se donne garde d'abuser les dons de Dieu et de cacher le talent en terre . . . Parquoy je me suis efforcé de mettre en lumière les choses qu'il a pleu à Dieu me faire entendre." Palissy, *Discours admirables*, 3.

95. Ibid., 4.

96. "[Méfiez-vous] de quelque livre escrit par imagination, de ceux qui n'ont rien pratiqué . . . prendre la peine de venir voir mon cabinet, auquel on verra des choses merveilleuses qui sont mises pour preuve de mes escrits, attachez par ordre et par estages, et avec certains escriteaux afin qu'un chacun puisse s'instruire pour soy-mesme." Ibid.

97. Hunt, *Garden and Grove*, 73.

98. O'Grady, "Huguenot Statement," 1.

99. Chambéry, *Fortifications*, xii.

100. "Rapportant les mesures que l'on voudra scavoir avec le compas sur l'eschelette . . . au profil on trouvera ce qu'on cerche tant au plan qu'en perspective." Ibid., x.

101. "Pseaume XCI. Qui en la garde du hault Dieu pour jamais se retire en ombre bonne et en fort lieu retire se peut dire conclu donc en lentendement. Dieu est ma garde sure ma haulte tour et fondement sur lequel ie massure. C'est du psaume XCI." Ibid., vi. It is also worth noting that these images and captions are very difficult to read. The reader must continually turn the book, to "square" the plate, as it were. The result is that the Word, by mere virtue of the attention it demands in order to read it fully, tends to usurp the image. The image seems part of a design, while the Word seems to be the essential element in the composition.

102. "Tu aimeras le seigneur ton Dieu de tout ton coeur, de toute ton âme et de tout ton entendement, c'est le premier et le grand commandement et le second semblable à icelui, est, tu aimeras ton prochain comme toy mesme de ces deux commandemens despendent toute la loy et les prophetes. C'est le sommaire de toute la loy. Exode vintiesme et mattieu vintedeuxiesme chapitre." Ibid., xiv.

103. "Vous tous Princes et Seigneurs remplis de gloire et dhonneur Rendez—Craignez Dieu—Rendez au Seigneur toute force Et toute honneur. Psaume vinteneufviesme." Ibid., title page.

104. "La grande ville de Paris a esté assiégée & prise . . . par le grand Roy Henri III, le 22 de mars 1594." Ibid.

105. "On a beau sa maison bastir si le seigneur ny met la main cela n'est que bastir en vain quand on veut villes garentir on a beau veiller sans Dieu rien ne profitera." Ibid., x.

106. "Et pour attestation des choses susdictes, j'en prens à tesmoing monseigneur le Duc de Montpansier, lequel se transporta dernierement qu'il estoit en Xaintonge à mon hastelier, accompaigné de plusieurs grands seigneurs. Lequel apres avoir veu la grandeur de l'oeuvre, ou partie, il mit en sauvegarde moy, & tous ceux de ma maison . . . Et partant que j'aurois esté accusé de la nouvelle reli-

gion (qu'on appelle) . . . qu'il en reservoit à luy la cognoissance. J'en prens aussi à tesmoing . . . Aussi ont veu ledict oeuvre feu le Roy, & la Royne de Navarre, accompaignez d[u] seigneu[r] . . . de Rohan." *RV*, 237.

107. "Quelque temps apres que j'eu consideré les horribles dangers de la guerre, desquels Dieu m'avoit merveilleusement delivré, il me print envie de designer et pourtraire l'ordonnance de quelque Ville, en laquelle on peust estre asseuré au temps de guerre." Ibid., 208.

108. I should note here that Patricia O'Grady, the only other North American scholar to my knowledge who has worked on *Des fortifications*, does not agree with me on this. She feels that the scriptural citations do not contradict the images that they circumscribe. Although not willing to go as far as I do, she does, however, concur that "these are projects . . . that represent a Huguenot mentality." Letter to author, 30 September, 1994.

109. "Tu as bien mal retenu mon propos: car je ne t'ay pas dit, que par le plan et pourtrait, on peust juger le total, mais avec le plan et pourtrait, j'ay adjousté qu'il estoit requis faire un Modelle." *RV*, 221; "Mais je me suis estudié d'escrire le plus bref que j'ay peu en ce petit dialogue, lequel se doit plutost appeler un abregé, ou epitome, que non pas dialogue." Ibid., 236. His emphasis on the need for brevity necessarily entails incompleteness; there is not sufficient space for untrammeled expression.

110. "Voulant edifier ma Ville en forme et ligne aspirale, et ensuivant la forme et industrie du pourpre: mais quand j'eu un peu pensé à mon affaire, j'apperceus que le devoir du canon est de jouër par lignes directes, et que si ma Ville estoit totalement edifiee, suivant la ligne aspirale, que le canon ne pourroit jouër par les ruës, parquoy . . . je commençay . . . en vironnant à l'entour, en forme carree." Ibid., 216.

111. "À fin de voir s'il y avoit quelque figure de labyrinthe inventee par Dedalus, . . . qui me peust servir à mon dessein." Ibid., 209.

112. Keith Cameron, editor of *RV*, x. Indeed, Cameron has suggested that Palissy's text and, by extension, the structures that it profiles constitute a sort of advertisement, both Huguenot and commercial self-promotion. If such is the case, that explains many things. We could then consider the book as displaying Palissy's qualities and aptitudes.

113. "Il me sembla que ma Ville se moquoit de toutes les autres: parce que toutes les murailles des autres Villes sont inutiles en temps de Paix, et celles que je fais, serviront en tout temps, pour habitation à ceux mesmes qui exerceront plusieurs arts, en gardant ladite Ville." *RV*, 217.

114. "Voila bien un pauvre corps de Ville, quand les membres ne se peuvent consolider et aider l'un l'autre . . . Il est fort aisé de battre le corps, si les membres ne donnent aucun secours." Ibid., 209.

115. See also ibid., 210.

116. Harpham, *Grotesque*, 94.

117. "De faire plaisir cest mon grand plaisir, faisons à tous comme nous voulons qu'il nous soit faict." Chambéry, *Fortifications*, 26.

118. "Ceste figure est de *divers* plans de fortifications & de *divers* profits pour contenter *diverses* opinions. Mais une grande importance & despence il se fault re-

soudre par une bonne consultation de gens capables, & bailler la charge à un seul pour commander." Ibid., 18.

119. "Les chrestiens enfans de Dieu sont le vray temple d'iceluy"; "peut bien servir pour un grand temple." Ibid.

120. See Phillippe Joutard, "The Museum of the Desert: The Protestant Minority" *Realms of Memory*, ed. P. Nora, vol. 1 (New York: Columbia University Press, 1992), 353–71. Such Protestant countercultural expressions continue even in our day; consider the unified opposition the Protestant town of Le Chambon made to Nazi persecution of the Jews in World War II. Their opposition was explicitly expressed as an offshoot of their faith. Professor Patrick Henry of Whitman College is working on this subject.

121. "Inventeur qui craint Dieu / Ne craint rien dautre." Chambéry, *fortifications*, 21.

Chapter 4. Philibert de l'Orme and the "Peculiar Problems" of Protestant Architecture

An earlier version of this chapter appeared as a monograph in the series edited by David Willis, *Philibert de l'Orme: Protestantism and Architecture*, Studies in Reformed History and Theology, 2 (Princeton Theological Seminary, 1997).

1. Philibert de l'Orme, "Instruction de Monsieur d'Yvry, dict de l'Orme," quoted in Blunt, *Philibert*, 150–51.

2. Interestingly, Calvin specifically inveighed against the Cercle de Meaux for nicodemism; he felt that their neo-Platonizing tendencies led them to dilute portions of Christian doctrine. Calvin was concerned that Marguerite, too, despite his extensive correspondence with her, might manifest a more weak version of the Christian faith.

3. "Nella bibliografia tournesiana de guegli anni non mancano Marot, la stessa Margherita di Navarra, la versione italiana del Nuovo Testamento del Brucioli." Carpo, *La maschera*, 102.

4. "Nel cinquecento l'architettura sicuramente era un mezzo di communicazione di massa." Ibid., 117. Serlio's strategies were particularly "subversive" in that architecture was a—perhaps *the*—mass medium in the sixteenth century, and thus could display monumental messages to many.

5. "Perciò Christo, per essere compreso soltanto dai fratelli, parlò in parabole . . . la simulazione religiosa, si vede, era a seconda dei casi una dottrina, un'ideologia, una strategia, o una necessità. *L'Extraordinario libro* Serliano è un caso di simulazione architettonica. Più o meno ambiguamente, l'autore offre al pubblico esempi deplorevoli—propaganda (apparentemente) l'errore ed il vizio; dice ciò che forse non pensa, e nello stesso tempo allude a ciò che pensa, ma non dice." Ibid., 116.

6. "Benché i verí templi siano I cuori dei pietosi cristiani . . . nondimeno ancora sono i templi materiali necessari al culto divino." Ibid., 85, quoting Serlio in his *Quinto libro*.

7. This is, incidentally, one way in which the later Calvinist architects ratio-nalized their construction of buildings for Catholic worship—as is the case, for instance, with the openly Calvinist Salomon de Brosse, who nonetheless built Catholic churches—nicodemism regards *adiaphora* as unessential accretions that cannot harm true faith. If one's Calvinism is unshakeable, the reasoning proceeded, what harm in erecting a Catholic church?

8. "Non a tutto si può dire la verità. Gli eletti sapranno troverla. I reprobi, predestinati alla dannazione, in ogni caso non potranno capirla. Perché dunque cercare di convincerli? . . . I topoi dell'interiorità della fede, della chiesa come as-semblea, di eletti, dell'inutilità della propaganda ante porcos . . . Anche fra gli architetti, come fra tutti I mortali, esistono eletti e reporbi. Anche in architettura esiste una verità, anzi, quasi una verità rivelata . . . solo, questa verità non è per tutti." Carpo, *La maschera*, 120.

9. "Un poco, come per intermedio, dell'architettura giudiziosa, e massi-mamente degli ornamentire del decoro, e per conoscere, per quanto potrà il mio piccolo intelletto, un'architettura soda, semplice, schietta, dolce e morbida da una debole, gracile, delicata, affettata, cruda, anzi oscura e confusa." Serlio, quoted in ibid., 56.

10. Among such factors are his title Abbé d'Ivry and the last rites that he received on his deathbed.

11. "Le dessous en avait été tellement travaillé par des carrières et par le mouvement des eaux." Prévost, *Philibert*, 32.

12. Blunt, *Philibert*, 86.

13. Prévost, *Philibert*, 40. "Il cherche un accaparement de l'espace, par des formes qui doivent rappeler celles du ciel."

14. Blunt, *Philibert*, 88.

15. Ibid., 93.

16. "His proposal to double the pavilions as adjacent to the corps-de-logis . . . was an arrangement widely to be followed in the seventeenth century, for instance, by Salomon de Brosse at the Luxembourg, although it had the disadvan-tage of making the side elevation asymmetrical." Ibid., 94.

17. Clouzot, *Philibert*, 152.

18. See, for instance, Philibert de l'Orme, *Nouvelles inventions*, II, i, 309.

19. Larissa Taylor, *Soldiers of Christ*, 118.

20. In one such possible borrowing, Philibert's allegory of the "Critic" visu-ally depicts *skandalon*, or stumbling blocks in the way of the comprehension or observance of a biblical life: a primary concern of *Des scandales*.

21. The dimensions for Solomon's temple are found in the Old Testament, and Philibert reproduces them exactly in his text.

22. He eventually aborts the project, seeming to recognize that no space exists within hostile Catholic France for an Old Testament structure with which Calvinists, conceiving of themselves as the Hebrew patriarchs, would identify.

23. Serlio uses the excuse of "novelty" to exculpate him for any fault that might be found with his work; such self-protective terminology also appears in Philibert's title.

24. "Laquelle neantmoins ie monstreray quelque iour, avec plusieurs autres

belles inventions que i'ay trouvées, s'il plaist à Dieu me donner l'esprit plus libre, & me mettre hors de tous ennuis & traverses que l'on m'a donné depuis le trespas du feu Roy Henry." Philibert, *Nouvelle inventions* I & X, "Conclusion," 308.

25. Blunt, *Art and Architecture*, 94.

26. *Ibid.*, 85.

27. See his will, published in Clouzot, *Philibert*, 81–84. It is also noteworthy that, during the Wars of Religion, Philibert was not banished, as were other Calvinist architects such as du Cerceau. This attests to a considerable degree of covert and secret sympathizing rather than overt or explicit confessional identity for Philibert.

28. Clouzot, *Philibert*, xiii. It is possible to limit the interpretation of Philibert's originality only to the architectural culture of the times. For instance, Philibert, like Borromini, was an imaginative and inventive architect who bent the established rules to create works that were unique yet still recognizably part of tradition. This architectural invention parallels the subversion that I see in Philibert's works, but both must be accounted for. It is not sufficient to take the buildings as structure; there is always a determining intention—and sometimes, several *warring* intentions and directives—behind their construction.

29. It is undeniable that Philibert's allegories and his entire text can be interpreted in another way, as simply epitomizing the contemporary struggle of artists and architects in society to establish the intellectual value of their profession in distinction from craftsmen. Read in comparison with the editions of Vitruvius or Barbaro or Serlio, such seems a more plausible case. However, while this context may be a parallel phenomenon, it is significant that Philibert's Calvinism has been overlooked and that all the other architects of the king were Calvinists. The confessional stance cannot fail to have had a theoretical and an actual impact. A fuller and more balanced picture of the complexities within which Philibert labored is produced through the mutual consideration of *both* contextual issues.

30. "Au reste, il n'est ia besoin de chercher par un long circuit quel sens il use de ces mots." (1552), IV, xvii, 412.

31. "Comme cousue de toutes pièces." IV, xix, 499.

32. "Les poutres estans tirées de tels centres, & assemblées par telles commissures qui en procedent, se trouvent d'une force incroyable quand elles sont construictes . . . Telles commissures & assemblages ne se voyent point pour les ornemens." II & XI, vii, 18.

33. See Carpo, *La maschera*, 70. "L'ironio serliana ha un sapore amoro . . . il libro nasce in un contesto ostile, nell'isolamente e nello solitudine."

34. "Quand toutes les poutres sont parfaictes & assemblées, comme ie vous ay descrit cy-devant, si elles sont pour servir à une salle ou chambre, aucuns ne trouveront beau de voir les liernes, clefs, chevilles, pouteaux & liens estre ainsi creux par le milieu de la poutre, & voudront dire que ce sera un amas d'ordures & nichées d'araignées, qui pourroit estre vray. Mais pour y obvier, il faut enrichir lesdites poutres de quelques lambris dorez, ou autres ornemens, tant riches que voudrez." Philibert, *Nouvelles inventions*, II & XI, v, 315.

35. "Modestia e semplicità non sono valori vitruviani . . . si limitano a ribadire un criteria di pertinenza, o di adequatezza decorativa." Carpo, *La maschera*, 60.

36. "Posez donques le cas, qu'il soit venu à quelque grand seigneur ou autre,

par succession hereditaire, ou par autre moien, un chasteau ou maison bastie par son grand pere . . . & l'heritier . . . ne trouve bon ce qui est faict, quelquefois avec iustes cause & raison, quelquefois sans aucune . . . pourquoy il en veult refaire un tout autre aupres du susdit, & le tourner d'une autre sorte, ains qu'il luy plaist, le semble mieux estre à sa volonté." Philibert, *Architecture* (1648), III, viii, 65.

37. "Souhaittant donques de faire un fort beau logis, il ne veut abbattre pour cela l'antique edifice de ses maieurs & predecesseurs . . . empeschent que le lieu ne se peult faire comme il [le veut]." Ibid., 66.

38. "En telle contrarieté, subiection & contraincte, il fault que l'Architecte ait bon entendement & qu'il ne parle comme font les ignorans, qui conseillent de tout abbattre incontinent . . . Mais il fault que ledit Architecte soit diligent à cognoistre l'assiette du lieu, & sçavoir où doit estre posée une chacune chose, selon qu'elle le requiert." Ibid., 65.

39. Fletcher, *Allegory*, 223.

40. "Qu'un bon Architecte desirant representer au naturel un bastiment, ne doit jamais faire, comme nous avons dict, un modelle fardé, ou si voulez, enrichez de peinture, ou doré d'or moulu, ou illustré de couleurs, ainsi que font ordinairement ceux qui veulent trompez les hommes." Philibert, *Architecture*, I, ix, p. 23.

41. "Leurs oeuvres ne sont en apres semblables à leurs modelles, lesquels ils fardent ainsi pour l'avarice, & pour decevoir les hommes . . . ils taschent d'attirer les yeux des regardans, à fin de destourner leurs iugements de la vraye consideration de l'oeuvre, & de ses parties & mesures . . . on doit proposer des modelles simplement unis & plustost imparfaictes." Ibid.

42. "Ie prieray les lecteurs . . . ne trouver estrange si ie use quelquefois en ces discours . . . des mots . . . autres. Car pour dire verité, nostre langue françoise en l'explication de plusieurs choses, est si pauvre & si sterile, que nous n'avons mots qui les puissent representer proprement, si nous n'usurpons le langage & mot estranger: ou bien que nous usions de quelque longue circonlocution." Ibid., III, vi, 137.

43. "En quoy ie veux omettre que la plus grande partie de [ces] mots, sont entendues [*sic*], receus & cogneus de plusieurs ouvriers." Ibid.

44. "L'Architecte donnera ordre de ne fascher personne, n'aussi d'estre faché d'aucuns, pour autant qu'estant travaillé d'autruy, jamais il ne peut rien faire ne ordonner qui soit à propos. De s'en vouloir pleindre au seigneur chacune fois, ne seroit jamais fait. Ie sçay par moy combien en telles choses on endure de fascheries." Ibid., I, iii, 12.

45. "Estant à tort chargé, rechargé, & surchargé de calomnies, traverses, ennuits & plaisirs, ie les ay virilement sousten us, & sans fleschir constamment portez." Ibid.

46. "Mais voirement quelqu'un me voyant commencer à escrire d'Architecture en ceste façon, dira que ie resemble celuy qui a une belle statue d'or ou d'argent, & pour l'amitié qu'il porte à la republique il luy en donne seulement un bras, qui est une chose imparfaicte de tout le corps, lequel n'est beau sans l'armonie entiere de tous ses membres & parties. Considerant cela, ie me deliberois ne donner le present oeuvre que premier ie n'eusse parfaict tout ce qu'il faut pour l'accomplissement du corps universel de ladicte *Architecture*, et non une partie d'icelle . . . Ce que j'eusse

faict, n'eust esté que plusieurs Seigneurs . . . m'ont tant pressé de mettre en lumière ceste dicte partie." Ibid.

47. "Mais quoy? Les auditeurs et assistans pour n'avoir ouy parler de si nouvelles choses & si grande invention, tout à coup me recullerent de mon dire: comme si i'eusse voulu faire entendre à ce bon Roy quelques menteries: lesquelles j'ay tousiours eu en grandissime horreur & detestation: estimant que tout ainsi que le corps vault peu sans l'ame, aussi fait la bouche sans verité." Philibert, "Au lecteur," *Architecture*, I, iii, 12.

48. "Qui m'a faict penser de longue main comme lon y pourroit remedier, pour satisfaire aux entreprinses de leurs Maiestez: et qu'il seroit possible en telle necessité trouver quelque invention de se pouvoir aider de toutes sortes de bois, & encores de toutes petites pieces, & se passer de si grands arbres que lon a coustume mettre en oeuvre." Ibid., 11.

49. "Ainsi que nous le deduirons ailleurs, Dieu aidant, avecques bonnes & suffisantes raisons, si nous n'en sommes destournez par quelques grands & urgents affaires." Ibid., V, vii, 137.

50. "Et quand à ceste mienne oeuvre & Invention que ie vous presente en toute humilité, faut que ie confesse, Sire, que s'il y a quelque chose de bien, ce n'est pas de moy, ains de la grace de Dieu, sçachant tres bien que de moy ie ne puis inventer, excogiter ou faire quelque chose, quelle quelle soit, sans estre prevenu de luy, & de sa pieté . . . mais il faut . . . protéger la vraye religion." Ibid., "Au lecteur," Aiiiij.

51. Prévost, *Philibert*, 59. He notes that Bernard Palissy called Philibert "le Dieu des maçons": "Palissy ne songea qu'à faire vivre les gens dans un univers artificiel, décoré de formes bizarres et de couleurs éclatantes."

52. "La colomne Thuscane . . . mais pour bien appliquer en oeuvre ladicte colomne, il fault noter qu'aux lieux où elle porte plus de charge & pesanteur, il est necessaire de la rendre plus grosse & massive, à fin de pouvoir mieux resister contre la ponderosité & charge qu'on luy voudra donner." Philibert, *Architecture*, V, viii, 138.

53. "Et pour cognoistre quand un arbre est abbatu, si dedans & au coeur, il est bien sain, apres en avoir couppé les bouts faut prendre un marteau & frapper par l'un d'iceux & si quelqu'un mettant l'oreille contre l'autre bout, entend le son lourd & cassé, c'est signe que le corps de l'arbre est dedans vicieux par pourriture, ou autrement. Mais si le son est clair & bien resonant à l'oreille, c'est signe qu'il est fort bon, sain & entier." Philibert, *Le Premier et dixiesme livre des oeuvres et nouvelles inventions pour bien bastir et à petits frais*, addendum to the *Architecture* (1648 edition), I & X, iii, 281.

54. If so, he would not be the first, or the only, Protestant creator to do so. One thinks of how Pieter Brueghel encoded the subversive Protestant content of his works. I thank the participants in, and the discussants at, the Calvin Studies Conference, Princeton Theological Seminary, May 1993, for these insights and for their helpful response to the paper I delivered there on Bernard Palissy's conception of Protestant architecture and strategies for subversion.

55. "Personne . . . n'a bien compris Philibert delorme . . . Cet homme a rendu la tâche difficile à qui veut l'aimer: il a menti . . . il a caché quels maî-

tres furent les siens, attribué à d'autres des influences qu'ils n'ont pas pu avoir sur lui. Pour pouvoir vivre et construire, fallait-il qu'il mentît?" Prévost, *Philibert*, 13. For instance, Philibert makes such misrepresentations in his will, the *Instruction de Monsieur d'Ivry*.

56. Clouzot, *Philibert*, 103, alleges that Philibert, "ce réformateur de bâtiments," acts like a theological reformer, and that some of his *charpentes* recall those of early Christian churches.

57. "Premier doncque commencer l'oeuvre vous considererez toutes ces choses, & n'y ferez aucunement trompez, mais bien fort asseurez . . . proufit & honneur tout le temps de vostre vie, & encores apres vostre mort . . . [du] bon ordre lequel vous avez tenu & gardé en toutes vos entreprinses." I, x, 22.

58. "Il [Saint Paul] dénonce que tous ceux qui auront adiousté quelque chose en l'édifice de l'Eglise qui ne sera point correspondant au fondement auront travaillé en vain." III, v, 155.

59. "Plusieurs beaux bastiments, lesquelz on faisoit edifier pour avoir la commodité d'aucuns autres vieux: mais apres qu'ils ont esté faicts, on a cogneu l'erreur, nuysance & commodité qu'ils portoient . . . Parquoy on a esté contrainct de les abbatre . . . ou contemner . . . mais il n'estoit temps de penser à l'erreur." Philibert, *Architecture*, I, ix, 21a.

60. "Car le commencement est de si grande importance, que si les premiers fondements ne sont bien droicts, & à l'équarre, le reste de l'édifice ne sera jamais sans avoir quelque deformité . . . et telle faulte en amenera plusieurs. Il est vray que tous n'ont pas le iugement de le bien cognoistre." Ibid., II, ii, 34.

61. "Paraventure pour figurer que la vie & salut devoit advertir aux hommes par la mort d'un seul mediateur Iesus Christ, qui seroit attaché au bois portant figure de croix, qui est la première que Dieu son père a figuré au monde. Mais nous laisserons tels propos aux Theologiens, & reprendons nos lignes & traicts de Geometrie, en tant que l'Architecte s'en peut ayder." Ibid., I, ii, 33.

62. Blunt, *Philibert*, p. 24.

63. "Pour sçavoir représenter l'Echo, & faire resonner et ouyr la parolle & voix, aussi bien de loing que de pres. Qui est chose requise aux Temples & Eglises pour les predications qui s'y font, & psalmes . . . qui se chantent." Philibert, *Architecture*, I, iii, 11.

64. Ibid., "Prologue," II, I, 31. Philibert speaks of "les orthographies," "les scenographies," and "faffades."

65. "Certains precepts & enseignements qui conduirent les Architectes & autres à choisir & eslire temps propre pour heureusement commencer fonder toutes sortes de bastiments. Remettant donques le tout à nostre dict livre *Des divines proportions*." Ibid., II, x, 48.

66. "Ie ne vous en escriray d'avantage, à fin d'eviter prolixité accompagnée le plus souvent d'ennuy. Si quelques uns desirent en cognoistre d'avantage, s'il leur plaist se retirer par devers moy, ie leur feray part de mon petit sçavoir & industrie, d'autant bon coeur qu'il me sera possible." Ibid., III, xv, 79–80.

67. "Quant à la reveuë de Vitruve, ie laisse à penser à ceux qui doctement dilegemment l'ont feuilleté & discouru, combien elle est necessaire pour le reduire à une facile, entiere & certaine methode: qui est si confuse & indigeste aux livres

que nous en avons, comme aussi aux figures & demonstrations, que ie laisse à tous gentils esprits accompagnez de bon iugement à en dire leurs advis: les priant affectionnément de vouloir emploier & donner quelque temps pour assembler & proprement recoudre les pieces de la robbe de ce grand & incomparable auteur . . . sous evident desordre, qui sera facile à estre reduict en bon ordre." Ibid., III, vi, 62.

68. "Il suffit, à ce qu'il me semble, d'en montrer seulement les principes & methode: pour autant que ceux qui en apres voudront prendre peine, en trouveront à tous propos, selon les oeuvres qu'ils auront à faire. De sorte qu'il ne se présentera chose tant estrange, ne tant difficile, qu'ils ne trouveront incontinent le moien d'en venir à bout par l'ayde de ces traicts estants accompagnez de Geometrie." Ibid., III, ix, 71.

69. "Ie n'use point icy du pied du Roy, ny du pied antique, ny moins des palmes Romains, ny autres mesures sinon des proportions lesquelles i'ay tirées de l'escriture saincte du vieil Testament, & (ce que ie diray sans aucune iactance) les mets en usage le premier . . . par le discours de nostre seconde partie d'Architecture, qui portera le tiltre & nom *Des divines proportions.*" V, xxx, 168.

70. De l'Orme claims (folio 168) to be the first person to have applied to modern architecture the system of proportion revealed in the Old Testament.

71. "Au second tome et oeuvres des Divines proportions (lequel i'espère faire imprimer si Dieu m'en donne la grace), vous verrez, non seulement le moyen et nouvelle invention de faire des corniches, mais aussi par mesures tout le corps humain, trouver toutes les proportions de toutes sortes de plans et montées de bastiments que vous desirerez, conformément avec les mesures et proportions qui se trouvent en la saincte Bible." Blunt, *Philibert*, 124, quoting Philibert.

72. "Helas! Peu d'Architectes reçoivent tant de graces & faveurs de Dieu, de les pouvoir cognoistre & entendre, ainsi qu'il luy plaist ouvrir les sens & l'intelligence à un chacun pour luy donner cognoissance de ses oeuvres, & des proportionnéess mesures, ie ne diray d'Architecture, mais aussi de toutes autres choses, lesquelles luy mesmes a ordonnées à la premiere creation . . . ainsi que plus à plein nous le deduirons quelque iour (Dieu aidant) en nostre Tome & oeuvre des *Divines proportions* . . . par consequent dignes d'estre plustost ensuivies, que celles qui ont esté escrites, inventées et faictes par les hommes . . . Car Dieu est le seul, le grand, & admirable Architecte." Ibid.

73. "Comme semblable à Ezechias de l'homme qui s'apparut à luy, resemblant estre d'airain, & tenant en une main une ficelle, & en l'autre un roseau ou canne, portant les mesures & proportions lesquelles Dieu seul luy monstra pour restaurer & redifier le Temple de Ierusalem. I'en pourrais alleguer assez d'autres qui se trouvent dans l'Escriture saincte, n'estoit que ie serois trop prolixe." Ibid., 126, quoting Philibert.

74. "Veritablement telles proportions sont si divines & admirables, que ie ne puis contenter mon esprit de les lire, relire, contempler & si ainsi ie dois dire, adorer, pour la grande maiesté & divinité de celuy qui les a données . . . O magnifique & supernaturel Architecte . . . prononcer de ta . . . bouche les vraies mesures & proportions." Ibid.

75. Larissa Taylor, *Soldiers of Christ,* 75.

76. Larissa Taylor provides the following figures in *Soldiers of Christ,* 196–

97. Protestant preachers' biblical quotation sources by percentage: Psalms, 25%; Isaiah, 21%; Genesis, 8%; Exodus, 6%; Matthew, 17%; Corinthians, 13%; Romans, 13%; Luke, 9%; Acts, 7%.

77. "Protestants, no doubt because of their desire to simplify sermons, used significantly fewer references, with an average of twelve per sermon. Of 611 citations, 99.5 percent are biblical." Ibid., 196.

78. Taylor says this reflected their concern with "law and grace." Ibid., 194.

79. Ibid., 197.

80. "Plusieurs choses, la faute de la bien entendre . . . je donneray bien tost le surplus pour la perfection d'*Architecture* illustree & accompaignee de tous ses membres necessaires. De sorte que tous ceux qui font profession de ladicte [vray, universel] Architecture . . . en tireront profit inestimable." Philibert, *Architecture*, "Au lecteur," viii.

81. "J'espere que les hommes vertueux, bons & pacifiques qui sçavent considerer et priser le bien, trouveront mon intention & invention bonne: & à tels j'addresse mes escripts, & non aux detracteurs . . . les oeuvres que j'ay commandé [sic] & ordonné [sic] faire depuis l'eage de quinze ans iusques icy, soubz diverses sortes & façons par vray art d'Architecture, ie ne diray en ce Royaume mais aussi en plusieurs autres, parleront suffisamment pour moy, & laisseront ample tesmoignage de mes capacitez." Ibid., "Au lecteur," viiij.

82. "Ce que ie dy non par iactance, ainsi plustost pour en rendre gloire & honneur à Dieu, autheur de tous biens . . . ainsi qu'escrivent les Apostres, Sainct Paul & sainct Jacques." Ibid.

83. "Je ne veux icy oublier que mon labeur & estude a tousiours tendu à ce but & fin . . . faire service . . . à ma patrie . . . Et jaçoit que communement on ne soit prisé et estimé en sa patrie, comme tesmoigne Jesus Christ." Ibid.

84. "En son Evangile, je n'ay pour ce delaissé y vouloir vivre, & luy communiquer liberalement mon industrie, & le talent que j'avois receu de Dieu, pour luy estre distribué, comme aux autres." Ibid., xix.

85. "Ie loue Dieu auteur de toutes graces, & le remercie humblement du bien & faveur qu'il me faict de pouvoir distribuer aux hommes une partie du talent lequel il a pleu à sa saincte bonté me departir à fin que les hommes de bon esprit en reçoivent quelque fruict & prouffit à sa louange, luy en donnant gloire & honneur à tout jamais." Ibid., III, xxi, 129.

86. "Et mesmes de celuy du temple de Salomon, & encores du lieu auquel il donnoit des iugemens: en attendant que ie vous en escrive bien au long en *nostre* oeuvre Des divines proportions, ce que ie vous ay bien promis." My emphasis. Ibid., VII, xiv, 224.

87. Blunt, *Philibert*, 123. This cultural climate of constraint and subterfuge is also experienced by the evangelical Serlio: "Ma questa strategia pedagogica non è un'invenzione serliano. Non è né innocente, né ingenua. Partecipe di un atteggiamento spirituale generale, di una sorta di spirito del tempo, comune agli ambiento culturali, ed editorali, che Serlio frequentava in quegli anni." Carpo, *La maschera*, 83.

88. "Doncques ie vous veux bien protester que ce que i'en escris ne tend à autre fin qu'à iustruire [sic] & apprendre les hommes de bonne volunté, & sig-

namment les ignorants, ausquels ie desire de bon cueur communiquer le talent lequel Dieu m'a liberalement donné." Philibert, *Architecture*, IV, I, 89; "à fin que les hommes de bon esprit en reçoivent quelque fruict" III, xxi, 129.

89. "Ce peu de discours me semble estre assez pour vous donner à entendre le reste de la figure & voute proposée: parquoy ie ne vous en feray autre escriture, vous asseurant que s'il vous plaist prendre le compas en la main, & chercher sur le plan & la montée ce que ie vous ay proposée, vous le trouverez, ainsi que ie vous ay dict." Ibid., III, xiii, 115.

90. "Ie prieray ceux qui auront quelque iugement de vouloir bien noter ce traict icy: car, s'ils l'entendent, ils en entendront plusieurs autres." Ibid., III, xx, 126.

91. "Mais quand ie considere la longueur de leurs descriptions & demonstrations, & la confere avec ce peu de loisir que i'ay, veritablement ie crains de n'y pouvoir vacquer, car il y faudroit employer si grandes escritures que l'explication que i'en ferois, ne me seroit seulement laborieuse, mais aussi aux bons esprits fort ennuyeuse, qui facilement conçoivent les descriptions & figures qu'on leur propose avec peu de paroles. Pource est il qu'il me semble qu'on se doit contenter de ce peu que i'en escris & figure le mieux qu'il m'est possible." Ibid., III, xvi, 119.

92. "Tels devroient avoir la sentence de sainct Paul devant les yeux, qui dict: SI QUIS SE EXISTIMAT SCIRE ALIQUID NONDUM COGNOUIT QUEMANDMODUM OPORTEAT EUM SCIRE. Qui signifie: Si aucun s'estime sçavoir quelque chose, il n'a encores cogneu ce qu'il luy convient sçavoir . . . les exhortans de demander conseil & ayde à Dieu, avant que de commencer aucune oeuvre." Philibert, *Nouvelles inventions*, II & XI, I, 309.

93. "Si la grandeur du papier pouvoit porter qu'on peust mettre & assembler toutes les parties & ornements des colomnes l'une sur l'autre, comme sur la base, la colomne, le chapiteau . . . à fin qu'elles fussent d'une grandeur competente pour cognoistre les mesures, ie les y mettrois voluntiers, comme aucuns ont faict, en representant par feuilles imprimées les ordres: mais cela seroit si petit, veu la capacité du papier de nostre livre, que malaisément le lecteur en pourroit tirer quelque fruict." Philibert, *Architecture*, V, x, 141.

94. "Par ainsi il m'a semblé pour le mieux . . . de les monstrer & enseigner par pieces l'une après l'autre, . . . en accompagnant le tout de figures plus petites les unes que les autres, & quelquesfois autant grandes que le fueillet du livre le peult porter." Ibid.

95. "Car ie procède tout ainsi qu'il plaist à sa maiesté le me commander, sauf les ornemens, symmetries & mesures, pour lesquelles elles me faict ceste grace & faveur de s'en fier à moy." Ibid., V, xxiii, 156.

96. "Complaincte & doleance de l'auteur, que les figures ne sont bien & iustement taillées . . . Qui a esté cause que i'ay prins grand plaisir de le designer & protraire beaucoup de fois: mais le tailleur n'a si bien conduit l'oeuvre sur la planche de bois, comme i'eusse bien voulu." Ibid., V, xxvii, 165.

97. ". . . grand-regret & desplaisir, pour l'envie que i'avois de donner plaisir avec proufit à ceux qui desirent apprendre." Ibid., 166.

98. "Et pource que ie voy que les tailleurs de mes figures & histoires ne m'ont faict les choses si nettement que i'eusse bien desiré, i'ay voulu reparer la faulte par multiplicité de desseings & protraicts que i'ay faict tailler." Ibid., VII, x, 213.

99. "A dire verité on doit craindre merveilleusement de faillir à une telle entreprinse, et signamment de bastiments, lesquelz on voit toujours durant la vie." I, i, 7.

100. "Qu'on doit choisir un expert Architecte, & de quelles sciences il doit estre accompagné, & que sa liberté doit estre exempte de toute contrainte & subiection d'esprit." I, iii, 10b.

101. "Quelquesfois on est contrainct de faire les choses contre raison, pour servir à la volunté du seigneur qui faict construire le bastiment." III, xii, 73.

102. "Le seigneur doit enquerir diligemment de la suffisance de l'Architecte, & aussi entendre quelles sont ses oeuvres, sa modestie, son asseurance, preud'hommie, gouvernement . . ." Ibid.

103. "Ie ne veux icy omettre, qu'on iuge l'entendement du Seigneur & la sagesse pour les oeuvres qu'il a faict faire, & la prudence pour bien sçavoir choisir les hommes & donner bon ordre à tout . . . Il advient aussi une faulte tres enorme pour mal considerer son entreprinse, laquelle souvent est si grande, & la despense si excessive, que le seigneur n'y peult satisfaire, et est constrainct que l'oeuvre demeure du tout imparfaict, ou bien long temps suspendue." Ibid., I, 71.

104. "Ie sçay une maison de Roy où les poutres ne valent rien & par dessus y a si grandes serrures qui traversent les murs, & retiennent les portiques ou galleries qui sont par les costez, que s'il faut remettre d'autres poutres, en grand danger seront lesdictes galleries qu'elles ne tombent, ou qu'elle les dementent, pour le moins . . . et si celuy qui en aura la charge n'est diligent, & n'entend bien son estat, qu'en peut-il advenir?" Philibert, *Nouvelles inventions*, I & X, iv, 285.

105. Recourse to nicodemism, as described by Carlo Ginzburg in *Il nicodemismo*, offers a rationalization for cases in which a Protestant sympathizer or believer is called to in some way cooperate with Catholics, in building a Catholic church, for instance. Nicodemites cite 1 Thessalonians 5:21 and Romans 12:17: "Tu omnia proba, si quod bonum est, tibi serva." What matters is not so much the outer manifestation but rather the inner orientation of the believer: "Deus respicit intentionem et cor." Ginzburg avers, "in base ad esse, la participazione a cerimonie religiose 'idolatriche' appariva lecita, purché venisse compiuta con intenzione buona, in purità di cuore" (135). Calvin himself opposed nicodemism prior to 1527, most notably in the *Excuse à Messieurs les Nicodémites*, but after that date he became much less categorically opposed to its use as a tactic or strategy. Ginzburg has shown, contrary to Calvin's initial argument (that nicodemism was a repugnant and cowardly response to the threat of martyrdom), that in many circles—especially the Strasbourg group centered around Otto Brunfels—nicodemism was, rather, a carefully thought out and doctrinally argued recourse in times of persecution (xv). This attitude became more widely accepted during the time of the second-generation architects.

106. "Laquelle trompe fut faicte par une contrainte, à fin de pouvoir accommoder un cabinet à la chambre où le feu Roy Henry logeoit estant audit chasteau. La contraincte estoit pour n'avoir espace ou lieu pour le faire au corps d'hostel qui ia estoit commencé . . . Voyant donques telle contraincte & angustie du lieu." Philibert, *Architecture*, IV, I, 88.

107. "Ie fus redigé en grande perplexité . . . Ie dressay ma veuë sur un angle qui estoit près la chambre du Roy . . . du costé du jardin, & me semble estre fort bon d'y faire une voute suspendue en l'air, à fin de plus commodément trouver place." Ibid.

108. "Among the technical achievements of which he was the most proud was his *cryptoporticus*, which was of far greater complexity than is usual for the sixteenth century." Blunt, *Philibert*, 50.

109. Ibid.

110. "Ce lieu me semble estre fort à propos pour mieux donner l'usage des traicts Geometriques, et monstrer la commodité qui les accompagne, pour eviter les empeschements ausquels on peult tomber quelquesfois: & aussi pour accommoder les vieils logis avec les neufs, ainsi que l'on en pourra avoir affaire, & que l'oeuvre le requerra pour sa perfection, beauté & decoration. Car par le moien desdicts traicts on n'oste pas seulement les faultes qui sont faictes, ny les contrainctes & subiections des pieces, mais encores on rend les logis plus admirables, forts & plaisants à voir, avec grande espargne pour faire servir les vieilles matieres, desquelles on se veult ayder." Philibert, *Architecture*, III, viii, 65.

111. "Avecques grande espargne pour faire servir les vieilles matieres, desquelles on se veult ayder, avecques les neuves, comme vous le cognoistrez." Ibid.

112. "La façon d'amender un fondement, quand on ne trouve terre ferme pour le bien asseurer." Ibid., II, ix, 46.

113. "Veritablement quand ie pense aux entreprinses faictes quelquesfois trop inconsidérément, & aux oeuvres de plusieurs ainsi précipitées & mal conduictes, ie ne sçay qu'en dire ny penser. Considerant donques tant d'incommoditez survenir à la plus part de ceux qui batissent, & si grandes fautes se commettre à l'Architecture, ie montreray . . . comme l'on doit proceder . . . pour se garder d'y faire faulte." Ibid., I, I, 8.

114. "Qu'il seroit contrainct de bastir en tels lieux . . . il faudroit que l'Architecte monstrast par son bon esprit les moiens & inventions de [l'améliorer] . . . les vrais fondements & plus asseurez sont sur la roche, comme chacun sçait." Ibid., II, ix, 46, and x, 47.

115. "Mais pour bien obvier à tant de peines, il doit aussi choisir un bon & sage seigneur qui le soutienne, qui le garde des envieux, & qui l'ayme et conserve." Ibid., I, v, 13.

116. "Les blasmes ou louenges, honneurs ou deshonneurs, communement accompagnent les grands bastimens & grandes oeuvres, & specialement celles qui sont publiques." Ibid., I, I, 9.

117. "Nous avons une infinité de beaux traicts en France, desquels on ne tient aucun compte, pour ne les entendre, & que pis est, lon ne se soucie gueres de chercher l'excellence de beauté des oeuvres [que] i'ay faict faire à Fontainebleau." Ibid., III, xix, 125.

118. "Comme si c'estoit une colomne Thuscane avec peu d'oeuvre, pour autant que au lieu où elle est, les pages & laquais qui sont indiscrets & malicieux, rompent ordinairement tous ce qu'ils y peuvent toucher à la main, ou pour le moins ils le barbouillent, et difforment. Parquoy il me semble qu'en ces bases la, on doit mettre le moins d'oeuvre qu'on peult." Ibid., VIII, vii, 241.

119. ". . . sottilinea che la libertà cristiana è un fatto spirituale, interiore, che può anche conciliarsi con la libertà esteriore—il non essere servì né poveri—ma non si identifica in nessun modo con essa." Ginzburg, *Il nicodemismo*, 44.

120. Blunt, *Philibert*, 20.

121. Ibid., p. 33.

122. "L'invention de la colonne française . . . ne pouvant se procurer de pierres assez considérables pour obtenir des colonnes d'un seul bloc, ou du moins des colonnes composées de peu de blocs, il accepte des pièces de faible hauteur; certains diront qu'il en dissimule la jointure par une décoration." Prévost, *Philibert*, 79–80.

123. Prévost, *Philibert*, 36. "Philibert affirme que cette structure donne à l'architrave plus de résistance que si elle était d'un seul bloc. A parler rigoureusement, cela est inexact . . . néanmoins ce procédé peut avoir l'avantage, s'il se produit de minimes affaissements de terrain . . . de permettre une souplesse."

124. Blunt, *Philibert*, 40.

125. Ibid., 72.

126. Ibid.

127. Ibid., 37.

128. Blunt, *Philibert*, 44, n. 1.

129. Ibid., 75.

130. The discussion of how private houses should be configured was of much interest to the Protestant community. Androuet du Cerceau devoted a considerable portion of his text to plans for townhouses, a focus not at all customary in contemporary (non-Protestant) architectural manuals.

131. Carpo, *La maschera*, 131.

132. Blunt, *Philibert*, 87.

133. Noted in Clouzot, *Philibert*, 81–84.

134. Blunt, *Philibert*, 106.

135. "Qui empeschera que nous Français n'en inventions quelques unes . . . comme pourroient estre celles que ie inventay & fis faire pour la portique de la chappelle qui est dans le parc de Villiers coste Rets, du temps & reigne de la maiesté du feu Roy Henry? Vray est que pour la necessité où ie me trouvay [contrainct] de ne pouvoir recouvrer promptement, & sans grands frais des colonnes toutes d'une piece, ie les fis faire de quatre ou cinq pieces, avec beaux ornements & moulures, qui cachent leurs commissures: de sorte qu'à les voir il semble qu'elles soient entierement d'une piece, se monstrans fort belles, & de bien bonne grace." Philibert, *Architecture*, VII, xiii, 219.

136. "Le remède fut pire . . . Au temps de du Cerceau, la couverture . . . s'était 'affoncée' de telle sorte que sa solidité en était compromise et que le château tout entier menaçait ruine . . . Il n'en reste aujourd'hui que le souvenir. Pareil sort était réservé à une autre entreprise de l'abbé d'Ivry: la chapelle du parc." Clouzot, *Philibert*, 128.

137. Ibid., 101.

138. Puttenham, quoted in Fletcher, *Allegory*, 77.

139. Blunt, *Philibert*, 85.

140. Here, too, the strategy that Philibert adopts appears to derive from

Brunfels's conception of legitimate nicodemism. Brunfels, for instance, states that scriptural exegesis should always be as clear and as direct as possible. Yet, when he feels threatened, his scriptural discussion becomes fragmented, convoluted, its interpretation difficult to perceive. Ginzburg notes, "se Brunfels dichiara di limitarsi a presentare la parola di Dio nella sua semplicità e nudità, le *Pandectae* sono ben alto. Il testo biblico è disarticolato e ricomposto, piegato a un'interpretazione precisa." *Il nicodemismo, 22.*

141. Philibert, *Nouvelles inventions*, I & X, and restated verbatim in *Architecture*, "Conclusion," XXVI, 308.

142. "Se garder des personnes qui ne sçavent bien faire, ny voir ce qui est bon de faire, ny ouyr ce qu'on doit entendre, ny moins avoir sentiment de ce qui est utile & proufitable, ainsi qu'il vous est representé par la prochaine figure." Philibert, *Architecture*, "Conclusion," IX, 281.

143. "L'Architecte est fort subiect à ouyr & recevoir plusieurs calomnies & faux rapports qui se disent de luy: parquoy il fault qu'il s'asseure, que tant plus il sera vertueux & sçavant, plus il sera envié & travaillé par mauvais rapports des ignorants & malicieux: & plus l'oeuvre s'avancera & augmentera en beauté, plus il sera calomnié & despesché en diverses sortes . . . avec une infinité de mensonges, ainsi que je l'ay souvent apperceu à mon grand desavantage: voire jusques à estre de telle sorte rendu suspect." Ibid., 282.

144. Fletcher, *Allegory*, 136.

145. Kenneth Burke, cited in Bloch, *Utopian Function*, 203.

146. Such strategies are discussed more broadly in Chambers, *Room for Maneuver*.

147. "C'est une chose superflue." Calvin, *Institution*, IV, xvi, 369.

148. "Comme cousue de toutes pièces" (ibid., IV, xix, 499), "Coudre pièce sur pièce" (IV, ix, 44).

149. "Par leurs circuits" (ibid., I, iv, 66 and 67), "Au reste, il n'est ia besoin de chercher par long circuit quel sens il use de ces mots" (IV, xvii, 412).

150. IV, xvii, 412. On the pope, see also III, v, 143.

151. A number of biblical proof texts could be cited (and were, by nicodemites like Brunfels) for the use of a non-Calvinist technique in order to protect, or to render into code, a stance that is, in reality, orthodox Calvinism. For example, Kings 5:18–19, in which Elisha lets Naaman adore an idol as long as he venerates God in his heart; I Corinthians 9:22; or Paul's permission that Timothy be circumcised. Such a scriptural network constructs a sort of theory of religious dissimulation when in a climate of constraint. In *On Christian Liberty* (1520), Martin Luther articulates a similar position (see Ginzburg, *Il nicodemismo*, 71–75) when he separates the soul of man—free, subject to none—from his body, which is determined by his circumstances, even enslaved by them. What matters is the soul's freedom, the interior confession. Ginzburg summarizes the argument in this way: "The interior, spiritual man knows that no external thing has any relationship with justification by faith and Christian liberty. What does it matter to the soul if the body is well or not? . . . If the body wears profaned garments, if it goes to profane places, the soul receives no damnation thereby."

152. "Estant à tort chargé, rechargé, & surchargé de calomnies, traverses, ennuits & plaisirs, ie les ay virilement soustenus, & sans fleschir constamment portez." Philibert, *Architecture*, III, iv, 138.

153. ". . . l'Architecte . . . sa liberté doit estre exempte de toute contraincte & subiection d'esprit." Philibert, *Architecture*, I, iii, 10b.

154. ". . . on est contrainct de faire les espaces . . . on est contrainct de chercher . . ." Ibid., VII, xv, 225.

155. "Voyant doncques telle contraincte & angustie du lieu, ie fus redigé en grande perplexité." Ibid., IV, I, 88.

156. ". . . et autres . . ." Ibid., III, I, 50.

157. "En premier lieu donques ie figure un Architecte habillé ainsi qu'un homme docte et sage (tel qu'il doit estre) & comme sortant d'une caverne ou lieu obscur." Ibid.

158. ". . . c'est a dire de contemplation, solitude & lieu d'estude." Ibid.

159. Crow, *Philosophical Streets*, 12.

160. ". . . à fin de parvenir à la vraye cognoissance & perfection de son art." Philibert, *Architecture*, III, I, 50.

161. "Il trousse sa robe d'une main, voulant monstrer . . ." Ibid.

162. ". . . un compas entortillé d'un serpent." Ibid. The serpent has a wide range of meanings; with the figure of prudence as death, with Minerva as wisdom, and also as death and immortality because of the way it sheds its skin. See Guy de Tervarent, *Attributs et symboles dans l'art profane: Dictionnaire d'un langue perdu, 1450–1600* (Geneva: Droz, 1997), and emblem books of the period. St. John uses the image of the serpent as a prefiguration for the crucifixion.

163. "Moyse montre que la puissance invincible de Dieu estoit de son costé, d'autant qu'il fait engloutir toutes les verges des autres par la sienne. Mais puis que telle conversion s'est faite à veue d'oeil . . . et aussi un petit après la verge retourna à sa premiere forme . . . Quant est de Moyse, . . . Dieu [a fait] d'une verge un serpent, et derechef d'un serpent une verge." Calvin, *Institution* (1552), IV, xvii, 392–93. Also see Exodus 7:12.

164. Matthew 10:16: "prudentes sicut serpentes." Here, Christ counsels his disciples about strategies for subverting hostile criticism, precisely my thesis.

165. Carpo, *La maschera*, 102. And Carlo Ginzburg, in his study of nicodemism and strategies of dissimulation, notes that the Strasbourg writer Otto Brunfels, author of the *Pandectarum veteris et novi Testamenti* (1527), used as the incipit to his text a scriptural citation that similarly praised recourse to wiles of deception for purposes of religious self-protection. The *Pandectarum* began, "When among unbelievers we must pretend . . . [that is not important as long as] God knows our heart."

166. This is the case with Serlio, as well; Carpo observes that "la dedica serliana ad Ercole d'Este contiene anche un curioso esercizio di esegesi neotestamentaria" (91).

167. ". . . conioncte avecques simplicité & modestie conduit l'homme à toutes bonnes & louables entreprises." Philibert, *Architecture*, III, I, 51.

168. "Celuy qui n'est fourni de ceste tant belle vertu de prudence ne sçaura recouvrer sa perte." Ibid.

169. Ibid., III, viii, 65.

170. "Mais encores on rend les logis plus admirables, forts & plaisants à voir: avec grande espargne pour faire servir les vieilles matieres, desquelles on se veut ayder, avecques les neufves." Ibid.

171. "Je desire que nostre Architecte soit de bonne ame, non trompeur, abuseur ou malicieux. Toutesfois il sera vituperé d'imiter le serpent, c'est à dire, estre cault et bien advisé." Ibid., III, I, 51.

172. "Aux grands entreprinses qui se font pour les Roys, Princes et grands seigneurs, il n'y a jamais faulte d'hommes & serviteurs, mais le plus souvent peu fideles . . . tels resemblent à ceste figure." Ibid., "Conclusion," ix, 281.

173. "Veritablement, ie vous Propose." Ibid.

174. While the skulls are a standard decoration in the Renaissance, Philibert's iconography is so coded, so overcharged with menace throughout, that it would be too simplistic to determine *any* of its components to be simply decorative.

175. "Quelques testes de boeuf seiches en son chemin." Philibert, *Architecture*, "Conclusion," ix, 281.

176. ". . . avecques plusieurs pierres qui le font chopper, & buissons qui le retiennent & dechirent sa robbe." Ibid.

177. "Ledit homme n'a point de mains, pour monstrer que ceux qu'il representent ne sçauroient rien faire." Ibid.

178. ". . . aucuns yeux dans la teste . . . ny oreilles, pour ouir et entendre les sages, ny aussi guieres de nez, pour n'avoir sentiment des bonnes choses." Ibid.

179. "Sono gli eletti cercheranno la verità, nascosta sotto l'inganno delle apparenze." Carpo, *La maschera*, 121.

180. "Et vous asseurez que telles personnes haïssent ordinairement & de leur naturel non seulement les doctes Architectes, mais aussi tous les vertueux, & la vertu mesme." Philibert, *Architecture*, "Conclusion," ix, 281.

181. ". . . les faultes qu'ils commettent; ils ne cessent de mesdire des Architectes envers les seigneurs." Ibid.

182. "Mais ie ne m'en suis pas beaucoup soucié, m'asseurant qu'il ne m'en pourroit venir aucun dommage." Ibid.

183. Angus Fletcher, *Allegory*, 236.

184. "Doncques nous reprendrons nostre Architecte, lequel ie desire estre si advisé qu'il apprenne à se cognoistre & sçavoir quel il est, avec ses capacitez & suffisances: & s'il cognoist qu'aucune chose luy defaille, ie luy conseille d'estre diligent de la demander à Dieu." Ibid., 282.

185. "Sur lesquelles preside Mercure." Ibid., III, I, 51.

186. "Toutesfois ie ne veux pas qu'il soit trop Mercurial, c'est à dire muable & babillard, se iongnant tantost à l'un, tantost à l'autre, par une je ne sçay quelle inconstance et legereté, ainsi plustost qu'il suyve et imite les bons, à fin d'estre bon." Ibid.

187. This image, like many of Philibert's, has various possibilities for interpretation, and since Philibert himself provides no key, the reader has to try on the different options. While it is likely that the statue is Mercury, since Mercury is discussed in the text, it is not inconceivable that related networks of symbolism, perhaps a reference to Minerva or even to Justice, might be intended.

188. In his comments on an earlier version of this manuscript, Robert Griffin noted that this depiction of the hands has many possible resonances, as well.

He listed the hand gestures, "which are found on nearly every Gothic Christ as part of the *Boon Bestowing* and *Gift Giving* ritual," as well as mentioning "common attributes of the Byzantine Sophia, and . . . even in the *mudra* of second-century Buddhas." (Letter to author, 4 March, 1993). I see no reason why Philibert would have referred to the last of these examples, but the Sophia is not incompatible with Philibert's portrayal of the Calvinist architect as possessing wisdom superior to that of his Catholic critics, nor is the reference to the Christ inconceivable.

189. For the scroll, see John on Patmos, Book of Revelation. Dürer customarily portrayed St. John with a book, not a scroll, but this was a sixteenth-century anachronistic rendering on Dürer's part.

190. Calvin, *Institution* (1552), III, ii, 47, cites Psalm 33:12: "Bien-heureux est le peuple duquel l'Eternel est le bien, et la gent qu'il s'est esleue pour héritage." Philibert, *Architecture*, III, viii, 65, "l'heritier."

191. "Representant ieunesse, qui doit cercher les sages & doctes, pour estre instruicte tant verbalement que par memoires, escritures, desseings & modeles." Philibert, *Architecture*, "Conclusion," ix, 282.

192. Serlio's *Extraordinario libro* possesses similarities with Philibert's program here, although Philibert's message, as expressed through the visual medium of the allegories, is even more bold and memorable. Serlio lauds "a simple sweet architecture . . . [over against] one that is affected, crude, obscure or confused . . . The register of a 'judicious' architecture is found, once again, in its moderate use of ornament, especially in a scarcity of detail. Serlio invokes rigor and austerity, instead, in the treatment of surface areas . . . this is a spiritual requirement, an interior desire, for him"; "un'architettura soda, semplice, schietta, dolce, e morbida, da una debole, gracile, delicata, affettata, cruda, anzi oscura e confusa . . . Il registro dell'architettura 'giudiziosa' . . . dispende ancora una volta dalla moderazione nell'ornamento, in particolate dalla scarsità degli intagli . . . Serlio invoco piuttosto rigore ed austerità nel trattamento delle superficie . . . Esigenza spirituale, o aspirazione interiore." Carpo, *La maschera*, 56–57.

193. "Et apres avoir ordonné ce qui est necessaire pour faire les oeuvres de sa charge, qu'il se retire et se tienne solitairement en son estude, cabinet, chambre, librairie ou iardin." Philibert, *Architecture*, "Conclusion," ix, 283.

194. Although many historians of the period can certainly confirm this specifically Protestant vocabulary (*temple*), it is interesting to note that vocabulary issues continue to have impact in modern times, where religion is concerned. See, for instance, Christian Makarian, "La grande revanche des protestants," cover essay of *Le Point* (27 January 1996): 50–59. He observes, "Toute tribu a son langage. Celui des protestants se singularise par un rejet du vocabulaire catholique traditionnel. Ainsi ne dit-on jamais qu'on se rend à l'église le dimanche, mais au *temple*, car on n'assiste pas à la messe, mais au culte" (52). Emphasis added.

195. ". . . les clefs . . . pour prevoir le futur et le temps advenir . . ." Philibert, *Architecture*, "Conclusion," ix, 283.

196. "Ie luy figure aussi quatre oreilles, monstrant qu'il fault beaucoup plus ouyr que parler." Ibid., 282.

197. ". . . ainsi que le commande Sainct Jacques au premier chapitre de sa premiere epistre canonique . . ." Ibid.

198. "En nous, car estans en ce monde nous n'avons cognoissance des arts & sciences, sinon que par petits loppins & morceaux." Ibid.

199. "Ie luy figure d'abondance quatre mains, pour monstrer qu'il a à faire & manier beaucoup de choses en son temps." Ibid.

200. "Maintenant ie desirerois vous monstrer une façon de bastiment . . . sous un ordre Corinthien . . . qui est pour monstrer le contraire de ce qu'on faict ordinairement." Ibid., VIII, xvi, 252.

201. "Labyrinth" is found throughout the *Institution*. See for example (1552) III, ii, 16, and I, vi, 89. Bouwsma, *Calvin*, offers a magisterial analysis of two structuring components of Calvin's personality and thought: the labyrinth and the abyss.

202. "Comme la dignité, origine et excellence d'Architecture est venue de Dieu, & du ciel, sans en arrester à un Dedalus." Blunt, *Philibert*, 126–27, citing Philibert.

203. Philibert, *Architecture*, "Conclusion," ix, 282. "(Lequel on dit avoir esté auteur & inventeur des premieres loges et maisons . . .)."

204. "Ie adiousteray que les choses ecrites ne donnent tant de delectation, plaisir & instruction, pour en retirer quelque fruict & prouffit, que celles qui sont pratiquées & monstrées du doigt . . . la matiere est fort difficile à pratiquer & mettre en oeuvre. Qui est cause que mal-aisément on les peult enseigner par livre et escriture." Philibert, *Architecture*, iv, "Prologue."

205. "Autres choses accompagnées d'un grandissime plaisir & prouffit: ainsi que vous le cognoistrez apres avoir diligemment leu et releu le present oeuvre." Ibid.

206. In 1525 Lefèvre d'Etaples left Paris for Strasbourg, seeking protection from persecution by Beda and the Sordonne for his evangelical perspective. He was accompanied by others from the Cercle de Meaux, among them Roussel and Caroli: Lefèvre knew Brunfels and stayed in the house of Brunfels's friend Capitone. Lefèvre agreed with the thesis of permissible dissimulation in the face of persecution, imitating the fragility of Christ's humanity in contingent situations (Ginzburg, *Il nicodemismo* 86–95) — as Philibert does, here, advocating a sort of subterranean proselytizing. While Calvin abominated nicodemism (Ginzburg, 121), it is possible to find in his radical distinction between interiority and exteriority, between the visible and the invisible church, and his privileging of the inner religious experience within the believer's heart, some implicit permissions for a nicodemite stance. Epigoni like Beza found what they thought signified predestination in Calvin's works, although scholars argue for a much softer position on Calvin's part in reality. Calvinist tyrannomachs construed portions of Calvin's writings as legitimizing tyrannicide, although Calvin, with his very traditional attitude toward the appointing of a monarch for the people by God, probably would have been appalled at their re-reading. It is equally possible that a second generation of Calvinist architects, operating within the politically fraught climate of France (unlike Calvin, secure in Genevan city-space), may have believed that they had found in Calvin the justification for political, artistic, and religious dissembling such as that proposed by the Nicodemites. "Eventually even Calvin . . . began to recognize, after some 25 years, how inadequate his characterization of Nicodemism had been . . .

he came to realize that lying behind Nicodemism was not the fear of martyrdom, but rather a precise [and reasoned] religious choice" (Ginzburg, 202). Followers of Calvin like Pierre Viret began to pen documents significantly more relaxed toward nicodemism, as was Viret's *Admonition et consolation aux fidèles qui délibèrent de sortir entre les papistes*. (Viret did, however, manifest some persistent concerns about nicodemites, whom he called "besaciers": those carrying sacks, which they place to the left, to the right, in front of them, or behind them, in accordance with their needs or circumstances.)

Chapter 5. The Second-Generation Calvinist Architects

1. In 1569, for instance, Charles IX dismissed all known Protestants from his employ. See Ward, *Architecture*, 162.

2. The artistic choices that these Calvinist architects made are, in large part, attributable to their practice of a form of architectural nicodemism which, by the mid-1550s, could be found in some form in most Reformed circles throughout Europe. Ginzburg, *Il nicodemismo*, 182.

3. Hill, *Bible*, 224, 108.

4. Pannier is quoting Lemonnier's comment of 1895 here. "La génération d'hommes qu'Henri IV a eus à son service pour la peinture, la sculpture et l'architecture est restée effacée entre devanciers et ses successeurs: aucuns des noms qui la composent n'est arrivé à la pleine renommée. Cette constation . . . [est surtout] vraie pour les architectes [parce que] l'époque s'efforça d'achever les constructions entamées . . . leurs oeuvres ne sont que des fragments d'un tout qui appartient à d'autres." Pannier, "Salomon de Brosse," 5–6.

5. "The effects of the Wars of Religion on architecture [were that] the great figures were thinned out one by one by death or exile. After 1578, Jacques du Cerceau was the only one left." Ward, *Architecture*, 162.

6. Blunt, *Philibert*, 120.

7. Ibid., 118.

8. O'Grady, "Huguenot Statement," 1.

9. Ballon, *Paris*, 80.

10. Ibid., 81–83.

11. Ibid., 73.

12. Hill, *Bible*, 224.

13. Ibid., 78.

14. Blunt, *Philibert*, 33. Rychier died in 1566.

15. See Chapter 3, on Palissy, for further details.

16. Incidentally, a similar situation obtained for Protestant architects in the early part of the seventeenth century in the New World. Protestantism was declared illegal in Quebec as of 1685 (the date of the Revocation of the Edict of Nantes), although as early as 1588 there was much legislation in favor of Catholicism. "Au-delà des édits et des ordonnances, la présence protestante fut d'une certain façon tolérée. Les hommes de métier étaient recherchés, et on devait les accepter . . . Ainsi,

Maisonneuve, le fondateur de Montréal, dont la ferveur catholique ne faisait aucun doute, accepta la présence d'hommes de métier protestants à Ville-Marie." Such effective toleration so as to capitalize on the skills of the Protestants corresponds to the situation of the first-generation Calvinist architects. However, increasingly "les protestants devaient se plier aux pressions des catholiques." And, of course, after the Revocation, there was active and explicit persecution. A. Tessier, *La ville de Québec: Un guide historique* (Quebec: S.H.Q., 1991), 103–6.

17. Carpo, *La maschera*, 107. "Il discorso nicodemita transmette un messagio diversi, più o meno sofisticati, permettono di creare testi ambiui, o ambivalenti."

18. Aiii. "Messieurs, pour rendre plus claire intelligence aux ouvriers, à ceste deuxième impression, ie me suis employé à tout ce qui m'a esté possible, de ce qui me sembloit estre demeuré obscur & caché aux figures de ce mien petit labeur & aussi à dire verité, quand quelque oeuvre est faicte, est facile à tous cognoistre les faultes: mais difficile sinon à peu de les amender . . . ie me suis mis en debvoir ce peu de practique que Dieu m'a donné."

19. Bullant wrote the *Petit traicté de Géometrie et d'Horologiographie* (1564) and the *Reigle générale de l'architecture des cinq manières de colonnes* (1568).

20. Blunt, *Philibert*, 143.

21. "It is characteristic of him that he should in a single building combine two apparently contradictory tendencies." Ibid., 136.

22. Coope, *Salomon de Brosse*, 20.

23. Blunt, *Philibert*, 139, 140. Others demonstrate this tension concerning the use of space. When Jean Goujon designed the Fontaine des innocents circa 1571, the space that he allotted to each of the decorative nymphs seemed insufficient for their bodies and the draperies of their garments. Anthony Blunt, *Art and Architecture*, observes that such treatment "contrasts sharply with the static court portrait" (141).

24. "Or ay-ie dit qu'en tout bastiment quel qu'il soit, l'on doibt songneusement prendre garde à ce que iamais rien ne porte à faulx, ains que tout ce qu'on met l'un sur l'autre, aist correspondance au massif. Et certes il y aura du faulx, si le rondeau à plomber mis contre la face de quelque moulure treuve en pendant du vuide entre luy & les autres choses qui seront au dessoubz." Bullant, *Reigle*, V.

25. Other Protestants felt the need to dramatize spatial constraints. Jean Goujon, a Calvinist, left France in 1563 due to persecution. Anthony Blunt describes his work as one in which lack of space, and a desire for space, resolve themselves in a strategy of overflowing, of surpassing limits: "his reliefs . . . show great freedom in their relation to the architecture. The upper figures break out of the field of the pediment and those at the side come over the zone of the capitals" (*Philibert*, 127).

26. As contrasted with the more customary location of Montaigne's scale and "Que scay-je?" at the beginning of the *Essais*.

27. "L'aage & le temps mettront en ouverture / Tout ce qui est en la terre cachée / Et musseront soubs noire couverture / Ce qu'on a veu, tenu, passé, marché." Bullant, *Reigle*, last page.

28. "Venez icy, & aux profits publiques / Imitez-en [les pratiques architecturales]. / Si qu'or' avant on voye enmy la France / Maintz beaux Pallais d'orgueilleuse apparence / Ne ceder poinct aux Babyloniens: / Comme or' BULLANT en

diverse maniere / Vous en prescrit la forme singuliere / Sur le patron des ouvriers anciens." Ibid., "Aux architectes français."

29. See Chapter 4, on Philibert de l'Orme, the allegories.

30. "Nouveau" invariably had a negative valence in sixteenth-century thought. See Cotgrave, *Dictionarie*: "strange . . . uncouth . . . lately done . . . unheard of before."

31. "Mon intention ne fust oncques autre, que de faire cognoistre (tant qu'en moy est) les choses qui sont *bien ou mal entendues . . .* je supplie estre excusé . . . si je *n'ay si clairement exposé le texte.*" Bullant, *Reigle*, Ai verso; my emphasis. "Opinion" is a term often used in the sixteenth century for "heresy"; Bullant thus distinguishes between a sympathetic Calvinist audience and a pejorative Catholic audience.

32. ". . . ny adiouster ny diminuer." Ibid., Aii recto.

33. "Il nous sera assez évident que ceste n'est point l'Eglise, laquelle en outrepassant les limites de la parolle de Dieu, s'ébat . . . 'Tu n'adiousteras à la parole du Seigneur et n'en diminueras' . . . Le Seigneur ne souffre point qu'on adiouste . . . ou qu'on en diminue." Calvin, *Institution* (1552), IV, X, 202.

34. "Car à quel propos se fascheroit-il du lieu auquel il doit passer sa vie? Peut-il convertir les montaignes en pleines, et les pleines en montaignes? Qu'il se console donc, en la providence de Dieu" (3). All citations of Serres are from the *Théâtre d'agriculture*.

35. The parable of the talents is probably the single parable most responsible for developing a Protestant consciousness about use and abuse of natural resources. The Puritans in the New World used it as a justification for taking the land away from the Native Americans, hunters and gatherers, who, to Puritan understanding, were not adequately developing the earth. See John Canup, *Out of the Wilderness: The Emergence of an American Identity in Colonial New England* (Middletown, Conn.: Wesleyan University Press, 1990), and, among other original sources, John White, *The Planter's Plea or the Grounds of Plantations examined and usuall objections answered* (1630), reprinted in *Transactions of the Massachusetts Historical Society*, June 1929.

36. Here is de Serres's reference to the parable of the talents: "Mais digne de loüange est l'homme, qui se voyant possesseur légitime d'un beau domaine, passant plus outre, s'esvertue non-seulement à luy faire produire des fruicts à l'accoustume, ains . . . constraint . . . sa terre . . . à luy rapporter plus que de l'ordinaire" (40).

37. "Mon inclination, et l'estat de mes affaires, m'ont retenu aux champs en ma maison, et fait passer une bonne partie de mes meilleurs ans, durant les guerres civiles de ce Royaume, cultivant la terre par mes serviteurs, comme le temps l'a peu porter. En quoy Dieu m'a tellement beny par sa saincte grace, que m'ayant conservez parmi tant de calamitez, dont j'ay senty ma bonne part, je me suis tellement comporté parmy les diverses humeurs de ma Patrie, que ma maison, ayant esté plus logis de paix que de guerre, quand les occasions s'en sont présentées, j'ay rapporté ce tesmoignage de mes voisins, qu'en me conservant avec eux, je me suis principalement addonnée chez moy, à faire mon mesnage" (1–2).

38. "Durant ce miserable temps-là, à quoy eusse-je peu mieux employer mon esprit, qu'à rechercher ce qui est de mon humeur? Soit donc que la paix nous donnast quelque relasche, soit que la guerre par diverses recheutes, m'imposast la nécessité de garder ma maison" (2).

39. "Mon intention est de monstrer, si je peux, brievement et clairement, tout ce qu'on doit cognoistre et faire, pour bien cultiver la Terre, et ce pour commodément vivre avec sa famille, selon le naturel des lieux, auxquels l'on s'habitue" (2).

40. "Et qui doit imaginer aux mesnages, quelque Paradis sans peine et incommodité, puisque les grands Estats du monde, sont enveloppez de tant d'espineuses difficultez?" (4).

41. "Il est plus aisé de souhaiter, que de rencontrer un lieu aux champs, accomply de toutes commoditez; c'est-à-dire, qui soit bon et beau, où le Ciel et la Terre s'accordans ensemble" (3).

42. "La Science est l'adresse au vray usage, la regle et le compas de bien faire" (3).

43. "Ainsi par degré appert, que quelque chemin qu'on tienne en ce monde, on vient finalement à l'Agriculture: la plus commune occupation d'entre les Hommes, la plus saincte et naturelle . . . Ce n'est donques aux habitants des champs que nostre Agriculture est particuliere: ceux des villes ont leur part" (8).

44. "Est requis à tout bon Mesnager, d'estre hazardeux à vendre, hastif à planter, tardif à bastir, diligent neantmoins à edifier . . . [il] n'entrera jamais en querelle avec aucun s'il est possible, pour le peril d'issue, semblable aux excès des guerres civiles, tirans en ruine le vainqueur avec le vaincu" (16).

45. "[Les paons] gardent le logis. De quoi ie suis fidele tesmoin car durant les guerres civiles ils m'ont fourni diverses preuves de telle loüable qualité: aians souventesfois esventé les secretes approches des ennemis en ceste mienne saison, durant l'obscurité de la nuict, estans perchés sur les arbres" (65).

46. Roper, *Holy Household*, 15, 147, and 267. The quote within the quote is from Konrad Sam, *Handtbuchlin darin begriffen ist die Ordnung une weiss, wie die Sacrament und Ceremonen der kirchen zu Ulm gebraucht und gehalten werden* (Ulm, 1631) fols. A/vii, b/i verso.

47. "Pa là nous apprendrons de policer nostre maison, specialement d'instruire nos enfants en la crainte de Dieu, nos serviteurs aussi: afin que . . . chacun . . . vive . . . religieusement, sagement, se comportans avec les voisins." Serres, 13.

48. "Le Père-de-famille aimera aussi ses *subiects*, s'il en a, les chérissant comme ses enfans, pour en leur besoin les soulager . . . mesmes en cas de nécessité, du passage des gens de guerre . . . les gardant de foules et sur-charges, d'exactions indeuës, et semblables violences" (13), my emphasis. The italicized term makes the equation between Protestant father and Catholic king explicit, inviting the latter's emulation of the former's model.

49. "Nostre père-de-famille sera averti de s'estudier à se rendre digne de sa charge: afin que sçachant bien commander ceux qu'il a sous soy, en puisse tirer l'obeïssance necessaire (ce qui est l'abrégé du Mesnage)" (9). "Mesnage" capitalized may be a reference to how this model is meant to be applied in the public sphere, while the term "abrégé" stresses the essential character of the household—obedience—as well as reinforcing the potential for public application. Cotgrave gives "abrégé" as "shortened, curtailed," demonstrating that de Serres feels his model has not received the broad emulation it merits.

50. "S'employer à pacifier les differens et querelles d'entre ses subjects et voisins . . . à ce que la paix estant conservée parmi eux" (13).

51. "Quelle chose plus laide y a-il au monde que la dissension et haine, sur

tout entre ceux qui mangent d'un mesme pain, et habitent en mesme maison, comme enfans d'un mesme pere? . . . Et comme il ne faut jamais faire mal, afin que le bien en advienne . . . ne laissera le pere-de-famille d'entretenir tous les siens en union paternelle" (45–46).

52. "Sur ce sujet dit le Poëte: Que son vers chante l'heur du bien aisé rustique / Dont l'honneste maison semble une Republique" (10).

53. "Et qu'il s'ajoute à son Mesnage quelque honneste negotiation, laquelle, compatible avec la culture de ses terres, fortifiera la recolte de ses fruits, d'où sortiront des moyens à suffisance, pour exercer tous offices honnestes, de charité, de liberalité . . . En somme, par là se rendra-il tel que Caton desire le pere-de-famille: assavoir, plus vendeur d'acheteur" (15).

54. "Sur ce propos alleguera les beaux dicts des Sages, mesmes de Salomon, 'Que la main du diligent l'enrichit: Qu'en temps de nécessité, il ne sera point confus . . . [autrement il aura] dissipé son heritage . . . le mangeant une piece apres l'autre" (23). See Chapter 4, on Philibert, for more on "heir" and "inheritance." The wolf-mother reference is from d'Aubigné, "Misères," *Les tragiques*, in *Oeuvres complètes*.

55. ". . . reformera sa maison." Serres, 38.

56. "Par telle correspondance la paix et la concorde se nourrissans en la maison . . . vous fera honorer . . . Et par telle marque estant vostre maison recogneuë pour celle de Dieu, Dieu y habitera, comme est promis en l'Escriture" (11).

57. "Des Paroles, il faut venir aux Effets, pour avoir contentement de nostre Agriculture. Et comme ce n'est que du papier peint, que le dessein du bastiment, sans pierre, chaux, sablon, bois et autres materiaux pour eslever l'edifice, aussi vainement aurions-nous representé le mesnage des champs, sans mettre la main à l'oeuvre. L'on a accoustumé de se moquer de ceux qui disent vouloir bastir . . . sans en voir l'avancement" (117).

58. Ballon, *Paris*, 26. I would add that Huguenots thus entered the realm of city planning, a *métier* with a high proportion of members of the Reformed faith up through the present day.

59. "L'ambition des hommes & leur avarice ont porté avec le temps les plus subtils esprits aux choses qu'ils ont estimé plus propres à leurs intentions, laissans le soin du labourage aux plus grossiers & durs de corps & d'esprit. De là l'ignorance est venuë en cet art, car ces pauvres maneuvres apprennans leur mestier de gens ignorans comme eux, en ont suivi le plus facile mais souvent le moins bon, ne pouvant penetrer à la raison des choses." "Avant-propos," *Traité*, I, a. All citations from Boyceau are from the *Traité*.

60. "Nous suivons un labeur tres ancien, car les premiers hommes cultivent la terre, leur ayant esté donné de Dieu cet exercice necessaire & ce travail ordinaire, pour une douce punition de leurs pechez: aussi ceux qui y sont occupez semblent mener une vie plus innocente" (a).

61. Boyceau's nephew and editor states: "J'ay representé son Visage selon mon art et mon pouvoir. Mais son Esprit et son Scavoir sont mieux despeints en son ouvrage" (d).

62. Ibid., 42.

63. "Parlerons-nous de ces oeuvres de Dieu merveilleuses sans admirer sa grandeur? Possederons nous son heritage sans luy rendre hommage? Penserons nous à elles sans craindre & reverer sa puissance? Et nous réioüyrons nous les voy-

ant sans chanter les loüanges de sa gloire et de sa bonté, qui les a faictes pour nous?" (aij).

64. "O Dieu d'un puissant secours seconde nostre peine" (aij).

65. ". . . auquel Jesus Christ comparoit les Apostres, leur disant, 'Vous estes le sel de la terre, et si le sel perd sa saveur, dequoy le selera-on?'" (aiij).

66. Ibid., 4.

67. "Ne dirons pas qu'il se desvoye de la droite voye d'architecture, laquelle dépend de l'ordre perpétuel de nature." Calvin, *Institution* (1552), II, xi, 229.

68. "On connoistra plus particulierement le goust des terres, si en creusant deux pieds de profond vous mettez une poignée de cette terre dans un verre la destrempant avec eau de pluye, ou autre bonne eau, puis laissent rassoir, & la terre estant au fonds du verre vous gousterez de cette eau éclaircie, qui tesmoignera si la terre est amere, sallée, ou a autre mauvaise goust ou odeur, qu'elle contribuëroit aux plantes qu'elle nouriroit; ce qu'on doit eviter, car le rabiller seroit malaisé ou impossible. Au contraire si vous trouvez odeur ou saveur plaisante & douce en cette eau, choisissez telle terre qui produira tous bons fruits." *Traité*, 9–10.

69. "Doncques s'il dépend de nous de choisir à nostre gré la situation du Iardin, nous aurons premierement égard au climat . . . mais chacun en approchera le plus près qu'il pourra, s'il veut iouïr des bienfaits de la nature avec moins de peine" (29).

70. "Employerons nous à cette manufacture tant importante, de grand art et de grande pratique, le premier qui se presentera, sans le connoistre & bien choisir? Quand avec grand soin nous le chercherons, à peine trouverons nous homme d'entiere connoissance & intelligence requises . . . aussi je croy que nous aurons plustost fait d'en dresser un que de le trouver accomply" (30). My emphasis.

71. Boyceau entitles this chapter "Des qualitez requises au Iardinier."

72. ". . . commençant à profiter en pourtraiture . . . Geometrie . . . voire . . . iusques à l'Architecture . . . & apprendra l'Arithmetique"; "afin qu'il ne se trompe" (30).

73. The gardener must be a "jeune garçon de bonne nature, de bon esprit" (29). See Chapter 4, on Philibert, for a discussion of the importance of *Ieunesse*.

74. "Encore il faut que le Iardinier sçache pour faire & pour enseigner les gens, car tant & tant de choses ne se font pas par un homme seul" (31).

75. "Ceci sera le subtil de nostre agriculture & le but de nostre intention, si avec bonne intelligence nous sçavons appliquer les choses, aydant la nature, & la guidant au chemin que nous voulons qu'elle tienne: estimant qu'elle est si riche en soy, que nous y pouvons choisir & puiser toutes les varietez qui peuvent venir en nostre fantaisie: Mais quittant les curiositez superflues, il suffira de nous arrester à oster les vices & defauts" (36).

76. "L'artifice ayde encor à cecy" (36).

77. "Il se fait de petits bosquets qui servent de grand embellissements aux Iardins, qui sont composez d'allées, sales & cabinets en lignes droites & courbes . . . vostre dessein estant faict & bien arresté le faudra tracer sur terre, & suivant la trace . . . long temps devant que de plantes, afin de rendre la terre plus aimable au plan, luy donnant moyen de se meurir & d'evaporer les mauvaises conditions qui se rencontrent d'ordinaire au second lit d'icelles" (65).

78. "Que si le Iardinier est ignorant du dessein, il n'aura aucune invention

ny iugement, pour les ornemens: s'il les emprunte d'autruy, comment les tracera-il sur la terre?" (68).

79. "Il y encor grand plaisir de voir de lieu eslevé les parterres bas, qui paroissent plus beaux, car d'en bas ils ne peuvent estre seulement discernez: la disposition & departement de tout le Iardin estant veuë de haut, est remarquée & reconnuë d'une seule veuë, ne paroist qu'un seul parterre, dans lequel sont distinguez tous les ornemens: vous jugez de là la bonne correspondance qui est entre les parties, qui toutes ensemble baillent plus de plaisir que les parcelles" (70).

80. "Les autres formes parfaites trouveront aussi leur lieu & leurs graces dans les Iardins, si elles sont disposées selon la nature du lieu . . . ces choses dépendantes de l'invention & gentillesse d'esprit du Designateur" (71).

81. Adams, *The French Garden: 1500–1800*, 151. "In Boyceau can be found a rigorous, intellectual approach to the subject . . . [which] first raises gardening to an art . . . Boyceau's analysis of garden art, like Palissy's, began with the fundamental elements of water, earth, fire and air, revealing a deeply religious belief in the rational workings of God through nature."

82. "Quand [ces formes] seront formées de bonne ordonnance d'architecture . . . placez avec ordre" (*Traité*, 74).

83. "Et n'entends pas pourtant qu'on les brouille ensemble, en les entremeslant confusément, ains qu'en iugeant de la convenance ou repugnance que les choses ont ensemble, on les approche ou les esloigne" (82).

84. "Disposés par bon ordre d'architecture" (80).

85. "Madame, si l'iniure du temps & troubles qui ont cours, n'eussent empesché mon accès & veuë des chasteaux & maisons, que vostre Maiesté desire estre comprins aux livres qu'il vous a pleu me commander de dresser & dessigner . . ." (Aii).

86. Du Cerceau, "Dans l'Europe du XVIe siècle, il est de loin le 'vulgarisateur' le plus prolifique en matière d'architecture et de décoration." *Les plus excellens*, 5.

87. Ludet notes in du Cerceau "Certaines extravagances, certains manques de proportions . . . dans ses recueils . . . les écarts dûs en général, à cette fantaisie à laquelle il [s']abandonne." Ibid., 239.

88. "Davantage ayant bien entendu ce petit livret, vous aurez l'intelligence non seulement de tous les livres de ceux qui en ont escript: mais encore voyant quelques desseings de maçonnerie, paysages, ou autres, vous iugerez aisément si les maistres [ou les] oeuvriers y ont mis la main." Du Cerceau, *Perspective*, Aiii.

89. "Comme un miroir lequel de soy ne fait les choses qui luy sont presentees meilleures ou pires qu'elles ne sont, mais seulement represente au vray ce qui luy est mis au devant ainsi & comme il est." Ibid.

90. F. Boudon, "Les livres d'architecture de Jacques Androuet du Cerceau," 367.

91. "Lorsqu'il trouvait sur son chemin un bâtiment bien entretenu, le souvenir laissait tomber: 'ce n'est pas des miens.'" Du Cerceau, *Les plus excellens*, 9.

92. Ibid., 13.

93. ". . . qui confessait sa foi, n'avait d'autre choix que de s'enfuir." Ibid., 8.

94. Ibid., 335.

95. Ward, ed. *French châteaux*, 42.

96. Du Cerceau, *Les plus excellens*, 9.

97. "J'estoye acheminé pour aller visiter les dicts bastiments [singuliers] et commencer ledict oeuvre, les misérables troubles survindrent en ce Royaume, qui me causèrent si grandes pertes et dommaiges, et à toute ma famille, que je n'ay eu depuis moyen, ne pouvoir de poursuivre mon desseing." Du Cerceau, *Premier recueil d'ornements et arabesques grotesques* (1566), 204.

98. "Nous sommes frappés de voir Androuet dédier encore trois de ses ouvrages, après la St-Barthélemy, à Catherine de Médicis. Faut-il voir là de la part d'un protestant un signe d'indifférence religieuse, ou le témoignage d'une grande misère qui le faisait dépendre entièrement de la Cour?" Geymuller, *Les du Cerceau*, 239.

99. "Sire . . . n'ayant moyen . . . de me transporter sur ces lieux, afin d'en prendre les desseings." Geymuller, 340.

100. There are many kinds of constraint: spatial, architectural, religious. He says, for example, "qu'avant que commencer l'édifice, on soyt adverty de la despense qu'il convient faire, & quel moyen on aura de la parachever, à faute de quoy, plusieurs se trouveront bien souvent trompez & abusez." Ibid., Geymuller cites du Cerceau's *Architecture*, ii.

101. ". . . une certaine originalité dans le système de hachure, employé pour modeler ses édifices, et dans les détails de tous genres qu'il réproduit . . . un sentiment très personnel dans l'interprétation de beaucoup de ses gravures." Ibid., 282.

102. "L'abondance et la spontanéité des détails et des fioritures." Geymuller, *Les du Cerceau*, 13.

103. "La naïveté des méthodes d'illustration et l'utilisation flexible des modes de perspective sont parmi les caractéristiques les plus surprenant du recueil." Ibid., 14.

104. In this, he is very different from the Catholic Le Muet, for example. "Le travail de du Cerceau n'est pas soutenu par un esprit de système comme le sera celui de Le Muet. Il travaille surtout par citation, par collages d'éléments, par accumulation. Il cherche la diversité et l'exploitation de tous les possibles . . . Les deux livres demandent à être utilisés avec la plus grande liberté." Boudon, "Les livres," 381.

105. Du Cerceau, preface, *Les plus excellens bastiments*, 337. "Madame, après qu'il a pleu à Dieu nous envoyer par vostre moyen une paix tant nécessaire et désirée de tous, j'ay pensé ne pouvoir mieulx à propos mettre en lumière le premier Livre des bastiments exquis de ce Royaume, esperans que nos pauvres Français (ès yeux et entendemens des quels ne se presente maintenant autre chose que desolations, ruines, et saccagements, que nous ont apporté les guerres passées), prendront . . . en respirant, quelque plaisir et contentement, à contempler ici une partie des plus beaux et excellens edifices, dont la France est encores pour le iour d'huy enrichie."

106. "J'ay toujours eu cette opinion . . . que la nécessité est la mère de tous arts et science, que la paix, richesse et abondance en sont les nourrices: et au contraire les longues seditions et guerres les vraies meurtrieres: ce qui se void encore plus clairement en l'art d'architecture . . . en l'architecture, durant une longue paix . . . une merveilleuse quantité de marbre, iaspe, et porphyre, et l'embellirent de tels et si grands édifices tant publicqs que privez . . . [mais] les divisions de l'Empire et guerres civiles . . . de toute ces merveilles à grand peine y peut on aujourd'huy re-

marquer ces places où elles estoient assises . . . emporté et du tout enseveli avec tels édifices, l'art et les maistres." Du Cerceau, preface, *Livre des edifices antiques romains*, 338–39.

107. "Le fait de feuilleter les deux volumes, le second d'entre eux en particulier, dut représenter pour elle un mélange de plaisir et d'amertume car, dans cet ouvrage, la moitié des 'maisons royales' . . . se révélaient être des projets de construction, ou d'agrandissement important, qui n'avaient progressé que très peu, ou pas du tout." Geymuller, *Les du Cerceau*, 11.

108. "J'ay composé, taillé et imprimé . . . qui sera pour enrichir & embellir de plus en plus cestuy vostre si florissant Royaume: lequel de iour en iour on voyt augmenter de tant beaux & somptueux edifices, que doresnavant vos sugectz n'auront occasion de voyager en estrange païs, pour en veoir de mieux composer. Et d'avantage vostre Majesté prenant plaisir & delectation, mesmes à l'entretenement de si excellents ouvriers de vostre nation, il ne sera plus besoing de recours aux estrangers . . . vostre . . . tresobeissant suject, & serviteur." Du Cerceau, *Architecture*, ij.

109. This theological description may provide the solution to what confuses critics in Cerceau's work: "L'absence totale de logique historique ou chronologique dans l'organisation des deux volumes ne laisse pas de nous intriguer." Geymuller, *Les du Cerceau*, 12.

110. "Considérant que la providence divine a voulu establir un ordre entre les creatures raisonnables, à ce que chacun, selon le don de grace qu'elle luy avoit distribué, laissait à la posterité quelque tesmoignage de sa vocation." Du Cerceau, *Les plus excellens*, "au lecteur," Aiiv.

111. Another Protestant, François de la Noue, in his *Discours politique et militaire* (1587), expresses similar concerns.

112. ". . . analyse en détails les pièges de la construction et de l'architecture . . . fustige ceux qui consacrent leurs maigres ressources à l'ostentation." Geymuller, *Les du Cerceau*, 10.

113. "Luy ayant senti se gratter où il lui démangeoit, a incontinent forgé en imagination un dessein qu'il a commencé avec plaisir, continué avec peine et despence, achevé avec douleur." Ibid., 10.

114. "Le titre même de son livre confirme au lecteur qu'il se trouve devant une démonstration intelligible de pratique très éprouvée plutôt que, devant un ouvrage de théoricien, on est au fond, en présence d'une sorte de prospectus technique." Geymuller, *Les du Cerceau*, 14.

115. F. Boudon, "Les livres," 371.

116. See many authors, "La grande revanche des protestants," *Le point*, 1219 (27 January 1996): 51–59. Such intermarriage is still the case today, in the essentially closed community of Huguenots. "La première caractéristique de la personnalité protestante réside dans le fait minoritaire, fruit d'une histoire douloureuse . . . Leur force se nourrit de leur faiblesse . . . un long cortège de persécutions . . . a forgé un tempérament de résistants et a appris aux huguenots à vivre seuls, en marge . . . [avec] une aspiration permanente à l'affranchissement et une quête de modernité . . . l'enclave protestante . . . des familles protestantes . . . la tribu . . ." The authors note a recent "faible endogamie, diminution de la taille des familles."

117. Pannier, "Salomon de Brosse," 22. "Ils [y] venaient le dimanche assister à l'exercice du culte public, interdit dans la ville épiscopale, mais autorisé à un lieu environ."

118. Ibid.

119. Gulczynski, "Les Tabourot," 61.

120. Ibid.

121. "Ce jeu gratuit d'accumulation de détails . . . con[vient] d'une large part d'imitation dans les oeuvres . . . de Sambin . . . Des emprunts à Jacques Androuet du Cerceau, pour les premières . . . sont incontestables. L'extravagance de la plupart des compositions gravées par l'artiste dijonnais outrepassait les limites de la vraisemblance et les rendait irréalisables telles quelles." Ibid., 61.

122. "Il est à noter que l'auteur représente toujours les objets de son intérêt se dressant au milieu d'un vaste espace, au contraire des géomètres et des mathématiciens qui tapinaient la *camera oscura* et qui dans la France ou l'Italie du seizième siècle, comme dans la Hollande du dix-septième, choisissaient plutôt de démontrer des intérieurs ou des paysages pour illustrer des problèmes de perspective." Boudon, "Les livres," 14.

123. ". . . [il] met en évidence à la fois sa conscience et son mépris des conventions." Ibid., 14.

124. "On a souvent mis en doute la précision des illustrations d'Androuet du Cerceau"; "Il a pris en diverses occasions des libertés avec ce qu'il voyait et s'est rendu coupable d'erreurs étranges et inexplicables . . . [Mais] ces aberrations . . . ne sauraient en aucun cas jeter un discrédit sur la valeur . . . de son travail."

125. "Il y a quelque chose de profondément satisfaisant dans le plan achevé de St.-Léger tel que le dessine Du Cerceau: 4 ailes autour d'une cour, reliées par 4 pavillons et enrichies, sur chacune de leur face externe d'un édifice en saillie chaque fois différent. C'est là un parfait témoignage tant de l'époque, fascinée par la régularité, que du génie de l'auteur, acharné à retravailler les formules acceptées en les traitant comme thèmes et variations, à les exprimer dans son propre langage." Boudon and Blécon, *Philibert*, 75.

126. "Ce château avait été terminé par les protecteurs du début de sa carrière, François Premier et Henri II, ce qui rend encore plus inexplicable l'espace vide où les structures omises devraient se trouver sur la gravure." Ibid.

127. It must be observed that, while du Cerceau apparently admired de l'Orme, frequently taking him as his model, even if he did revise his works, Philibert de l'Orme seems not to have cared for du Cerceau's work: "Il tourne souvent en ridicule ceux qui versent dans cet art sans avoir produire beaucoup plus que d'agréable desseins." Ibid., 11.

128. Blunt, *Philibert*, 64.

129. Ibid., 143.

130. Ibid., 64, 94.

131. "Parfois Du Cerceau, sous des dénominations antiques, donnait des monuments qui ne l'étaient point du tout." Geymuller, *Les Du Cerceau*, 196.

132. Coope, *Salomon*, 22.

133. Geymuller, *Les du Cerceau*, 40, "une transformation méthodique."

134. "Plusieurs de ces combinaisons et variantes offrent parfois des défauts de

proportion qui sautent aux yeux . . . plusieurs d'entre elles peuvent être envisagées comme le résultat d'expériences qu'il entreprenait précisément pour faire mieux ressortir . . . l'incompatibilité de certains éléments, et la nécessité d'avoir recours en ce cas à des combinaisons d'un autre ordre." Ibid., 60.

135. ["C'est] une série de réflexions et d'expérimentation en chaîne . . . l'idée de la symétrie . . . a pour corollaire un essai de systematisation de la distribution des circuits. L'organisation intérieure se transforme par une évolution complémentaire de l'enveloppe murale." Boudon and Blécon, *Philibert*, 82.

136. "Mascherare, o occultare un insegnamento interiore era un sotterfugio commune, ma alcuni autori non fecero una virtù—o almeno una prova di abilità. Portare il lettore, o il discepolo alla verità attraverso la contraddizione e l'inganno era una pratica corrente per molti degli umanisti, teologi ed editori—con cui Serlio era in contatto." Carpo, *La maschera*, 8.

137. "Loin de copier servilement le modèle qu'il se proposait de réproduire, il en ressentait si vivement les mérites, qu'il le concevait en quelque sorte à nouveau et le rendait comme il l'aurait fait pour une de ses propres créations." Geymuller, *Les du Cerceau*, 226.

138. "Prenez en considération l'architecture de Verneuil, les archivoltes, les guirlandes, les masques . . . ce détail diffère sensiblement de tous les autres édifices représentés dans *Plus excellents*. [Ce sont] . . . figures fantastiques . . . [et des] bizarreries de forme attribuables aux accents personnels de l'artiste." Ibid., 83.

139. "[Serlio was] an author who apparently wanted to publish in book form a catalogue of models *not* to be followed—or, rather, to follow only in part." Carpo, *La maschera*, 14.

140. "Ceste leçon vous donne à cognoistre la maniere de raccourcir pilastres avec leurs ornemens qu'on voit de la veuë du costé, parce qu'ils sont seuls & separez d'autre oeuvre. Il est vray que si à l'opposite y avoit autant de pilastres, & que sur le tout fussent assis arcs ou bien planchers, toute l'oeuvre ioncte ensemble se diroit veuë du front: mais separez comme ils sont, sont veuë de costé, comme on voit par le dessing, lequel est sur le raccours du front, mais la veuë nous apparoist du costé." Du Cerceau, *Perspective*, leçon xxx, 8. See also leçon xvii, 6v: "Et fault noter, que tant plus vos estages se haulseront de la ligne visuale, tant moins apparoistra-il de raccours: ce qui semble estre contraire en la Perspective theorique, mais en nostre Positive, tant plus les estages s'approchent de nostre ligne visuale, de tant plus ils raccourcissent: qui est la cause que ne pouvez voir en iceux ce qui y est figuré si amplement comme apparoist par ces desseings." The designs can be decoded, he tells us; they are an optical illusion with a deeper meaning than the trickery that they cause.

141. "Or sur chacune de ces quatre veuës on peut considerer & arrester trois assiettes, haute, moyenne, & basse, ainsi nommees du respect de l'oeil du regardant, qui dessigne les choses selon son milieu, non pas selon celuy des autres. Basse assiette ou veuë commune, est comme quand le regardant est en une rue devant un temple pour le dessiner. La haulte . . . plus haulte qu'iceluy. Mais . . . entre le haut et le bas . . . moyenne assiette." Ibid., Aiii (v).

142. "Vostre ligne visuale est assise au deuxiesme estage. Et fault noter & entendre, que toutes lignes qui renfondent pour le raccours, leurs lignes sont su-

biectes à se rendre au visual, n'estoit que la place ou quelque partie de l'oeuvre bien fait: car le biais causeroit poincts accidentaux & faudroit dessigner le biais en vostre plan . . . il me semble que si avez bien compris ce qu'en ay dit, vous ne fauldrez . . . de vous-mesmes en ferez de differente." Ibid., xlix, 10.

143. Carpo calls this, at the artistic level, a "dialectic between convention and invention" [dialettica fra convenzione ed invenzione; saussurianamente, fra langue e parole]. *La maschera*, 16; Paul might term it the difference between the letter that kills and the spirit that gives life.

144. "Vous avez . . . en ce dessing la moitié du plan . . . que de toute l'édifice . . . les leçons . . . bien entendues vous monstreront non seulement et les moyens pour mettre en execution ceste leçon, mais d'autres inventions que de vous-mesmes vouldrez dessigner sur la circonference." *Perspective*, li, 9.

145. Blunt, *Art and Architecture*, 143.

146. "Les doubles entrelacs . . . les petites irrégularités d'exécution de cet ornement si régulier en lui-même fournissent au dessinateur l'occasion de révéler sa touche, la manière habituelle qu'il s'est faite pour représenter cette forme." Geymuller, *Les du Cerceau*, 10.

147. Coope, *Salomon*, 24.

148. "Face du dehors . . . laquelle n'a este parachevee." Partial caption on du Cerceau's engraving, to the left.

149. Du Cerceau, *Les plus excellens*, 18. Ludet's remark: "Jamais nous ne saurons pourquoi il montre une oeuvre si renommée autre qu'elle n'est dans la réalité!"

150. ". . . l'incarnation monumentale des aspirations . . . de la monarchie française à l'hégémonie . . . un peu décevante." Ibid., 29.

151. Coope, *Salomon*, 23.

152. "Du Cerceau's elevations . . . were in part extremely elaborate and sometimes fantastic . . . As with so many of Du Cerceau's elevations, one feels that altogether too many things have happened." Ibid., 27.

153. "Being Zwingli's junior by a generation, Calvin was far less willing to jettison the arts. It was under Calvin's direction that stained glass windows were ordered for the cathedral of St. Peter, which may have been designed by Duvet. The latter is also known to have prepared designs for the Church of the Magdalen and tapestries for the Maison de ville." Eisler, *Master*, 15. See also 83: "A contemporary of Duvet named Loys Chocquet . . . wrote a mystery play devoted to the *Revelation of St. John* (1541) . . . *L'Apocalypse de Saincte* [sic] *Jehan Zebedee* . . . The play contains veiled protests against the censorship and religious intolerance of François Ier and Henri II . . . The increasingly rigid censorship by the French Counter-Reformation frowned upon the *mystère de sainctes sainc* [sic] whose presentation of the sacred was found too free, almost casual, providing artists with a vehicle to convey Protestant sentiments." We see that many media cooperated in introducing the subversive Protestant message within the Catholic realm.

154. Coope, *Salomon*, 2.

155. Cited by Geymuller, *Les du Cerceau*, introduction, iv. "A ceux qui ne font que commencer dans l'architecture, [ses oeuvres] sont plus dangereux qu'utiles, à cause des licences qu'il s'est données dans ses inventions." Du Cerceau, *Les plus excellens*, 24.

156. Ibid., 37.

157. Ibid., 38.

158. Ballon, *Paris*, 42.

159. The first to criticize Jacques II's work was Henri Sauval, circa 1660, regarding the former's work on the Louvre. See Ballon, *Paris*, 40.

160. Schama, *Landscape*, 278. De Caus was rumored to have been locked up in the Bicêtre prison by Richelieu.

161. Ward, *Architecture*, 224.

162. Ibid., 7.

163. "Comme tant d'autres huguenots . . . la persécution étant rude . . . sa famille s'éloigna . . . [prenant] diverses courses and changements de lieu." Quoted in Pannier, "Salomon," 30.

164. Coope, *Salomon*, 7. Coope does acknowledge that "it is not possible to assess whether or not his religious beliefs affected de Brosse's character and outlook . . . it is not possible to say whether . . . he especially favored employing his co-religionists, and he certainly had no scruples whatsoever in working for Catholic patrons." Most of the patrons with power and money were Catholic, however, so de Brosse's ability to compromise should not be a surprise. He was simply dealing with reality.

165. "Jacques II . . . assumes responsibility for training the young Salomon de Brosse . . . Queen [Marie de Médicis]'s architect . . . connected with important commissions in Paris . . . inherited Jacques II du Cerceau's position and pension on the royal payroll . . . collaborated in 1619 in reediting Jean Bullant's *Reigle* . . . De Brosse's parents, his maternal grandfather . . . his du Cerceau uncles . . . were Protestants . . . They worshipped at the Temple near Senlis." Ibid., 3–7.

166. "En 1606, les protestants n'étaient admis à célébrer leur culte à Charenton que par simple tolérance; les catholiques protestaient contre la construction d'un temple; ils n'auraient pas permis qu'on lui donnât la forme ordinaire d'une église." Pannier, "Salomon," 237.

167. "Les protestants eux-mêmes, à cette époque en France, n'étaient pas bien fixés sur la disposition à donner à leurs édifices religieux. Salomon de Brosse devait, ici plus que nulle part ailleurs, faire oeuvre créatrice." Ibid., 238.

168. "La prédication occupant en effet dans le culte des Eglises réformées de France, au XVIIe siècle plus encore qu'au XXe, une place très importante, et d'autre part le nombre des lieux de culte autorisés par l'Edit de Nantes étant excessivement limité, c'était des milliers d'auditeurs qu'il fallait mettre à même de bien entendre chaque dimanche les pasteurs de Charenton. De là cette rangée de galeries sur trois côtés rappelle plutôt une salle de conférence." Ibid.

169. Pannier, notes that Geymuller, concerning Charenton, "trouve remarquable l'effort fait par Salomon de Brosse pour s'affranchir des traditions séculaires concernant la disposition intérieure d'une église chrétienne" (238).

170. Patricia O'Grady, "Jacques Perret," 6.

171. G. German, *Der protestantische Kirchenbau in der Schweiz* (Zurich: Orell Fussli, 1963), 26.

172. Blunt, *Art and Architecture*, 176.

173. See the chapter on Calvinism's elevation of daily life to a superior, almost spiritual status (the "priesthood of all believers," of which Luther was so fond of speaking) in Charles Taylor's *Sources of the Self* (Cambridge: Harvard University Press, 1991).

174. Coope, *Salomon*, 13.

175. "Il a terminé sa grande oeuvre du Luxembourg après avoir reçu 'peu de chose' . . . nous n'avons trouvé aucun document permettant d'insinuer qu'il ait été malhonnête; au contraire nous l'avons vu subir maintes fois des retards longs et injustifiés dans les paiements qui devaient lui être faits par ses nobles clients." Pannier, "Salomon," 66.

176. "Nous le verrons chargé de construire quelques-uns des plus importants monuments de cette époque." Ibid., 48.

177. Pannier asserts the case that Janine Garrison has refuted: that there was toleration, at least on the commercial or mercantile level, of Calvinist artisans. He claims, rather naively, as we can now see in light of Garrison's archivally based findings, that "entre protestants et catholiques, surtout dans le domaine artistique ou littéraire, les rapports étaient, à cette époque, beaucoup meilleurs qu'on ne se le figure ordinairement, meilleurs peut-être qu'ils ne l'ont été à aucune autre époque avant la nôtre, et tout à fait indépendants des passions religieuses" (86). Garrison, however, has instructed us, some years later, that such was emphatically *not* the case. See 224–27 in her *Guerre civile*, in which she states, "on verra de quelles difficultés seront faits pour les huguenots friands de charges [royaux, ou de commissions] les lendemains de l'Edit de Nantes" (224).

178. Some of his works, such as the aqueduct at Arceuil, were "interrompues par les troubles." Pannier, "Salomon," 68.

179. "Salomon de Brosse était chargé par ses coreligionnaires de l'Eglise réformée de Paris de reconstruire leur temple à Charenton, et cette coïncidence expliquerait d'une manière très plausible la mauvaise volonté de la reine mère . . . à l'égard de Salomon de Brosse au sujet du Luxembourg . . . la reine, docile aux instructions de son confesseur, ne pouvait être favorable à l'architecte chargé de relever le principal monument où l'hérésie allait se maintenir aux portes de la capitale." Ibid., 87.

180. "L'abus des bossages sur les murs et les colonnes, l'emploi persistant de toitures aux profils trop raides, donne aux bâtiments quelque chose de pesant, un aspect écrasé." Ibid., 136.

181. "The manipulation of space in the comparatively small chapel . . . must have been . . . impressive." Coope, *Salomon*, 51.

182. "De Brosse s'y est permis . . . des disparités qu'on n'aime pas à rencontrer dans un genre d'architecture dont la régularité fait la principale condition . . . quelque chose d'irrégulier." Ibid., 152, quoting the art critic J. B. de St. Victor's assessment.

183. Ibid., 110, describing the Palais du Luxembourg. "Characteristically, . . . there is a certain carelessness in detail, in the juxtaposition of various parts of the building . . . de Brosse has ignored the fact that the asymmetry and indeed slight imbalance of the lateral façade . . . is even further stressed by the different propor-

tions of the pavilions at the entrance end and the different treatment of their upper storeys." (115).

184. "[He] has led himself into certain complications . . . a criticism which might be made of the façade is that it is too open-ended." Ibid., 125, describing the Church of St-Gervais.

185. "De Brosse's besetting weakness [was that] he would compose splendidly in mass, and would design fine details, but he so often failed to consider the relationships between the details of one part of a building and another." Ibid., 102.

186. "Parquoy ie supplie les ouvriers de bon iugement, & tous autres qui se delectent en cest art, avoir esgard à la maniere seulement, quant viendra à mettre en oeuvre; car l'oeuvre faict autrement que les desseings." Bullant, *Reigle*, last page. Bullant, of course, has been solidly identified by many as a "true follower" of Philibert de l'Orme (Blunt, *Philibert*, 136). Here we have the Calvinist line of filiation stretching incontestably from de l'Orme through Bullant and now de Brosse. Blunt further underscores this link, observing that "it is in de Brosse that we find a real continuation of [Philibert's] methods." He pairs Blérancourt and the Château Neuf, and views the Palais du Luxembourg as a second St.-Maur (137).

187. "Souvent de père en fils, on était à la fois maçon, entrepreneur, architecte . . . ils sont comme tant d'autres artisans et artistes . . . devenus protestants." Pannier, "Salomon," 30.

Chapter 6. Conclusion: Constrained Creations

1. Blunt, *Art*, 162.

2. Ibid., 164.

3. "Premierement je fis la figure d'une grande place . . . et à l'entour de laquelle je fis le plan d'un nombre de maisons . . . il n'y aura qu'une rue, et une autre . . . par lignes directes, d'anglet en anglet, jusques à la place." Palissy, *Recepte véritable*, 217–18.

4. Ballon, *Paris*, 38. For what follows, I am indebted to Ballon's analysis.

5. Ibid., 39, notes that "their *oeuvre* as a whole is almost entirely undocumented."

6. Ibid., 83, 42.

7. Ibid. Does the lack of monuments signify a power void? If such is the case, does the power then shift to the public domain? Is this a Calvinist iconographic strategy designed to show that power does not inhere absolutely in the monarch?

8. Ibid., 320, n. 102.

9. "A new spatial concern permeated the *grand dessein* and marked the emergence of planning on an urban scale in Henri IV's Paris." Ibid., 46.

10. Ibid., 115.

11. Ibid., 123.

12. Ibid., 128.

13. "Il eut été à souhaiter que ceux qui ont eu l'inspection de cet ouvrage eussent placé cette statue en face de l'ouverture de la Place Dauphine et la porte du Palais." Ballon, citing Jaillot's *Recherches*, I: 182. Ibid., 327, n. 39.

14. Quoting Sauval. Ibid., 129.

15. Ibid., 127, 133.

16. Ibid., 135. My emphasis.

17. Ibid., 137.

18. Ibid., 84.

19. Coope, *Salomon de Brosse*, 42. I would add that this unencumbered aspect also memorialized the brief, former Protestant investiture of the town, providing a nostalgic look back to those few historical moments of Calvinist strength.

20. Coope, quoting the language of the document. Ibid., 43.

21. Ibid., 12.

22. Jacques Lemercier was Catholic. He succeeded de Brosse as *architecte du roi* and was Cardinal Richelieu's private architect. He represents an arch-Catholic, extremely conservative trend in contemporary architecture and was called a "reverent" architect because he conformed to the ideological expectations of his patrons. Ward, *Architecture*, 225, 226. He is known for having constructed the church of the Sorbonne (1635–53). Lemercier and most of the other Catholic architects of the period do not seem to have been as involved with the production of architectural manuals as were Calvinists, for reasons that should be clear by this point. In addition, Catholics trained under the great Calvinist architects, which in some measure explains why the former were not the authors of the great architectural manuals of the day.

23. "A l'image de Richelieu, le bourg conçu et construit sur l'ordre du cardinal, dont les rues en damier, les maisons identiques signifient l'ordre nouveau et géométrique d'une nature désormais écrite en langage mathématique . . . chacun sait à présent 'qu'on réduit toutes choses à l'autorité' et que l'Etat est une puissance définie en termes de pouvoir et de commandement, une puissance visible aussi . . . Mais rien n'est jamais aussi simple que le plan—fut-il réalisé—d'une cité-idéale . . . éclatante . . . et l'immensité de l'écart . . . qui sépare la théorie et la pratique du pouvoir." Joël Cornette, "Fiction et réalité de l'état baroque (1610–52)," in Méchoulan, *L'état baroque*, 9–10.

24. Blunt, *Art*, 201.

25. "Pour la littérature, pour le texte littéraire, l'objet architectural (au sens large, ville, jardin, maison, machine, habit, meuble, monument) semble doté d'un statut sémantique complexe. Il peut être, d'abord, conçu essentiellement comme un objet herméneutique, dans la mesure où un dedans (toujours plus ou moins caché) s'y distingue nécessairement d'un dehors . . . d'un côté, la façade, de l'autre, la crypte . . . les stratégies du savoir . . . Tout objet architectural pourra être appréhendé par le texte littéraire comme un objet discriminateur, différentiel, analysant l'espace par cloisons et contiguïtés . . . Enfin, tout objet architectural peut être conçu . . . comme un objet hiérarchisé, comme un système de contraintes, des organisations" (7).

26. Such is also the case for Sebastiano Serlio, in whose writings "the truth . . . is hidden away in a box of surprises . . . The 'prudent architect' must go beyond

the 'letter to the mystery'; . . . nell'*Extraordinario libro* la verità . . . è chiusa iù una scatola a sorpresso . . . il 'prudente architetto' serliano dovrà 'passare dalla lettera al mistero.'" Carpo, *La maschera*, 127.

27. Lefèbvre, *Production of Space*, 33. He is quoting Nietzsche here.

28. Carpo, *La maschera*, 129. "Inutile insegnaro a chi non può caprire."

29. Bell, *Ritual Theory*, 84–85. While this comment is taken from Bell, much of this page is informed by a conversation in 1993 with the Reverend William Russell Coats in which we talked about the goal of Christianity and its relationship to politics. He observed that the Calvinist architects were making a statement that amounted to the encapsulation "Read My Witness"; that, unable to possess power, these men were witnessing, instead. We see this in the second-generation architects, not in Calvin, since he still was convinced that he could, ultimately, obtain and redirect power. The second-generation architects may have decided to critique the very notion of power (this is consistent with their contemporaries, the tyrranomach writers). Coats asked, "Isn't the critique of power the Christian goal, anyway, when all is said and done? They're saying to the Catholics, 'we don't want your kind of power.' Theirs is a metaphysical hope and perspective. That is the ultimate, lasting power."

30. This is Carpo's main thesis in *La maschera*: "ma, per concludere, non si puo escludere che lo stesso atteggiamento [e] spirituale" (136); [but, in conclusion, we can never forget that his attitude [is] spiritual].

31. Coope, *Salomon de Brosse*, 32.

32. "Les architectes, volontiers, se présentent eux-mêmes . . . d'une part à l'écoute des consignes du client, d'autre art produisant à la fois des lieux-récits et des lieux de récit . . . Qui dit récit dit transformation et orientation . . . l'architecte pense à travers et grâce à la narrativité." Hamon, "Texte," 33.

33. "Nous sommes ceux qui sont separez de telles gens, non par distinction de naissance, de teint de visage ni de prolation, mais par la profession de pureté en creance, en moeurs et par observation de telle justice que nous mesprisons biens et vies pour le service de Dieu." D'Aubigné, *Histoire universelle*, 10:314.

34. "De Brosse's last known work, and his most curious creation, is the architectural setting which he designed (and signed) for an engraving by Michel Lasne in honor of Pope Gregory XV. It is strange to find this respected member of the Paris Protestant community, and the designer of their new Temple, engaging in so uncompromisingly Catholic and ultramontane an undertaking. Not that de Brosse objected any more than his fellow Protestant architects and artisans to working for Catholic patrons, embellishing Catholic churches or building Catholic chapels, . . . but since this is the only surviving engraving from de Brosse's design, its theme seems ironic." Coope, *Salomon de Brosse*, 187.

35. "Quant au mot de Religion, combien que Cicéron le deduise tres bien du mot de *Relire* . . . les serviteurs de Dieu ont tousiours releu et diligemment médité ce qui estoit de faire . . . car la vraie pieté . . . se recueille en ses limites." Calvin, *Institution* (1552), I, xii, 140.

36. Peter Burke reproduces this illustration, among others, in his *Fabrication of Louis XIV*.

37. "Persecution of the Protestants was intensified around 1680 . . . In 1685,

the Edict of Fontainebleau was issued, revoking that of Nantes . . . The Revocation, intended to root out the last remnants of dissent, had the opposite effect . . . dissent began to grow [despite the dispersal] . . . the Huguenots in exile were the most out-spoken." Keohane, *Philosophy*, 312.

38. Burke, *Fabrication*, citing first Bossuet, then *Soupirs* (1689): "tout l'Etat est en lui . . . le roi a pris la place de l'Etat."

39. Ballon, *Paris*, 6.

40. "What kind of Protestant church is this? Duban identifies it only with the subscription, 'Temple consacré au culte protestant.' It does not resemble in layout or scale any of the impressive Protestant churches erected in Europe after 1800 . . . It is a simple double-cubic volume without balconies or interior complexities of form. Seats rear up on three sides, and the altar table, pulpit, and organ are set vertically one above the other on the axis of the fourth. Behind is a bell tower and a room for the minister and the consistory . . . The Académie shook its head in dismay at this simplicity . . . in a number of details Duban's project shows that it embodied ideas even more worrisome to the architectural bureaucracy of the Restoration. This particular plan, with everything in a single space arranged for ease of hearing and seeing, is Calvinist, and more specifically Swiss Calvinist . . . Protestantism was otherwise a catchword for liberalism and resistance to the Bourbon monarchy. Protestants led the liberal opposition in parliament." Van Zanten, *Designing Paris*, 19–23. I owe this information, and much else, to David Van Zanten, of Northwestern University, who graciously and generously shared his knowledge, expertise, and encouragement with me on several occasions.

41. Ibid., 26.

42. As was the case for so many Calvinist architects, fragmentation and juxtaposition were part of Haussmann's arsenal of stylistic tools.

43. Du Cerceau, *Les plus excellens*, 25.

Bibliography

Abray, Lorna. *The People's Reformation: Magistrates, Clergy, and Commons in Stras-bourg, 1500–1598*. Oxford: Blackwell, 1985.

Adams, Frank Dawson. *The Birth and Development of the Geological Sciences*. London: Baillere, 1938.

Adams, William Howard. *The French Garden, 1500–1800*. London: Scolar, 1982.

Adorno, Theodor. *Aesthetics and Politics*. Trans. R. Taylor. London: New Left Books, 1977.

———. *Aesthetic Theory*. Trans. C. Lenhardt. Minneapolis: University of Minnesota Press, 1997.

Ahmed, Ehsan. "Pierre de Ronsard's *Odes* and the Law of Poetic Space." *Renaissance Quarterly* 44, no. 4 (1991): 757–76.

Aillaud, E. "L'espace d'un récit." *Cahiers de la recherche architecturale* 6–7 (Oct. 1980): 55–78.

Alpers, Svetlana. *The Art of Describing: Dutch Art in the Seventeenth Century*. Chicago: University of Chicago Press, 1983.

Appignanesi, Lisa, ed. *Postmodernism: ICA Documents*. London: Free Association Books, 1989.

Aston, Margaret. *The King's Bedpost: Reformation and Iconography in a Tudor Group Portrait*. Cambridge: Cambridge University Press, 1993.

Augoyard, J.-F. *Pas à pas: Essai sur le cheminement quotidien au milieu urbain*. Paris: Editions du Seuil, 1979.

Augustine. *City of God*. New York: Doubleday, 1958.

Autin, Albert. *L'Echec de la réforme en France au XVIe siècle*. Toulon: Tissot, 1917.

Autin, J. *Louis XIV Architecte*. Paris: Lanore, 1981.

Babelon, J.-P. *Demeures parisiennes sous Henri IV et Louis XIII*. Paris: Le Temps, 1965. Reprint, Paris: Hazan, 1991.

———. "Documents inédits concernant Salomon de Brosse." *BSHAF* (1962): 67–82.

———. *Paris au XVIe siècle*. Nouvelle histoire de Paris. Paris: Les Beaux Arts, 1986.

Ballon, Hilary. "Constructions of the Bourbon State: Classical Architecture in Seventeenth-Century France." *Cultural Differentiation and Cultural Identity in the Visual Arts*. Studies in the History of Art 27. Washington, D.C.: National Gallery of Art, 1987.

———. *The Paris of Henri IV: Architecture and Urbanism*. Cambridge, Mass.: MIT Press, 1991.

Ballot, Marie J. *La Céramique française: Bernard Palissy et les fabriques du XVIe siècle*. Paris: Morancé, 1924.

Baltrusaitis, Jurgen. *Aberrations: Les perspectives dépravées*. Paris: Flammarion, 1983.
———. *Réveils et prodiges: Le gothique fantastique*. Paris: Colin, 1960.
Barbiero, Daniel. "Rereading the Classics." *Diacritics* (summer 1990): 40–53.
Barthes, Roland. *Mythologies*. London: J. Cape, 1972.
Battles, Ford Lewis. *An Analysis of the Institutes of the Christian Religion of John Calvin*. Grand Rapids, Mich.: Baker Book House, 1980.
Baxandall, Michael. *Patterns of Intention*. New Haven, Conn.: Yale University Press, 1985.
Bayley, Peter. *French Pulpit Oratory, 1598–1650*. Cambridge: Cambridge University Press, 1980.
Beaune, Jean-Claude. "The Classical Age of Automata: An Impressionistic Survey from the Sixteenth to the Nineteenth Centuries." In *Fragments for a History of the Human Body*, ed. Michael Feher. 3 vols. Cambridge, Mass.: MIT Press, 1989.
Bedouelle, Guy. *Le "Quincuplex Psalterium" de Lefèvre d'Etaples: Un guide de lecture*. Geneva: Droz, 1979.
Beguin, Sylvie. *L'Ecole de Fontainebleau: Le maniérisme à la cour de France*. Paris: Editions d'art Gonthier-Seghers, 1960.
Bell, Catherine M. *Ritual Theory/Ritual Practice*. New York: Oxford University Press, 1992.
Bellenger, Yvonne, ed. *La métamorphose dans la poésie du XVIe*. Paris: Nizet, 1989.
Benedict, Philip. *Rouen During the Wars of Religion*. Cambridge: Cambridge University Press, 1981.
Bénouis, Mustapha Kémal. *Le dialogue philosophique dans la littérature française du XVIe siècle*. Paris-La Haye: Mouton, 1976.
———. "Un livre contre les livres: La *Recepte* de Bernard Palissy." *Romance Notes* 18, no. 1 (1977): 115–19.
Bercé, Yves-Marie. *The Birth of Absolutism: A History of France, 1598–1661*. New York: St. Martin's Press, 1996.
———. *La naissance dramatique de l'absolutisme, 1598–1661*. Nouvelle histoire de la France moderne. Vol. 1. Paris: Seuil, 1992.
———. *Révoltes et révolutions dans l'Europe moderne*. Translated as *Revolt and Revolution in Early Modern Europe: An Essay in the History of Political Violence*. New York: St. Martin's Press, 1987.
Berkenhagen, E. "Entre Jean Goujon et Philibert de l'Orme." *Berliner Museen* 1 (1971): 9–23.
Beza, Theodore. *The Life of John Calvin*. Philadelphia: Whetham, 1836.
Bèze, Théodore de. *Du droit des magistrats sur leurs sujets* (1574). In *Constitutionalism and Resistance in the Sixteenth Century*, ed. Julian Franklin. New York: Pegasus Books, 1969.
Bloch, Ernst. *The Utopian Function of Art in Literature*. Trans. Jack Zipes. Cambridge, Mass.: MIT Press, 1988.
Bloomer, Keith. *Body, Memory, and Architecture*. New Haven, Conn.: Yale University Press, 1977.
Blunt, Anthony. *Art and Architecture in France, 1500–1700*. 5th ed. Harmondsworth, England: Penguin Books, 1970, 1988.

———. *Philibert de l'Orme*. London: Zwemmer, 1958.

Bornert, René. *La réforme protestante du culte à Strasbourg au XVIe siècle, 1523–1598: Approche sociologique*. Leiden: Brill, 1981.

Bossuet, J.-B. *Politique tirée des propres paroles de l'écriture sainte (1709)*. Ed. J. LeBrun. Geneva: Droz, 1967.

Bossy, John. *Christianity in the West, 1400–1700*. Oxford: Oxford University Press, 1987.

Boudon, Françoise. *Richelieu*. Paris: Hachette, 1975.

———. "Les livres d'architecture de Jacques Androuet du Cerceau," in *Les Traités d'architecture*. Paris: Librairie de l'Art, 1982, 367–96.

Boudon, Françoise, and Jean Blécon. *Philibert Delorme et le château royal de Saint-Léger-en-Yvelines*. Paris: Librairie de l'Art, 1985.

Boudon, Philippe. *Sur l'espace architectural, essai d'épistémologie de l'architecture*. Paris: Dunod, 1971.

Boullée, E. L. *Architecture: Essai sur l'art*. Paris: Hermann, 1968.

Bourdieu, Pierre. *Ce que parler veut dire: L'économie des échanges linguistiques*. Paris: Fayard, 1982.

———. *The Field of Cultural Production*. Trans. Randal Johnson. New York: Columbia University Press, 1993.

———. *Language and Symbolic Power*. Trans. J. B. Thompson. Cambridge, Mass.: Harvard University Press, 1991.

———. *Outline of a Theory of Practice*. Cambridge: Cambridge University Press, 1977.

———. "Symbolic Power." Trans. R. Winge. In *Identity and Structure*, ed. Denis Cleason. Driffield, England: Nafferton Books, 1977.

Bouwsma, William. *John Calvin: A Sixteenth-Century Portrait*. New York: Oxford University Press, 1989.

Boyceau, Jacques. *Traité du jardinage selon les raisons de la nature et de l'art*. Paris: Michel Vonlochom, 1638.

Brady, Thomas. *Handbook of European History, 1400–1600: Late Middle Ages, Renaissance, and Reformation*. Leiden: Brill, 1994.

———. *Ruling Class, Regime, and Reformation at Strasbourg*. Leiden: Brill, 1978.

Bratt, John H. *The Rise and Development of Calvinism: A Concise History*. Grand Rapids, Mich.: Eerdmans, 1959.

Brightwell, Cecilia. *Palissy the Potter, or the Huguenot Artist and Martyr*. New York, 1858.

Brodsky, Claudia Lacour. *The Imposition of Form: Studies in Narrative Representation and Knowledge*. Princeton: Princeton University Press, 1987.

———. "The Impression of Movement: Jean Racine, Architecte." In *Autour de Racine*, ed. Richard Goodkin. *Yale French Studies* 76 (1989): 162–81.

———. *Lines of Thought: Discourse, Architectonics, and the Origin of Modern Philosophy*. Durham, N.C.: Duke University Press, 1996.

Brown, Peter. *The Body and Society*. New York: Columbia University Press, 1988.

Bryson, Norman. *Word and Image: French Painting of the Ancien Régime*. Cambridge: Cambridge University Press, 1981.

Bucher, Bernadette. *Icon and Conquest: A Structural Analysis of the Illustrations of De Bry's "Great Voyages."* Chicago: University of Chicago Press, 1981.

Bullant, Jean. *Reigle générale d'architecture de cinq manières de colonnes.* Paris: Marnef et Cavellat, 1564; reprint 1568.

Bullet, Pierre. *L'architecture pratique qui comprend le détail du toisé, & du devis des ouvrages de massonerie, charpenterie, menuiserie, serrurerie, plomberie, vitrerie, ardoise, tuille, pavé de grais, & impression.* Paris: Michallet, 1691.

———. *Traité de l'usage.* Paris, 1692.

Bunyan, John. *Grace Abounding to the Chief of Sinners.* Harmondsworth: Penguin Books, 1987.

Burgelin, Pierre. *Jean-Jacques Rousseau et la religion de Genève.* Paris: Vrin, 1962.

———. *La philosophie de l'existence de Jean-Jacques Rousseau.* 2d ed. Paris: Vrin, 1973.

Burke, Peter. *The Fabrication of Louis XIV.* New Haven, Conn.: Yale University Press, 1992.

Burridge, Kenneth. *New Heaven, New Earth.* New York: Schocken Books, 1969.

Butor, Michel. "La ville comme texte." *Répertoire* 5 (1960): 3–21.

Calvin, John. *Calvin's New Testament Commentaries: Paul to Thessalonians and to Romans.* Trans. H. L. Parker. Grand Rapids, Mich.: Eerdmans, 1971.

———. "The Catechism of the Church of Geneva." In *Library of Christian Classics*, vol. 22, ed. John Baillie. Philadelphia: Westminster Press, 1954.

———. *Catechism, or Manner to Teache Children the Christian Religion.* Amsterdam: Theatrum Orbis Terrarum, 1968.

———. *L'excuse à Messieurs les Nicodémites sur la complainte qu'ils font de sa trop grande rigueur.* Geneva, 1544.

———. *Institutes of the Christian Religion.* Ed. and trans. F. L. Battles. Grand Rapids, Mich.: Eerdmans, 1986.

———. *Institution de la religion chrestienne.* Geneva, 1552.

———. *Institution de la religion chrétienne.* Ed. J. Benoist. Paris: Vrin, 1969.

———. *The Necessity of Reforming the Church* (1545). Trans. Thomas Beveridge. Edinburgh, 1844.

———. *Réponse à un certain Hollandais lequel sous ombre de faire les chrestiens tout spirituels, leur permet de polluer leurs corps en toutes idolâtries. Calvini opera*, ed. J.W. Baum, ix. Brunswick: Schwetschke, 1863. Rpt. New York: Johnson, 1964.

———. *Des scandales.* Ed. O. Fatio. Geneva: Droz, 1984.

———. *Treatises Against the Anabaptists and the Libertines.* Grand Rapids, Mich.: Baker Books, 1982.

———. *Commentaire sur les pseaumes.* Geneva, 1561.

Calvin et les génévois, ou, la vérité sur Calvin, par un citoyen de Genève. Geneva: Findig, 1908.

Calvino, Italo. *Invisible Cities.* Trans. William Weaver. New York: Harcourt Brace Jovanovich, 1974.

Cameron, Euan. *The Reformation of the Heretics.* Oxford: Clarendon Press, 1984.

Camille, Michael. *Image on the Edge: The Margins of Medieval Art.* Cambridge, Mass.: Harvard University Press, 1992.

———. "Visual Signs of the Sacred." *Word and Image* 5 (1989): 111–30.

Carlson, Marvin. *Places of Performance: The Semiotics of Theatre Architecture*. Ithaca, N.Y.: Cornell University Press, 1989.

Carnac, Pierre. *Architecture sacrée: Le symbolisme des premières formes*. Paris: Ed. Dangles, 1978.

Caron, Antoine. Entry in *Catalogue de l'école Fontainebleau*. Paris: Ecole Fontaine-bleau, 1972.

Carpentier, Jacques, ed. *Histoire de France*. Paris: Editions du Seuil, 1989.

Carpo, Mario. *La maschera e il modello: Teoria architettonica ed evangelismo nell' "Ex-traordinario libro" de Sebastiano Serlio*. Milan: Jaca Book, 1993.

Caus, Isaac de. *New and Rare Inventions of Water-Works*. London: Moxon, n.d.

———. *Rare Inventions of Water-Works*. London, 1659.

Céard, Jean. *La nature et les prodiges: L'insolite au XVIe siècle en France*. Geneva: Droz, 1977.

———. "Les talents de Bernard Palissy." In *L'intelligence du passé: Mélanges offerts à Jean Lafond*. Tours: Presses universitaires de Tours, 1991.

Certeau, Michel de. *The Mystic Fable. Vol. 1, The Sixteenth and Seventeenth Centuries*, trans. Michael Smith. Chicago: University of Chicago Press, 1992.

———. "L'oralité, ou l'espace de l'autre: Léry." In *L'écriture de l'histoire*. Paris: Gallimard, 1975; trans. Tom Conley as *The Writing of History*. New York: Columbia University Press, 1988.

———. *Une politique de la langue*. Paris: Gallimard, 1965.

———. *The Practice of Everyday Life*. Trans. S. Rendall. Berkeley: University of California Press, 1984.

Chambers, Ross. *Room for Maneuver: Reading (the) Oppositional (in) Narrative*. Chicago: University of Chicago Press, 1991.

Chambéry, Jacques Perret de. *Des fortifications et artifices d'architecture et perspective*. Paris, 1601. Reproduction Verlag Uhl, 1971.

Chapuis, A., and E. Droz. *Les automates figures artificielles d'hommes et d'animaux*. Neuchâtel: Plon, 1949.

Chastel, André. "Bernard Palissy: Mythe et réalité." *Catalogue d'exposition*. Niort, 1978.

———. *La crise de la Renaissance*. Geneva: Droz, 1968.

———. "French Renaissance Art in a European Context." *Sixteenth-Century Journal* 12, no. 4 (1981): 77–103.

Chastel, André, and J. Guillaume. *La maison de la Renaissance*. Paris: Presses uni-versitaires de France, 1983.

Châtelet-Lange, Liliane. "L'architecte entre science et pratique: Le cas de Jacques Gentillâtre." In *Les traités d'architecture à la Renaissance*, ed. Jean Guillaume. Paris: Picard, 1988.

———. "Jacques Gentillâtre et les châteaux de Thons et de Chauvigny." *Le pays lorrain* 2 (1978): 65–95.

Chatenay, Léopald. *Vie de Jacques Esprinchard, Rochelais et journal de ses voyages au seizième siècle*. Rennes: Oberthur, 1957.

Chatman, Seymour, et al., ed. *A Semiotic Landscape*. The Hague: Mouton, 1979.

Chiffoleau, Jacques. *La comptabilité de l'au-delà*. Rome: Farnese, 1980.

Choisy, Eugène. *L'église de Genève de 1535 à 1909: De la réformation à la séparation.* Geneva: Kuntdig, 1911.

———. *L'état chrétien calviniste à Genève au temps de Théodore de Bèze.* Geneva: Georg, 1909.

Christin, Olivier. *Les réformés: Luther, Calvin, et les protestants.* Paris: Gallimard, 1995.

———. *Une révolution symbolique: L'iconoclasme huguenot et la reconstruction catholique.* Paris: Editions de Minuit, 1991.

Christol, M. G. "La fresque du château de Tanlay." *Bulletin de la société de l'histoire du protestantisme français* 101 (1951): 231–36.

Church, William F. *Richelieu and Reason of State.* Princeton: Princeton University Press, 1972.

Ciprut, E.-J. "Le premier grand Temple de Charenton." *Bulletin de la société de l'histoire du protestantisme français* (Jan.–Mar. 1968): 115–32.

Clouzot, Henri. *Artistes huguenots: Les frères Huaud, peintres en émail.* Paris: Fishbacher, 1907.

———. *Un client de Philibert de l'Orme.* Paris: Leclerc, 1910.

———. *Philibert de l'Orme.* Paris: Plon, 1910.

Coffin, David. *Le colloque de Fontainebleau.* Paris, 1972.

———. *Gardens and Gardening in Papal Rome.* Princeton: Princeton University Press, 1991.

Comito, Tomaso. *The Idea of the Garden in the Renaissance.* Sussex: Harvester Press, 1979.

Congar, Yves. *Luther, sa foi, sa réforme.* Paris: Cerf, 1983.

Conley, Tom. *The Graphic Unconscious.* Cambridge: Cambridge University Press, 1994.

Coope, Rosalys. *Salomon de Brosse and the Development of the Classical Style in French Architecture from 1565 to 1630.* University Park: Pennsylvania State University Press, 1972.

Coope, Rosalys, and Catherine Grodecki. "La création d'Henrichemont." *Cahiers d'archéologie et d'histoire du Berry* 41 (June 1975): 21–48.

Costabel, Pierre, ed. "Vers une mécanique nouvelle." In *Sciences de la Renaissance.* Paris: Vrin, 1973.

Cotgrave, Randle. *A Dictionarie of the French and English Tongues.* London: Dent, 1611.

Crockett, Bryan. "Holy Cozenage and the Renaissance Cult of the Ear." *Sixteenth-Century Journal* 24, no. 1 (1993): 47–67.

Crouzet, Denis. *Les guerriers de Dieu: La violence au temps des troubles de religion vers 1525–vers 1610.* Paris: Seyssel, 1990.

Crow, Dennis. *Philosophical Streets: New Approaches to Urbanism.* Washington, D.C.: Maisonneuve Press, 1990.

Dars, Christine. *Images of Deception: The Art of "Trompe l'Oeil."* Oxford: Phaidon, 1979.

Daston, Lorraine. "Marvelous Facts and Miraculous Evidence in Early Modern England." *Critical Inquiry* 18, no. 1 (1991): 93–125.

d'Aubigné, Agrippa. *Histoire universelle*. Vols. 1–10. Ed. André Thierry. Geneva: Droz, 1995.

———. *Oeuvres complètes*. Ed. Henri Weber. Paris: Gallimard, 1969.

Davis, Natalie Zemon. "The Sacred and the Body Social in Sixteenth-Century Lyon." *Past and Present* 90 (Feb. 1981): 56–69.

Debus, Allen G., ed. *Science, Medicine, and Society in the Renaissance*. New York: Neal Watson Academic Publications, 1972.

De Caus, Isaac. *Nouvelle invention de lever l'eau*. London: T. Davies, 1657.

De Caus, Salomon. *La perspective avec la raison des ombres et miroirs*. Paris, 1612.

———. *Les raisons des forces mouvantes*. Paris, 1624.

De Croix, Pierre. *Le miroir de l'amour divin*. Ed. Lance Donaldson-Evans. Geneva: Droz, 1990.

Defaux, Gérard. "Evangelism." In *A New History of French Literature*, ed. Denis Hollier. Cambridge, Mass.: Harvard University Press, 1991.

Desan, Philippe. *Les commerces de Montaigne*. Paris: Nizet, 1992.

———, ed. *Humanism in Crisis: The Decline of the French Renaissance*. Ann Arbor: University of Michigan Press, 1991.

Di Cesare, Mario, ed. *Reconsidering the Renaissance*. Binghamton, N.Y.: Medieval and Renaissance Texts and Studies, 1992.

Diefendorf, Barbara. "Prologue to a Massacre: Popular Unrest in Paris, 1557–1572." *American Historical Review* 90 (1991): 167–91.

———. "Simon Vigor, A Radical Preacher in Sixteenth-Century Paris." *Sixteenth-Century Journal* 18 (1987): 399–410.

Diehl, Huston. "The Image of the Labyrinth." *Journal of Medieval and Renaissance Studies* 12 (1989): 35–78.

Dodge, G. H. *The Political Theory of the Huguenots of the Dispersion*. New York: Vintage, 1947.

Donville, L., ed. *De la mort de Colbert à la Révocation de l'Edit de Nantes: Un monde nouveau?* Marseilles: Presses universitaires, 1985.

Du Bartas, Guillaume Salluste. *La sepmaine*. Ed. Yvonne Bellenger. Paris: Nizet, 1980.

DuBois, Claude-Gilbert, ed. *L'invention au seizième siècle*. Bordeaux: Presses universitaires, 1987.

du Cerceau, Jacques Androuet. *Collection d'estampes (Praecipua)*. Trans. C. Ludet. Paris: Sand, 1988.

———. *Détails d'ordres d'architecture*. n.p. 1679.

———. *French Châteaux and Gardens in the Sixteenth Century: A Series of Reproductions of Contemporary Drawings Hitherto Unpublished*. Ed. W. H. Ward. London: Batsford, 1909.

———. *Leçons de perspective positive*. Paris: Patisson, 1576.

———. *Livre d'architecture de Jacques Androuet du Cerceau: Auquel sont contenues diverses ordonnances de plans et elevations de bastiments pour seigneurs, gentilshommes, & autres qui voudront bastir au champs, mesmes en aucuns d'iceux sont desseignez les basses courts, avec leurs commoditez particulieres: Et aussi les iardinages & vergiers, tres-utile et necessaire a ceux qui veulent bastir, a ce qu'ils soient instruits,*

& cognoissent les frais et la despense qu'il y convient faire. Paris: For Jacques Androuet, 1559. Reprint, 1582.

———. *Livre pour bastir aux champs*. Paris, 1572.

———. *Petites habitations ou logis domestiques*. Paris, 1885.

———. *Plan de la ville de Paris au XVIe siècle: Plan en perspective de la ville de Paris telle qu'elle estoit sous le règne de Charles IX, gravé d'après une tapisserie conservée dans l'Hôtel de ville*. Paris: Tardié, 1908.

———. *Les plus excellens bastiments de France*. 2 vols. Paris, 1576–1579.

———. *Les plus excellens bastiments de France*. Ed. and trans. C. Ludet. 2 vols. Paris: Aventurie, 1955. Reprint, Paris: Sand, 1988.

———. *Premier recueil d'ornements et arabesques grotesques*. 1566. Reprint, Paris: Jombert, 1794.

———. *Oeuvres: 62 petits arabesques*. Paris: Librairie de l'Art, 1884.

Ducolombier, Pierre, and Pierre D'Espezel. "L'habitation au XVIᵉ siècle d'après le sixième livre de Serlio." *Humanisme et Renaissance* (1934): 31–49.

Du Four, Alain. "Le mythe de Genève au temps de Calvin." In *Histoire politique et psychologie historique*. Geneva: Droz, 1966.

Eco, Umberto. "Function and Sign: The Semiotics of Architecture." *Vista internationale architetture*, 2. New York, 1973.

Edgerton, S. Y. *The Renaissance Rediscovery of Linear Perspective*. New York: Basic Books, 1975.

Eire, Carlos. *War Against the Idols: The Reformation of Worship from Erasmus to Calvin*. Cambridge: Cambridge University Press, 1986.

Eisler, Colin. *The Master of the Unicorn: The Life and Work of Jean Duvet*. New York: Abaris, 1979.

Eliade, Mircea. *Architecture sacrée et symbolisme*. Paris: Cahiers de l'Herne, 1978.

———. "Centre du monde, temple, maison." In *Le symbolisme cosmique des monuments religieux*. Rome, 1954.

Entrikin, J. Nicholas. *The Betweenness of Place: Toward a Geography of Modernity*. Baltimore: Johns Hopkins University Press, 1991.

Estèbe, Janine. "The Rites of Violence: Religious Riot in Sixteenth-Century France. A Comment." *Past and Present* 67 (1977): 127–30.

———. *Tocsin pour un massacre: La saison des Saint-Barthélemy*. Paris: Editions du Centurion, 1968.

Estienne, Charles. *Maison rustique, or the countrie farme*. Trans. R. Surfler. London: Norton, 1600.

Estienne, Henri. *Conformité des merveilles anciennes avec les modernes*. Paris, 1566.

Fagiolo, Marcello. "Effimero e giardino della citta e il teatro della nature." In *Il Potere e lo spazio la scena del principe*. Florence: Electa Editrice, 1980.

Farge, James. *Orthodoxy and Reform in Early Reformation France*. Leiden: Brill, 1985.

Farr, James. *Hands of Honor: Artisans and Their World in Dijon, 1550–1650*. Ithaca, N.Y.: Cornell University Press, 1991.

Febvre, Lucien. *Amour sacré, amour profane: Autour de "l'Heptaméron."* Paris: Gallimard, 1944.

———. *The Problem of Unbelief in the Sixteenth Century*. Cambridge, Mass.: Harvard University Press, 1982.

Feher, Michael, ed. *Fragments for a History of the Human Body*. 3 vols. Cambridge, Mass.: MIT Press, 1990.

Fenoaltea, Doranne. *Du palais au jardin: L'architecture des Odes de Ronsard*. Geneva: Droz, 1990.

———. *"Si haulte architecture": The Design of Scève's 'Délie.'* Lexington, Ky.: French Forum Publishers, 1982.

Fichet, F. *La théorie architecturale à l'âge classique*. Brussels: Mardaga, 1979.

Finke, R. A., and H. S. Kurtzman. "Mapping the Visual Field in Mental Imagery." *Journal of Experimental Psychology* 110 (1981): 510–17.

Fisher, Alan. "Three Meditations on the Destruction of Virgil's Statue: The Early Humanist Theory of Poetry." *Renaissance Quarterly* 40, no. 4 (1987): 607–35.

Fletcher, Angus. *Allegory: The Theory of a Symbolic Mode*. Ithaca, N.Y.: Cornell University Press, 1964.

Forster, Robert, and Orest Ranum, eds. *Ritual, Religion, and the Sacred: Selections from the "Annales."* Vol. 7. Baltimore: Johns Hopkins University Press, 1982.

Foucault, Michel. *Technologies of the Self*. Ed. L. H. Martin. Amherst: University of Massachusetts Press, 1988.

Fournier-Marcigny, Edouard. *La vie ardente du 1ᵉʳ refuge français, 1532–1602: Genève au XVIᵉ siècle*. Geneva: Editions du Mont-Blanc, 1942.

Fragonard, Marie-Madeleine. "Les meubles de Palissy." In *L'intelligence du passé*, ed. Jean Céard. Geneva: Droz, 1993.

Francastel, Pierre, ed. "L'urbanisme d'Henri IV et de Sully." In *L'urbanisme de Paris*. Paris: Plon, 1969.

Friedlander, Max. *Landscape, Portrait, Still-Life: Their Origin and Development*. Trans. R. F. C. Hull. New York: Schocken Books, 1963.

Frugoni, Chiara. *A Distant City: Images of Urban Experience in the Medieval World*. Princeton: Princeton University Press, 1991.

Gabarée, J. *Histoire de l'Eglise de Genève*. 3 vols. Geneva, 1858.

Gamble, Richard, ed. *Articles on Calvin and Calvinism*. Vols. 4, 7, 17. New York: Garland, 1993.

Garrison, Janine. *L'Edit de Nantes et sa révocation*. Paris: Editions du Seuil, 1985.

———. *Guerre civile et compromis, 1555–1598*. Nouvelle histoire de la France moderne, 2. Paris: Editions du Seuil, 1992.

———. *Royaume, Renaissance, et Réforme, 1483–1559*. Nouvelle histoire de la France moderne, 1. Paris: Editions du Seuil, 1992.

Garrison-Estèbe, Janine. *Protestants du Midi, 1559–1598*. Toulouse: Privat, 1977.

Garside, Charles. *Zwingli and the Arts*. New Haven, Conn.: Yale University Press, 1973.

Gasches, Jacques. *Mémoires sur les guerres de religion, 1555–1612*. Paris, 1894. Geneva: Slatkine Reprints, 1970.

Gebelin, François. *Les châteaux de la Renaissance*. Paris: Beaux Arts, 1927.

Geertz, Clifford. *The Interpretation of Cultures*. New York: Basic Books, 1973.

Geisendorf, Paul-François. *Le livre des habitants de Genève*. 2 vols. Travaux d'humanisme et renaissance, 26 and 56. Geneva: Droz, 1957, 1963.

Genette, Gérard. "Espace et langage." *Figures*. I. Paris: Editions du Seuil, 1966.
———. *Introduction à l'architexte*. Paris: Editions du Seuil, 1979.
———. "La littérature et l'espace." *Figures*. II. Paris: Editions du Seuil, 1968.
Gerrish, Brian. *Calvin's Eucharistic Theology*. Philadelphia: Fortress Press, 1992.
Geymuller, Baron Henri von. *Les du Cerceau: Leur vie et leur oeuvre*. Paris, 1887.
Giacometti, Jeanne. "The Influence of China and the Dominance of Delft, 1630–1700." In *World Ceramics*, ed. R. Charleston. New York: McGraw-Hill, 1968.
———. "Renaissance Pottery: France." In *World Ceramics*, ed. R. Charleston. New York: McGraw-Hill, 1968.
Gideon, Sigfried. *Space, Time, and Architecture: The Growth of a New Tradition*. Cambridge, Mass.: Harvard University Press, 1967.
Gille, Bertrand. *Les Ingénieurs de la Renaissance*. Paris: Hermann, 1964.
Gillot, Hubert. et al. *La satyre ménipée*. Tours, 1593.
Ginzburg, Carlo. *Il nicodemismo: Simulazione e dissimulazione religiosa nell'Europa del '500*. Turin: Einaredi, 1970.
Golson, L. "Primaticcio, Serlio and the Architectural Grotto." *Gazette des Beaux Arts*, 6th ser. (1971): 35–59.
Gombrich, E. H. *Art and Illusion: A Study in the Psychology of Pictorial Representation*. Princeton: Princeton University Press, 1969.
Goujet, Abbé Claude-Pierre. *Mémoire historique et littéraire sur le Collège Royal de France*. Paris, 1758.
Goujon, Jean. *C'est la deduction du sumptueux ordre, plaisantz spectacles et magnifiques theatres dresses, et exhibees par les citoiens de Rouen . . . a la sacree maieste du Treschrestien roy de France, Henry Second . . . et a sa tres illustre dame Katharine de Medicis*. Rouen: Robert Le Hay, 1551.
———. *Oeuvre de Jean Goujon gravé au traict d'apres ses statues et ses bas reliefs*. Reprint, Paris: Audot, 1844.
Grant, Edward, ed. *A Source Book in Medieval Science*. Cambridge, Mass.: Harvard University Press, 1974.
Greenberg, Mitchell. *Subjectivity and Subjugation*. Cambridge: Cambridge University Press, 1993.
Greenblatt, Stephen. *Renaissance Self-Fashioning*. Berkeley: University of California Press, 1986.
Greengrass, Mark. *France in the Age of Henri IV: The Struggle for Stability*. Oxford: Blackwell, 1984.
———. *The French Reformation*. Oxford: Blackwell, 1987.
Grimsley, Ronald. *Rousseau: Religious Writings*. Oxford: Clarendon Press, 1970.
———. *Rousseau: The Religious Quest*. Oxford: Oxford University Press, 1968.
Groupe 107. *Sémiotique de l'espace*. Paris: Denoel, 1979.
Guicharnaud, Helene. *Montauban au XVIIᵉ, 1560–1585: Urbanisme et architecture*. Paris: Picard, 1991.
Guillaume, Jean. *Les traités d'architecture à la Renaissance*. Paris: Picard, 1988.
Gulczynski, Henri. "Les Tabourot et l'architecture." In *Tabourot, seigneur des accords*, ed. François Moureau. Paris: Klinkseick, 1990.
Guye, Samuel, and Henri Michel. *Time and Space: Measuring Instruments from the Fifteenth to the Nineteenth Century*. New York: Praeger, 1970.

Habermas, Jürgen. *The Structural Transformations of the Public Sphere*. Cambridge, Mass.: MIT Press, 1989.

Hall, Basil. "The Reformation City." *Bulletin of the John Rylands Library* 54 (1971): 103–48.

Hamon, Philippe. *Exposition: Littérature et architecture au XIXe siècle*. Paris: José Corti, 1989.

———. "Texte et architecture." *Poétique* 73 (Feb. 1988): 3–27.

Harbison, Richard. *The Built, the Unbuilt, and the Unbuildable*. Cambridge, Mass.: MIT Press, 1991.

Harpham, Geoffrey. *On the Grotesque*. Princeton: Princeton University Press, 1982.

Hauser, Henri. "Le système de Barthelémy de Laffemas." *Revue bourgignonne de l'enseignement supérieur* 12, no. 1 (1902): 113–31.

Hazelhurst, Franklin Hamilton. *Jacques Boyceau and the French Formal Garden*. Athens: University of Georgia Press, 1966.

Heidegger, Martin. *Bâtir, habiter, penser: Essais et conférences*. Paris: Gallimard, 1958.

Heller, H. *The Conquest of Poverty: The Calvinist Revolt in Sixteenth-Century France*. Leiden: Brill, 1985.

———. "Marguerite de Navarre and the Reformers of Meaux." *Bibliothèque d'humanisme et renaissance* 33 (1971): 271–301.

Hersey, John. *The Lost Meaning of Classical Architecture*. Cambridge, Mass.: MIT Press, 1988.

Hexter, J. H. *More's Utopia: The Biography of an Idea*. New York: Harper, 1952.

Heyer, Henri. *L'Eglise de Genève*. Geneva: Jullien, 1909.

Higman, Francis. "Premières réponses catholiques aux écrits de la Réforme en France, 1525–circa 1540." In *Actes du XVIIIe colloque internationale d'études humanistes à Tours, Histoire du livre*. N.p., 1988.

Hill, Christopher. *The English Bible and the Seventeenth-Century Revolution*. Harmondsworth: Penguin Books, 1993.

Hollier, Denis. *Against Architecture*. Trans. B. Wing. Cambridge, Mass.: MIT Press, 1989.

Höpfl, Hans. *The Christian Polity of John Calvin*. Cambridge: Cambridge University Press, 1982.

Höpfl, Haro, and M. P. Thompson. "The History of Contract as a Motif in Political Thought." *American Historical Review* 84, no. 4 (1979): 112–38.

Horowicz, Maryanne, ed. *Privileging Gender in Early Modern England*. Kirksville, Mo.: Sixteenth-Century Studies Publishers, 1993.

Huarte, J. (1575). *L'examen des esprits pour les sciences où se monstrent les différences d'esprits qui se monstrent parmi les hommes*. Trans. Vion Dalibray. 1668.

Huber, Martin. "Sebastiano Serlio: Sur une architecture civile alla parisiana." *L'information de l'histoire de l'art* (1965): 9–17.

Hughes, P. E. *The Register of the Company of Geneva in the Time of Calvin*. Grand Rapids, Mich.: Eerdmans, 1966.

Humbert, Michele. "Serlio: Il sesto libro e l'architettura borghese in Francia." *Storia dell'arte* 43 (1981): 199–240.

Hunt, John Dixon. *Garden and Grove*. London: Methuen, 1986.

————. "Ut pictura poesis, ut pictura hortus, and the picturesque." *Word and Image* 1, no. 1 (1985): 87–108.

The Idea of the Renaissance in France. Special issue, *Journal of Medieval and Renaissance Studies* 22, no. 1 (1992).

Jackson, John Brinckerhoff. *The Necessity for Ruins and Other Topics*. Amherst: University of Massachusetts Press, 1980.

Jacob, Christian. "Ecritures du monde: Points de vue, perspectives et catalogues." *Catalogue d'exposition: Cartes et figures de la terre*. Paris: Centre Pompidou, 1980.

Jaillot, Jacques. *Recherches critiques, historiques, et topographiques sur la ville de Paris*. 5 vols. Paris, 1772–74.

Jameson, Fredric. "Architecture and the Critique of Ideology." In *Architecture Criticism Ideology*, ed. Dimitrii Porphirios. Princeton: Princeton Architectural Press, 1987.

Jencks, Charles. *The Language of Postmodern Architecture*. New York: Rizzoli, 1981.

Jestaz, Bertrand. *L'art de la Renaissance*. Paris: Mazenod, 1985.

Johnson, Jerah. "Bernard Palissy, Prophet of Modern Ceramics." *Sixteenth-Century Journal* 14, no. 4 (1983): 399–410.

Jordan, Elisabeth. "Inigo Jones and the Architecture of Poetry." *Renaissance Quarterly* 14, no. 2 (1991): 280–317.

Joukousky, Françoise. *Paysages de la Renaissance*. Paris: Presses universitaires de France, 1974.

Joutard, Philippe. "The Museum of the Desert: The Protestant Minority." In *Realms of Memory*, ed. Pierre Nora, Vol. 1, trans. Arthur Goldhammer. New York: Columbia University Press, 1996.

Kaufman, Peter Iver. *Redeeming Politics*. Princeton: Princeton University Press, 1992.

Kayser, Wolfgang. *The Grotesque in Art*. Princeton: Princeton University Press, 1981.

Keller, A. G. *A Theatre of Machines*. London: Chapman and Hall, 1964.

Kelley, Donald. *The Beginning of Ideology: Consciousness and Society in the French Reformation*. Cambridge: Cambridge University Press, 1981.

Keohane, Nannerl O. *Philosophy and the State in France: The Renaissance to the Enlightenment*. Princeton: Princeton University Press, 1980.

Kertzer, Daniel. *Ritual, Politics, and Power*. New Haven, Conn.: Yale University Press, 1988.

Kingdon, Robert. *Geneva and the Consolidation of the French Protestant Movement*. Geneva: Droz, 1967.

Kingdon, Robert, and Jean-François Bergier, eds. *Registres of the Compagnie des pasteurs de Genève au temps de Calvin*. Geneva: Droz, 1962–64.

————. *Geneva and the Coming of the Wars of Religion in France, 1555–1563*. Geneva: Droz, 1956.

Kisch, Yves de. "L'Ecrivain." *Bernard Palissy, mythe et réalité*. Catalogue de l'exposition présentée à Agen, Niort et Saintes, 1990.

Knapp, Bettina. *Archetype, Architecture, and the Writer*. Bloomington: Indiana University Press, 1986.

———. *Machine, Metaphor, and the Writer*. University Park: Pennsylvania State University Press, 1989.

Kostof, Spiro. *The City Shaped*. New York: Bullfinch, 1992.

Kubovy, Michael. *The Psychology of Perspective in Renaissance Art*. Cambridge: Cambridge University Press, 1985.

Laborde, Léon. *Les comptes des bâtiments du roi, 1528–1571*. 2 vols. Paris: Librairie de la société, 1887–80.

LaBoullaye, E. J. de. *Etudes sur la vie et les oeuvres de Jean Duvet*. Paris, 1876.

La Charité, Raymond, ed. *Rabelais's Incomparable Book*. Lexington, Ky.: French Forum Publishers, 1986.

Ladurie, Emmanuel Le Roy. *L'état royal: De Louis XI à Henri IV*. Paris: Hachette, 1987.

Ladurie, Emmanuel Le Roy, ed. *La ville classique: Histoire de la France urbaine*. Vol. 3. Paris: Hachette, 1981.

Languet, Ulrich. *Vindiciae contra tyrannos*. French transl. 1581. A. Jouanna, et al., eds. Geneva: Droz, 1979.

Laquenne, Fernand. *Olivier de Serres*. Paris: Presses universitaires de France, 1983.

Lazzaro, Claudia. *The Italian Renaissance Garden*. New Haven, Conn.: Yale University Press, 1990.

Leach, Eleanor. *The Rhetoric of Space*. Princeton: Princeton University Press, 1988.

Leblanc, Paulette. *La poésie religieuse de Clément Marot*. Paris: Nizet, 1955.

Lecointe, Jean. "Structures hiérarchiques et théorie critique à la Renaissance." *Bibliothèque d'humanisme et renaissance* 52, no. 3 (1990): 529–60.

Lecoq, Anne-Marie, "Les peintures murales d'Ecouen." In *Actes du colloque internationale sur l'art de Fontainebleau*. Paris: CNRS, 1975.

———. "La symbolique de l'état," In *Les lieux de mémoire*, ed. Pierre Nora. 4 vols. Paris: Gallimard, 1992.

Leeman, F., and M. Schuyt. *Hidden Images: Games of Perception, Anamorphotic Art, Illusion*. New York: Abrams, 1976.

Lefebvre, Henri. *The Production of Space*. Trans. D. Nicholson-Smith. London: Blackwell, 1991.

Leftow, Brian. *Time and Eternity*. Ithaca, N.Y.: Cornell University Press, 1991.

Lemos, Ramon. *Rousseau's Political Philosophy*. Athens: University of Georgia Press, 1977.

LeMuet, Pierre. *Manière de bien bastir pour toutes sortes de personnes*. Ed. Claude Mignard. 1623.

Lenoble, Robert. *Histoire de l'idée de la nature*. Paris: Albin Michel, 1969.

Leroux, Désiré. *La vie de Bernard Palissy*. Paris: Champion, 1927.

Leroy, Louis. *De la vicissitude ou variété des choses en l'univers*. Paris: Pierre l'Huillier, 1578.

Léry, Jean de. *Histoire d'un voyage faite en la terre du Brésil*. Ed. Jean-Claude Morisot. La Rochelle: Antoine Chuppin, 1578. Geneva: Droz, 1975.

———. *History of a Voyage to the Land of Brazil*. Trans. Janet Whatley. Berkeley: University of California Press, 1990.

Lestringant, Frank. *André Thevet: Cosmographe des derniers Valois*. Geneva: Droz, 1990.

———. "L'art imite la nature, la nature imite l'art: Dieu, Du Bartas, et l'Eden." In *Du Bartas, poète encyclopédique du XVIᵉ siècle*, ed. J. Dauphiné. Paris: La Manufacture, 1988.

———. "Bernard Palissy à Saintes." *Bulletin de la société de l'histoire du protestantisme français* 7, no. 136 (1990): 642–44.

———. *Bernard Palissy, 1510–90: L'écrivain, la réforme, le céramiste, journées d'études 29 et 30 juin 1990*. Saintes: Abbaye-aux-dames, 1992.

———. "Calvinistes et cannibales. I. Jean de Léry ou l'élection." *Bulletin de la société de l'histoire du protestantisme français* 126 (1980): 9–26.

———. "L'Eden et les ténèbres extérieures de la *Recepte véritable* aux *Discours admirables*." In *Albineana*, 4. Actes du colloque Bernard Palissy, 1510–1590. Niort Presses de l'université, 1992.

———. "L'excursion brésilienne, note sur les trois éditions de *l'Histoire d'un voyage* de Jean de Léry." In *Mélanges sur la littérature de la Renaissance à la mémoire de V.-L. Saulnier*. Geneva: Droz, 1984.

———. "The Philosopher's Breviary: Jean de Léry in the Enlightenment." *Representations* 33 (winter 1991): 200–212.

———. "Le prince et le potier: Introduction à la *Recepte véritable* de Bernard Palissy (1563)." *Nouvelle revue du seizième siècle* 3 (1985): 5–24.

Lestringant, Frank, and Krystyna Szykula. *Géographie du monde au moyen age et à la Renaissance*. Ed. M. Pelletier. Comité des travaux historiques et scientifiques. Paris: BN, 1989.

Lestringant, Frank, and C. Jacob, eds. *Arts et légendes d'espaces: Figures du voyage et rhétoriques du monde*. Paris: Plon, 1981.

Lincoln, Bruce. *Discourse and the Construction of Society*. New York: Oxford University Press, 1992.

Linde, Charlotte, and William Labov. "Spatial Network as a Site for the Study of Language and Thought." *Language* 51 (1975): 924–39.

Linder, Robert. "Pierre Viret and the Sixteenth-Century French Protestant Revolutionary Tradition." *Journal of Modern History* 38 (1966): 125–37.

Lipietz, A. "Approche théorique des transformations de l'espace français." *Espaces et société* 16 (1975): 3–14.

———. "Structuration de l'espace foncier et aménagement du territoire." *Environment and Planning* 7 (1975): 415–25.

Lloyd, Howell A. *The State, France, and the Sixteenth Century*. London: Allen and Unwin, 1983.

Lyons, John. *Semantics*. Cambridge: Cambridge University Press, 1977.

MacDougall, Elizabeth, ed. *Fons sapientiae: Garden Fountains in Illustrated Books, Sixteenth–Eighteenth Century*. Washington, D.C.: Dumbarton Oaks, 1977.

Magnin, I. *Histoire de l'établissement de la réforme à Genève*. Paris, 1844.

Maiorino, Giancarlo. *The Cornucopian Mind and the Baroque Unity of the Arts*. University Park: Pennsylvania State University Press, 1993.

———. *The Portrait of Eccentricity: Archimboldo and the Mannerist Grotesque*. University Park: Pennsylvania State University Press, 1991.

Malssen, P.-J. W. *Louis XIV d'après les pamphlets répandus en Hollande*. Amsterdam, 1936.

Marcheix, M. "Les Emaux à l'Exposition de l'Ecole de Fontainebleau." *Bulletin de la société archéologique et historique du Limousin* 100 (1973): 163–92.

Marienstras, Richard. *Le proche et le lointain*. Paris: Editions de Minuit, 1981.

Marin, Louis. "Classical, Baroque: Versailles, or The Architecture of the Prince." In *Baroque Topographies: Literature/History/Philosophy*, ed. T. Hampton. Special issue, *Yale French Studies* 80 (1991): 167–83.

———. *Food for Thought*. Trans. Mette Hjort. Baltimore: Johns Hopkins University Press, 1989.

———. *Portrait of the King*. Trans. Tom Conley. Minnesota: University of Minnesota Press, 1988.

———. *Sémiotique de la passion*. Paris: Aubier, 1971.

———. *Utopiques: Jeux d'espace*. Paris: Editions de Minuit, 1973.

Marion, Emile. *Souvenir de la réformation à Genève*. Geneva: Droz, 1936.

Marot, Clément. *Oeuvres poétiques*. Ed. Yves Giraud. Paris: Garnier-Flammarion, 1973.

Mastai, M.-L. *Illusion in Art. "Trompe-l'oeil": A History of Pictorial Illusionism*. New York: Abaris Books, 1975.

Mayer, Christine. *La religion de Marot*. Geneva: Droz, 1960.

McCauley, Robert, and E. T. Lawson. *Rethinking Religion*. Cambridge: Cambridge University Press, 1990.

McGowan, Margaret. *Ideal Forms in the Age of Ronsard*. Berkeley: University of California Press, 1985.

McGrath, Alister. *A Life of John Calvin*. London: Blackwell, 1990.

McKenna, Andrew J. *Violence and Difference: Girard, Derrida, and Deconstruction*. Urbana: University of Illinois Press, 1992.

Méchoulan, Henry, ed. *L'état baroque, 1610–1652*. Paris: Vrin, 1985.

Metman, Yves, ed. *La construction du Pont-Neuf, le Registre ou Plumitif de la construction du Pont-Neuf*. Paris, 1987.

Meyer, Jean. *Noblesse et pouvoirs dans l'Europe de l'Ancien Régime*. Paris: Hachette, 1973.

Meylan, Henri. *D'Erasme à Théodore de Bèze*. Geneva: Droz, 1975.

Michel, M. M. "Bernard Palissy, hydrologue et géologue: Etude historique et critique." Thesis, Département de Pharmacie, Ph.D. diss. Université de Bordeaux, Bordeaux, 1951.

Miernowski, Jan. *Du Bartas: Travaux d'humanisme et renaissance*, 257. Geneva: Droz, 1992.

Miller, Naomi. *French Renaissance Fountains*. New York: Garland, 1977.

———. *Heavenly Caves: Reflections on the Garden Grotto*. New York: Braziller, 1982.

Milner, Benjamin. "Calvin's Doctrine of the Nature of the Church." Ph.D. diss., Harvard University, 1965.

Monter, William. *Calvin's Geneva*. New York: Wiley, 1967.

———. "The Consistory of Geneva, 1559–1569." *Bibliothèque d'humanisme et renaissance* 38 (1976): 467–84.

Moore, James. "Geologists and Interpreters of Geology in the Nineteenth Century." In *God and Nature*, ed. David Lindberg and Ronald Numbers. Berkeley: University of California Press, 1986.

Moore, W. G. *La réforme allemande et la littérature française*. Strasbourg: La faculté des lettres, 1930.

Moussiegt, Paul. *Hotman and Du Plessis*. Geneva: Slatkine Reprints, 1970.

Muchembled, Robert. *L'invention de l'homme moderne*. Paris: Fayard, 1988.

Murray, R. H. *The Political Consequences of the Reformation*. New York: Russell and Russell, 1960.

Naef, Henri. "Un artiste français du XVIᵉ siècle: Jehan Duvet, le maître à la licorne." *Bulletin de la société d'histoire et archéologie de Genève* 5 (1925): 86–98.

———. "La vie et les travaux de Jean Duvet le Maître à la licorne." *Bulletin de la société de l'histoire de l'art français* 2 (1934): 145–73.

O'Grady, Patricia. "A Huguenot Statement in Architectural Terms." Manuscript, University of Toronto, 1994.

Olin, John. *The Catholic Reformation: Savanarola to Ignatius Loyola, Reform in the Church, 1495–1540*. New York: Harper, 1969.

Omodoe, G. *Giovanni Calvino e la riforma in Ginerva*. Bari: Laterza e figli, 1947.

Orth, Myra. "Radical Beauty: Marguerite de Navarre's Illuminated Protestant Catechism and Confession." *Sixteenth-Century Journal* 24, no. 2 (1993): 383–425.

Ostrowetsky, H. "Logiques du lieu." In *Sémiotique de l'espace*. Paris: Denoel, 1979.

Owens, Craig. "The Allegorical Impulse: Toward a Theory of Postmodernism. Part 2." *October* (1992) 13: 59–80.

Ozment, Stephen. *The Age of Reform*. New Haven, Conn.: Yale University Press, 1980.

———. *The Reformation in the Cities: The Appeal of Protestantism to Sixteenth-Century Germany and Switzerland*. New Haven, Conn.: Yale University Press, 1975.

Palladio, Andrea. *The Churches of Rome*. Trans. E. Howe. Syracuse, N.Y.: Medieval and Renaissance Texts and Studies, 1991.

Palissy, Bernard. *Architecture et ordonnance de la grotte rustique*. In *Oeuvres complètes*. Reprint, Paris: Blanchard, 1961.

———. *Discours admirables de la nature des eaux et des fonteines*. Paris, 1580.

———. *Oeuvres complètes*. 2 vols. Reprint, Paris: Blanchard, 1961.

———. *Recepte véritable*. Ed. Keith Cameron. Textes littéraires français. Geneva: Droz, 1988.

Pannier, Jacques. "Salomon de Brosse." Ph.D. diss., Université de Paris, 1911.

Paré, Ambroise. *Des monstres, des prodiges, et des voiages*. Reprint, Paris: Club français du livre, 1964.

Parker, Charles. "French Calvinists as the Children of Israel." *Sixteenth-Century Journal* 24, no. 2 (1993): 227–49.

Patry, Henri. "La Captivité de Bernard Palissy, 1562–63." *Bulletin de la société de l'histoire du protestantisme français* 70 (1921): 6–25.

Patterson, Annabel. *Censorship and Interpretation*. Madison: University of Wisconsin Press, 1984.

———. *Reading Between the Lines*. Madison: University of Wisconsin Press, 1992.

Payot, Daniel. *Le philosophe et l'architecte*. Paris: Aubier, 1982.

Pelikan, Jaroslav. *The Christian Tradition: A History of the Development of Doctrine:*

Reformation of Church and Dogma (1300–1700). Chicago: University of Chicago Press, 1984.

Perez-Gomez, Alberto. *Architecture and the Crisis of Modern Science*. 5th ed. Cambridge, Mass.: MIT Press, 1983.

Perrault, Pierre. *On the Origin of Fountains*. Paris, 1674.

Perrot, F. "Les vitraux du château d'Ecouen." *Le Colloque de Fontainebleau*. Fontainebleau, 1978.

———. "Vitraux héraldiques venant du chateau d'Ecouen." *Revue du Louvre* (1973): 77–82.

Philibert de l'Orme. *Architecture de Philibert de l'Orme oeuvre entiere, contenant onze livres, augmentee de deux, et d'autres figures non encores veues, tant pour dessins qu'ornementer de maisons, avec une belle invention pour bien bastir, et a petit frais.* (1626). Rouen: David Ferrand, 1648; Brussels: Mardaga, 1648. Reprint, London, 1981.

———. *Le premier tome d'architecture*. Paris, 1567.

———. *Traité d'architecture: Nouvelles inventions pour bien bastir et à petits frais.* Paris: Leonce Laget, 1561. Reprint, London, 1988.

Pierron, Gérard. *Salomon de Brosse: Discours*. Rennes: Les nouvelles, 1968.

Pinet, Antoine du. *Plantz, pourtraits, et descriptions et plusieurs villes et forteresses, tant de l'Europe, Asie et Afrique, que des Indes, et terres neuves*. Lyons: Ian D'Ogerolles, 1569.

Porteous, J. D. *Landscapes of the Mind: Worlds of Sense and Metaphor*. Toronto: University of Toronto Press, 1990.

Porter, Roy. *The Making of Geology*. Cambridge: Cambridge University Press, 1977.

Potter, G. R., and M. Greengrass. *John Calvin*. New York: St. Martin's Press, 1983.

Prest, John. *The Garden of Eden: The Botanic Garden and the Re-creation of Paradise*. New Haven, Conn.: Yale University Press, 1990.

Prévost, Jean. *Philibert Delorme*. Paris: Gallimard, 1948.

Price, Susan. *Rituals and Power*. Cambridge: Cambridge University Press, 1984.

Py, Albert, Alain DuFour, and Jean Barbier. *Ronsard et la Rome protestante*. Catalogue d'exposition à Genève, 1985.

Rabelais, François. *Oeuvres complètes*. Ed. Jacques Boulenger. Paris: Pléiade, 1968.

Radding, Charles. *Medieval Architecture, Medieval Learning*. New Haven, Conn.: Yale University Press, 1992.

Ranum, Orest. "Encrustation and Power in Early Modern Baroque French Culture." *Yale French Studies* 80 (1991): 202–26.

Reiss, Timothy J. *The Meaning of Literature*. Ithaca, N.Y.: Cornell University Press, 1992.

Richelieu, Armand-Jean du Plessis, cardinal de. *Mémoires*. 10 vols. Paris: Société de l'histoire de France, 1908–31.

Rochal, Claude-France. *Catalogue général des cartes, plans, et desseins d'architecture*. Paris: Archives nationales, 1978.

Roger, Jacques. *Les sciences de la vie dans la pensée française du dix-septième siècle*. Paris: Colin, 1963.

Roper, Lyndal. *The Holy Household: Women and Morals in Reformation Augsburg*. Oxford: Clarendon Press, 1989.

Rosci, Mario. *Il trattato di archittetura di Sebastiano Serlio*. Milan: Jaca Book, 1967.

Ross, Kristin. *The Emergence of Social Space*. Minneapolis: University of Minnesota Press, 1988.

Rothschild, Germain de, and Serge Grandjean. *Bernard Palissy et son école*. Paris: T. Schmied, 1952.

Roussel, P. D. *Histoire et description du château d'Anet*. Paris, 1875.

Roy, Maurice. *Artistes et monuments de la Renaissance en France*. Paris: Champion-Picard, 1929.

Rudwick, Martin. "The Shape and Meaning of Earth History." In *God and Nature*, ed. David Lindberg and Ronald Numbers. Berkeley: University of California Press, 1986.

Rykwert, Joseph. *The First Moderns: The Architects of the Eighteenth Century*. Cambridge, Mass.: MIT Press, 1980.

Sabatier, Georges. "Imaginaire, état et société: La monarchie absolue de droit divin en France au temps de Louis XIV." *Procès: Cahiers d'analyse politique et juridique* 4 (1979): 163–82.

———. "Versailles, un imaginaire politique." In *Culture et idéologie dans la genèse de l'état moderne*. Rome: Fabri, 1985.

Sambin, Hugues. *Oeuvre de la diversité des termes*. Lyons, 1572.

Sauzay, Alexandre. *Monographie de l'oeuvre de Bernard Palissy, suivie d'un choix de ses imitateurs*. Paris: Lemercier, 1862.

Savot, Louis. *L'architecture françoyse des bastimens particuliers*. Ed. F. Blondel. Paris, 1624. Reprint 1673.

Schama, Simon. *Landscape and Memory*. New York: Knopf, 1995.

Scheflen, Albert, and Norman Fishcraft. *Human Territories: How We Behave in Space-Time*. Englewood Cliffs, N.J.: Prentice-Hall, 1976.

Schnapper, Antoine. *Le géant, la licorne, la tulipe: Collections et collectionneurs dans la France du XVIIe*. Paris: Flammarion, 1988.

———. "The King of France as Collector in the Seventeenth Century." *Journal of Interdisciplinary History* 18 (summer 1986): 189–95.

———. *La scenografia barocca*. Bologna: CLUEB, 1982.

Scruton, Roger. *The Aesthetics of Architecture*. Princeton: Princeton University Press, 1979.

Seltzer, Mark. *Bodies and Machines*. London: Routledge, 1992.

Serlio, Sebastien. *The Five Books of Architecture*. Facs. 1611 Eng. ed. New York: Dover, 1982.

Serres, Olivier de. *La cueillete de soye par la nourriture des vers qui la font*. Paris, 1599.

———. *Le théâtre d'agriculture et le mesnage des champs*. Rouen: Jean de la Mare, 1600.

Sill, Gertrude. *A Handbook of Symbols in Christian Art*. New York: Collier, 1975.

Skinner, Quentin. *The Foundations of Modern Political Thought*. Cambridge: Cambridge University Press, 1978.

Soman, Alfred, ed. *The Massacre of Saint Bartholomew: Reappraisals and Documents*. The Hague: Nijhoff, 1974.

Southorn, James. *Power and Display*. Cambridge: Cambridge University Press, 1988.

Stauffenegger, Roger. *Eglise et société: Genève au XVIIe siècle*. 2 vols. Geneva: Droz, 1983.

Strong, Roy. *Art and Power: Renaissance Festivals, 1450–1650*. Woodbridge: Boydell, 1984.

Sturm, Florence, and Anne Winter-Jensen. *Montres génévoises du XVIIe siècle*. Geneva: Musée d'art et d'histoire, 1982.

Sully, Duc de. *Sages et royales Oeconomies d'Estat*. 2 vols. Ed. H. Michaud and F. Poujoulat. Paris, 1837.

Sutherland, N. M. *The Huguenot Struggle for Recognition*. New Haven, Conn.: Yale University Press, 1980.

Le symbolisme cosmique des monuments religieux. I.S.M.E.D., 1957.

Taylor, Charles. *Sources of the Self*. Cambridge, Mass.: Harvard University Press, 1991.

Taylor, Harrison B. "A Historical Study of the Mission of the Church in Geneva, 1536–1564." Ph.D. diss., University of Michigan, 1984.

Taylor, Larissa Juliet. "The Influence of Humanism on Post-Reformation Catholic Preachers in France." *Renaissance Quarterly* 50 (1997): 119–35.

———. *Soldiers of Christ: Preaching in Late Medieval and Renaissance France*. New York: Oxford University Press, 1992.

Taylor, Mark. *Disfiguring: Art, Architecture, Religion*. Chicago: University of Chicago Press, 1992.

Therborn, Goran. *The Ideology of Power and the Power of Ideology*. London: Verso, 1980.

Thompson, H. R. "The Geological and Geographical Observations of Bernard Palissy the Potter." *Annals of Science* 10 (1954): 149–65.

Thomson, David. *Renaissance Paris*. Berkeley: University of California Press, 1984.

Toesca, Ilaria. "Drawings by Jacques Androuet du Cerceau the Elder in the Vatican Library." *Burlington Magazine* (May 1956): 153–57.

Torrance, Thomas. *Space, Time, and Incarnation*. Oxford: Oxford University Press, 1969.

Trentler, Thomas. *Sin and Confession on the Eve of the Reformation*. Princeton: Princeton University Press, 1977.

Trudeau, Danielle. "Ronsard côté cour, côté jardin." *Poétique* 80 (Nov. 1989): 445–59.

Turner, Victor. "The Center Out There." *History of Religions* 12 (1976): 191–230.

Vachon, Marius. *Philibert de L'Orme*. Paris: Librairie de l'art, 1884.

Vallée, Léon. *Catalogue des plans de Paris*. Paris: Champion, 1908.

Vallet, Pierre. *Le jardin du roy très chrestien Henry IV*. Paris, 1608.

Van Till, Howard J. *Portraits of Creation: Biblical and Scientific Perspectives on the World's Formation*. Grand Rapids, Mich.: Eerdmans, 1990.

Van Zanten, David. "The Beginnings of French Romantic Architecture and Felix Duban's Temple Protestant." *Festschrift for Henry Russell Hitchcock*. Princeton: Princeton University Press, 1980. 64–84.

———. *Designing Paris*. Cambridge, Mass.: MIT Press, 1987.

Vasari, Giorgio. *Lives of the Most Eminent Painters, Sculptors, and Architects*. New York: Abrams, 1979.

Vaucher, Pierre. *Calvin et les génévois*. Geneva: Findig, 1908.

Venturi, Robert. *De l'ambiguité en architecture*. Paris: Dunod, 1976.

————. *Complexity and Contradiction in Architecture*. New York: New York Graphic Society, 1977.

Virèt, Pierre. *Admonition et consolation aux fidèles, qui délibèrent de sortir d'entre les papistes, pour éviter idolâtrie*. Geneva, 1547.

————. "Cosmographie infernale." In *Disputations chrestiennes*. Geneva: Girard, 1552.

————. *Dialogues du désordre*. Geneva, 1545.

Vitzthum, Walter. "Jean Goujon." In *I maestri della scultura*, 10. Milan: Fratelli Fabbri, 1966.

Wallace, Ronald S. *Calvin, Geneva, and the Reformation*. Edinburgh: Scottish Academic Press, 1988.

Waltzer, Michael. *Revolution of the Saints: A Study in the Origins of Radical Politics*. Cambridge, Mass.: Harvard University Press, 1965.

Wandel, Lee Palmer. "Envisioning God: Image and Liturgy in Reformation Zurich." *Sixteenth-Century Journal* 24, no. 1 (1993): 21–41.

Ward, W. H. *The Architecture of the Renaissance, 1495–1830*. 2 vols. London: Batsford, 1911.

Weibenson, Dora. *The Mark J. Millard Architectural Collection: The French Books*. New York: Braziller, 1991.

Whiteman, John, et al., eds. *Strategies in Architectural Thinking*. Cambridge, Mass.: MIT Press, 1992.

Williamson, Loretta. "Art and Propaganda During the French Wars of Religion." Ph.D. diss., University of Illinois, 1986.

Wilson, Dudley. "Dessein, réalisme, et imagination dans le jardin d'Eden de Du Bartas et dans le commentaire de Claude Duret." In *Du Bartas: Poète encyclopédique du XVIᵉ siècle*, ed. James Dauphiné. Paris: La Manufacture, 1988.

Wittkower, Rudolph. *Architectural Principles in the Age of Humanism*. New York: Norton, 1971.

Wolf, A. *A History of Science, Technology, and Philosophy in the Sixteenth and Seventeenth Centuries*. New York: Macmillan, 1935.

Zapalac, Christina. *In His Image: Political Iconography in Sixteenth-Century Nuremburg*. Ithaca, N.Y.: Cornell University Press, 1990.

Zerner, H. *École de Fontainebleau: Gravures*. Paris: Arts et Métiers graphiques, 1969.

Acknowledgments

As always, I owe everything to my family. Without them, I could do nothing.

Caroline Bynum told me that everything I have written is somehow autobiographical, and I guess that is true, because I certainly was sorely aware of pushing against a system and working within constraint, at the time I conceived of this project and brought it to fruition. I want to thank her for encouraging me to believe in my insights, even when they seemed idiosyncratic, and to trust "my Calvinists" to deliver the material. I did, and they did, and I learned a lot about their century, and the vagaries of ours, in the process.

I am indebted to Joyce Benkov, of San Jose State, for a brief conversation in which she recommended that I read Bernard Palissy and in that way got me started, unbeknownst to her, on this whole project. Hilary Ballon talked over early stages of my argument with me and offered valuable suggestions and bibliography, including her own excellent work. François Cornilliat, Ed Bensen, and Ehsan Ahmed offered suggestions as I was formulating my ideas for this book (whether during a friendly conversation, or as a question or comment in the course of one of my talks).

I wish I could emulate the beauty and clarity of Randall Balmer's prose style; hopefully, an occasional portion here and there in this text will approach something resembling a well-told story; if so, that is attributable to his influence. (So is the survival of this manuscript.)

Robert Cottrell, always ready with an intelligent perspective, encouraged my work on this project. He included me in the sixteenth-century session at the Modern Language Association in Toronto in 1993, where I delivered an early version of the chapter on Philibert de l'Orme and the Calvinist use of allegory. Jim Basker and Gita May opened the forum of the Columbia University Seminar in the Eighteenth Century, welcoming me as a speaker on Calvin and Rousseau. Bill Sharpe, literary critic and Renaissance man *extraordinaire*, shared my interest in architecture and commented on a draft of Chapter 2, on Calvin's use of city-space. Robert Griffin made detailed comments on the first draft of Chapter 4, on Philibert;

these were invaluable to me as I was revising. Patricia O'Grady graciously shared her research through the mail with a scholar she had never met. The Reverend William Coats helped me to formulate many of the preliminary ideas of this book. Daniel Martin's ground-breaking theoretical work on literature and architecture was an early influence on my project. Dan Russell, my first mentor, remains my best and kindest.

Kathleen Perry Long and Tom Conley are friends and kindred spirits; their interest in this project, and our sharing of similar styles and idioms, mean very much to me. Lance Donaldson-Evans is a faithful friend who never quite seems able to see my shortcomings. He is incredibly gracious and willing to share his own work: in short, an ideal colleague. He invited me to talk about Charlotte de Mornay, wife of the famous Calvinist statesman, at the University of Pennsylvania, where I shared a portion of Chapter 1, on code and Calvinists. David Van Zanten read substantial portions of this manuscript and provided invaluable perspectives, both as to the Reformed faith and concerning architecture. David Willis, at the Princeton Theological Seminary, published one of the chapters in this book, in revised form, as a monograph. He and so many colleagues in theology and religion have been extraordinarily welcoming to me, an interloper in their midst. Brian Armstrong invited me to present a portion of this manuscript, Chapter 2, on Calvin, in Edinburgh, where it stimulated much comment and controversy.

Several institutions facilitated and funded my work on this project. The Folger Library provided a fellowship for the work on gardens and grottoes as well as support for the illustrations; the National Endowment for the Humanities made possible my participation in an NEH Seminar on the Reformation, led by Hans Hillerbrand, at Duke University, where the other seminar participants, especially Bodo Nischan, were welcoming and enthusiastic about my work; and the Center of Theological Inquiry at Princeton paid for a semester's leave, during which I completed revisions of the entire manuscript. The staff of the Avery Art and Architecture Library (and its Rare Book Room librarians) were extremely helpful to me, and tireless in searching out manuscripts. Hans Hillerbrand also invited me to speak on Calvinist architecture at Duke University in 1992.

I am grateful to all my students, at Rutgers University, Barnard College, and Fordham University, who listened to bits and pieces of my theorizing over the past ten years. The warmth, excitement, and intellectual rigor of my undergraduate and graduate students, especially Holly Folk, in the Seminar on the Reformation that I taught in 1994 and again in 1996, were a great inspiration to me. Thanks to Jack Hawley, Alan Segal, and Randall Balmer for affording me that opportunity.

My colleagues at Fordham have been encouraging and supportive, especially Dean McShane, Fred Harris, Thelma Fenster, Nicole Kaplan, and Astrid O'Brien. In addition, I want to thank the many colleagues in the field, whose kindness, encouragement, and lively intellectual interchange—whether through actual conversations or through my readership of them—have enriched my life and work over the past seven years: Mary McKinley, Mike Latham, Lynn Chancer, Hope Glidden, Cynthia Skenazi, Deborah Lesko-Baker, Kathleen Bauschatz, Tim Hampton, Michael Randall, Patrick Henry, Ellen Ginsberg, David Rubin, John Lyons, Mario Carpo, and Peter Stallybrass. And I am grateful to Jerome Singerman, of the University of Pennsylvania Press, for being always encouraging, and such a thoughtful reader.

I hope that this study will encourage others to explore more fully the provocative intersections of theology and literature, and their style, idiom, structure, and spirit.

Index

Building Codes